THE URBANISTS,
1865–1915

**Recent Titles in
Contributions in American Studies**

Politics, Democracy, and the Supreme Court: Essays on the Frontier of
Constitutional Theory
Arthur S. Miller

The Supreme Court and the American Family: Ideology and Issues
Eva R. Rubin

Heralds of Promise: The Drama of the American People during the Age of Jackson,
1829–1849
Walter J. Meserve

The Line of Duty: Maverick Congressmen and the Development of American Political
Culture, 1836–1860
Johanna Nicol Shields

The Course of American Democratic Thought,
Third Edition with Robert H. Walker
Ralph Henry Gabriel

The Golden Sword: The Coming of Capitalism to the Colorado Mining Frontier
Michael Neuschatz

Corporations and Society: Power and Responsibility
Warren J. Samuels and Arthur S. Miller, editors

Abortion, Politics, and the Courts: *Roe v. Wade* and Its Aftermath,
Revised Edition
Eva R. Rubin

The Secret Constitution and the Need for Constitutional Change
Arthur S. Miller

Business and Religion in the American 1920s
Rolf Lundén

Modular America: Cross-Cultural Perspectives on the Emergence of an American Way
John G. Blair

The Social Christian Novel
Robert Glenn Wright

THE URBANISTS, 1865–1915

DANA F. WHITE

Contributions in American Studies, Number 94
Robert H. Walker, Series Editor

Greenwood Press

NEW YORK • WESTPORT, CONNECTICUT • LONDON

Library of Congress Cataloging-in-Publication Data

White, Dana F.
    The urbanists, 1865-1915 / Dana F. White.
        p. cm. — (Contributions in American studies, ISSN 0084-9227 ;
    no. 94)
    Bibliography: p.
    Includes index.
    ISBN 0-313-25256-4 (lib. bdg. : alk. paper)
    1. Urbanization—United States—History—19th century.   2. City
    planners—United States—History—19th century.   I. Title.
    II. Series.
    HT384.U5W46   1989
    307.7'6'0973—dc19   88-24703

British Library Cataloguing in Publication Data is available.

Library of Congress Catalog Card Number: 88-24703
ISBN: 0-313-25256-4
ISSN: 0084-9227

First published in 1989

Greenwood Press, Inc.
88 Post Road West, Westport, Connecticut 06881

Printed in the United States of America

∞

The paper used in this book complies with the
Permanent Paper Standard issued by the National
Information Standards Organization (Z39.48–1984).

10   9   8   7   6   5   4   3   2   1

Copyright Acknowledgments

The author and publisher gratefully acknowledge the following source for granting permission to
use the following material:

Figures 11 and 12 entitled ''A Municipal Exhibition'' are courtesy of *American City and County*.

Every reasonable effort has been made to trace the owners of copyright materials in this book,
but in some instances this has proven impossible. The publisher will be glad to receive
information leading to more complete acknowledgments in subsequent printings of the book and
in the meantime extend their apologies for any omissions.

Contents

Illustrations		vii
Preface: The Modern City: Real and Perceived		ix
1	**Widening Urban Vistas, 1865–1885**	1
	The Urbanist	35
2	**Comprehending Metropolis, 1885–1900**	37
	Concept for a Plan	88
3	**Governing Great Cities, 1885–1900**	99
	Packaging a Plan	142
4	**Cities of Extremes, 1885–1900**	151
	A Social Survey	195
5	**Toward Equilibrium, 1885–1900**	207
	Agenda for a New Century	254
	Appendix: A Note on Method	269
	Bibliographical Essay	275
	Index	279

Illustrations

Figures

1 Frederick Law Olmsted Plan for Buffalo, 1876   92

2 Frederick Law Olmsted Plan for Boston, 1896   94

3 Senate Park Commission, Washington, D.C.: Diagram of a Portion of City Showing Proposed Sites for Future Public Buildings   146

4 Senate Park Commission, Washington, D.C.: Model of the Mall, Showing Present Conditions   147

5 Senate Park Commission, Washington, D.C.: Model of the Mall, Showing Treatment Proposed   148

6 University of Pennsylvania: Condition of the Negroes of Philadelphia, Ward Seven: Individual Schedule and Home Schedule   198

7 The Seventh Ward of Philadelphia: The Distribution of Negro Inhabitants Throughout the Ward, and Their Social Condition   200

8 Migration of the Negro Population, 1790–1890   203

9 Wacker's Manual of The Plan of Chicago: CHICAGO. Plan of the Complete System   258

10 Wacker's Manual of The Plan of Chicago: CHICAGO: The Great Central Market   260

11–12 A Municipal Exhibition—Adaptable to Your City   264

Table

1 Magazine Selections, 1865–1900   272

Preface:
The Modern City: Real and
Perceived

"The 'modern city,' " urban historian Gunther Barth has written, "constitutes a rapidly expanding urban world in a uniquely American context, characterized by striking physical and human contrasts. Like all concepts," he continues, "it is an abstraction that has no separate historical existence. It comes to life through the accounts of people who experienced its features in the metropolitan centers of the United States." Their records and acts are the bases for his *City People*. The phrase "modern city," Barth elaborates, traces its provenance to the 1890s: "In the context of the history of urbanization, the rise of the modern city was a phenomenon of the nineteenth century; but by the time people actually recognized the new urban phenomenon they had been so busily living, the twentieth century was already shaping the world."[1] Their dawning recognition is the subject of *The Urbanists*.

To observe urban America in its entirety—as its contemporaries saw and described it—is the purpose of this book. Burning issues, major personalities, light-hearted impressions, local problems, national movements, metropolitan proposals—all appear in these pages. What follows is, as well as I have been able to portray it, the view of an evolving urban culture as perceived by an important segment of its citizenry, chiefly those who contributed to the periodical press.

The period covered is 1865 to 1915, but the sharpest focus is on 1885 to 1900. All told, thirty-seven magazines and journals constitute the essential text: eleven of them started before 1885, twenty-six after.[2] Selection and periodization combine to give this body of literature a definite flavor and bias. For one thing, the representation for 1865 to 1885 is less comprehensive than that for 1885 to 1900. The body of ideas on urban matters was so circumscribed during the first twenty years that a more intensive investigation would probably have unearthed little more of significance. Because magazine writing about cities in the two post–Civil War decades was essentially reportorial and seldom analytical and because it failed to advance from the particular to the general, it has a secondary role in this study—mainly as backdrop for the periodical literature of the closing years of the century.

This is the literature of the emerging metropolis. Thus, that other urban America of small towns and cities, commercial and industrial both, is poorly represented in these pages. The emphasis here was dictated by national growth trends, levels of awareness and, most directly, conditions in the field of magazine publication. The most dramatic aspect of urban growth during this thirty-five-year period was the emergence of the giant center of population concentration, the *Millionstadt*. Thus, national attention was drawn increasingly and ceaselessly to the largest cities—whether by the challenge of rebuilding Chicago after the 1871 fire, the drama of the exposure of the Tweed Ring in the same year, or the creation of a Greater New York in 1898—always, the great cities seemed to dominate the national stage. The major (and the vast majority of the lesser) magazines of the period, significantly, were published in and covered the progress of great cities, increasingly New York itself, the metropolitan center most frequently the subject of the periodical press.

A recognizable urban frame of mind invigorated a developing periodical press. Ideas, therefore, take precedence over individuals in these pages. Whenever possible, brief identifications have been provided contributors. Still "magazinists," as Frank Luther Mott has dubbed them, were a fugitive lot, and no extra effort has been made to search them out beyond standard sources.[3] Their relative anonymity serves in one sense to provide them a stronger group identity. Thus, magazine contributors may be characterized as having approached their subjects with an enthusiasm and vigor that gave life to their times and shaped the imagery of their writings. But their words and ideas have all too often been ignored by later generations of urbanists and critics who, unimpressed by the lessons of the past, seem intent upon rediscovering an "urban crisis" for each generation. Here, these early spokesmen for the nation's cities have been allotted space to speak out about their own age, in their own terms. Here, I hope, the contributions of these proponents of a better urban America have been provided another hearing that will reveal them as perceptive, imaginative, and intelligent at their best; typically and predicably human at their worst. Lincoln Steffens did not discover the American city. Urban America stood, many years before his day, fully conscious of itself and justly unashamed.

The Urbanists, like the traditional novel, has a beginning, middle, and end. It opens with a background chapter on the civic concerns expressed during the two decades following the American Civil War, proceeds to four chapters detailing the full range of urban affairs during the final fifteen years of the century, and concludes with the suggestion that the ideas developed by 1900 framed the conventional wisdom of urban America for the next half-century. So much for narrative qualities. There is also a dramatic structure here. Five shorter scenes or interludes, each more narrowly focused, supplement the sweep of the periodical literature with close-up readings. They encompass a profile of the urbanist, a scheme for metropolitan reordering by Frederick Law Olmsted, a promotional plan for civic enhancement by Daniel H. Burnham, an area impact study by W. E. B. Du Bois, and an agenda for urban research and metropolitan rebuilding for the new century. Three of these five interludes stem directly from the periodical press; the other two were noted in it. Together, they provide the microcosm to balance the macrocosm of the major chapters. What is more, through their dramatic intensity, they offer an additional focus for carrying the narrative forward to 1915.

Three individuals, one of them twice, helped carry me forward toward the completion of this manuscript. On the High Plains of Wyoming, within the first hour of our initial meeting, Robert H. Walker gave me sound advice about research and writing, which I hold to this day, some thirty years later. After we both removed to the District of Columbia, he not only continued to direct my work, but also interested me in the period of this study, prescribed against the malady of scholarly "Oblomovism," guided me into the new field of urban history, and advised that I attach myself to someone who spoke this new (to us) language of the city. In his Pennsylvania Avenue office, a block from the White House, I soon encountered Frederick Gutheim, who instructed me in the vocabulary of urban studies and who drew me beyond the confines of the library, out into the city streets. From metropolitan Washington to rural England, from coastal Maine and Washington State and back to Baltimore, we would continue our working association for the next two decades. Together, then, Bob Walker and Fritz Gutheim guided me through "The Self-Conscious City," the initial version of this study.[4]

On a streetcorner in Philadelphia, on an evening during an unmemorable academic conference, Sam Bass Warner, Jr., the contemporary whose work in the field I most admire, first heard me out concerning the development of urban self-awareness. In a Chicago subway car several years later, Sam indicated that he had recently read "The Self-Conscious City" and advised that I prepare it for publication, supplementing the chapters on periodical literature with new interstitial materials. When I questioned this advice, he countered: "Have you read your manuscript recently?" I hadn't. But upon my return to Georgia, I did. There, on a July night in Frederick Law Olmsted's Druid Hills, I subsequently discussed a proposal for the present book with the editor of the series in which my *Olmsted South* had appeared, Walker of Wyoming and Washington.[5] Since then, Bob has encouraged, exhorted, cajoled, cautioned (Oblomovism!), and advised—for example, about transforming the undefined interstitial materials into the present interludes. His contributions as editor, in sum, have transcended the professional to include the personal.

Blake McKelvey provided an early reading and, in his book *American Ur-*

banization, indicated a refocus for "The Self-Conscious City."[6] A reader of that manuscript for the MIT Press, whom I honor as The Unknown Reviewer, made many thoughtful and workable suggestions about revision, for which I remain grateful. Tim Crimmins, my longtime collaborator in writing about Atlanta, provided a late and helpful critique. And John Fondersmith provided books, plans, and encouragement.

Emory University's Graduate Institute of the Liberal Arts graciously provided typing assistance for this manuscript, with Julie Sabin completing the major chapters and Elaine Hardigree and Justine Busto the interludes. The Frederick Law Olmsted National Historic Site at Brookline, Massachusetts, advised on photographs, with Anne Jordan making every extra effort to search out just the right shot. Greenwood Press—especially Cynthia Harris, Alicia S. Merritt, and Elizabeth L. Hovinen—helped me transform a manuscript into a book—a feat, as every author knows, that has magic in it. George Washington University's Center for Washington Area Studies, housed then in the Division of Experimental Programs (of fond memories), provided me time for writing and editing when I held the Benjamin Banneker Professorship there during the spring term of 1984. Students in my seminar "City, Metropolis, Region: Theories & Theorists of American Place & Space, from 1865 to the Present" at GWU reviewed with me and helped me reaquaint myself with these urbanists. Should I ever carry their story all the way "to the Present," as threatened in that course subtitle, I shall owe these institutions and individuals in them even more than I do today. And that is considerable.

Two final acknowledgments: to the memory of my parents, Dana White and Mary Porter White, who brought me up urban, and to the presence of Yvonna, who brings laughter, warmth, and caring.

NOTES

1. Gunther Barth, *City People: The Rise of Modern City Culture in Nineteenth-Century America* (New York: Oxford University Press, 1980), 4, 7–8.

2. See Appendix, "A Note on Method," for selection procedures and historical background concerning the periodicals examined here.

3. Frank Luther Mott, *A History of American Magazines*, vol. 2: *1850–1865*, 26, and vol. 3: *1865–1885*, 17–18 (Cambridge: Harvard University Press, 1938), for origins of the term.

4. See Appendix, "A Note on Method."

5. Dana F. White and Victor A. Kramer, eds., *Olmsted South: Old South Critic/New South Planner* (Westport, Conn.: Greenwood Press, 1979).

6. Blake McKelvey, *American Urbanization: A Comparative History* (Glenview, Ill.: Scott, Foresman, 1973), 80: "A new generation of progressives was emerging in many cities around the turn of the century. Dana White has called them urbanists, whose detached concern for city problems distinguished them from the earlier mugwumps animated generally by moral indignation."

1

Widening Urban Vistas,
1865–1885

"I shall always respect War hereafter," wrote Ralph Waldo Emerson during the closing months of the American Civil War. "The cost of life, the dreary havoc of comfort & time are overpaid by the Vistas it opens of Eternal Life, Eternal Law, reconstructing & uplifting Society."[1] Hope, progress, reform, optimism—the familiar rallying cries of antebellum philosophers, pundits, and politicos—would indeed brighten the horizons of the reunited nation-state at peace with itself within a few months after the American Scholar penned these words; however, five years of stormy conflict had also darkened the skies of a disrupted democracy and threatened the survival of a *nation* of Americans. Civil war had served, to adopt Emerson's imagery, to "open" and to "break up" the old pattern of society, to drive "rifts" into American life itself. Then, in 1865, the fighting stopped. The end of the war marked what has been variously termed a national turning point, a watershed, a year of decision: commonplace, over-worked, and banal as these historical clichés may seem, 1865 was a special and noteworthy year, for it marked the end of an old and the beginning of a new era in American life and thought. The national character, the condition of con-temporary civilization, and the structure of American society came to be viewed as pressing issues in the two decades following the war.

After Appomattox, the "wider vista" to American life was essentially urban. This is not to argue that there was any abrupt and catastrophic "rise of the city" in the postwar period; quite the contrary, the urban experience had always been a shaping force in American life and thought. During the formative period, from the early seventeenth to the opening of the nineteenth century, towns and cities, both seacoast entrepôts and interior trading centers, exercised an influence pow-erful enough to shape the colonies and the new nation into a society based upon commerce as well as agriculture. This long tradition in city living, to some extent, served to cushion early nineteenth-century American society against the combined shocks of urbanization and industrialization that rocked Western civilization at the conclusion of the Napoleonic wars. The building of industrial cities nevertheless, as sociologist Leonard Reissman observed, "formed the wave of the most thoroughgoing social revolution we have ever known."[2] The wave seemed to crest when, between 1860 and 1910, the urban-industrial transformation of the United States entered its most crucial phase, when the number of cities over 100,000 rose from nine to fifty and those from 10,000 to 25,000 increased from 58 to 369. These five decades witnessed, Charles N. Glaab and A. Theodore Brown suggested in their classic text (the initial survey in the field), "the emergence of a national urban network—a complex, interrelated system of national and regional metropolises, specialized manufacturing cities, and hundreds of smaller subordinate cities of varying size and function."[3] Most importantly, the decades after the Civil War marked the coming of age of that urban area of heavy population concentration, the seeming focal point of change itself, the burgeoning "modern city."

After 1865 social change had so unsettled the United States that, according to Frank Luther Mott's diagnosis, "it was as if the nation had eaten a tremendously big meal and was suffering from a painful indigestion." Diagnoses and proposed treatments of these internal rumblings increasingly came to be the concerns of traditional general practitioners as well as rising specialists of the periodical press. Magazine publishing was, to change the metaphor, being revolutionized: the volume of publication skyrocketed, then burst to new heights, with the 700 periodicals in print during 1865 increasing to over 1,200 by 1870, about 2,400 in 1880, and some 3,300 in 1885. New York City, firmly established as the national publishing center by 1865, continued to extend its domination over the printed word throughout the next two decades; traditional quarterlies were abandoned in favor of the more popular monthlies and weeklies. This journalistic revolution was evident, according to Mott, in that most basic element of magazine publishing, the writing itself, as the "old Johnsonian style" was rejected by a new, and abler, school of authors who turned to a lighter, more readable, more popular prose.[4] Between 1865 and 1885, the city-based periodical press became increasingly professionalized and urbanized, and the magazine literature of the age shifted perceptibly from the reportorial to the analytical. In these two decades, magazine publishing developed into a major national industry, one that was situated in and reflected the life-style of urban America. Magazine publishing was approaching its apogee: its influence increasingly pervasive; its message, in the words of historian Gunther Barth, that "the greatest news story of the nineteenth century [was] modern city life."[5]

THE AMERICAN CHARACTER AND URBAN CHARACTERISTICS

"To-day, ahead, though dimly yet, we see," wrote Walt Whitman, "in vistas a copious, sane, gigantic offspring. For our New World I consider far less important what it has done, or what it is, than for results to come.'' Present and future were much on the American mind in the decade following the Civil War; the troubled days of antebellum America were dead and forgotten, the immediate past seemingly historyless. In the new surge of nationalistic writing that appeared between the surrender at Appomattox in 1865 and the celebration of the Centennial in Philadelphia in 1876, analysts of the Union attempted to sketch its uniqueness, the character of its citizens, and the structure of its society.[6] The one element common to the American experience in this period of change, all agreed, was change itself.

Democracy struck painter-critic Eugene Benson, much as it did Walt Whitman, as the key force in an evolving civilization. Democracy, for good or ill, had ''invaded the whole of life, and forced the modern man constantly to keep himself open to the incessant come and go of curiosity and equality.'' The democratic spirit was a ''modern spirit,'' Benson proclaimed, advanced by ''communicativeness'': ''the multiplication of means of intercourse, of exchange, . . . constantly at work levelling and elevating, uniting outlying places of life and thought with the great social centres of the world—the great cities.'' The spirit of the day, Benson continued, had been urbanized: it seemed ''public, noisy, full of light, full of hope, but without a single trait of an ancient spirit, or the mellow and harmonious tones which we discover in things venerable and mysterious''; it offered ''no room for anything but men of action and men of pretension,'' men for whom this traditionalist had little sympathy.[7] Yet these same ''men of action'' were distinctive if only for their excess of motion and drive, and their energy permeated American society in the late 1860s. These were the men who were to shape modern urban America.

The dynamism of the age was, many felt, a mixed blessing, since the building of a new order would result, inevitably, in the destruction of the old. To the editor of the *Galaxy*, for example, the social climate of the postwar years was in a state of rapid deterioration: ''In the course of the last twenty-five years, the period during which our wealth has so notably increased,'' he asserted, ''there ha[s] been a great and wide-spread deterioration in our manners and in the tone of our society.'' This degeneration had resulted from a too-rapid change in national attitudes toward life-styles: to the American of the late 1860s, the simpler life of the preindustrial farm, village, or town was no longer adequate; now, ''unless we can get rich and go to court—that is, to some great city, which is the court of now-a-days—we are in a parlous state, a state of poverty and provincialism.'' The character of many city dwellers seemed especially abrasive, concluded this spokesman for one of the nation's most cosmopolitan magazines, because ''our urban folk, who are in haste to shake off their provincialism,'' had managed not to overcome, but only to disguise their selfishness and materialism with a veneer of social polish.[8] The negative results of urbanization seemed to be social disorganization and, paradoxically, a loss of urbanity.

The inevitability of progress was the positive side of urbanization. ''There is a looking up in all social interdealings over all the world. Let croakers say what they will,'' wrote a contributor to *Scott's Monthly Magazine* in 1868, ''the rights of man" and "the finer claims upon our sympathy and charity, our brotherly kindness and neighborly help" were "now more fully recognized than ever" before. Human knowledge and skill would be marshaled to create a better environment: "Is the denseness of city life found to be repugnant to a free development of body and soul? Science and art will pu[t] it in the power of a city's populace to enjoy suburban freshness in their homes and metropolitan advantages in their centers of business."[9] The new urban order promised, in addition, more social cohesiveness: "The club, the guild, the coterie, the fraternity, the corporation, the church, the State—if, indeed, all these shall not be merged into one full orb of society, normal, organic, adjusted, [they] shall all work together with a harmony consistent with specialty of purpose and a proper subordination to the good of the whole."[10]

Change had produced social degeneration; change promised social amelioration: between these poles of opinion, the argument ran from 1865 to 1885. The Union, its citizens, and their society were subjected constantly to intense and extended analysis, as observer after observer offered his individual answer to Hector St. Jean de Crèvecoeur's challenging question, "What then is the American, this new man?"

The editors of Scott's Monthly Magazine maintained that "the unprecedented development of the material resources of this mighty continent, the rapid expansion of our commerce, the vast strides of our manufacturing industry, and, perhaps, more than all else, the continued expansion of our national territory have greatly modified, if they have not completely moulded, American civilization into forms which have no analogue in any other quarter of the globe." The culture of the United States, these same editors continued, employing a popular point of departure for the period, stood in especially sharp contrast with that of its parent culture, the British. The uniqueness of American civilization arose out of social mobility: "The family which yesterday lodged on the third floor of a tenement, to-day is installed in a brown-stone residence on Fifth Avenue." America's open avenues of opportunity made its citizens, unlike their English cousins, gamblers in real estate and stocks, individuals with a "love of adventure" and a "passion for excitement." Money, the measure of success, led to an emphasis upon quantity instead of quality; as a result, shoddiness was to be expected in manufactures and services, for "the Shoddyite is, as much as the bison, a peculiarity of our American Fauna."[11] Money was certainly the great leveler; perhaps it was also the great homogenizer. To the renowned Justin McCarthy, who practically made his living by comparing the characters of Brother Jonathan and John Bull, it seemed that Americans and American places were remarkably alike: "I venture to think that a man may observe far broader dissimilarities of habit, and character, and speech, who travels from Cornwall in England to Dundee in Scotland, or from London to Galway, than he can find in journeying from Broadway, New York, to Montgomery Street, San Francisco."[12] This lack of variety, of individuality, in cities and in citizenry was the result, physician-travel writer Titus Munson Coan suggested, of American "timidity." "We have, indeed, free speech in politics," he was prepared to admit, "but there are things which are quite as important to us as our privilege to vote. Upon the questions of religion and social science, there is less real freedom of debate among us than in almost any European country." Alexis de Tocqueville's "tyranny of the majority" seemed very much in evidence in postwar America. Because of democracy, urbanization, and social mobility, personal relationships and marks of status were uncertain; therefore, the timid American felt insecure. His social responses were limited to remaining silent, attempting to domineer, or pretending superiority. "The American scale of rank is," Coan lamented, "a scale of surliness." Since money was the "recognized proof of merit," it was "essential to have at least the appearance of wealth. Hence our slavishness toward the fashions, our deference to tradesmen, our fear to challenge exorbitant prices, and, in consequence, our unhesitating surrender to all manner of extortion. Hence, too, our ostentatious wastefulness."[13] In situations requiring spontaneous public action, Coan asserted, the "natural timorousness" of the American submerged him in "apathy." "There is among us," he lamented, "none of that bluff and sturdy assertion of our rights, that demand for equal justice, which is to be found among more than one of the Old World nations." Yet, at the same time, hope was not to be found in a retreat from urban America into the countryside. Security would develop in the major cities: "For here," Coan reasoned, "the social elements are so numerous that they spontaneously classify themselves into *sets*, in each one of which people meet freely; either wealth, fashion, family, or culture being the attraction in the particular circle."[14] Life in the large city would improve, Dr. Titus Munson Coan implied, because the American metropolis was becoming more like the European cosmopolis.

The Europeanizing—especially the Anglicizing—of city and citizen was also a cause for alarm. The urbanite who aped English manners, the editors of *Every Saturday* cautioned, was "no longer a Bostonian or a New Yorker; nor yet is he a Londoner." He became, simply, "Smithers." "In attempting to be an English 'gent,' he has not only failed egregiously, but has spoiled a commonplace American. Smithers says there are no ruins in America. Smithers is a ruin."[15] As the Centennial celebration drew nearer, however, the recognizably—almost blatantly—indigenous qualities of American life were glorified. Upon entering Philadelphia, according to *Galaxy*'s "Philip Quilibet" (editor George E. Pond), "The centennial hackman drives you in his coach, 'The Centennial,' to a centennial hotel, where your furniture and food are centennial; and if this be true in June, 1875, what shall be expected of June, 1876?" But the banalities of boosting were unimportant when measured against the "zeal and pride" of Philadelphians in the coming world's fair, their "elaborate plan of civic improvement" of streets and parks, their city's " 'fresh start, in all her *metropolitan* attire.' "[16] All Americans shared this sense of pride: "Society moves together in solid phalanx," wrote Washington correspondent Mary Abigail Dodge, under her customary pseudonym Gail Hamilton. "Rich and poor, bond and free, country and city, we have all marched down the hundred years together.''[17] Because of this century of shared experience, suggested Gail Hamilton's fellow Washingtonian Jane Grey Swisshelm, the American had developed a distinctive national character, one personified in the "impersonation" of Columbia. The American was unique, this outspoken abolitionist and feminist commented, in his treatment of the gentler sex: he invariably rose to the occasion, whether it meant surrendering his scalp on the frontier, or his seat on a city streetcar. The American was marked also by his "personal cleanliness, which springs from that self-respect born of self-government." Indeed, "the use of soap and water follows the ballot, and the superiority of the United States masses in this respect to those of other lands is sufficient to constitute a feature of national life."[18] The Centennial Exposition provided, *The Western*'s editor Horace H. Morgan counseled, an immense "supply of *data* for a reasonable judgment of the past; the present and immediate future are occupied with complicated problems which cause anxiety to all thoughtful persons, while they also incline us to consider the extent and grounds of our civil obligations." On balance, the national account seemed to be in the black: on the debit side, the country was accused of extravagance and materialism; in the credit column, Americans could boast a wise use of their "opulence of natural resources" and a healthy utilitarianism for material possessions. The nation's "unhappy politics" could not be ignored, but at the same time, the general level of social morality seemed higher, according to Morgan at least, in 1878 than at any time previously.[19] Julian Hawthorne, short story writer and biographer of his illustrious father Nathaniel, would, a half-dozen years later, qualify Morgan's optimism with the reservation that America was at its best as an idea or as a spirit, that the concept was superior to its actuality. So that the spirit might be made flesh, the United States in the mid–1880s had to turn not to Nature, but to Civilization. America's future resided not in its fields and forests, but in its towns and cities. "When our foreign visitors begin to evince a more poignant interest in Concord and Fifth Avenue than in the Mississippi and the Yellowstone," Hawthorne advised, "it may be an indication to us that we are assuming our proper position relative to our physical environment."[20] Coming to terms with a new urban environment, he failed to recognize, meant more than an attitudinal change. It also required both a new frame of reference and a fresh vocabulary.

URBAN THEORY VERSUS CITY PLACE

After the war men came to cities, and by their coming they made these cities great. New York, boasted one of its chroniclers, was by 1867 the "acknowledged Metropolis of the Western Hemisphere," "a polylingual, cosmopolitan capital— a half-way house for gregarious races." In describing this city, exaggeration seemed to be impossible, for hyperbole was the expected figure of speech: "The New Yorker is certainly proud of his noble city; but he feels that its greatness is manifest and everywhere known; that to doubt such greatness would be to doubt the daylight with the sun at meridian; and he is quite content that his city and her people should manifest and approve themselves in what they have done and will yet do for this country and the world."[21] Down East, the Athens of the North continued its dominance: " 'Sub-Hub' is the appropriate name suggested," *Scott's Monthly Magazine* noted, "for the Roxbury district recently annexed to Boston." Out west, according to this same journal, a real estate boom in Chicago had resulted in the sale of a lot valued at $3,000 some fifteen years previously for $165,000 in 1868.[22] Clearly, *Scott's* asserted, George Berkeley's maxim, "Westward the star of empire takes its way," was especially appropriate to postwar America: "The population of the world is sweeping like a mighty tide across the western continent. New York City is already claimed as the commercial center of the earth, and the present generation shall witness a rival for the supremacy of the seas in the ambitious capital of the Pacific States."[23] To a contributor to the *Galaxy* in the same year, it seemed that there were two major forces that alternately governed the destinies of people and nations: "One tending to concentration or centralization, the other to division or diffusion." In the late 1860s, the centripetal force seemed to be "in the ascendant; great cities are eating up small ones, and are growing greater; great nations are moving in the same direction, and great businesses, and great fortunes. . . . Paris now devours France; London, England; and New York, America."[24] North, south, east, west, the people moved on; their towns ate up the countryside, their cities devoured the towns.

The movement of people, the growth of cities, an increasingly wealthy nation—all these changes were anticipated in American periodicals during the two decades following the war. Significantly, however, the components of change were seldom investigated, and general theories of urbanization were rarely formulated. Occasionally, scattered through the magazine literature of the period, one finds brief attempts to conceptualize the processes of urban development. Thus the editors of *Every Saturday* in 1870 noted correctly that, according to the recent census, "the great cities have not, with a few exceptions, increased in population in the same ratio as our small towns and newer settlements," only to attribute this result, somewhat quixotically, to wasteful, incompetent municipal governments and abnormally high prices that were maintained through monopolies over food and services.[25] One year later, *Every Saturday* asked whether the "townward tendency" was merely a "feature of the age." "Or is it the product or concomitant of a certain stage of civilization, with a durability extending over generations and ages, and possibly increasing in vigor as it lasts?" It brushed aside theories that migration to cities was a fashion, that technical innovations would make agriculture a more profitable and more appealing calling, that the increasing scarcity of land would enhance the status of agrarian living and promote a counter migration to rural America. "The substance of the whole matter seems to be this: if civilization is a good thing, you—that is, the average you—are apt to get more of its features in the city than in the country—more intellectual and moral facilities; more opportunities for employment, amusement, and locomotion; more resources against drudgery and monotony; better division of labor, better household appliances, more order, neatness, and control of one's time.'' Until this situation changed, *Every Saturday* asserted, the ''townward tendency'' would prevail.[26]

The census of 1880 demonstrated, as had its predecessor, that newer settlements were eclipsing established centers in the race for population gains. ''The increased percentage of the town population to the rural population is not, to my belief,'' the future editor of the *International Review*, Robert T. Porter, wrote in the *Journal of Social Science*, ''due so much to the overcrowding of our cities as to the springing up of manufacturing centres in the West.'' In a two hundred-mile radius around Chicago, for example, more agricultural machinery was manufactured than in any other section of the country. The growth of towns and cities at the expense of farms and metropolises was, Porter argued, inevitable and beneficial: ''In 1850, less than one-quarter of the population of the United States lived in cities; now cities and towns contain upward of one-third. The change may be almost entirely accounted for by the change in the industrial condition of the West.''[27] A nonindustrial condition of the West, town promotion on a giant scale, was also held to be a mainspring of urbanization. In thirty-one stanzas of satiric verse, for example, the popular balladeer Charles G. Leland retold the familiar tale of land speculation in a mining boomtown. ''Gloryville'' was born with the discovery of ''shining metal'' in its environs. ''Little boots or little shoes it to inform you,'' the poet sang, ''how like crows / To a carcass, folks came flying, and the town of Glory rose.'' But as ''all the pay-dirt vanished,'' so did the residents. Efforts to restore land values by floating bonds led to fraud and chicane; in the end, the citizens of Gloryville, leaving behind them a debt of $1 million, removed to ''Splendorbug'' and a new dream of instant prosperity.[28]

Still another tentative hypothesis on urban growth was offered by the editors of the *Banker's Magazine*. Cities, they suggested, experienced not ''slow, steady, and imperceptible growth,'' but ''crises and fits of growth.'' ''They appear for years to be quite stationary, and all at once they move on again, as we even see to-day.''[29] New York City in the mid–1880s was undergoing just such a crisis of growth, since the opening of the Brooklyn Bridge in 1883 made the anticipated consolidation of the independent municipalities of New York and Brooklyn seemed ever more likely. ''Whether it is desirable that a large city should keep growing larger may reasonably be a matter of doubt,'' wrote the editors of *The Manhattan*. Growth in itself, they conceded, guaranteed more wealth. ''But,'' they added, ''how far such a vast aggregation of human beings increases the sum of happiness in the world is not so clear.'' Population concentration raised property values, taxes were then increased, and home owners were forced to move into newer settlements to the north and east of an increasingly commercial city center. This ''nomad life'' destroyed the roots of the home and the feeling for community and thus was an increasingly divisive force in American life.[30]

Small cities outstripped major centers, towns and cities cut into the country-side, and a metropolis could possibly outgrow its bounds: these, in sum, were the major unifying concepts offered for the study of urbanization between 1865 and 1885. One of the few contemporary explanations for the period's failure at conceptualization and generalization on urban affairs was offered in *Hours at Home* during 1870. Influenced by "the reiterated and somewhat commonplace fancies and argumentations of poetry" and by "the more practical representations of health and scenery," Americans, it was suggested, had attached their "admiration and affections upon fields and pastures, and the more open and extended inducements supposed to be held out by country life." The nation's cities, moreover, "up to a comparatively recent period, . . . have presented few attractions to the cultivated eye"; as a result, according to this interpretation, "we of the Western Continent have not always hitherto been accustomed to pride ourselves overmuch upon our cities, or upon the abstract attractions of city life."[31] A traditional involvement with patterns of rural living and an unfamiliarity with urban amenities together constituted the first probable reason for the dearth of general concepts of urban growth. Another was what historian Charles L. Sanford has termed America's inherent "optimistic fatalism," its unfailing confidence in present problems working themselves out gracefully in the near future.[32] Thus, in the *North American Review* of 1866, after a long and doleful account of corruption and waste in the administration of New York City, an unsigned article could conclude, on a paradoxically optimistic note, that "one half of civilized mankind were going henceforth to live in towns," that the United States had long displayed a "talent" for urban living, and that the passage of time would obliterate current problems.[33] Theories of urban growth remained unformulated owing to inadequate methods for the measurement of urbanization and the resulting lack of a scientific (that is, value-free) vocabulary for recording and analyzing the processes of population movement and settlement. Only the development of professional skills and an increased specialization in defined urban disciplines could begin to remedy this deficiency. A narrow view of the growth and progress of cities, one limited strictly to a single municipality, was a final obstacle in the path that led toward the conceptualization of general theories of urbanization and urbanism. In the two postwar decades, for the most part, observers wrote about a single city, not a nation of cities—about an urban place, not an urban America. Their writings often captured the style of life in a municipal center, but generally their perceptions were bounded by the walls of a singular city.

Strident boosterism, as has been indicated above, was typical of postwar comment on the nation's largest municipality; however, praise was just as easily turned into ridicule. Immediately after the war, New York (along with Boston) became for Atlanta's *Scott's Monthly Magazine* the incarnation of Yankeedom. Gotham, the editors of this journal reported gleefully, spent $70 million for "ardent spirits" in 1865 alone.[34] Furthermore, this sinful urban center contaminated the South by regularly sending its "courtesans" to New Orleans, and the parasitic tendencies of its residents were so pronounced that a municipal bureau had to be set up for "the protection of greenhorns."[35] Finally, its streets were so dangerous that in broad daylight a woman stopped a gentleman in the street, asked him for the time, "clapped a handkerchief to his nose saturated with chloroform, and when he recovered he found that he had been relieved of his watch and six hundred dollars in greenbacks."[36] New York, a gentler and more optimistic critic asserted, was "as vigorously engaged in doing the work of a nation as either London or Paris, yet as compared with those cities it is raw and unfinished, and in the most important features of a commercial capital, is wholly unreconstructed." Imperial Rome, commercial Venice, and "colossal" London had all risen to represent nations dwarfed by comparison with the United States; with these cases in mind, then, "what must the grand Republic of the West require for a national heart?"[37] It was an easy matter, the editors of the *Galaxy* admitted, to attack the vices and imperfections of New York City but, at the same time, accusations of this sort were based on "a one-sided view of things."[38] A more balanced judgment of the great port city, others repeatedly asserted, was that, despite its social and economic ups and downs, New York was the nation's chief city, and every effort had to be made to improve its condition.[39] Perhaps only the poet could express the power and potential of this:

> The peerless mistress of the puissant West,
> In gathered splendors of the ages drest, . . .
> In her all glories of all climes are blent,
> The crowned sovereign of the Occident.[40]

" 'Cosmetropolis,' " complained the editors of Philadelphia's *Continent*, was what New York vainly called itself; such conceit, they continued, was evidence not of cosmopolitanism, but parochialism.[41] Yet, only six weeks later, editor Albion W. Tourgée announced that his magazine was about to open a second branch in "Cosmetropolis" itself, inasmuch as that city had become "the intellectual as well as the financial metropolis of the country."[42] The pull of New York, then, by the early 1880s, was not to be resisted.

Boston, too, Tourgée noted, had once been the intellectual center of the nation, its true "Hub."[43] "O happy town beside the sea," Emerson had greeted it in 1876, "Thou darling town of ours!"[44] "Darling" of New England, possibly; beloved of the nation, no longer. Boston's reputation, as well as its rank in the country's urban hierarchy, was in sharp decline in the twenty years after the war. The voice of the South could be heard in the reports from *Scott's Monthly Magazine* about immorality in the Puritan citadel: there was, for example, the account of the fifteen-year-old girl who had stood trial there for bigamy, and the moral for that self-righteous "Hub" was "Physician, heal thyself."[45] There were further stories, dutifully recounted by *Scott's*, of a dozen infanticides committed in the region within a fortnight.[46] Thus was Boston the victim, on the one hand, of the scorn of the South, a sectional phenomenon, and the target, on the other, of competitive jibes from New York, an urban happening. Boston might call itself "the Athens of America," *Galaxy* claimed, but this was a "rather cheap provincial sobriquet," one that had been self-proclaimed and was therefore not "really deserved." While Boston was still the nation's foremost "intellectual" center, it was certainly not America's most "urbane" city. Boston, *Galaxy* gloated, was becoming increasingly commercial and markedly less intellectual; soon, it seemed, New York would be assured of unchallenged intellectual, as well as commercial, supremacy.[47] Surprisingly, however, Bostonians had little to say in their city's defense. Charles Francis Adams, Jr., provided one of the few comprehensive analyses of the city's growth and its future as a regional center; even here, perhaps not surprisingly, since these essays were written by a member of the lugubrious Adams family, one finds a gloomy and reluctant acceptance of Boston's new role as a city of the second order.[48] As the period drew to a close, moreover, the stalwart scions of the Shawmut Peninsula were characterized as "those horrid Boston 'stiffies,' " with their " 'dreadful, knowing, superior, better-than-you-look,' " men whose "banter" was lifted from the mouldy pages of the *Atlantic Monthly* and, therefore, whose ideas were "skin-deep."[49]

If Boston was experiencing a genteel decay, Chicago was undergoing a vital transformation. In 1871, this city's efforts to rebuild after the great fire captured the imagination of the American people. Chicago, the editors of *Galaxy* proclaimed, was "the fastest of all modern cities";[50] its efforts at self-help had served to unite its sister cities, who had learned "that a neighbor's calamity is a calamity for all."[51] The response of the country to Chicago's misfortune had been, *Every Saturday* agreed, "an exhilarating experience"; it had demonstrated that Chicago was more than a commercial rail center, that "in her moral and intellectual energy, in all the force and scope of genuine public spirit, Chicago might well be considered a worthy representative of the whole country."[52] Chicago, according to the same magazine, was a model for an optimistic nation, since "in all modern history there is nothing more marvelous and captivating than the growth of Chicago." When its inhabitants suffered discomfort and disease from its low-lying swamps, "it lifted itself to six or eight feet of higher level." When Chicagoans needed water, "it burrowed for two miles under the Lake, and audaciously drew a supply from the oceanic fountain." In short, "there was no project too bold, no enterprise too great, for it to undertake." "As its growth had been the superlative in modern history, so was its destruction."[53] And so would be its resurrection: "The man who thinks Chicago has been destroyed," an observer noted, "has only to cross the river into the burnt district to be undeceived. Labor and skill, directed by energy and enterprise, are working like bees in the hive, and when spring comes the desolate places will be desolate no longer, and from the ashes will have arisen new monuments of industry and faith."[54] Chicago's fate was not only of national concern; it was also discussed abroad. Journalist-lyceum lecturer Kate Field summarized Justin McCarthy's speech to the Social Science Association, meeting in London, in November 1871. Before the fire, McCarthy maintained, the city had been "a mark for satire and abuse"; afterwards "she was the shorn lamb to be sheltered and loved.'' The noted Irish essayist, according to Field, predicted that ''in five years Chicago would rise from her ashes more beautiful than ever,'' and he judged 1871 to be ''not a year of calamity, but a year of reorganization; a year of unbounded sympathies; a year of good-will between England and America, begun by treaty, and cemented in fire.''[55] Justin McCarthy's emphasis on the national significance of the Chicago fire was correct, for the Windy City was ''newsworthy'' in 1871, but not between 1865 and 1870 or from 1872 to 1885. Its growth and rebirth were symbolic, it was hoped, of the reunited American nation: Chicago and the Union would be reborn, rebuilt, and revivified.

The reconstruction of Chicago began at the halfway point of the Reconstruction of the southern states. For *Scott's Monthly Magazine*, the rebuilding of the former confederate cities was one of the major topics of the postwar period. Atlanta, the city in which this journal was published, had been destroyed by Sherman, ''with a malice hard to be understood, . . . from centre to circumference.'' That it would—like the phoenix (its official symbol), from the ashes (its motto)— soar to the heights predicted for it before the war was inevitable, *Scott's* asserted, since ''Atlanta, like New York, St. Petersburg and Rome, is one of the pre- destined capitals of the world.''[56] *Scott's*, as one in a handful of spokesmen for the South, took every opportunity to boost the region's cities; it noted proudly, for example, a rumor that President Andrew Johnson had expressed ''a strong desire'' to visit major southern cities.[57] It took pride in reports that Washington society had become increasingly ''Southernized.''[58] Yet, it held to a resolve to maintain its ''traditions of our race and lineage,'' to reject utilitarianism, and to refuse to be ''Yankeeized.''[59] With the end of political Reconstruction, these beliefs evolved into what historian Paul M. Gaston has described as ''the New South creed.''[60] By freeing the region from those outside ''forces over which her own people had no control''; by adjusting the system of slavery, which in ancient Rome represented a luxury but in the South stood as a nascent form of industrial development, to a free-labor system based upon racial separation; by adapting the ''Northern method'' which ''tended to produce intellectual acute- ness, to stimulate invention, to foster speculation'' to the ''Southern'' which served to ''develop the judgment, to enlarge the powers of combination and to strengthen the faith''—by doing all of these things New South spokesman Wil- liam L. Trenholm promised, the region was assured ''great prosperity.''[61] Its focal point, newspaper editor Henry Woodfin Grady predicted late in the 1880s, would be in one of the earlier-proclaimed ''predestined capitals of the world'': Atlanta, Georgia.[62]

Single city and urban America were jumbled together in the magazine literature of the period. The Gothamite's galling parochialism might rankle the out-of- towner, but all Americans had to take pride in New York's high rank in the world hierarchy of cities. The gradual but inevitable decline of proud Boston might give pleasure to the outsider, but the intellectual achievements of mid- century were not to be forgotten. The legendary boastfulness of the Windy City on the frontier's edge might shock the genteel sensibilities of older municipalities on the Atlantic seaboard, but Chicago's spirited efforts to rebuild after the great conflagration were a source of pride to the nation and an indication of the strength of the national character. The perverse refusal of Confederate communities to adopt Yankee ways might irk victorious and resentful Unionists, but the determination of southern urbanites to reconstruct their cities according to their own ideas seemed to be evidence of the revival of that region. Attention to the progress of the individual city could thus serve national ends, as an urban community became the focus for national pride. From such a point of view, however, it was impossible to generalize on cities as types; indeed, the viewpoints examined above tended to emphasize rather than minimize individual municipal peculiarities. Generalizations upon urban conditions would be developed only after characteristics common to all cities had been clearly defined and logically categorized.

A CITY CLEAN AND GREEN

That large cities could prove to be unhealthy and unpleasant places in which to live was the most obvious of general postwar urban conditions. That they should remain so was challenged with increasing vigor. Once again, the Civil War opened new vistas, toward healthy and happy cities.

"Wartime service in the Army, the Sanitary and Christian Commissions, the YMCA, the Loyal Leagues, and the Protestant churches' home-front network," historian Harold M. Hyman has pointed out, "taught ways to gain such new goals as communicable-disease containment. . . . These lessons centered on marrying the goals, managerial talents, and professional expertness of voluntarily associated improvers to government's powers."[63] Veteran "sanitarians," inspired by their wartime victories, sought after the war to evangelize American cities with a "gospel of public health."[64]

A nationwide cholera epidemic during 1866 provided an immediate test for the war-born sanitary science. This dread disease killed thousands of city dwellers across the country, but in New York, the urban center generally regarded as being among the most susceptible to the spread of contagious diseases, deaths from cholera declined from an 1849 high of 5,017 to 591 in 1866. This remarkable 900 percent drop in the mortality rate was directly attributable to the able administration of sanitary regulations by a newly constituted Metropolitan Board of Health. Its success in New York, together with the previous wartime record of sanitarians, guaranteed the future of their science in the nation's cities. "For the first time," historian Charles E. Rosenberg has noted, "an American community had successfully organized itself to conquer an epidemic. The tools and concepts of an urban industrial society were beginning to be used in solving this new society's problems."[65] Imitated by towns and cities across the continent, the institution of the powerful municipal board of health held out the hope that urban America could rid itself for good of major epidemics. The "sanitary elite," as historian George M. Fredrickson described the group, had demonstrated its leadership and expertness both immediately and dramatically.[66]

By the early 1870s, the gospel of public health had become so generally accepted that writers on urban affairs were prepared to argue that the city was more conducive to good health than was the country. The editors of *Every Saturday*, for example, termed the idea that rural living was healthier and safer than urban a "popular fallacy," and as evidence, significantly, they turned, in true sanitarian fashion, not to polemics but to statistics on comparative mortality rates.[67] Dr. Francis Bacon, Union surgeon and supporter of the Sanitary Commission during the war and later a Yale Medical School faculty member, also rejected the idea that city dwelling was injurious to the health of the citizen of the "modern city." The "ancient city," it was true, "like one of those microscopic monsters whose only function seems to be to swallow what is next to it, took in everything, and gave out nothing." And it was also clear that for "almost every considerable modern town" there came "a critical and dangerous period": "It has ceased to be a rural community, its population has become close, perhaps even crowded; but those public works, and that strict police, and that sense of individual responsibility in the people which are indispensable conditions of civic welfare, have not yet been established." During this transition period, the party of progress had to marshal its forces against the defenders of the older, simpler order. Debate over specific sanitary conditions would be clouded with "much idle and delusive talk about natural and unnatural modes of life." Fact had to replace fancy, the romantic had to give way to the real. In the new urban order, a new frame of reference was required. With great American cities well past their transition stages, the "modern city" had come of age in the 1870s, and the future seemed to offer infinitely more sanitary communities with heretofore undreamed of amenities.[68]

Throughout the 1870s and into the mid–1880s, the case for the sanitary city was strongly reenforced. John A. Church, a professor of minerology at the Columbia School of Mines, promoted the major structural innovations of Dr. Benjamin Ward Richardson's utopian "Hygeia, or the City of Health."[69] Elisha Harris, a founding member of the Sanitary Commission and a national leader in municipal sanitation, examined the progress made by state-appointed boards of health and recommended additional fields for their expansion.[70] Noted political critic Charles F. Wingate similarly traced the history of New York's water supply and, on another occasion, examined the sanitary arrangements in the homes of the wealthy.[71] Again, the period's foremost sanitary engineer, Colonel George E. Waring, Jr., translated the technical vocabulary of the new sanitary science into layman's terms and in a magazine for the general reader.[72] Throughout this literature, point by point, the evidence was amassed to demonstrate that the quality of life—no longer mere survival—was the major concern of the resident of the "modern city." Individual writers would continue to complain of dirt and disease in a single city at a particular time, but the problems that they raised were those of degree, not kind. That urban America *could* be made a healthy place was no longer a matter for serious dispute; the record of the immediate postwar years was proof of that. The question that remained to be answered was whether it *would*.

Even after the question of improving the city's physical health had been answered satisfactorily, there remained doubts as to its moral health. The postwar era was, after all, but one generation removed from the Romantic movement in literature and the arts, which had so influenced life and ideas on both sides of the Atlantic earlier in the century. Moreover, the finest writers of America's Golden Day were, for the most part, still alive—physically, if not always artistically. Their simple dichotomy between a beneficient Nature and a destructive Civilization had become by 1865 part of the conventional wisdom. That nature (that is, the nonurban) exerted a strong emotional "pull" on the city dweller during the two decades after the war remains certain; that there existed a dominating anti-city tradition seems doubtful. Much of the magazine literature of the period on the joys of country life dealt with the genteel manners of some ruralized or countrified form of urban living. The benefits of a *rural* residence were recognized readily enough, but *agricultural* life was seldom endorsed. To the sophisticated urbanite, there was no necessary dichotomy between city and country: the two, he believed, could and should be experienced and enjoyed together for the attainment of a balanced mode of urban living.

Traditional defenses of agriculture as the salvation of American democracy were still published regularly in postwar magazines, particularly when an urban interest group, most often immigrant, was under attack. When needed, the sturdy yeomen could still serve as a stock figure for simple virtue. His very simplicity, on the other hand, had an increasingly troublesome quality about it in a complex urban-industrial order, a civilization based upon sociability. The isolation of the farmer and his dependence upon the unpredictable vagaries of nature frequently drove him, the editors of *Hours at Home* commented, to a "miserable impecunious insanity."[73] *Every Saturday* argued, to the contrary, that any idea of the country's constituting "the abode of simplicity and primitive unworldliness" was "wholly erroneous," that "the simple swain as he really is could, metaphorically, extract the eye-teeth from an Italian relic-seller, and teach him that he had not got beyond nouns in the grammar of shrewdness." The unique purity of agrarian virtue had, this magazine claimed, "been tenderly fostered by the pastoral poets, who, for the most part, have lived and died in cities. Their bucolics differing from other colics in being contagious." While dissociating itself from any claims that "Simple Simon is any worse than his metropolitan relation," *Every Saturday* was careful to note that the records of the Civil War had demonstrated that the farmer's "pale-faced city-cousin" had been able to "out-walk him, out-ride him, and out-fight him." "Simple Simon" was often "strong of limb; but he is liable to break down suddenly, to collapse, like your crack stroke-oar. He sometimes lives to be very old. So does a man with one lung."[74] The publication of Dugdale's study of the Jukes in the mid–1870s was welcomed by the *Galaxy* as further evidence that rural America bred not only the inept, but also the vicious. While it accepted Dugdale's data, this magazine rejected his basic hypothesis: environment and not heredity, it countered, had produced such families as the Jukes. People of this caliber, moreover, came from the rural areas into the cities to make up "a very considerable part, if not the majority of the active and habitual criminals in cities."[75] By the early 1880s, the *Continent* was welcoming the formation of rural improvement societies, organizations directed and promoted by "wealthy men from our large cities" who were intent upon exploiting the "varied charms of the country" for suburban homes and summer vacations.[76] By the end of this period, it is sad to relate, the sturdy yeoman would appear in a pastoral poem in what was, at best, a contradictory role: "This plodding churl grows great in his employ, / God-like, he makes provision for mankind."[77] This uneasy counterpoint of the brutish and the divine was indicative, perhaps, of an urban frame of mind which, although it gave lip-service to traditional values, was developing a more serviceable value system of its own.

Again, the advantages of country living were not ignored between 1865 and 1885; plans for their enjoyment, however, were related closely to urban life itself and drawn primarily for the city's more prosperous inhabitants. The eight-part *"De Rebus Ruris"* by farmer, founding editor of *Harper's* "Easy Chair," and creator of the comic-philosopher "Ik Marvel," Donald Grant Mitchell, provided a detailed overview of the life-style.[78] Mitchell's "Mr. Urban," the hero of his account, was to be transformed into a "ruralist"; yet, he was to be transplanted not to the wilds of the West, but to land near a pleasant town. By "ruralist" the author meant "gentleman farmer," for Mitchell had no use for "the scrubby farmers of New England" or federal "charity" in the establishment of state schools for agriculture. Mr. Urban was so far removed from the yeomanry, in fact, that his rural guide had to advise him against the temptation of trying to create "a repetition of a bit of Central Park upon his own grounds."[79] "Sylvan," the hero of James Manning Winchell's "A Day at a Country Home on the Hudson," maintained an even wider social distance from the yeomanry. Whereas Mr. Urban retreated to the suburban farm, Sylvan maintained an exurban retreat. Far removed from the chaotic scramble of Manhattan Island, this admitted disciple of Henry David Thoreau (with, it should be noted, far more concern for creature comforts) lived with his family on the banks of that metropolis's lifeline, the Hudson River, and managed to "spend a part of every winter in New York." The action of this story was built around the initiation of visiting cousin "Celia" into the pleasures of exurban or, in Sylvan's terms, "genuine suburban life." Celia's education in the mysteries of country life involved, inevitably, a series of pompous lectures from Sylvan on the full gamut of rural lore, from bird watching to the preparation of "natural" meals; significantly, again, the choice was not between country and city but between two modes of cosmopolitan living. Sylvan's defense of his own preference for life in the exurbs was prefaced with the advice that "If one wants a city life, let him go to New York: he had there a genuine metropolis, with its innumerable advantages, and the Hudson and East rivers and the Narrows, with the ocean beyond, all at his service."[80] At the story's conclusion, moreover, Celia remained as a guest, not a resident. The periodic vacation to the country was, then, a possible alternative to suburban or exurban living.[81]

Still another approach to the question of balancing the urban with the rural was to be found in the crusade for the preservation of downtown open spaces, a movement that sought a basic readjustment in the rapidly changing land uses of the central city. At a certain juncture in a city's growth, Donald Grant Mitchell wrote in the final essay of "De Rebus Ruris," the need for clearly defined open spaces became vital. Once a city had reached a certain size and concentration of population, that is, when its distances from open land had been widened, the need for public spaces in its core area became inescapable. At that point, there came "to all denizens of cities a resurrection of those earlier rural instincts which crave growth and food—an outburst, through all the stony interstices of pavement, of the love for trees and green things."[82] Landscaped cemeteries and parks were frequently proposed to meet this need.

As early as the 1830s, the residents of crowded municipal centers had used landscaped urban cemeteries as public recreation areas.[83] These "cemeteries for the living" maintained their fascination for the urbanite in the postwar period. Indeed, so popular had the "fashionable drive" through the cemetery become that D. G. Mitchell warned against its becoming a "*voyant*, inviting chance-comers, offering views of sea or environs, cheating one into the belief that he is in a well-kept garden and not among graves, lured thither by views or prettinesses of landscape design and not by the memories or the sentiment of the place—that is awkward."[84] The novelty of the "cemetery-park" as a recreation center was largely a prewar phenomenon, and it had diminished in the postwar years; yet, upon the planting of New York's Woodlawn Cemetery, one Absalom Peters, in the spirit of Edward Young's *Night Thoughts*, composed an ode to his own "city of the silent": "A vast *necropolis*, a city under ground,/Concealed and dark below, but beautiful above."[85] The landscaped cemetery thus remained usable urban space.

A more significant amenity in postwar urban America was the landscaped park or, as architectural sociologist Galen Cranz has categorized it during its initial stage, "the pleasure ground."[86] The first and finest of this form had been created in the twin cities of the Empire State—"the" Central Park in New York City, as contemporaries dutifully called it, and Prospect Park in Brooklyn. To "the great Central Park, and the Brooklyn Park of hills" came Walt Whitman, "musing, watching, absorbing . . . the assemblages of the citizens in their groups, conversations, trades, evening amusements, or along the by-quarters—these, I say, and the like of these, completely satisfy my senses of power, fulness, motion, &c., and give me, through such senses and appetites, and through my esthetic conscience, a continued exaltation and absolute fulfilment."[87]

To Frederick Law Olmsted, co-creator with Calvert Vaux of both New York and Brooklyn pleasure grounds, this response of the "good, gray poet" would have come as no surprise, for the landscape architect saw his work as part of an international "*park movement*," "a common, spontaneous movement of that sort which we conveniently refer to [as] the Genius of Civilization." And its advent was timely, for in an age of progress threatened by "excessive materialism," with a resulting "loss of faith and lowness of spirit," the "contemplation of beauty in natural scenery," Olmsted taught, could serve effectively in "counteracting and alleviating these evils."[88]

To the writer of *The Manhattan's* "Town Talk," by the period's close *the* Central Park had become "the most precious possession that New Yorkers own in common." For the weary Gothamite it was "like a plunge into a refreshing bath to leave the hard, monotonous street and rumbling wheels behind; the dust, the grime, and the turmoil; the bustle of those imperiously rapid and persistent äerial car meteors or shuttles that go whizzing and thundering above your head, and taste the quiet and comfort and *dolce far niente* of this luxurious haunt of peace. . . . The scent of shrub and flower, the 'splendor of the grass,' as Wordsworth phrases it, woo you at the entrance."[89] This vast expanse of greensward in the center of Manhattan Island both stimulated the ambitions of those who proposed to shape the contours of the future metropolis, and captured the fancies of ordinary New Yorkers—no mean feat in itself.

The most significant aspect of postwar writing about the relationship between *rus* and *urbs* was its underlying recognition that the city was taking on a radically new shape, that—figuratively and literally—the walls of the traditional city were being broken down. Because of technological innovations in transportation and communications, the constricted radius of the preindustrial city could be pierced: the city, that is, could be moved out into the countryside. Postwar expansion of short-distance rail lines, both steam-powered and horse-drawn, made movement to the suburbs possible.[90] It also encouraged population concentration in municipal centers. With land values on the rise, the use of all available intown space was inevitable: hence, on the one hand, the insistence by park advocates on the crucial need for public open spaces; and, on the other, the recognition that the single-family urban residence might be impossible to sustain. American cities required, critic and sometime Olmsted spokesman Richard Grant White asserted, "more separate, comfortable houses" than were to be found in European cities;[91] the editors of *Every Saturday* expressed concern over the "flimsy" construction of most urban housing;[92] Donald G. Mitchell described morosely a "class" that seemed "always afloat" and found "all their home appetites in those great caravansaries which we call hotels, and whose local attachments must be of a very vague and illusory character";[93] a contributor to *Every Saturday* noted that a "vast number of buildings" were being erected on the "French plan," "which mainly consists of furnishing as little room and as many inconveniences as is possible for the money."[94] The examples could be multiplied, but the conclusion would remain the same: Living conditions in cities were being revolutionized. A new order was emerging to replace the old. This drastic change might be judged as an "uglifying process" or as the precursor

to a higher stage of civilization; in either case, it could not be ignored.[95]

The physical transformation of the city was hardly ignored in the two postwar decades. A source of national pride, evidence of national progress, the major urban center was examined, described, and cherished by its chroniclers. Ill-equipped though they were to develop a working theory of urbanization, these writers managed nevertheless to grasp the fundamentals of sanitary science, something of the relationship between central city and its outlying suburbs, and the basics of landscape design and architecture. They were moving toward what Leonard Kip termed in 1870 "a more metropolitan taste," a recognition "that uncleanliness, inordinate disproportion of crime, and a dingy absence of beauty, are not of themselves the necessary concomitants of city life, but are rather mere unholy parasites which long neglect has allowed to cluster around it; and that it is possible, with good management, to retain the advantages afforded by large massing of population, and not necessarily to assume its disadvantages also.... So, little by little," Kip concluded, "the stream of cultivation is beginning to set citywards."[96] This awareness that people could indeed shape their cities was the major precondition for the foundation of modern planning and the applied social sciences.

THE SPECTER OF URBAN DEMOCRACY

The new urban order demanded a new order of government, and one of the most frequently noted facts about the governing of large cities in the postwar years was that heavy financial expenditures in capital investments for public utilities and the establishment of extensive administrative bureaucracies were inescapable. That the growth of cities would entail greater expenses and stronger municipal governments was generally, if sometimes reluctantly, accepted. The amount to be spent, the type of administration to be instituted, and the character of the governors were the questions at hand.

Municipal indebtedness was a burning issue during the 1870s and 1880s. The editors of *Banker's Magazine*, for example, commented regularly upon "temptations to municipal extravagance." They noted approvingly, in one instance James G. Blaine's warnings about current "extravagance and prodigality" in public finance, an administrative pattern that could lead only to "calamity"; they seconded the "Plumed Knight's" advice that a local government ought to "bide its time and patiently await its well-assured prosperity" before investing on credit; and they repeated verbatim his judgment that "Credit, prudently used and safely guarded, is one of the great engines of modern civilization and advancement.... But I think our cities have been too ready to draw on the future."[97] Equally noteworthy to *Banker's Magazine* were the plans of "demagogues" for increased tariff charges, the repudiation or the lowering of interest rates ("semi-repudiation") on federal bonds, the taxation of commercial or

industrial stocks and state or municipal bonds, and a " 'graduated taxation,'
which would treat the industrious, prudent capitalist as if he were a public
nuisance, and not a benefactor, as he really is." Public monies could be raised
without problem by taxing all real and personal property; such a fiscal policy,
together with a "prudent" administration of these funds, would check current
abuses.[98] Two years later, in 1876, this journal noted that "the temptations to
municipal extravagance are no longer so strong as they once were, and various
circumstances are keeping it in check." Yet "dangerous facilities" still existed
for major debt increases as the financial history of New York demonstrated. In
that city, the ratio of the debt to the valuation of real property had risen from
0.62 in 1830, to 3.21 in 1860, to 10.60 in 1875, and it threatened to go still
higher.[99] A disproportionate burden in taxes had been placed upon real property,
a situation that this journal of the banking fraternity would classify in 1882 as
"barbaric," a system that placed the entire burden of supporting a municipality
upon one form of property and upon one class of its citizenry.[100] Two years
later, in a summary statement on municipal finances since the 1850s, the *Banker's
Magazine* judged that "many of the improvements for which the indebtedness
was incurred, were very necessary." Future plans for public investment, this
journal counseled, should be based upon needs of public health, the promotion
of business prosperity, matters of general convenience, and, most importantly,
the capability of the community to be taxed. Once again, prudence was the key
element: each generation must pay its own way.[101]

Most contemporary observers lacked the financial knowledge and the temperate
disposition of the editors of *Banker's Magazine*; most critics were less concerned
with monies spent than they were with monies misspent. Whereas the country's
leading financial journal usually presented municipal indebtedness in strictly
economic terms, some urban observers were more inclined to see it as a moral
condition, like the explanation for the soaring costs of governing American cities
offered by Robert P. Porter. "A debt of $1,000,000,000—half the sum of the
national debt, an annual expenditure of $220,000,000—within $40,000,000 of
the national expenditures—liabilities increasing at the rate of $50,000,000 yearly,
involving an additional charge of $3,000,000" were the totals. These fortunes
"handled by reckless men, and expended in ways unknown to the taxpayer"
was the indictment.[102] With the sin proclaimed, the sinner was not difficult to
identify.

Municipal indebtedness, most Americans would have agreed, was only the
most visible moral problem in the governing of great cities. The depths of postwar
political degradation were probably unfathomable, but one critic after another
did attempt to plumb them until the terms corruption, dishonesty, rottenness,
immorality, thievery, and baseness had become the accepted lexicon for any
analysis of municipal government. The moral judgments underlying this litany
of abuse might also have been captured in either of two phrases: the "Ring" or
"Tammany Hall."

Brendan Behan, an Irish visitor to the United States during the 1960s, was amazed and amused to find that "the Americans, and the New Yorkers in particular, . . . are always boasting about bribery and corruption, as if it was their own special invention and as if nobody else had any."[103] One hundred years before Behan's visit, American magazine writers wrote as if New Yorkers, and the braves of Tammany Hall in particular, had invented systematized bribery and corruption and as if no other city had any to match it. And, to an extent, they were correct. The New York of the mid–1860s was a special case. "New York," as Daniel Patrick Moynihan has observed, "became the first great city in history to be ruled by men of the people, not as an isolated phenomenon of the Gracchi or the Commune, but as a persisting, established pattern. Almost to this day the men who have run New York City have talked out of the side of their mouths."[104] Between 1865 and 1885, Tammany Hall became the vehicle for the immigrant Irish and, although it was not actually representative of big-city political organizations nationwide, it came to symbolize what many saw as a threatening and seemingly "foreign" form of municipal polity.

In 1866 *North American Review* captured in a simple sentence the emotional response of genteel America to the Democratic administration of New York City: "It is a dishonor to belong to it." Whereas, "the time was when the city was governed by its natural chiefs,—the men who had a divine right to govern it," it was ruled in the postwar years by a new class, " 'our ruling class,'—butcher-boys who have got into politics, bar-keepers who have taken a leading part in primary ward meetings, and young fellows who hang about engine-houses and billiard rooms." The extension of the suffrage in the Jackson–Van Buren era, *North American* judged, had marked the beginnings of this downward trend. Once "ignorant foreigners and vicious natives" had recognized that their fortunes were to be made in municipal government through the sale of public service franchises, particularly with the expansion of the street railroads beginning in the 1850s, the course of corruption had been set. The only hope for New York and other large cities that were certain to follow its bad example, this magazine concluded, was "a great and glorious revival of public spirit."[105] The problem was a moral one, the voice of genteel America proclaimed; therefore, its solution had to be a moral one, too. Throughout this fifty-three-page article, based though it was on nineteen books and pamphlets on municipal government and upon its author's detailed observations of the city's council in action, there is no mention of the unifying force behind New York's corrupt administration. *North American Review* offered judgment in place of investigation at the ward and precinct levels. From its Olympian heights, the "Old North" looked over, but not into the city. For it, Tammany was literally an overlooked presence.

With the exposure of the Tweed Ring in 1871, the existence of a well-organized political machine in New York City was made manifest. *Every Saturday* was typical in its response to the uncovering by the New York *Times*—if it was "to be believed"—of a "class of men, . . . who are 'complacent' in their infamy. They are so degraded as not only to have lost all sense of shame, but to pride themselves on their superiority to it." Clearly, this magazine asserted, New York had fallen into the clutches of "the Rascal-Power."[106] Throughout 1871, in articles and cartoons, *Every Saturday* followed the Tweed case. It noted, in one instance, that Tammany had fostered the extension of crime and violence in the city, but it refused "*as yet* to believe that roughs and pimps and thieves and gamblers and blackguards are a majority, *even* in the city of New York."[107] It suggested, at a later date, that as a science of "Comparative Anatomy" had been initiated in the schools, one in "Comparative Rascality" might well be instituted.[108] It warned, yet again, against the notion that "successful fraud can long be confined in official circles; it will burst the thin barriers between private and public life, and invade every department of business and society until the city itself becomes a very Babylon of corruption."[109] Whether its enemies were clever and patient enough to combat the Ring, whether local citizens' clubs and political factions might attempt to exploit the scandal for their own gains, whether national and state leaders felt it necessary to protect their own interests and settle for a token cleanup and a few sacrificial victims from the New York Democracy—these, too, were questions to be answered.[110]

The most persistent note in *Every Saturday*'s coverage of the exposure of the Ring was one of incredulity at the gargantuan extent of this organized swindling: "That any thing whatever is left of cash or credit is at once a mercy and a mystery, which can be explained only on the ground that there is a limit to the capacity of robbers for stealing. The Tammany crowd apparently did all that men could possibly do in a given time." There is, indeed, an epic quality in *Every Saturday*'s description of these relentless brigands who "plundered day and night with the utmost energy and activity" and who, had they not been stopped in 1871, would have bankrupt the city in another year.[111] Yet, behind these thieving Brobdingnabs were New York's own Yahoos—the "wild Irish."[112] Municipal corruption, it seemed obvious, was the result of democratic rule in the large cities.

A self-evident solution to perceived democratic excesses was oligarchic control.[113] Historian Francis Parkman, in "The Failure of Universal Suffrage," lamented that the United States was shackled with a new royalty, "the many-headed one that bears the name of Demos, with its portentous concourse of courtiers, sycophants, and panders."[114] Civil service reform advocate Dorman B. Eaton labeled the contemporary system of office-holding a "communistic theory of giving everybody a chance to get into office."[115] Municipal government, he had urged nearly a decade earlier, had to be free from politics: it was "a sphere for personal honesty and business capacity, rather than for political policy or party principles." A well-governed city, then, would be controlled by its wisest and wealthiest citizens. Such an ideal municipality—and Eaton had a Tammany-free New York in mind—would be assured of "abundant wealth, irresistible physical power, [and] the largest population that ever bowed its neck to any human sovereign."[116] And bow its neck, such a population would indeed be forced to do. The proposals of the most vociferous opponents of the big-city machine were aimed at the disenfranchisement of nonproperty holders and the centralization of power in the office of the strong mayor.[117]

The anti-majoritarianism of these patrician reformers was always apparent in their attitudes toward the Irish-American electorate, who came to symbolize the urban masses, ethnic and native-born alike. The editors of the *Banker's Magazine*, for example, noted that Ireland, with its high fertility rate, had been frequently called the world's *"piggery."*[118] A contributor to *North American Review* complained of immigrant contributions to the Fenian cause and quoted approvingly General Butler's charge to a New York mob that "You are not fit for the exercise of the elective franchise."[119] But perhaps the most extreme confession of this prejudice was made shortly after in the same journal. "The idea of unqualified or 'tramp' suffrage, like communism, with which it is closely allied, seems to be of modern origin," William L. Scruggs argued, "and like that and kindred isms, it usually finds advocates and apologists in the ranks of the discontented, improvident, ignorant, vicious, depraved, and dangerous classes of society." Their philosophy "originated in the slums of European cities, and, like the viper in the fable, has been nurtured into formidable activity in this country by misdirected kindness."[120] " 'Tramp' suffrage, like communism" seemed demonstrably un-American.

This genteel or patrician view of municipal government dominated magazine literature between 1865 and 1885. A few dissenters offered somewhat different interpretations. Political economist-sociologist William Graham Sumner, for example, saw the "Boss" as "the last and perfect flower of the long development at which hundreds of skillful and crafty men have labored, and into which the American people have put by far the greatest part of their political energy"; he was, in short, "the product of a long process of natural selection."[121] This blithe acceptance of the deterministic processes of social Darwinism, however, was limited solely to this proponent of the survival of the fittest. Editor Horace H. Morgan was closer to the genteel viewpoint when he distinguished between the politician and the "professional" politician: to accept the latter as typical of his calling, Morgan suggested, was similar to picking a Shylock to represent the business world.[122] Finally, Gail Hamilton maintained that "total depravity crops out in politics no more and no less than it crops out in ecclesiasticism"; that government, in effect, was a reflection of the social body from which it emanated.[123] Hamilton, as did Morgan and others of like mind, however, turned to the genteel solution for good government: good men.

That adherents to this patrician ideal were so threatened by the boss and the machine was inevitable given their failure to develop workable alternatives to what they decried as "boss rule." The strong-mayor system and civil service reform—the latter still proposed more often at the national than at the local level—were such legal mechanisms, but they were barely a beginning. The reform element was, as yet, so concerned with the morality of politics that it ignored the matter of power. It lacked a sure grasp on the structure and workings of the political machine. Political theorists of the period both underestimated and overrated its place in municipal polity: on the one hand, they miscalculated the broad base of voter support available to the machine and hence its durability as a political force; on the other, they exaggerated its power to control the political, social, and economic life of the city.

A sharp awareness that such entities as the "Ring" and the "Boss" had become a part of the nation's major municipalities had developed by the early 1870s. Boss Tweed and the Chicago fire shared the headlines in 1871, but the former, unlike the latter, did not cease being newsworthy in the years that followed. Indeed, it might not be too much of an exaggeration to say that the specter of the elephantine bulk of the Boss—his bediamonded paunch thrusting ominously forward, his crafty and piglike eyes leering over his bulbous nose— became a dominant image of urban America.

THE CLASSES VERSUS THE MASSES

"Foreign travellers" to the United States, wrote *Galaxy* editor George E. Pond in 1868, "are struck with the careless, slap-dash style of living here; with the extravagance of the well-to-do and the squandering of the rich; with waste of materials and resources everywhere." These national traits, he conceded, had long been associated with the American character; however, they had been exaggerated still more by "eight years of business invaded and controlled by chance, and the excitement of a long and fluctuating war" and, more importantly, by the emergence of "new society leaders and 'new rich' lately thrown to the surface, whose profusion and extravagance equal the speed wherewith fortune came to them."[124] Nine years later this same column expressed the hope that future historians would not mistake its own times for a "Golden Age of commercial honesty"; it would be more accurate, it was suggested, to "style it the Brazen Age."[125] Later generations, of course, would attempt to characterize the period neither with this title nor with Godkin's "Chromo Civilization," but as the Gilded Age.

The rise of the "new rich" in American cities was a popular topic in postwar magazine literature. For example, *Scott's* in 1867 reported that "New York rejoices in seven citizens whose collective wealth is estimated at $150,000,000"; a year later, it noted that there were 126 men with incomes exceeding $10,000 in St. Louis, 220 in Cincinnati, and 302 in Chicago.[126] In New York itself, a contributor to that city's *Galaxy* claimed, ten men owned one-tenth of the municipality's taxable property. They had achieved their wealth, he maintained, not by "*earning*" money, but by "*making*" it. Making money was accompanied by "GRAB"—that is, through the organization of economic power into a "RING": "These Rings have been many, and under varied names.... War, Government, Religion, Civilization, Progress, Commerce, Banks, Railroads, City Fathers, Dispensing Boards, Free-trade, Protection—these and many other good names have expressed, or do express, valuable Rings."[127] "An American

Positivist," writing in the *Galaxy*, cautioned that, since it had been demonstrated that major business firms were often guilty of bribing public officials, there would come pressure from all levels of society to organize against the monied powers. These opponents of the capitalistic plutocracy, the Positivist warned, had to learn that "every scheme to limit the power of wealth will inevitably fail," that "the capitalist is the true king of the industrial era." His reign thus far, it had to be admitted, had been less than perfect; however, as the system developed, conditions would improve. Capitalists, this *Galaxy* contributor continued, could not be satisfied with economic power only: "They desire to control also the political powers of the State and the nation. Well, they are right. They ought to have it." They were also "profound disbelievers in the whole republican or democratic theory of government. But we," he continued, shifting conspirationally from the third to first person, "are not, therefore, either Imperialists or Monarchists. We do not advocate going back to any obsolete political institutions. . . . There is something in the future as much better than republicanism as republicanism is better than monarchy, and that is the rule of wealth controlled by moral considerations. . . . Our king has come," the Positivist celebrated. "He rules already, but it is in such hideous shapes as the Lobby—the Ring. Let us recognize, tame, and ennoble him, so that he may serve the highest interests of humanity."[128] Such, in exaggerated and extreme form, was the argument of proponents of a benevolent plutocracy. Their case was proclaimed loudly during the postwar years and, indeed, it gained still greater favor in the final fifteen years of the century. It did not, however, go unchallenged.

Titus Munson Coan, for example, likened the powers of the "New American Plutocracy" to those of the feudal barony: "They cannot be deprived of their wealth without a social convulsion; and they cannot be lynched, for they could raise regiments of armed bravos. No aristocrat in modern days has had anything like the power of the American plutocrat; and no aristocrat in any days has been more completely beyond restraint."[129] The advent of aristocracy in the United States seemed imminent, warned lawyer and railroad builder Richard B. Kimball, since "every essential element" or its introduction was already present in the makeup of its largest corporations—"to wit, exclusive powers, rights, and privileges in perpetuity"; the aristocratic quality that was still lacking, unfortunately, was responsibility.[130] Indeed, the failure of the new wealth to respond to the needs of the municipality was particularly noted and criticized; upon the deaths of New York's "three monstrously rich men"—Vanderbilt, Astor, and A. T. Stewart—for example, the *Galaxy*'s "Philip Quilibet" observed that their "master passion of acquisition" had worked to "outwit death." These great fortunes, in other words, had been reinvested in business—not in the municipality.[131] The critics of the system feared that the meteoric rise of a plutocracy, its proud display of wealth, and its failure to exercise civic responsibility, taken together, constituted a threat to the social peace.

"The fact and the perception of a widening class rift," the fear "that America was in the grip of alien forces," an Alan Trachtenberg has described it, pervaded magazine writing about cities between 1865 and 1885.[132] "Fear," a contributor to the *Journal of Social Science* confessed, "not of danger from without, . . . but of internal disquiet, of disorderly movements, which may seize on the heart of a great city and may cost money if not blood to put it down,—this fear, the mother and the child of tyranny, is chronic and sleepless." Fear of the "dangerous classes," who were in "a state of war with social interests," was widespread.[133] Because the United States had never known before the dangers of class conflict, *Banker's Magazine* warned, its municipal governments were "not armed with powers and the machinery necessary to cope with these dangerous classes, when they are concentrated and organized, as they seem likely to be before long in our large cities."[134] To *Galaxy* also, it was equally obvious that the nation's cities required "the constant presence of organized force to protect us from domestic violence. The powers of disorder are in a certain way organizing themselves against society." Police powers had to be defined and formalized.[135]

The "powers of disorder" or "dangerous classes," as Charles Loring Brace had stigmatized them in his influential tract, *The Dangerous Classes of New York* of 1872, were, quite simply, the urban working and lower classes. More numerous, more visible, and seemingly more alien in the postwar years, they threatened to become a permanent proletariat. A booming industrialization, an expanding commercialization, the influx of European immigrants and native inmigrants, and the development of urban democracies could create an unstable social order. The great danger to urban America, most observers agreed, was that it would become the battleground for class warfare. While a postwar metropolis like New York City, for example, housed the nation's wealthiest people, there existed in that same city "squalid wretches who burrow in the worst class of tenement houses and in the old worm-eaten sheds of the dirtiest portions of the town."[136] Nor did this seem to be a passing phase of urban development. As an anonymous contributor to *Galaxy* noted, the celebration of the "dignity of labor" was still ritualistically repeated; however, by the late 1860s, this was merely "a fine phrase—it seems to be nothing more." A new value system seemed to determine that "*manual labor is disreputable in this community*; and indeed in all communities where great cities prevail."[137] The social distance between the opposed classes, plutocracy and proletariat, was, Titus Coan asserted in the mid–1870s, a worldwide phenomenon: "In the great cities of Christendom the wretchedness of human life has reached a degree which outdoes all the previous record of modern history, and probably even of the cruelest ancient tyrannies."[138] Such conditions, most Americans agreed, could no longer be tolerated in their urban centers.

An immediate response to the call for a new and better urban order was the moralistic one of individual regeneration. In the magazine literature of the two postwar decades, this answer to social (and, of course, political) problems was frequently voiced. More importantly, however, there appeared a developing awareness that the creation of a new urban order depended ultimately upon the fashioning of new approaches and institutions.

Education was, as always, a popular cause: "The school-room," a contributor
to *The Western* noted, "is the place for reform without ruin." "Education fights
the battle of truth, love, and light against darkness, hatred, and crime. It is the
hope of the patriot." Moreover, "the rich and poor it benefits alike."[139] The
poor, the dangerous classes themselves, were the objects of reform: from immigration restriction, to eugenics, to religious crusades in the tenement districts.[140] In most instances, reformers sought to avoid charitable giving: Charles
Loring Brace's widely imitated Children's Aid Society, for example, taught self-
help because its founder "dreaded the effect of almsgiving."[141] Still another
contributor to the *Journal of Social Science* sought to make unnecessary the
"soup-houses" of the winter by providing beforehand "penny banks" for the
city's "extravagant and prodigal" lower classes in the summer.[142] More ambitious still were plans for the provision of improved urban housing through
cooperative building societies for the middle class and in the erection of model
tenements for the lower class.[143] An outspoken housing reformer warned, for
example, that the "social see-saw" had to be balanced or Americans would be
faced with the "danger of Communism." Well-planned and well-constructed
model tenements were, he advised, a safeguard against the massing of dangerous
elements in the slums and, therefore, a necessary investment for the community's
leadership.[144] The building of model tenements with limited dividends to investors—"philanthropy and five per cent," declared one of this movement's ablest
spokesmen, Robert Treat Paine, reached and aided those at the "*very bottom*."[145]
In each case, it should be noted—in education, in philanthropic programs, in
housing—the leadership for those at the very bottom would come from the very
top—a patrician elite.

The recognition that there was a wide gap between the classes was, in itself,
an important insight. An awareness of this basic flaw in the social fabric, as in
the political, was the first step in its repair. A moralistic approach toward social
and economic ills, as toward the political, remained dominant during this period;
nevertheless, there was a reaching out for more tangible, more concrete solutions
to the problems of urban America. The technical advances made in public health,
the new confidence in human control over the urban environment, and the beginnings of a science of politics were lessons to all urbanites in their quest for
better and more livable cities, a more efficient and effective municipal administration, a prosperous and stabler economy, and a sounder and safer society.
Between 1865 and 1885, only a beginning had been made: the magazine literature
of the period was still more reportorial than analytical. Yet, by the middle of
the 1880s, a shift was under way—a change in direction recognized by at least
one contemporary, the editor of *Northwest Magazine*, Eugene Virgil Smalley.
"We are in a transition period," he wrote, "when old questions have been
settled and new questions . . . ,although looming spectre-like on the horizon of
the prophetic eye, are not seen clearly by the multitude. As they approach
nearer," he predicted, "the light and gossipy epoch of journalism will give place
to one of earnest thinking and vigorous writing."[146] That transition was made.

"Light and gossipy" magazine writing about urban America gave way to the professional and the specialized; and it was, without doubt, "vigorous writing." A new habit of mind was to transform the literature of urban awareness. The urbanist was in the process of becoming.

NOTES

1. Letter to Thomas Carlyle, Sept. 26, 1864, in *The Correspondence of Emerson and Carlyle*, ed. Joseph Slater (New York: Columbia University Press, 1964), 542.

2. Leonard Reissman, *The Urban Process: Cities in Industrial Societies* (New York: The Free Press, 1964), 18.

3. Charles Glaab and A. Theodore Brown, *A History of Urban America* (New York: Macmillan Company, 1967), 108–09.

4. Frank Luther Mott, *A History of American Magazines*, vol. 3: *1865–1885* (Cambridge: Harvard University Press, 1938), 3, 5, 25–26, 31–32, 17–18.

5. Gunther Barth, *City People: The Rise of Modern City Culture in Nineteenth-Century America* (New York: Oxford University Press, 1980), 58.

6. "Democratic Vistas," in *Walt Whitman: Representative Selections, with Introduction, Bibliography and Notes*, ed. Floyd Stovall, rev. ed. (New York: American Book Company, 1939), 377. Published in 1871, *Democratic Vistas* was drawn largely from his earlier essays in the *Galaxy*: "Democracy," 4 (December 1867): 919–33, and "Personalism," 5 (May 1868): 540–47. For "the increasingly popular concept of the national character" early in the period, see John Tomsich, *A Genteel Endeavor: American Culture in the Gilded Age* (Stanford, Calif.: Stanford University Press, 1971), esp. pp. 64–72.

7. Eugene Benson, "Solitude and Democracy," *Galaxy* 4 (June 1867): 165, 166–67.

8. The Editor, "The Manners of the Day," *Galaxy* 5 (March 1868): 376, 377.

9. N. L. L., "The Progress and Destiny of Man," *Scott's Monthly Magazine* 5 (June 1868): 323, 322.

10. Ibid., 324. The near realization of this prophecy in the final fifteen years of the century constitutes the major theme of this study.

11. "Our Tripod. Our American Civilization," *Scott's Monthly Magazine* 8 (March 1869): 229.

12. Justin McCarthy, "American Men and Englishmen," *Galaxy* 9 (June 1870): 759.

13. Titus Munson Coan, "American Timidity," *Galaxy* 10 (August 1870): 181, 177.

14. Ibid., 182, 177.

15. "English-Plated Americans," *Every Saturday*, n.s. 3 (July 8, 1871): 43.

16. "Drift-Wood. The Centenary," *Galaxy* 20 (July 1875): 118, 119. This short article contains an excellent statement of the condition of the city's parks and transportation system, as well as a clear program for federal and state aid to the municipality in this international exhibition (esp. pp. 119–21).

17. Gail Hamilton, "The Display of Washington Society," *Galaxy* 21 (June 1876): 763.

18. Jane Grey Swisshelm, "The American Character," *Galaxy* 22 (November 1876): 618–23.

19. Horace H. Morgan, "Grounds for American Patriotism," *The Western*, n.s. 4 (January–February 1878): 1, 2–11.

20. Julian Hawthorne, "Emerson as an American," *The Manhattan* 4 (August 1884): 207.

21. F. J. Ottarson, "New York and Its People," *Galaxy* 4 (May 1, 1867): 53, 60, 64.

22. "Monthly Gleanings," *Scott's Monthly Magazine* 5 (May 1868): 315, 314.

23. "Our Tripod," *Scott's Monthly Magazine* 6 (August 1868): 568. Significantly as was the case in the next article cited, this editorial linked urban expansion with international acquisition. This analogy between urbanization and imperialism, as will be demonstrated below, became even more common between 1885 and 1900.

24. T. W., "Our Millionaires," *Galaxy* 5 (May 1868):535.

25. "City Living," *Every Saturday*, n.s. 1 (November 19, 1870): 739.

26. "The Townward Tendency," *Every Saturday* n.s. 3 (October 21, 1871): 402.

27. Robert T. Porter, "Recent Changes in the West," *Journal of Social Science* 11 (May 1880): 49.

28. Charles G. Leland, "The Rise and Fall of Gloryville," *Our Continent*, 1 (April 12, 1882): 136–37.

29. "Luxury" [adapted from the French text by M. Bërard-Varagnac], *Banker's Magazine* 37 (February 1883): 575.

30. "Town Talk," *The Manhattan* 3 (May 1884): 518–19.

31. Leonard Kip, "The Building of Our Cities," *Hours At Home* 11 (July 1870):206.

32. Charles L. Sanford, *The Quest for Paradise: Europe and the American Moral Imagination* (Urbana: University of Illinois Press, 1961), p. 176 ff.

33. "The Government of the City of New York," *North American Review* 103 (October 1866): 464–65. The examples cited of successful experiments in town living included the ordering of New England villages; the vigor displayed by municipalities such as Nashville, Detroit, Cleveland, Buffalo, Rochester, and at least fifty other cities; and the civic projects of Boston and New York, especially the Croton Aqueduct and Central Park of the latter.

34. "Monthly Gleanings," *Scott's Monthly Magazine* 1 (May 1866): 432.

35. Ibid. 3 (January 1867): 79.

36. Ibid. 4 (December–January 1868): 958.

37. Col. O. Vandenburgh, "The City of New York Ten Years Hence," *Hours At Home* 7 (August 1868): 350, 357. A similar view was expressed in "The Future of New York," *Galaxy* 9 (April 1870): 545–53.

38. "Nebula/e," *Galaxy* 7 (May 1869): 772. Complaints of urban shortcomings, this same journal pointed out on another occasion, were to be found in any period for any great city (ibid. 8 [August 1869]: 290–91).

39. William R. Martin provided two of the better in-depth analyses of the city: "The Financial Resources of New York," *North American Review* 127 (November–December 1878): 427–43, and "Cities As Units in Our Polity," 128 (January 1879):21–34.

40. Frederic D. Storey, "Manahatta," *The Manhattan* 2 (July 1883): 77.

41. "Migma," *Continent* 4 (September 19, 1883): 379.

42. Albion W. Tourgée, "Migma. A New Departure," *Continent* 4 (October 31, 1883): 570.

43. Ibid.

44. Ralph Waldo Emerson, "Boston," *Atlantic Monthly* 37 (February 1876): 196, 197.

45. "Monthly Gleanings," *Scott's Monthly Magazine* 1 (April 1866): 361.

46. Ibid. 3 (May 1867): 400.

47. "Nebula/e," *Galaxy* 2 (December 1, 1866): 673–74, 675.

48. Charles Francis Adams, Jr., "Boston," *North American Review* 106 (January, April 1868): 1–25, 557–91. This is not to say, however, that the Hub's boosters were no longer to be heard from; for a general defense of that city, see "Town-Talk. A Boston Notion," *Every Saturday*, n.s. 2 (May 20, 1871): 475.

49. Nora Perry, "A Boston Man," *The Manhattan* 3 (June 1884): 586–87.

50. "Nebula/e," *Galaxy* 8 (October 1869): 578.

51. "Drift-Wood. Chicago," *Galaxy* 12 (December 1871): 855–56.

52. "Chicago and the Country," *Every Saturday*, n.s. 3 (October 28, 1871): 410.

53. "Burned Chicago," *Every Saturday*, n.s. 3 (October 28, 1871): 409.

54. "Chicago Revived" [reprinted from the Chicago *Tribune*, n.d.], *Every Saturday*, n.s. 3 (November 18, 1871): 490.

55. Kate Field, "Justin McCarthy on 'Chicago and the Prairie Fires,' " *Every Saturday*, n.s. 3 (December 16, 1871): 595.

56. "Reviews, Notes, Etc.," *Scott's Monthly Magazine* 2 (September 1866): 724.

57. [Edit.], *Scott's Monthly Magazine* 2 (October 1866): 790.

58. "Monthly Gleanings," *Scott's Monthly Magazine* 2 (November 1866): 868.

59. "Our Tripod. Labor in the South," *Scott's Monthly Magazine* 8 (August 1869): 630.

60. Paul M. Gaston, *The New South Creed: A Study in Southern Mythmaking* (New York: Alfred A. Knopf, 1970).

61. William L. Trenholm, "The Southern States: Their Social and Industrial History, Condition, and Needs," *Journal of Social Science* 9 (January 1878): 80, 82–83, 84, 91.

62. *The New South: Writings and Speeches of Henry Grady*, with an Introduction by Mills Lane (Savannah, Ga.: The Beehive Press, 1971), p. 119.

63. Harold M. Hyman, *A More Perfect Union: The Impact of the Civil War and Reconstruction on the Constitution* (New York: Alfred A. Knopf, 1973), p. 309.

64. An expanded discussion of the sanitary movement, which draws on these same materials, will be found in Dana F. White, "Landscaped Atlanta: The Romantic Tradition in Cemetery, Park, and Suburban Development," *Atlanta Historical Journal* 26, nos. 2–3 (Summer/Fall 1982): esp. 96–99.

65. Charles E. Rosenberg, *The Cholera Years: The United States in 1832, 1849, and 1866* (Chicago: University of Chicago Press, 1962), pp. 114, 209, 193.

66. George M. Fredrickson, *The Inner Civil War: Northern Intellectuals and the Crisis of the Union* (New York: Harper & Row, 1965), pp. 98–112.

67. "Notes," *Every Saturday*, n.s. 3 (December 2, 1871): 547.

68. Francis Bacon, "Civilization and Health," *Journal of Social Science* 3 (1871): 67–68, 70, 76.

69. John A. Church, "Scientific Miscellany. A City of Health," *Galaxy* 21 (February 1876): 273–74.

70. Elisha Harris, "The Public Health," *North American Review* 127 (November–December 1878): 444–55.

71. Charles F. Wingate, "The Water Supply of Cities," *North American Review* 136 (April 1883): 364–74; "The Unsanitary Homes of the Rich," *North American Review* 137 (August 1883): 172–84.

72. George E. Waring, Jr., "Sanitary Drainage," *North American Review* 137 (July 1883): 57–67.

73. "Leisure Moments," *Hours at Home* 9 (August 1869): 378.

74. "Simple Simon," *Every Saturday*, n.s. 1 (August 27, 1870): 546. Army doctors during the war, Francis Bacon maintained, had discovered that the healthy, ruddy appearances of country-bred soldiers often masked weak constitutions and poor emotional states; "while men of less bulk and stature and of paler skins, skilled workmen from factories, mechanics, and even clerks from the large towns, would take the same unaccustomed tasks with a cheerful alacrity, and endure them with hardihood, seeming none the worse for them when they were finished, but 'coming up smiling' at the end, to use the expressive phrase of the prize-ring" (*Journal of Social Science*, 3: 75).

75. "Nebula/e," *Galaxy* 24 (October 1877): 577.

76. B. G. Northrop, "Rural Improvements," *Our Continent* 1 (March 29, 1882): 111.

77. Charles G. D. Roberts, "The Sower," *The Manhattan* 4 (July 1884): 61.

78. Donald Grant Mitchell, *Hours at Home* 3 (June–September 1866): 101–08, 197–205, 347–54, 447–54; 4 (November 1866, February–April 1867): 1–7, 306–13, 429–39, 538–44. The individual sections were: "I. An Old-Style Farm"; "II. English and American Wayside"; "III. Mr. Urban and Fifty Acres"; "IV. Fifty Acres Again: A Commission of Inquiry"; "V. A Country House"; "VI. On the Laying of Grounds"; "VII. Village Greens and Railway Gardens"; and "VIII. Parks, Gardens, and Graves."

79. Ibid., 3: 104–08, 454.

80. James Manning Winchell, *Galaxy* 24 (July 1877): 85, 93.

81. The summer vacation for the city dweller became a popular topic around 1870. Typical articles on this subject in *Every Saturday* were: "Town Talk," n.s. 1 (December 10, 1870): 794–95; "In Town and Out of Town," n.s.1 (September 3, 1870): 562; "The End of the Season," n.s.1 (September 24, 1870): 610; and "Saratoga: The American Baden-Baden," n.s. 3 (September 9, 1871): 257, 260–62. All dealt with the summer vacation as a refreshing interlude in urban living; all assumed that the city dweller would return happily to his urban residence.

82. "*De Rebus Ruris*," *Hours at Home* 5 (April 1867): 538.

83. Stanley French, "The Cemetery as Cultural Institution: The Establishment of Mount Auburn and the 'Rural Cemetery' Movement," *American Quarterly* 26 (March 1974): 37–59.

84. "*De Rebus Ruris*," *Hours at Home* 4 (April 1867): 543.

85. Absalom Peters, "The City of the Silent," *Hours at Home* 3 (May 1866): 81.

86. Galen Cranz, *The Politics of Park Design: A History of Urban Parks in America* (Cambridge, Mass: MIT Press, 1982), pp. 3–59.

87. "Democratic Vistas," *Walt Whitman*, pp. 386–87.

88. "The Justifying Value of a Public Park," *Journal of Social Science* 12 (December 1880): 153, 163–64. Olmsted's theories concerning parks as vital elements in urban development are the subject of "concept for a plan," below, following Chapter 2.

89. "Town Talk," *The Manhattan* 4 (July 1884): 123.

90. During the late 1860s and into the 1870s, increasing attention was given to streetcar travel, especially to the crowded conditions of the lines and the lack of manners among the passengers. See, for example, *Galaxy*: "Nebula/e," 3 (March 15, 1867): 686–87; the poem "Riding in a Street Car," 12 (November 1871): 728; and "Nebula/e," 24 (September 1877): 436.

91. Richard Grant White, "Gateways of the Central Park" (Review of *Gateways of*

the Southern Entrances of the Central Park, by Richard M. Hunt), *Galaxy* 1 (August 1, 1866): 653–54.

92. "Our Houses," *Every Saturday*, n.s. 3 (July 15, 1871): 67.

93. "*De Rebus Ruris*," *Hours at Home* 4 (November 1866): 1.

94. John Paul, "Things," *Every Saturday*, n.s. 2 (January 28, 1871): 91.

95. The two extremes may be found in "The Uglifying Process," *Every Saturday*, n.s. 1 (January 29, 1870): 77, and in Francis Bacon's essay in the *Journal of Social Science* 3 (1871): 58–77.

96. Leonard Kip, "The Building of Our Cities," *Hours at Home* 11 (July 1870): 206.

97. "Mr. Blaine on Municipal, State and County Debts," *Banker's Magazine* 29 (November 1874): 356–57, 359.

98. "Simple, Equitable Taxation," *Banker's Magazine* 28 (February 1874): 605–07. Churches and other such institutions, "which have hitherto been excused on supposed charitable grounds," should also, this journal suggested, be taxed "equitably" (607). *Banker's Magazine* was not alone in this demand: the argument over the taxation of nonprofit organizations continued throughout the century as a minor but persistent theme.

99. "The Growth of Municipal Debts," *Banker's Magazine* 31 (September 1876): 181, 183.

100. "New York City and State Taxation," *Banker's Magazine* 36 (March 1882): 655.

101. "City Indebtedness," *Banker's Magazine* 38 (May 1884): 823, 824–25. Because of its long-term commitments, New York's sinking-fund system, it was noted here, threatened to "immortalize" public debts.

102. Robert P. Porter, "The Municipal Debt of the United States," *Galaxy* 24 (September 1877): 399.

103. *Brendan Behan's New York* (London: Hutchinson & Co. [Publishers] Ltd., 1964), p. 13.

104. Nathan Glazer and Daniel P. Moynihan, *Beyond the Melting Pot: The Negroes, Puerto Ricans, Jews, Italians, and Irish of New York City* (Cambridge, Mass.: MIT Press and Harvard University Press, 1963), p. 223.

105. "Government of the City of New York," *North American Review* 103 (October 1866): 415, 446, 419, 447–59, 462.

106. "Municipal Corruption," *Every Saturday*, n.s. 2 (January 7, 1871): 3.

107. "Street-Car Ruffianism," *Every Saturday*, n.s. 2 (May 20, 1871): 458. (italics added).

108. "The Science of Comparative Rascality," *Every Saturday*, n.s. II (May 27, 1871): 498.

109. "The Exposure of the New York Tweed Ring," *Every Saturday*, n.s. 3 (August 1871): 146.

110. "Dangers That Threaten," *Every Saturday*, n.s. 3 (October 7, 1871): 338–39.

111. "How Much Was Stolen," *Every Saturday*, n.s. 3 (November 18, 1871): 482. The most detailed contemporary account of the Tweed scandals was Charles F. Wingate's *North American Review* series "An Episode in Municipal Government": "I. The Ring," 119 (October 1874): 359–408; "II. The Reign of the Ring," 120 (January 1875): 119–74; "III. The Ring Charter," 121 (July 1875): 113–55; "IV. The Shattering of the Ring," 123 (October 1876): 362–425.

112. The "monkey Irish," made famous in Thomas N. Nast's brilliant satiric cartoons

in *Harper's Weekly*, may also be found in the drawings in this magazine; see, for example, "The Broadway Squad," *Every Saturday* n.s. 1 (March 5, 1870): 160; two cartoons on Irish street laborers, n.s. 3 (October 21, 1871): 388, 391; and "Tammany at Bay," n.s. 3 (October 28, 1871): 421. This ethnic stereotype was also prominent in the poems "The Situation in Gotham. By Ex-Councilman Terrance O'Toole," n.s. 3 (October 14, 1871): 367, and "The Ballad of Boss Billee" [reprinted from the New York *Tribune*], n.s. 3 (November 18, 1871): 487.

113. See, for example, Samuel L. Clemens (Mark Twain), "The Curious Republic of Gondour," *Atlantic Monthly* 36 (October 1875): 461–63.

114. Francis Parkman, *North American Review* 127 (July–August 1878): 2.

115. Dorman B. Eaton, "A New Phase of the Reform Movement," *North American Review* 132 (June 1881): 558.

116. Dorman B. Eaton, "Municipal Government," *Journal of Social Science* 5 (1873): 11, 34–35.

117. James Parton, in "The Power of Public Plunder," *North American Review* 133, (July 1881): 43–64, argued that all civic progress had come either from a nobility or an upper class. Therefore, so that American society might advance, it would be necessary for men of wealth, distinction, and family to govern. In the same journal, John A. Kasson, in "Municipal Reform," 137 (September 1883): 218–30, asserted that a city's largest taxpayers ought to make up its governing body, and Gamaliel Bradford, in "The Proposed Charter for the City of Boston," 123, (July 1876): 1–25, stated the case for the strong-mayor system of municipal government.

118. "Population of the United States," *Banker's Magazine* 37 (May 1883): 826.

119. Edward Self, "The Abuse of Citizenship," *North American Review* 136 (June 1883): 556.

120. William L. Scruggs, "Restriction of the Suffrage," *North American Review* 139 (November 1884): 493.

121. William Graham Sumner, "Politics in America, 1776–1876," *North American Review* 122 (January 1876): 82.

122. Horace H. Morgan, "Grounds for American Patriotism," *The Western*, n.s. 4 (January–February 1878): 11.

123. Gail Hamilton, "The Display of Washington Society," *Galaxy* 21 (June 1876): 766.

124. "Philip Quilibet," "Drift-Wood," *Galaxy* 6 (August 1868): 273–74.

125. "Drift-Wood. The Times and the Customs," *Galaxy* 23 (May 1877): 696.

126. [Notes], *Scott's Monthly Magazine* 3 (February 1867): 159; ibid. 5 (May 1868): 316.

127. T. W., "Our Millionaires," *Galaxy* 5 (May 1868): 529–33; 536.

128. "What to do with Wealth," *Galaxy* 8 (November 1869): 707, 708.

129. Titus Munson Coan, "American Timidity," *Galaxy* 10 (August 1870): 183.

130. Richard B. Kimball, "What Are Our Aristocratic Institutions?"*Galaxy* 17 (February 1874): 262.

131. "Drift-Wood. The Wills of the Triumvirate," *Galaxy* 23 (March 1877): 411.

132. Alan Trachtenberg, *The Incorporation of America: Culture and Society in the Gilded Age* (New York: Hill and Wang, 1982), pp. 79, 71.

133. T. D. Woolsey, "Nature and Sphere of Police Power," *Journal of Social Science* 3 (1871): 109, 111.

134. "Emigration and Public Wealth," *Banker's Magazine* 30 (April 1876): 770.

135. "Nebula/e," *Galaxy* 24 (September 1877): 433.

136. F. J. Ottarson, "New York and Its People," *Galaxy* 4 (May 1, 1867): 63.

137. "Is Labor a Curse?" *Galaxy* 6 (October 1868): 539.

138. Titus Munson Coan, "Reforming the World," *Galaxy* 22 (August 1876): 163–64.

139. L. Soldan, "To Ruin is Not to Reform," *The Western*, n.s. 5 (May–June 1879): 290.

140. Almost every article on immigration surveyed for this study contained some recommendation for exclusion. Titus Coan, in "Reforming the World," *Galaxy* 22: 164–68, stated the case for eugenics. Protestant action programs in the large cities were given little space in secular magazines, perhaps because most denominations were indifferent to applied Christianity and were therefore unable to supply literature on the subject. (It proved impossible to select a representative religious journal from the thousands published during this period.)

One of the few postwar evaluations of the urban minister in the magazines examined here noted that "the position of the popular city clergyman, warmly beloved and highly paid, is, in a worldly sense, the most enviable one that a professional man can desire" ("The City Clergyman," *Every Saturday*, n.s. 3 [July 29, 1871]: 114). So shallow an observation would not be made after 1885.

141. Charles Loring Brace, "Child-Helping as a Means of Preventing Crime in the City of New York," *Journal of Social Science* 18 (May 1884): 289.

142. John P. Townsend, "Savings Banks," *Journal of Social Science* 9 (January 1878): 60–62.

143. See, for example, "Philadelphia Building Societies," *Banker's Magazine* 34 (July 1879): 26–27.

144. C. E. Illsey, "Homes for the People," *The Western*, n.s. 4 (July–August 1878): 450, 457, 457–70.

145. Robert Treat Paine, "Homes for the People," *Journal of Social Science* 15 (February 1882): 114. The problem faced by the housing movement in this first twenty-year period, as in the second fifteen-year one, was summed up in the *Galaxy*: "A speculative society needs cheap houses and low rents, in order that it may have more to speculate with" ("Nebula/e," 15 [January 1873]: 147). Such an attitude, and it was widespread, effectively limited the appeal of housing reformers for a limited dividend of 5 percent.

146. Eugene Virgil Smalley, "Recent Tendencies in American Journalism," *The Manhattan* 3 (April 1884): 365.

THE URBANIST

By the turn of the century, the United States was fast becoming an urban nation. Unsettling challenges and undreamed of opportunities seemed all-pervasive: the colossal metropolis, with its tight massing of inner-city residents and loose ties with suburban dwellers, shattered the walls of the historic city and invaded virgin countryside; science and technology introduced complex and untested devices for sheltering, maintaining, and transporting both urbanite and suburbanite; the forces of social change tested time-honored municipal institutions, found them wanting, and demanded modern ones in their place. New ideas, leaders, ethnic and racial groups, social classes, economic interests,and professional organizations confronted, then broke with the traditional. The United States had become, one journal proclaimed, "A Land of Great Cities." "One may truly call this century not only the age of cities," another observer boasted, "but also," invoking the familiar title of Briton Robert Vaughan's 1843 study, "the age of great cities."[1] And those great cities, a new generation of urban observers argued, could be planned, shaped, and controlled. What historian Robert H. Wiebe christened a "search for order" was in progress.[2]

A new habit of mind transformed periodical literature on urban themes during the final fifteen years of the century. The emerging metropolitan civilization lent impetus to the advancement of specialists in established disciplines, the professions, the new social sciences, all phases of technology, and the developing area of professional administration. Theorists, scholars, scientists, administrators, involved citizens, and experts came together to form their own organizations and to establish their associations' periodicals. This age of associationalism, under way by the mid–1880s, produced in the field of magazine publication, as Frank Luther Mott has observed, "an era of multiplicity, if not plenty." Every group published "its own journal or journals—all the ideologies and movements, all the arts, all the schools of philosophy and education, all the sciences, all the trades and industries, all the professions and callings, all organizations of importance, all hobbies and recreations."[3] Each of these journals, moreover, was distinguished by a marked specialization. In sharp contrast with older magazines, such as *Atlantic Monthly* and *Galaxy*, with their obvious appeal to the catholic interests of the well-educated reader, the limitation of subject matter and its consequent detailing in these more recent periodicals mark them clearly as a new type of publication. Of the twenty-six magazines upon which the chapters that follow are, for the most part, based, thirteen may be classified as professional and trade publications and seven others as strictly urban journals; the final six, although more mixed, also evidenced narrow and particular emphases (see Table 1, Appendix). These journals served as media of communication from each particular association to the reading public and as sounding boards for new ideas within each individual organization. Innovators within each field, as they began to define its outer boundaries and explore its inner ranges, evidenced a progressively surer grasp of fundamentals and of detail, as well as a growing tendency toward further specialization within the field itself.

For American cities, the urbanist was to be the prime mover in the period's search for order. His first task was to inventory the information and skills within his area of expertise; then, after this initial stock-taking, he was to recommend improvements in the structuring of organizations and in the formation of policies. His role was to be practical as well as theoretical. Assured that he would have sufficient opportunity to apply his analyses to immediate civic concerns, the urbanist expounded an optimistic creed of efficiency that permeated his writings. He prompted "the feeling," as Gunther Barth described it, "that something new was afoot."[4]

The periodical writings of the urbanist covered all aspects of city living— from shaping its physical environment, to administering its public business, to determining its social balance. This is not to argue that he led a formal movement for reshaping urban America; instead, the urbanist reflected a new mood or frame of mind. He responded differently to each urban challenge: with assurance and dispassion toward planning, with confidence and aggressiveness in politics, with concern and uncertainty toward class antagonisms and the social balance. His ideas are not readily categorized, for the voices of the periodical press were many—some adhering tenaciously to the past, more looking optimistically to the future; nevertheless, a general pattern emerges, an orientation toward the future metropolis. His emergence is the story of a new American urban self-consciousness.

NOTES

1. "A Land of Great Cities," *World's Work*, 1 (December 1900): 138–39; Edmund J. James, "The Growth of Great Cities in Area and Population," *Annals of the American Academy of Political and Social Science* 13 (January 1899): 8; Robert Vaughan, *The Age of Great Cities* (London: Jackson & Walford, 1843).

2. Robert H. Wiebe, *The Search for Order, 1877–1920* (New York: Hill and Wang, 1967).

3. Frank Luther Mott, *A History of American Magazines*, vol. 4: *1885–1905* (Cambridge: Harvard University Press, 1957), p. 10. Mott estimates that 4,400 periodicals were in print in 1890, 5,100 in 1895, 5,500 in 1900, and 6,000 in 1905. Between 1885 and 1905, according to his estimates, nearly 11,000 different periodicals were published.

4. Gunther Barth, *City People: The Rise of Modern City Culture in Nineteenth-Century America* (New York: Oxford University Press, 1980), p. 36.

2

Comprehending Metropolis, 1885–1900

METROPOLITAN THEORY, CITY AND SUBURB

Fin-de-siècle musings over the future of cities became a specialty for late-century urbanists. "The population of the twentieth century will be predominantly urban," Francis H. McLean predicted. "It will be the cities and the city vote which will decide great elections. It will be city ideas and ideals which will sway the nation. Calculating the relative increase of urban over rural population upon the basis of growth of the last fifty years the ultimate supremacy of cities can be foretold with the measure of the decades."[1] The turn of the century also provided opportunities for reflection upon the past and for fresh perspectives on the present.

Most American citizens in 1900 would most likely have agreed with their fathers that the greatest of their great urban centers was New York City. Here was the money; here was the power. Here, *The Public* of Chicago lamented, was the country's "capitalistic center, and our national life is now a capitalized affair." The East ruled the nation, "and New York is the east."[2] But Gotham's title to national leadership depended on more than mere material wealth, claimed New York's official bookkeeper Comptroller Bird S. Coler. His turn-of-the-century New York was "a great city, splendid in all that represents the grandest achievements of human genius, and the mind of man can scarcely grasp the possibilities of the future." Indeed, those very possibilities indicated that the New York of the twentieth century would become "the greatest city on earth, not only in population and wealth, but in the perfect development of all the grand opportunities of nature and science that tend to better the condition of mankind and to insure happiness and prosperity." New York City, Coler predicted, would advance on all fronts, material and spiritual, "until the people of all countries in years to come shall bow in reverence and admiration before the achievement of American genius.''[3] The prophecies of one of Comptroller Col-er's fellow civil servants, that indomitable sanitarian Colonel George E. Waring, Jr., were also called into witness by the editors of *Public Improvements* in the opening year of the new century as testimony to the future greatness of the Empire City. Waring, at that point the City's commissioner of street cleaning, had proclaimed his city of the late 1890s vastly superior to the Manhattan of the late 1860s, and held out the hope for continued, almost unlimited, improvement in the twentieth century. Even before the close of the coming century, Waring predicted, New York's population would number 10 million. Significantly, the city of which he wrote was part of a new order: its commercial center would, unfortunately, ''be given over entirely to architectural monstrosities devoted almost entirely to business''; however, the future of its residents would be a happier one, since, after they had been displaced from the central city, they would move into outlying communities, especially on Long Island, to enjoy healthier and more productive lives in homes of their own. Suburban living would guarantee them, as *Public Improvements* paraphrased Waring, ''air, light and sanitary arrangements,'' conditions that would be made possible when rapid transit became ''something more than a name'' and when the automobile came to play ''a prominent part in transportation problems.''[4] With singular prescience, then, Waring anticipated the transformation of the crowded nineteenth-century commercial and industrial city into a more open twentieth-century metropolis through the agency of an, as yet, unachieved automobile revolution.[5] As remark-able as these turn-of-the-century hopes and predictions for the Greater New York of the future might have been, the optimism from which they stemmed was not merely a local phenomenon; rather, it expressed the mood in all of urban America.

On the continent's other coast at the turn of the century, the urban spokesmen of California shared this national optimism. Here, the growth of cities had also proved constant; here, too, the opportunities for the future seemed limitless. Population gains in the closing decades of the century, particularly in the San Francisco Bay region and in the towns of Southern California, were not attributed to commercial reasons alone. The booming urban aggregations of the Pacific coast, the editors of *California Municipalities* proclaimed, had developed a new precondition to growth, which they labeled ''the esthetic idea.'' California cities ''have appealed not to men's pockets but to men's lives. They have said 'Here is the place to live!' and have called attention that the climate is not only agreeable but that it produces rare and beautiful trees, shrubs and flowers the year round.''[6] A native troubadour assured the readers of this same journal that quality, not quantity, was vital in urban California: ''No city or town of the Golden West/ Is willing to rest till it gets the best.''[7] In California, its propagandists proclaimed, ''the Coming City is the Artistic City.''[8]

This inclination toward predicting the future of urban America, the coming city of the twentieth century—whether it was to be shaped by commercial growth and a revolution in transportation, as in New York, or by the cultivation of climatic and scenic advantages, as in California—was symptomatic of the new habit of mind made manifest in the final years of the century. Although the subjects of these articles were individual cities, the emphasis throughout was upon the general process of urbanization. No longer did merely descriptive accounts suffice; in their place, the late-century urbanist substituted conceptual analysis and generalization, the beginnings of a systematic approach to urban studies.

In the spring of 1900, Dr. Leo S. Rowe of the University of Pennsylvania attempted to put late-nineteenth-century urbanization into proper historical perspective by demonstrating that the city had always played a dominant role, sometimes positive and sometimes negative, in the development of civilization. "In every system of social philosophy from Aristotle to Spencer," Rowe maintained, "the relation of city growth to national progress has occupied an important place." Classical civilization was "centered in the city. Beyond its limits life was stunted and incomplete." In the Middle Ages, he continued, a reaction had set in against "the conventionality and artificiality of city life," and the urban center had been "looked upon as the center of vice and crime"; however, the balance had been righted by the eighteenth century's "revolt against the excesses to which the temptations of city life had led." Now, at the close of the nineteenth century, Rowe asserted, the role of the city had once again been recognized as a positive one, for "the changes accompanying the industrial revolution had demonstrated that economic progress and city growth were connected as cause and effect." The nineteenth century had rediscovered the truth that it was " 'the crowd, the hum, the shock of men' that sharpens the intellect, develops inventive genius, stirs commercial activity, and arouses the spirit of cooperation." The city of the nineteenth century had brought together into a working partnership the rational control of the classical world and the individual initiative of the industrial; its development would, as a result, create "such a change in the life and thought of the people as will bring an increasing number of city services into organic, vital relation with the daily life, the pleasures and recreations of the population."[9]

This same "organic" and "vital" relationship had become the focus in the 1890s of a popular metaphor for urbanization, one known as "organicism." This "germ theory" of historical development, which suggested the image of society as "a living, self-perpetuating integral and adaptable totality," bolstered a native American faith in progress with imported Darwinian environmentalism.[10] Its major appeal lay in its wide utility. Kansas State Professor of Political Economy Thomas E. Will, for example, could employ it to encompass all urban society: "A healthy city is an organism with all its parts bound together like the various organs and members of the human body, all parts conscious of and responding to an impulse given to a single part."[11] Economist John R. Commons referred to this set of ideas when he declared in 1893 that all major socioeconomic issues were "laced and interlaced" because of the "organic nature of society."[12] This was also the conceptual framework upon which Mrs. Cornelius Stevenson based her optimistic prediction, made before the Civic Club of Philadelphia in

March 1894, that a natural social balance would be achieved in American cities because of the "unwritten law governing the social organism."[13] The official journal of the American Federation of Labor, too, although it challenged the inevitability of attaining this equilibrium, was prepared to accept organicism. While it was ready to grant that society might be "likened to the human body, composed of nerves, tissues, glands, cells, each dependent upon the other, in which individuality and regularity are one and the same," *American Federationist* cautioned, that "should the organism demand from any one of these more than its capability, the whole system becomes deranged." At that point the parts that did not function would be transformed into "glandular secretions being made up of cast-off cells,—barnacles excluded from the cell-republic. The difference between the human and social organism is," *Federationist* warned, "that the barnacles are not so easily got rid of in the latter."[14] Significantly, three of the four sources cited above employed the imagery of organicism to convey a sense of social unity; the fourth, the labor journal, used it to emphasize the threat of disintegration. The adaptability of the vocabulary of organicism was thus its primary virtue. So functional, in fact, was this analogy between the social group and the animal organism that few contemporary writers dared to point out that this relationship was purely metaphorical. A contributor to *Municipality* in 1900, primarily because he sought radical change in the social order, did so dare. The self-preserving organism possessed passive characteristics that assured its survival, Joseph Loeb asserted, but a social organization demanded active components in its makeup in order to meet ever-increasing demands. The urban community, because it was positive and not negative, was then an organization and not an organism. Moreover, the innovation that Loeb proposed, municipal socialism, could be achieved not by evolutionary and long-term change, but only by revolutionary and immediate action, which in turn could be effected only through a more complex urban organization.[15] Therefore, the serviceability of organicism depended ultimately upon whether or not its user was prepared to work within the existing political and socioeconomic framework. If he was, organicism served as a convenient framework. His journals suggest that, with few exceptions, he was. Evolutionary, not revolutionary, change was his design.

The student of the American city at the opening of the new century, in his attempt to comprehend nineteenth-century urbanization, was generally less concerned with any biological analogy of society than he was with the mechanics of urban growth, the patterns of and motivation behind the creation of community; logically, he turned from intuitive response to quantitative analysis. The federal census of 1900 provided, the editors of *California Municipalities* suggested, a starting point for such inquiries. It demonstrated, in the first place, that population increases in major urban centers had leveled off in the 1890s. This development, the journal advised, was neither surprising nor regrettable, because too often the "big city" had become "a crowded place with smoky and impure atmosphere; its streets are dusty and frequently ill paved; its moral atmosphere is unwholesome; living is expensive, especially in the matter of rents; its schools are overcrowded and generally not the best—in fact, a score of discomforts and disagreeable features may be charged against the modern metropolis." The expansion of rapid transit had made available to city dwellers and rural in-migrants an alternative mode of urban living by the promotion of "the small suburban town." "The smaller town has a pure atmosphere; there evil temp-tations are not prevalent to the extent that beset the youth of the big city; its municipal government is better; politics do not control the schools; there is more physical freedom, and those who have families to raise give these matters grave consideration." The metropolitan future of its state, the official journal of the League of California Municipalities concluded, was a bright one: suburban towns would expand on their own account; it remained only for the core cities to provide their residents with beautiful and functional urban centers.[16] Frederick L. Hoffman, in an address before the New Jersey Sanitary Association in that same year, turned also to the census of 1900, noted with approval the same "suburban trend," and was even more optimistic about the metropolitan future of his own state. He applauded "the tendency of recent times on the part of the more intelligent people to leave the large cities and settle in the more healthy and more advantageous portions of the surrounding territory, where under semi-rural conditions they can enjoy a degree of happiness and health such as under the best conditions is not possible in the crowded centres of population."[17]

Historically, the suburb had always adjoined the city: Many preindustrial cities, from the middle of the fourth millennium B.C. to the middle of the second millenium A.D., had boasted residential villas scattered about beyond the walls or confines of the cities themselves. However, the process of suburbanization, a mature phase of urbanization, could not begin in earnest until the urban-industrial complex had come of age; until, that is, population concentration in the core cities had reached a certain high density, transportation and commu-nication networks had been established, and home-owning by the middle and lower middle classes had been made practicable by new building and mortgaging procedures.[18] One of the most perceptive and original urban scholars of the period, statistician Adna Ferrin Weber, viewed "the rise of the suburbs" as a dual process: first, one of " 'city building,' the tearing down of dwellings to make room for business blocks"; second, one resulting from "the improvements in transportation, which enable an increasing proportion of the city's population to reside at a distance from their places of business. The double movement is relieving the congested districts and filling up the suburbs." Suburbanization, he asserted, was "by far the most cheering movement of modern times. It means an essential modification of the process of concentration of population that has been taking place during the last hundred years and brought with it many of the most difficult political and social problems of our day." The suburb, Weber concluded, was the hope of urban America, for it united "the advantages of city and country. The country's natural surroundings, the city's social surroundings—these are both the possession of the suburb."[19] For Weber, then, suburbanization was the optimum stage of urbanization.

By the mid–1890s, this new phase of city growth was widely recognized. Franklin H. Giddings, founder of Columbia University's Department of Sociology, noted that "the concentration of population in cities of monstrous dimensions" signaled a "transition stage" in urban living patterns, one marked by electricity scattering "much that steam has concentrated."[20] Levi Gilbert, too, commented upon "the constant centrifugal tendency, increased by electric rapid transit enormously, to get away from business centers and deteriorated streets, to find cheaper rent on the outskirts, to buy or build a house more eligibly located, in better neighborhoods."[21] Perhaps the imagination and wit of Edwin W. Sanborn's description of a suburbanized greater Boston best captured the mood created by this "centrifugal tendency":

If some supernatural observer could have taken a bird's eye view of New England in 1850 and again in 1900, he would read the story of change in plain character. Approaching New England, as would become a Superior Intelligence, by way of Boston, he would find the region for some fifteen miles around the gilded dome of Beacon Hill, so "filled in" as to form a continuous city with a million people, nearly half of them—figuring back for three generations—being Irish, about one-sixth "Old Americans," and the rest Germans, British, Scandinavians, Italians, Frenchmen, Chinamen, and citizens generally. . . . In river valleys the smoke of factory chimneys would draw attention to busy cities, wherever water power had fixed a site for manufacturing. In their suburbs he would mark the hard roads, with their maze of wires and buzz of trolleys and lines of thrifty dwellings.[22]

The quality of life in these "lines of thrifty dwellings" was of major interest at the close of the century, and satiric glimpses of the new suburbia filled the pages of the humor magazine, *Yellow Kid*. The modernity of the new domesticity was evident in the threat of an "Irate Suburban Resident" to his next-door neighbor that he would order his daughter to practice the piano before breakfast "if you don't stop getting out that infernal lawn mower at four o'clock."[23] Or again, "Mr. Suburb" explained to "Mrs. Suburb" that he was two hours late for dinner because he had "missed the five-seventeen train and had to take the five-nineteen. Mrs. S.—But that is only two minutes. Mr. S—Yes, my dear, but the five-seventeen comes straight through, and the five-nineteen stops at one hundred and seventy-three stations before it gets there."[24] A short story in the *Yellow Kid*, "My Suburban Sweetheart," telescoped the processes of the initial exodus from core to ring and a hasty retreat back again. The unnamed hero-narrator of the tale left Manhattan for the promise of a tranquil life in the verdant acres of Ferndale, New Jersey. He had hoped "to escape the din and roar of the metropolis, to find repose from its nerve-unstringing intensity of life. There should be no more clanging gongs of cable cars, no climbing to the 'L' road and sitting in stifling hot cars." He found, instead, that his daily trips into the city were marked by missing his trains, losing his commutation ticket, slapping mosquitoes on the station's platform, and dodging bicycles on his walk home; thus, he related, "when I recalled the push, shove and general maul of the suburbanites going to the station and returning therefrom day in and day out except Sunday, it appeared to me that it would be preferable to wear out my human machine, if anywhere, in some quiet undiscoverable lodging of the city of my childhood and my heart."[25] Yet, for every prodigal son who returned gratefully to the city of his childhood and his heart, a handful of his contemporaries retreated each to their own Ferndales and stayed there. How, asked serious students of society, would this pattern of movement affect the quality of urban life?

The central city, the Rev. Amory H. Bradford answered, was, because of this emigration of its natural leadership, a victim of suburbanization: "A large part of the property in cities," he observed, "is owned by those who dwell in the suburbs, and a large proportion of the business is done by those who live, vote and exert all their influence there, apart from business hours"; moreover, not only had men of political and business ability "gone to the suburbs, but many of the best Christian workers also." What this exodus of its elite did to a major city such as New York, Bradford warned, was to transform it from an urban community into a mere gathering point for the "masses," a "congeries of hotels, boarding-houses, apartment houses and tenements, with a comparatively small number of dwellings which, in the best sense, may be called home." In the metropolis, family life became "more and more impossible," as the family unit gave way to two inherently irresponsible groups: "The young who own nothing, and go with the hope of earning a livelihood in a more easy and respectable way than is possible in the rural districts" and "those who seek the city because it is the capital of pleasure." Its cities, Bradford insisted, were "the hearts of the nation." Should the present trend continue with "the best in the cities . . . emigrating to the suburbs, and the worst of the rural districts . . . flocking to the cities," urban America might soon become the abode of the proletariat and the plutocracy, with the former constantly menacing the latter. The challenge was clear: "If the best citizens slumber in the suburbs, the worst will run and ruin the cities." The necessary response of the Christian churches in the suburbs was equally clear to this determined minister, for the churches themselves were the victims of suburbanization: the comforts of an affluent, semi-rural life had "limited fields for the exercise of Christian energy." Suburban church members were able to "build churches and study the Bible, but opportunities of personal intercourse with the suffering and sinning—the means by which the most splendid character is developed—are not at hand." The suburban churches, then, were menaced by "spiritual destitution," and they needed "the cities as fields for the exercise of superfluous spiritual energy."[26]

To Samuel M. Lindsay, a political scientist from Columbia University and later director of the New York School of Philanthropy, suburbanization was less a curse than a blessing, for it promised relief for the urban poor from the congestion of pestiferous tenement districts. The example set by the City and Suburban Homes Company of New York, a benevolent investment corporation that adhered strictly to the principles of model housing, in its building of the

Homewood Estate in the Thirtieth Ward of Brooklyn, was a case in point. A "suburban colony of homes" on 530 city lots had been erected on the plains of Flatbush by this housing reform group, and its Second Annual Report predicted that "when completed, Homewood will be an ideal suburban village." This new Brooklyn community, Lindsay claimed, boasted of a modern sewage system, convenient transportation lines, and a well-planned system of interior roads and streets. Nor, he added, did it lack amenities: "The style of architecture is exceedingly tasteful, unified without being uniform. A well-known real estate editor has described Homewood as a Shakespearean village. The aptness of his characterization, technically considered, is complete."[27]

In the age of associationalism, two conflicting views of the movement from the core to its rings were articulated: the suburb as the probable destroyer of the central city or as the potential creator of a more civilized metropolis. The debate begun in the 1890s has continued to the present, and the image of the suburb as destroyer has become increasingly the emphasis of urban experts and popular writers alike. At the close of last century, however, most urbanists emphasized the role of the suburb as creator, since the opening up of the municipality's outlying rings promised both relief from the inner city's congestion and a greater mobility for all but the poorest of its dwellers. Suburbanization, in short, held out the hope for a democratization of opportunity: the gentlemen farmers and pseudo-squires of the postwar decades were to be joined now by a new breed of pioneers—professionals, clerks, shopkeepers, and skilled laborers—all in their own search for environment.

One final viewpoint of suburbanization was possible. Some observers were simply intrigued by the day-to-day process itself, the comings and the goings of thousands of commuters. The half million of "Manhattan's Suburbanites" from Brooklyn and New Jersey who daily almost depopulated the city's outlying rings were in themselves, Grace Goodwin maintained, a cause for wonder. "That such large masses can be handled within the space of a few hours without confusion, without accident, and almost without friction, is proof conclusive of the superb executive powers of those officials who have the matter in charge." It was, more importantly, "a test of the good nature of an American crowd, which endures without complaint innumerable discomforts for the comfort of reaching a home in the suburbs where it may sleep and return anon for its daily labor in the great metropolis."[28] Whether they lamented, applauded, or merely wondered at the pull of the suburbs, contemporary observers of urban America could not ignore it. It had shaped the metropolis of 1900, and it promised to remain a major force in the years ahead.[29]

Although the pull of the suburb (the centrifugal force of urban growth) interested the student of the city at the century's close, the ever-compelling lure of the central city (the centripetal drive of urbanization) fascinated even more. To study this phenomenon, the urbanist could turn with confidence by 1900 to the most ambitious study of urbanization yet undertaken in the United States, Adna Ferrin Weber's *The Growth of Cities in the Nineteenth Century*, an analysis that documented statistically, for the first time, the lure of the city.[30] William Z. Ripley pronounced it a "remarkably well-executed monograph," one that demonstrated that "men, once grafted upon urban life, permanently acquire the social habit, just as industrial promoters tell us they take on the telephone, the typewriter, and the street-car habit." Weber's study indicated, too, Ripley claimed, that the city dweller also acquired the "ambition habit."[31] People removed to and remained in cities, then, because of a desire for close social ties with their peers, or an urge to advance themselves materially, or a combination of both motives.

In December 1900, Samuel T. Dutton wrote that while it was "customary to ascribe [the] social change from rural to urban conditions" during the late nineteenth century "entirely to the influence of industry," it was equally important to recognize that there was another cause involved in this transformation, the fact that "people are naturally gregarious." Moreover, this human trait had been a mark of all civilized societies. "The valleys of the Tigris, of the Euphrates, and of the Nile," Dutton continued, "contained vast cities, when industrial conditions were distinctly different from what they are to-day. The same thing is noticeable among all ancient nations as well as in later times."[32] People had always lived in cities, then, because urban life had something unique to offer; indeed, George E. Bissel noted, "Were all the advantages of the city possible in the country, there would be no cities."[33] Thus, to the demographic process of *urbanization* it was necessary to add the abstract appeal of *urbanism*.

By the turn of the century most students of this nation of cities would have subscribed to Aristotle's dictum that "men come together in cities to live, but they remain together in order to live the good life." The socialization of the rural in-migrant to the large city, University of Chicago sociologist Albion W. Small suggested, was a case in point. In one in a series of articles on the state of contemporary sociology—subtitled "Some Incidents of Association," Small observed that the agriculturalist became "the city man, not alone by virtue of changing his location; he remains the farmer still, until he specializes his individuality. He accomplishes this change by adjusting his individuality more minutely with some minutiae of the social process." The citizen of urban America was bound, in short, to adjust his own individuality to the special personality of his own city, for each great metropolis was itself an active force in the socialization or conditioning of its residents. The great city possessed, according to Small, a "continuity of influence."

Boston is essentially a state of mind. . . . Increase and Cotton Mather, Governor Winthrop and Sam Adams, John Hancock, Garrison, Phillips, and Sumner, Longfellow, Whittier, Lowell, and Emerson, are more of today's Boston than its geographic site, and its natural structures, and its mayor, and its commissioner of public works, and its superintendent of schools, and its editors and its teachers and its ministers. Boston is a standard of thinking, a set of conceptions and emotions, a body of conclusions about the conduct of life. This is the fact about every community that has not forfeited its birthright in the human family.[34]

People came together in cities to live; their act of living together created community; community, in turn, shaped the lives of its members. What kind of people, the students of its cities asked next, did urban America produce?

As in the two postwar decades, late-century urbanists continued to speculate about the effects of city living upon the health—both physical and moral—of urban dwellers. To Grace Peckham, M.D., the answer was grim: lack of air, improper diets, widespread diseases, and nervous disorders were the lot of the city's children. "Who does not recall," she asked, "the pale, pinched features of city infants, fragile flowers, fading and withering in an uncongenial atmosphere?" But, she admitted, there was another side to city living in which the environment played a positive role, and that was the intellectual. Although the mental strains of urban living threatened an "obliteration of individuality" for children of school age, adults were "better for city life . . . because . . . generally they are so circumstanced in it that they can best exercise their mental faculties"; indeed, for her mature citizen, life in the city offered "change and vitality" that served to "quicken the pulses to increase vitality." The older the individual, the better was life in the city: in the country, older people retired early to the chimney corner to die; in the city, older people kept active. "In the city," Dr. Peckham asserted, "age is ignored until it is something to be proud of, as when one is a nonogenarian. . . . Mental activity is conducive to longevity."[35] Walter B. Platt, M.D., was more concerned with the purely physical defects of the urban environment, conditioning factors that affected all, young and old, rich and poor. These were: "the disuse of the upper extremities for any considerable muscular exertion," "the incessant noise of a large city," and the "jarring of the brain and spinal cord, by continual treading upon the stone and bricks which make up our sidewalks and streets." These conditions led eventually to the "degeneration of the individual and his offspring, by producing progressive feebleness, and to ultimate extinction of such families as are long subjected to their force"; nevertheless, these deleterious factors were not inescapably a part of the urban environment, for their roots were to be found "in faulty municipal arrangements, which can be largely corrected by intelligent action and supervision." The "disuse of the upper extremities" could be corrected by proper medically prescribed exercise. "The incessant noise" of the metropolis could be moderated by municipal regulation of transit and traffic. Noise abatement, Dr. Platt recognized with commendable foresight, could be achieved only by what would later develop as zoning. In residential areas "elevated railroads" should be replaced by "under-ground roads." "Certain streets, or blocks at least," Platt urged, "should be reserved for business purposes, others for dwelling alone, and heavy wagons allowed only on the first named, unless they are to leave their freight in the block."[36] The final problem, "the jarring of the brain and spinal cord," could be met only when people recognized that they "were designed to tread upon soft Mother Earth" but had become, instead, "a race of dwellers upon rocks and stones." The remedy that the good doctor prescribed was not a return to the nature, but the adoption of softer paving materials, preferably asphalt, and the shodding of urbanites with half-inch rubber heels.[37]

These concerns of medical practitioners for the health of the inhabitants of cities answered only part of the original question about the development of the citizenry of urban America. In addition to its conditioning of the human body, city living acted also upon the spirit. After all, the city was, Thomas E. Will proclaimed, "the center of civilization's light and heat," "the dynamo that drives the vast machinery of the nineteenth century world." "Whatever touches the city," he proclaimed, "touches civilization itself. It is in the ancient city that civilization first found its seat; it is in the modern city that civilization has attained its highest expression." Language itself attested to "the favored position of the city's man. . . . The 'polished' man lives in the *polis*, the city; the 'urbane' gentleman is from the *urbs*; the 'civil' man is the *civis*, the citizen, the city dweller; and from the root comes the word civilization itself." Within the walls of the modern city "the extremes meet"; here, Will declared, were "the abodes of the blest" and "the prison-houses of the lost." For urban America, "the problem of the city is the problem of civilization. This problem, in a word, is how to abolish, or at least how to mitigate, the terrible poverty that festers in the slums; how to provide economic occupation for the unemployed; how to eliminate the vice and crime; how to modify the fierceness of the competitive struggle; how to establish popular government; how, in short, to present a clean bill of health." That the American city could solve its problem of civilization, Will never doubted, since the lesson of the city in history was a clear one: "When the city societies of ancient Greece fell it was that they might give place to another civilization whose center and soul was a city—the Eternal City—Rome."[38] The modern American city might and should produce an even finer urbanite, one to eclipse even the proud citizen of imperial Rome.

Frederick J. Kingsbury's analysis of the advantages of city living in his presidential address before the American Social Science Association was similar to that of Thomas E. Will; however, Kingsbury began his own examination with the criticisms of the enemies of the city, "the possibly somewhat prejudiced people who"—from Genesis to Jefferson—"did not live in cities" but who arrived at "firmly settled conclusions in regard to their deleterious influence." These critics of urban living ignored, in the first place, the natural "gregariousness" of humankind for an expanded social existence. "The countryman, boy or girl," Kingsbury asserted, "longs for the village, the villager for the larger town, and the dweller in the larger town for the great city; and having once gone, they are seldom satisfied to return to a place of less size." Their living together tended "to make all the people who are subject to its [the city's] influence alike. They do and see and hear and smell and eat the same things. They wear similar clothes, they read the same books, and their minds are occupied

with the same objects of thought. . . . In the end they even come to look alike
. . . so that they are at once recognized when they are seen in some other place."
Yet, at the same time, urbanization had produced centers of civilization with an
abundance and variety of good food, advanced medical facilities, and improved
sanitary measures; as a result, the best in American life was to be found in and
around its urban centers, in cities that were improving yearly—as were their
citizens.[39]

By the turn of the century, an increasing number of urbanists were proclaiming
city dwelling to be a positive force. Improvements in the health sciences, the
promised easing of inner-city congestion by migration to the suburbs and by the
creation of more public parks, a central-city building boom, and the confidence
of urbanists in their ability to shape their environment all contributed to the
optimism of the age. An anonymous reviewer in *Gunton's Magazine*, for example, suggested that "city life is one of the greatest stimulators of new desires
and expanding social experience,"[40] an editorial in *Public Improvements* cited
with approval the hypothesis of "Prof. William T. Sedgwick of Boston" that
"with proper sanitary improvements city life may be made even healthier than
that of the country."[41] Dr. A. E. Winship reported that in his survey of 1,014
"representative men whose success is assured," he found a "much larger portion" of the urban-born "than our social philosophers have thought." Not only
was being born in the city no hindrance to success, Dr. Winship continued, it
was in itself beneficial: "The advantages offered by life in the cities, educational,
commercial, professional, and social, give the fortunately born city boy a better
start and a better equipment for his life's work than the country lad has. He
learns to work more effectively because of the better organized machinery of
life all about him, and the opportunities to cultivate any talent he may have are
greater."[42] The people who came together in cities to live seemed, by the turn
of the century, well on their way to achieving the good life.

EXPERIENCING CITIES

Sprawl and speed were two often-noted characteristics of late-century urban
living—with Boston typifying the former and New York the latter. The mean-
dering streets of the "Hub of the Universe" were frequently the subject of satire,
as when "Bacon" offered to support the candidacy of "Beans" for a position
as guide in Kentucky's labyrinthine Mammoth Cave: "You piloted me about
Boston once so I guess I can recommend you."[43] Still another critic of the Hub
pointed out that "Causeway Street, Commercial Street, Atlanta Avenue, Federal
Street and Foundry Street are not five distinct streets as heretofore supposed but
in reality one street"; that "North Street runs in every direction except north";
that the city's street plan was designed "to deceive strangers and missionaries";
that "the best way to get from one given point to another in Boston is to
telephone"; and that, finally, "the most practical use we can make of Boston
is to cover it with plate-glass mirrors and exhibit it through our country as the

Crystal Maze.''[44] If movement in Boston was labyrinthine, in Manhattan it seemed aqueous. Here were "whirlpools of traffic, the central places of the city, the meeting of mighty ways, the crossing of thronged thoroughfares"; here, "year by year, as the city grows northward for homes and concentrates itself southward for business, the whirlpools grow greater and roar and seethe the more.''[45] Not only was there more traffic, but it moved faster: "Even for short distance rides the New Yorker demands sureness and swiftness.''[46] Speed was called for, and it was increasingly available.

The urban rapid-transit revolution that began during the closing years of the century repeated at the local level the sweeping changes effected by railroad expansion on a national scale at mid-century. It fostered new settlement patterns in both central cities and their suburban rings; led to the relocation of business enterprises, both industrial and commercial; opened up opportunities for political venality and corruption, since many millions of dollars in investment capital were spent often without adequate institutional safeguards against graft and outright theft; and changed the living patterns of a great majority of city dwellers. The urban transportation revolution, in sum, shaped the modern metropolis: it tore down the walls of the walking city but, at the same time, kept alive the inner core. The movement into suburban rings made it unnecessary to create new central cities.

The major requirement of an urban transportation system was, the editors of *Municipal Affairs* advised, "largely one of rapid communication between business and residential districts," and attempts to furnish this link had been made both on and below the city's streets. The first method had failed: surface transit, both horse-drawn and power-driven, was not "sufficiently rapid"; steam-powered railroads had necessarily "been excluded from most centers because of the noise, smoke and ugliness of the trains." The second choice, the tube or subway, which had been tested successfully in London, Paris, and Boston, seemed to be the answer.[47] Still a third alternative, the elevated rail line, was possible. Unlike subsurface transit, which separated the traveler entirely from the city's everyday life, the "el," according to one of its few propagandists, encouraged participation in it. "The New York Elevated Railway," which "cuts its way like a relentless torrent through the very heart of the city's traffic; . . . crashes past the homes of the rich and the poor alike; . . . skirts the greenery of our parks, . . . and at the southern terminus is only held in bounds by the ocean" was a case in point. So intriguing was its progress that "even the absorbed New York business man . . . is compelled, in spite of the temptation of his daily paper, to watch the changing panorama of city life in all its phases as it unfolds itself through the windows of the car." Confronting him was "a story of irresistible interest," which "brought the extreme classes of rich and poor men in touch with each other and within a shorter space of time than all the preceding years of agitation on the subject of laborer and employer.''[48]

Such uncritical praise for the democratic and picturesque benefits of the elevated lines could scarcely go unchallenged because the "el" was, as James

Argyle Robinson noted, not only a public carrier but also a general nuisance: "Its unsightly structures were displeasing to the eye as its noises offended the ear." As a result of public pressure, municipal officials had held back from "the building of more overhead iron viaducts" and "even those existing—so hopes the aesthetic mind—may in time be torn away." The future of rapid transit, Robinson concluded and the vast majority of urban theorists and planners agreed, should and would be found beneath the city's streets.[49]

Another "mid-air" public transportation facility, the suspension bridge, was regarded with unanimous favor. The magnificent Brooklyn Bridge, judged since its completion in 1883 to be a wonder of the modern urban world, was heralded as the prototype of all future cross-river transportation and communication. There were thousands of "Brooklynites who daily cross the East River to Manhattan," wrote J. Herbert Welch in *Everybody's Magazine*, "in quest of the alluring dollar. They are drawn off, so to speak, by the system of trolley and elevated lines, which spread out over Brooklyn like the branches of a great tree, whose trunk is the Brooklyn Bridge."[50] Magnificent and important though it was, this "greatest bridge on earth" seemed to mark only the beginning of a new era in cross-river construction; indeed, New York City itself would soon boast an even more important structure, "the greatest piece of architectural engineering . . . in any part of the world," a proposed "North River Bridge" that would join Twenty-Third Street with Hoboken. Spanning the Hudson, the editors of the business-minded *Social Economist* predicted, would guarantee "the future development of the wholesale and retail trade, manufacturing and general rebuilding and architectural style of New York City"; moreover, such a project would assure for the metropolis "its general boom of transformation and remodelment."[51] New York Congressman John DeWitt Warner added yet another dimension to the function of the suspension bridge in an industrial metropolis: the great bridge must come to symbolize the city of the industrial age, as the cathedral and fortress had the medieval town. The "Twin Cities" of New York and Brooklyn, specifically, Warner advised the members of the National Sculpture Society in December 1899, would be shaped by the building of functional and beautiful suspension bridges across the East River, and the future of Greater New York would depend upon these undertakings. The alternatives, he continued, were clear: "it is for us to say whether by adequately improving it we shall be entitled to credit for the most beautiful, happy and prosperous City ever imagined by man; or whether, ignoring the opportunity or spoiling it, we shall be first among those whose sins of omission or commission have cursed their fellow men."[52] The island city, Warner wrote in *Municipal Affairs*, must now determine those improvements that would give "it a character helping to make it great instead of merely large"; the metropolis should, he recommended, create "a net work of swinging steel as in our Brooklyn Bridge makes a veritable pathway of the gods for men to travel on."[53] Although The Bridge clearly belonged to one city, the technology of bridge building was the property of all water cities in urban America.

The horsecar, the street railway, the elevated line, the subway, and the suspension bridge provided the dynamics for the city's horizontal expansion; the high-speed hydraulic elevator was a major factor in its vertical growth. Perhaps the "perpendicular" or "vertical railroads" of New York City had been, the editors of *Public Improvements* speculated, a "greater factor" in that city's growth than had been its transit system: "The elevators of the city have a right to be considered as a rapid transit system." By the turn of the century an estimated 3,055 passenger and 7,000 freight elevators in Manhattan alone transported 1.5 million people and thousands of tons of goods every day. "The daily trip of every first-class elevator car in the city, if there were no descents to offset its ascent," *Public Improvements* calculated, "would lift it above the clouds, above the highest flight of a balloon, thirty miles from earth and indeed almost out of the atmosphere."[54] The new buildings in which they were housed, moreover, presented an equal—and also equally metaphorical—threat to the same sky, for in the last fifteen years of the century, the modern skyscraper had come of age.

Montgomery Schuyler, the nation's leading architectural critic, judged in 1899 that "the general treatment of the 'sky-scraper' " had already become "conventional, in the sense of being agreed upon. It is nearly as distinct an architectural type as the Greek temple or the Gothic cathedral. . . . The elevator doubled the height of office buildings, and the steel-frame doubled it again, and yet," Schuyler concluded, "there is less of eccentricity and freakishness; more of conformity and homogeneousness, among the twenty-story buildings than there used to be among the five-story buildings."[55] From a purely technical standpoint, the skyscraper presented a challenge to traditional architecture. Its practitioners, Louis De Coppet Berg asserted, had now to add to their existing expertise the crafts of the artist, civil engineer, electrician, sanitary engineer, plumber and financier.[56] From a monetary standpoint, increases in property values would be accompanied by increases in building heights. Here, most architectural critics agreed, some limits had to be set. "Nobody, except owners of land upon which they propose to erect sky-scrapers, and have not yet effected their purpose," claimed the editors of *Architectural Record*, "will dispute that it is high time to put a legal limitation upon the height of buildings, and a legal limitation that means something." Washington, D.C., because of the erection there of one "single soaring aberration," had imposed a municipal height limit of 120 feet, a limitation that was not "oppressive." It seemed logical to this journal that other cities would follow the lead of the nation's capital.[57] If such codes were not drawn up and enforced, Montgomery Schuyler warned, other large American cities would soon resemble New York, which had "no skyline at all. It is all interruptions, of various heights and shapes and sizes, not even peaks in a mountain range, but scattered or huddled towers which have nothing to do with each other or with what is below." To curb the profit motive, it was necessary to adhere to aesthetic standards.[58]

Although architectural critics, in their efforts to achieve building height limitations, rightly exposed the crassness of landholding and construction interests, they were generally blind to the broader implications of the land-use revolution they were witnessing. That the concentration of workers in block after block of skyscrapers would intensify demands upon municipal services, public utilities, transportation networks, and service industries was all but ignored. They overlooked, as well, another very important characteristic of the skyscraper: it was a focus for municipal pride. Thus, the same skyline view that so appalled Montgomery Schuyler enthralled Louis Curtin. "No city in the world presents the attractive profile disclosed in a first glimpse of New York. No other town has the same number of tall office buildings displayed to equal advantage." Indeed, this Manhattan booster proclaimed, if Washington could aspire to the title of the "City of Magnificent Distances," New York "might appropriately be named the City of Magnificent Altitudes."[59]

The skyscrapers of a metropolis offered contemporaries, another contributor to *Metropolitan Magazine* exulted, "a thrill of superiority" with their "bird's-eye view of men, women, and things—the kind of exhilaration that springs from a sense of isolated perfection." Skyscrapers gave would-be observers the opportunity of—as the title of the essay in the *Metropolitan* phrased it—"Looking Down on Humanity." "The sudden perspective, the quaint form of all things seen from this perpendicular view-point," this enthusiast continued, "imbues the most commonplace objects with a new and strange interest. It is quite a new world and a different race of people we see from the ledge of a high building." The emotional appeal from the skyscraper might even be termed hallucinatory:

For example, a hunched-back man looks for all the world like a Newfoundland dog walking upon its hind legs, and the horse presents more the spectacle of the clothes-basket stuffed with a huge tarpaulin than a living creature with four legs and a desire to stand upright. Men, women, children, and animals are legless, so far as the perpendicular sight-seer is concerned; wagons and carriages have no wheels to his view, and an umbrella is brother to the pancake from his elevated perch.

It is a healthful pastime—mentally healthful—to see life distorted; it gives one the feeling that the things which the human mind cannot understand may not prove their non-existence, and lays great stress upon the fact that things are not always what they seem. More often than not it is our own mental astigmatism that makes the world look crooked or stale or flat. To clarify the mind or tickle the fancy, merely thrust your face over the window-sill of a sky-scraper and watch the living tumult below.

This somewhat bizarre observation concluded with the challenge that it was "all very well to say that we are superior animals, but even if that were true we have not succeeded in two thousand years in getting any higher from the dirt than a few hundred feet in a balloon."[60]

This essay by its very exaggeration, underscored the fascination of the age with the "prospect" or aerial view of the metropolis. In Victorian England, Asa Briggs has suggested, the city dweller ascended in a balloon or climbed a high building in order to obtain "a new and more ordered vision" of his environment.[61] In late-century urban America, too, the gigantic cathedrals of commerce contributed to "a new and more ordered vision" of society: they offered the assurance that humanity had indeed risen more than a few hundred feet "from the dirt"; they were evidence of progress, visible signs of the transformation from the old order into the new urban-industrial complex. The late nineteenth-century version of this century's space race, the competition for the world's highest structure, was even more than a contest between nations; it was a rivalry with the human past. Thus, a New York booster claimed that his city's reigning champion, the Park Row Building, was "the tallest building ever erected by man, with the possible exception of the Tower of Babel, and even that some Biblical scholars declare never rose more than two hundred feet in the air."[62] This new monarch of skyscrapers, the description continued, was 31 stories and 380 feet high, had its foundations 75 feet below street level in bedrock, was constructed of 8,000 tons of steel and 8 million bricks, contained 1,014 offices and 2,080 windows, was illuminated by 7,500 electric lights, and provided a 30-mile view of Gotham: Park Row Building was "literally a town by itself."[63] Fact was added to fact, detail was bolstered by still more detail—all presented as evidence of the progress of urban America. New York City, this booster article proclaimed, was not only the world's largest city, but also its most gigantic: "Here is located the greatest suspension bridge—the New York and Brooklyn; the largest elevated structure—the Manhattan 'L' road, having a total length of thirty miles."[64] Here, of course, was the world's tallest skyscraper; here, by extension, was the world's greatest city in a nation of cities.

In his celebration of the city, the booster of urban America could readily exploit the excitement inherent in the soaring skyscraper, "cloud-scraper," or "cloud cathedral." Stylistic devices, such as the "bird's-eye" or balloon view and "extension" of urban characteristics until they seem unique, what is more, were and are necessary contrivances for the writer in his attempt to approximate a comprehension of his city, because, as social psychologist Anselm Strauss has suggested, "These methods of portraying the city space are expressive declarations of its literal incomprehensibility. The city, as a whole, is inaccessible to the imagination unless it can be reduced and simplified."[65] The city's frantic movement, its high-speed transit, its monumental bridges, its giant skyscrapers containing tons of artifacts represented, in themselves, that reduction and simplification. Such image-making was constant throughout the period.[66]

This celebration of the immense and the magnificent led, at the same time, to a neglect of the human scale in the metropolis. A great city, Montgomery Schuyler warned, must be more than a jumble of giant buildings; it had also to be, he counseled, a community of pleasant and comfortable homes. Urban America, in general, and New York City in particular, were sorely lacking in the latter. Looking back upon the development of downtown building at the close of the century, he observed that the land laws and property values of large cities had combined to make the small city home practically obsolete. The deep and narrow lots on the blocks of the city's gridiron street pattern and the frantic demand for land in the business districts had resulted in the disappearance of the "decent," even "elegant" homes of the gentry and mechanics of early nineteenth-century American cities and towns; these simple, unpretentious homes gave way, in turn, to costly, ornate late-century dwellings.[67] Yet, in his initial article in *Architectural Record*, Schuyler had judged the new architectural style of the Romanesque, "in the Norman, the German and the Provencal phases of it, . . . an architectural language that is applicable to all our needs, for there is no mode of building, from the ecclesiastical to the domestic, in which we have not already successful examples of it to show, and in which we may not hope for still more signal successes in the future."[68] Four years later, in a eulogistic review of the works of Richard Morris Hunt, whom he praised as "one of the most conspicuous and distinguished American architects," Schuyler noted that the contemporary architect's work was shaped by "the steady and rapid increase of the magnitude and costliness of the buildings he is called upon to rear." By the mid–1890s, then, "the bourgeois mansion . . . [had] expanded to a palace."[69] By the end of the century, Schuyler lamented, the urban dweller was condemned to either the brownstone row house, "that scandalous edifice," or the cheap apartment building, a step lower still in comfort and amenities.[70] The future of downtown dwelling would continue to be grim, he predicted in the last year of the century, unless and until his professional colleagues designed and developed a reasonable alternative to the row house and apartment. That they could and would do so, Montgomery Schuyler doubted. Perhaps, as historian Carl Schorske has suggested, nineteenth-century architects, who were singularly creative in their "new utilitarian style" for bridges and factories and grossly imitative in their domestic buildings, were afraid "to face the reality of their own creation" and "found no aesthetic forms to state it."[71] Perhaps traditional domestic architecture imparted a sense of security, a tie with the past, in a rapidly changing metropolitan order.

The apartment house or "French flat," despite the strictures of a Schuyler, was regarded increasingly as a promising form of home-building. The lesson of French apartment living, an early article in *Architectural Record* advised, was social. "In France the social status of each individual is generally so clearly defined that a freedom of intercourse exists between the various classes of society, utterly unknown in this country. Poor artisans frequently occupy the upper floors of houses the lower floors of which are rented to people of high social standing." In American cities, this analysis continued, "things are different. All claims to social superiority are bitterly resented by people who regard the elevation of those above them as a mere accident of fortune that a day may reverse, while the favored few strive, through an excessive exclusiveness, to guard their dearly-cherished state of exaltation." The atmosphere of the French flat was marked by spaciousness, privacy, comfort, and ease—in short, "home"; that of the American apartment was characterized by crowding, noise, discomfort, and class-consciousness. Americans, this analysis concluded, had to learn the graces of living in multiple-unit dwellings; the French experience, moreover, provided an example worthy of emulation.[72]

The cliff dwellers of Gotham were the butt of as many jibes in the late 1890s as were contemporary suburban squatters. "The Happy One," for example, celebrating his "fifteenth year of existence in a New York flat," drew up a "Schedule, To Be Blown in a Christmas," a listing that provided standard gratuities for the corner policeman, the postman, the iceman, the gas company collector, and the "little boy who raises Cain daily and nightly in the apartment above."[73] "The Flatter," who lived in a "model flat" and boasted of a "model janitor" advised his readers to: "Put the motto 'God Bless Our Flat' on the wall and get your janitor to adopt this schedule." The gratuity list began with a two-dollar "regularly weekly fee (this of course means simply being janitor. Cheap enough)" and proceeded to detail the bribes necessary for all services beyond this first step.[74] Coupled with the high costs of apartment living was a new life-style, one marked by a shortage of space. Again, "The Flatter" was spokesman for the new condition, but this time in verse:

> We live in a rather uncomfortable flat—
>   It's so disagreeably small;
> In fact, it's so tiny we've come to that
>   It's best to turn 'round in the hall.
> My wife doesn't view with a rapturous glee
>   A life of such awful restraint;
> But she never complains, for the reason that she
>   Has not any room for complaints.[75]

This good-natured raillery indicated that apartment living was becoming ac-ceptable. Cliff dwelling and suburban camping out generally were judged as inevitable, if slightly comic forms of urban living: although they might not equal the simplicity and "elegance" of the traditional town house, their life-styles did, nonetheless, reflect the space requirements and the mobility of the new, proud metropolis.

More than a functional role, as had been indicated, was assigned to the paths, buildings, and dwelling places of the metropolis; these objects were expected to serve a civic end as well. Proponents of a coming urban renascence, in their attempts to measure contemporary signs of progress, turned repeatedly, therefore, to the past for comparison and inspiration. Was our metropolis, they asked, as magnificent as had been Periclean Athens, Imperial Rome, Renaissance Venice? How might it surpass their storied grandeur?

History was sometimes called to witness through the device of resurrecting long-dead heroes to criticize the present. Thus, Ictinus, designer of the Parthenon, was called back from the Underworld by staff critic Henry W. Desmond in an early issue of *Architectural Record*, so that he might consult with the contem-porary "Classicist," "Goth," "Romanesquer," "Archaeologist," "Eclectic," "Western Architect," and "Architect" (the tale's narrator). The modern prac-titioners of his craft received little encouragement from their Greek master. "Goth" and "Romanesquer" he dismissed out of hand; "Classicist" he ridiculed as "my slave." "Western Architect" did not ask for advice but, instead, boldly offered it: "In the West, you will be interested to know, several of our brainiest architects are now engaged in the creation of an original 'American Style,' and what with the Chicago system of construction on one hand, and the inventive genius of our people on the other, this copying of effete forms is about ended."[76] Ictinus did not answer the boastful Midwesterner; instead, he directed his criticisms against the most representative member of his profession, "Eclectic." " 'These tenements and office buildings of which you speak can—be—made—artistic—I—suppose,' " he granted, " 'but they cannot inspire great art. . . . Your office buildings and factories and stores are matters of percentage. Art is not.' " The final entreaty of the Athenian master was that modern architects concern themselves less with details of individual buildings and devote themselves more to the building of a "city of the Purple Crown."[77]

The creation of this urban imperium, A. D. F. Hamlin of Columbia University's Department of Architecture advised, would have far-reaching effects on all city dwellers, since "architecture surrounds and frames our lives, meets us at every turn and bounds our horizon." Good architecture would make possible the good city. "To encourage the growth of good taste in architecture is the duty of every good citizen," Hamlin asserted, "to exemplify good taste by just criticism, wise praise and merited condemnation, the duty of every critic; to insist upon it, the duty of every promoter, director or owner of any building enterprise; to exhibit by good designing and workmanship, the duty of every architect and artisan." Architecture, the most public of the arts, was therefore a conditioning factor in the creation of a better community. The craft, it followed, reflected the shortcomings of society: in the commissioning of his city's public buildings, Hamlin accused, the firm of Hogan and Slattery was little more than a front for Tammany Hall; in private construction, both commercial and domestic, gross individualism prevailed.[78] As he had complained in an earlier essay, the "pesterings of stupid, self-conceited and unreasoning clients" threatened a "universal commercialism."[79] His own profession, architect Leopold Eidlitz declared, was itself largely to blame for the descent into urban commercialism. The "architect of fashion" was "ubiquitous," Eidlitz asserted; he "no longer pretends to be a man of learning, of varied attainments, of a liberal education, of studious habits, retiring, modest, shrinking from contact with the world, devoted solely to his art. No, he is a man of business, a man who startles the world with his bold combinations of architectural bric-a-brac."[80]

Seldom did a professional critique omit reference to the poverty of inventiveness in the craft and to the corrupting nature of the spirit of commerce; at the same time, positive programs for reform were also offered. Architect Ernest Flagg, for one, recommended that an American equivalent of the *École des Beaux Arts* be established and that, further, each city should appoint its "most distinguished architect, City Architect, and let it be his duty to pass upon all proposed structures in regard to their artistic fitness for the place they are to occupy."[81] Charles Rollinson Lamb, designer of the Dewey Arch, invoked the

argot of imperialism in his proposal for architectural control in his own city of
New York: "Races are compared primarily for their art, and in the competition
of time, of race against race, we shall rank in the future as we leave behind us
such records." Leadership in this endeavor, Lamb echoed Nietzsche, had to
come from an elite, from citizens of genius. "Genius is akin to madness. True,"
he admitted, "and the madmen of yesterday have been elevated, as a rule, to
the pedestals of the public approval of to-day." The rebirth of the Empire City,
Lamb asserted, "rests on the united professions of New York, and legal mind
and business head must, with artistic thought and engineering skill, combine to
give, not the 'Greater New York' of the Charterists, not even the 'Better New
York' of the Religionists, but both in one, the dream of the Idealist, 'THE CITY
BEAUTIFUL.' "[82] Lamb's vision of the City Beautiful was of a center of power,
an island force that resembled "a great living monster."

Any one crossing the ferry line from the New Jersey depot of the Pennsylvania Railroad
to West Twenty-third street in the late evening, and watching the myriad lights as they
show the varied forms of the "steel-cage" construction, can easily imagine the contour
of the heroic skeleton. The skull formation of lower New York, the neck, the shoulders
at Twenty-third street, the hips of the upper city at Morningside Park and Riverside Drive,
and the tail as it swings northward, across the Harlem River. As this formation is studied,
the observer will appreciate how the concentration of muscular and nervous energy finds
expression in the development of building or muscle as the case may be, and that
constructive architecture is but the symbol of that bone and sinew, nerve and blood vessel,
suggested by such a great dragon like creature.[83]

Had Charles Rollinson Lamb chosen to call an Ictinus from the Underworld, the
master would probably have warned him that ancient Greece had a special name
for his "idealism": hubris. A contemporary and colleague, William Nelson
Black, did, in fact, caution that the emphasis of the architectural profession upon
the imperial facade of urban America, in the face of the existing and appalling
contrast between the rich and the poor, might lead to the "Final image of
reconstructed Parthenon surrounded by slums: the story of every city."[84]

Perhaps the American architect, too, as Walter L. Creese has stated the case
for his opposite number in industrial England, "was driven to extremes of
intensity by the very excess of realism he encountered in the conventional,
everyday urban environment."[85] The English professional turned to romantic
forms, the American to classical. In any event, the search for civic amenities in
art, sculpture, color, monuments—all prefaced with the key word "municipal"—
was a vigorous one. Thomas Tryon, for one, lamented the "mediocrity or worse"
in his city's "municipal decorations." New York's Municipal Art Society, in
which Tryon served as treasurer, had begun, he asserted, to replace the bad with
the good by introducing "the elevating influence of beauty in our public thoroughfares and on our public buildings." The society's motto was "To make
us love our city, we must make our city lovely."[86] Charles Rollinson Lamb
promoted municipal art from a different viewpoint: "Art is not a luxury, it is

an essential. Art is not exotic; any art which is will never live.''[87] Noted muralist
Edwin Howland Blashfield was still blunter: ''Art pays.''[88] Indeed, Municipal
Art Society Secretary Frederick S. Lamb agreed, ''news which ought to appeal
to every American'' was that art could be '' 'profitable' '': ''that by increasing
the beauty of their city, they have increased its advantages and attractiveness,
and that modern art thus applied 'enhances the prestige of a nation, and by
encouraging the best instincts of the people, raises their whole moral tone.' ''
What Frederick Lamb found difficult to understand was that ''until recently,
everything has been done, or left undone, to make our city [New York] as
unattractive as possible.'' It was time, he urged, to rescue art from its present
condition as a meaningless diversion of a spoiled aristocracy and return it to its
vital place as the expression of the lives of the citizens of the metropolis.[89] One
means for achieving municipal beautification, Frederick Lamb suggested in a
later essay, was by experimentation in color. The ''so-called dark ages,'' he
observed, had employed it as ''a medium of expression''; for medieval society,
''Color became a language.'' Industrial cities, on the other hand, because of
their drabness, had produced ''a dead language'': ''As in the boiler factory the
repetitive blows of the hammer eventually deafen the worker, so constant association with injurious and unrelated color sensation had deadened the receptive
sense until the power of appreciation is in a measure lost.'' Technological advances had, in themselves, destroyed much of the visual diversity of the preindustrial city: fire-proof building materials were less suitable for painting than
were older wooden structures; concentration of population had resulted in the
elimination of trees and lawns; and the chimneys of factories and shops had
covered large sections of cities with soot. Conversely, Frederick Lamb pointed
out, the new technology had also introduced a new diversity with terra cotta,
tile, bricks, faience, variegated stones, and methods for toning and coloring
building materials, which would provide an escape from the ubiquitous brown-
stone and red brick. ''What a field lies before us when we contemplate the
embellishment of a great city by the use of color as an ornamentation. Here is
the true field for the individual's selection. Here he may express his personality.''
Color, finally, could teach, since it ''could be used not only as color in mass
and color in ornament, but as color in symbolic figure-work.'' Color could project
the varied themes of urban life and, thereby, ''supplant signs. . . . Color in proper
relation to its surroundings will arrest and hold the attention when form passes
unnoticed.''[90] Frederick Lamb's Ruskinian approach to form and symbol was
bolder than that of most of his contemporaries. Yet, what united all the advocates
of municipal beautification—the supporters of art, sculpture, and monuments—
was a desire to advance what the twentieth century would term ''urban design,''
a wide-ranging humanistic approach to the technical problems and way-of-life
potentialities of modern city living.

It remained for muralist Edward Howland Blashfield to resurrect another spirit
from the past, this one a fifteenth-century Florentine. This ghostly tourist of
Gotham was shocked by its ''gigantic buildings, twice as high as our Giotto's

bell tower and twenty times as big,'' but he was even more surprised that these structures were not "municipal buildings," since it was "incredible that private citizens should have built such huge piles.'' He was even more perplexed to have the city's administrative center pointed to him: "*That* little thing the City Hall? Incredible! . . . No, I cannot understand it. What have you done with your public money?'' In the quarters of the "artisans and laborers" who had constructed the massive downtown buildings, the spectral critic expected to find "the lovely shrines at the street corners, the scores of sculptured fountains, the many colonnades under which the poor can sit at ease on Sundays and holidays and look at the statues and wall paintings about them.'' When he found instead "corner grocery stores and ash barrels,'' the Florentine exploded:

Your laboring men eat meat three times a day, do they? Let me tell you that there was not one mechanic or shopman or workman in Florence who would not have been ashamed to eat meat three times a day in such a wilderness of brick and mortar hideousness as you have here. He would have made one meal simpler and put the extra money into the building fund. And your richer men, whose counting-houses are in tall towers, have they no eyes, then, for beauty in public buildings also? Ah, you have no public spirit, no civic patriotism.

His New York host could only agree with his dissatisfied ghostly guest and bid him: "Creep back under your gravestone of the dim Florentine church; rest there for fifty years; or, if you an unquiet spirit, come sooner, come in a quarter of a century, and you shall see.''[91]

"ACRES OF ABSTRACT GREENSWARD"

The parkite crusade of mid-century took on a new dimension in the final fifteen years of the century, one that was articulated in housing expert E. R. L. Gould's address before the members of the American Statistical Association in May 1888. Gould began by outlining the established demands of open-space advocates of the preceding generation concerning the need for the creation of "breathing spaces'' and "air-holes in large towns.'' However, as he spelled out the details of the new program, his emphasis was less upon the need for large central parks, with their prohibitive " 'keep-off-the-grass' air,'' than it was upon the necessity of providing small neighborhood parks for all sections of a city, specialized open spaces that would serve the cultural, social, and recreational needs of all city dwellers.[92] The parkite crusade between 1885 and 1900 shifted increasingly from its earlier stress upon the aesthetic value of the large landscaped park or "pleasure ground'' to an emphasis upon the renewal of downtown living areas through the agency of a planned system of specialized local parks. No longer was it expected that the urban poor must come to the parks; the parks would now be brought to them. The era of the "reform park,'' as Galen Cranz has called it, had arrived.[93]

The editors of *The Social Economist* were particularly vehement, for example, about what they termed Frederick Law Olmsted's "rapt devotion to scenery," which was, they claimed, self-defeating. In the first place, his artistic settings for ponds required the absence of running water, the lack of which, in turn, resulted in the stagnation of the same ponds and the concommitant danger of creating breeding places for diseases. Second, by decree of the park authorities nut and fruit trees had been judged "unartistic," and their scarcity had resulted in a dearth of blooms and birds. Because "the park management could not eliminate the earthworms," these angry gentlemen continued, "a few robins will come in spring. But grass nesting birds cannot rest where the lawn-mower moves once a week and humming birds will not come where there are no blossoms. And what business," finally, "has a lawn mower in a public park anyway?" In essence, the major thrust of the criticism of this magazine was that "the health, instruction and intelligent enjoyment of the people are considerations more important, even, than the artistic construction of its landscapes," that a public park had to serve all of the people, not just the lovers of lush lawns. Public parks, *The Social Economist* asserted, should serve to uplift the people. Central Park, on the contrary, depressed them with its ersatz rural landscapes. "It cannot give them the mountains and the sea"; therefore, "it is belittling and of the nature of twaddle to give them as substitutes a cliff merely high enough to kill a baby, a pool merely deep enough to drown a boy, and wildwood of evergreen shade merely dark enough to shield the lascivious at night and gloomy enough to invite suicide by day."[94] Central Park was especially oppressive to children "doomed to the toil of drudgery in cities" who came "out from the sweat-shops and the sales-rooms without any longing for dignity. The jingle of the silver chains on the prancing horses of the rich [in the park] makes them wish they too were horses so that they might be groomed and petted and cared for lovingly and tenderly." The landscaped central parks, this editorial concluded, "are virtually wrested from the people and are confiscated to the representatives of gigmanity, to the Hon. Mr. and Mrs. Veneering and their set."[95]

Sociologist Charles Zueblin was not so harsh in his indictment of the landscaped park movement for, he maintained, " 'A return to nature' " was "as necessary a demand for the modern city as it was for the romanticists of the eighteenth century." His own city of Chicago, he was nevertheless quick to add, had planned poorly in its provision of open spaces on a city-wide basis. The existing parks, to begin with, were not spaced according to population densities and needs. In addition, Chicago had failed to take full advantage of its unique physical assets: its long lake front, which might be transformed into a park complex; its river which, instead of serving the people of the city, was fast deteriorating into "a great sewer." A sensible long-range plan for the development of open spaces in the nation's second city would provide for, Zueblin suggested, a system of local parks for the most densely populated districts of the city, with a network of boulevards connecting them. The primary aim of these neighborhood parks would be social betterment. Each would be staffed with a trained supervisor who would relax existing playground rules, so as to open it up to the children of the poor, who had hitherto regarded parks and playgrounds as part of the municipal correctional system; each would supplement the work of neighborhood schools by expanding activities during after hours and vacations; and each would serve to bring together in harmonious play the young of all nationalities, children who were separated not only by ethnic traditions, but also by their attendance in parochial as well as public schools, a condition that often proved to be socially divisive. Such a park and playground system, Zueblin promised, would not only socialize the citizenry of Chicago, but it would also serve the economic end of reducing a growing "juvenile criminality."[96]

Numerous proposals were advanced for a more efficient use of public open spaces. The editors of *Public Improvements*, for example, recommended that certain "beautiful garden spots" be equipped with library facilities, so that all age groups among the urban poor might be given access to good books and periodicals.[97] A writer for *Municipal Affairs* urged that trees be planted in "every street and avenue not in that portion of the city devoted strictly to commerce and industry."[98] Morris Loeb suggested that large American cities follow the example of Copenhagen and convert at least one small park "into a neighborhood garden, in which, in one form or another, the dwellers in the nearby tenements could actively participate in the tilling of the ground, or in which their children could be taught the rudiments of horticulture."[99] All these proposals were based upon the felt need that innovations in the use of inner-city land patterns were essential; at the same time, they represented a basic change in the meaning of the word "park" as it had been defined by Frederick Law Olmsted and his successors. Recreation was to replace aesthetics as the uplifting element, but the park was still to serve a moral purpose; thus, a search for order established continuity between the mid- and turn-of-the-century parkite crusades.

Innovations in the planning of parks shared with the growing movement for the conservation of national resources a spirit demanding preservation of the country's physical heritage. Prior to mid-century in most cities—at least until the 1820s, in even the largest eastern centers—*urbs* and *rus* had never been completely separate; to this point, an urban-rural continuum had been maintained. Only with the coming of age of the urban-industrial complex toward the end of the century did a true polarity between the two modes of living seem possible. This seemingly final step toward complete urbanization was regarded, understandably, with considerable trepidation; the probability of its coming was certainly one motive force behind the park movement, for the park preserved—actually simulated—the "natural." Without the benign influence of an ever-present nature, many urbanists wondered, what would be the nature of man? "And if the sad experience of the Ancient Mariner who shot the albatross is destined to come to man when he has destroyed all nature, and it is perhaps not too much to believe that the death of sympathy in man might make life of little worth, then," Henry Leslie Osborn philosophized, "we can see that our care for nature is not without higher compensations, additional to those which can be measured by means of the money standard."[100] Nature could not easily be ignored, but its meaning could be readily reassessed.

"Let us inquire," Ralph Waldo Emerson had asked some half-century before, "to what end is nature?" The ponderings of the vast majority of late-century urban theorists on this matter would, most probably, have baffled the American Scholar. He would have found in the first place, abundant evidence of pure romanticism, the stock celebration of a sentimentalized nature in the magazine literature between 1885 and 1900; an overwhelming proportion of this material, significantly, was written not in prose but in verse. The primary theme of the poetry of the city was one of contrast between rural virtue and urban degradation, and the major personnae were the children of the city.

> Summer has come.
> List to the hum!
> Bees, birds, and butterflies, sweet-scented breeze,
> Clover-blooms bending, and fruit-laden trees,
> Blossoms and grasses refreshed by the showers,
> Old-fashioned gardens run-over with flowers,
> Wheat-fields all golden, and hay-mows all sweet,
> Cool plashing brook, for the small, dimpled feet,
> *Rich* are the children, in Summer.

> Summer has come.
> List to the hum!
> Rumbling of truck-wheels and traffic and cries;
> Fetid and stifling the odors that rise;
> Gaunt little children are swarming the street,
> Seeking the shadows, to hide from the heat.
> Pitiful wailings of babies in pain,
> In pestilent rooms, where the Fever hath lain.
> *Doomed* are the children, in Summer.[101]

Another poem in the same vein began with the invocation, "God help the boy who never sees/The butterflies, the birds, the bees," and all of the other impedimenta of nature; for the child deprived of the boundless, beauteous bounties of greenery, the poet prayed, "For such a hapless boy I say/God help the little fellow."[102] Even the adult, claimed still another bard, should close his "eyes to the throng of the street" and his "heart to the thud of the stone,/And wander back to the meadow-sweet,/Where the young mint-stalks are sown."[103] The unsophisticated response of the versifier to urban life was most typically voiced by "Mamma" on the occasion of a day's excursion into the countryside with her brood, for there she recalled "the proverb handed/From our fathers down/ 'God made the country,/Man made the town.' "[104]

The verse published in magazines during this period differed in no way, either in style or message, from that examined by Robert H. Walker in his definitive study of the poetry of the Gilded Age. Walker's conclusion that the poetry of the period betrayed "preponderantly negative reactions to urban conditions and characteristics" holds true equally for that published in magazines.[105] It must be emphasized, however, that the verse published in these magazines was never representative of the general policy on urban affairs of *any* of the magazines under study. In all cases, poetry served primarily as marginalia. It seems likely, although this inference cannot be proved, that it was published in magazines for the purposes of editorial convenience and as "filler" to complete type-set pages with paragraphs of uneven length.[106] In the years ahead, ironically, these isolated snatches of pastoral song would be replaced increasingly by that most citified of prose forms, the block advertisement.

Directly opposed to the bucolic imagery of country life stood the popular and irreverent version of rural America as a wasteland inhabited by the rube and the hayseed. In fact, the words "rube" and "hayseed" were coined during the 1890s, and the standard "hick," although it originated in 1690, became a common slang word again toward the end of the nineteenth century.[107] Popular periodicals, especially those like *Yellow Kid* and *Metropolitan Magazine*, regularly featured cartoons about lank, weed-chewing, dungaree-wearing bumpkins who were unable to cope with the city of the city slicker. The visiting farmer was consistently the fool: he compared skyscrapers to haystacks; expected to find armed robbery on Wall Street; and mistook the theatrical play for real life. In short, he supplied the vaudeville and burlesque comedian of a later period with his repertoire of jokes about rural America—from the rube's purchase of the Brooklyn Bridge to the traveling salesman's conquest of the farmer's daughter. Husbandry itself was being transformed from the pursuit of "Nature's nobleman" to the condition of H. L. Mencken's *boobus Americanus*. Thus, city "Wife" would ask city "Husband" if a certain individual had ever been a farmer. The answer was no. "Wife—But he's always talkin' about the delights of livin' in the country. Husband—Exactly. That's what shows he never was a farmer."[108] No longer, moreover, was the great frontier the land of unlimited opportunity. In a railroad depot, "First youth" asked "Second youth" if he had traveled far. The latter answered, "Not yet, but I expect to before I stop. I am going West to seek my fortune. First youth—I just got back. Lend me a dime, will you?"[109] The time had come, *Bookman* editor Harry Thurston Peck recommended in a more serious vein, to renounce "that rant of Ruskin's about the country being better than the city," a doctrine that was nothing more than "rubbish and tommyrot," and to recognize that the city was "the perfect flower of the century." A nation of cities should turn for enlightenment, he continued, not to romanticism but to classicism: "Nature is never as fine as Art. It needs the suggestion of man's presence to make the landscape really sympathetic."[110]

The urban theorist was also concerned with the new relationship between city and country brought about by a half century of urbanization. His investigations and speculations may be divided into two categories: first, the impact of cityward migration on rural America, upon both in-migrants to urban centers and those

who remained behind in depleted agricultural areas; second, the social and cultural implications for the United States in its transition from rural to urban patterns
of living.

The rural ideal of a democratic society made up of independent yeomen whose
agrarian virtues served to counterbalance urban vices was still fostered in the
final years of the century. "Nature sets moral safeguards about those who are
near her," an advocate of the rural ideal asserted. "Honesty and orderliness are
not the result of precept, but of right conditions of life." Turn-of-the-century
Nebraska, this Jeffersonian continued, was the most fortunate state because it
was the most agricultural state. With half of Nebraska's wealth invested in
farmland and the other in cattle, "the Garden of Eden was not more purely
pastoral."[111] Marriott Brosius repeated the ruralist's dogma that "local self-
government had its origin in the institutions of farmers long before the birth of
cities; our Saxon ancestors created the models on which were formed the representative institutions which at length, under the modifying influence of environment, developed into the splendid system of free government under which
we now live in a perfect and harmonious union of individual freedom, local
independence, and national control." Unfortunately for American democracy,
he continued, urban areas were fast outstripping the agricultural in population
and power, and it was crucial that the farmer regain his moral lead by the wise
use of his vote and by guiding public opinion. It was the rural communities,
"where fresh air, pure blood, and good morals unite in preserving the physical
and intellectual vigor of the citizens" which had to serve, Brosius concluded,
as "breakwaters to protect our institutions in case the fountains of discontent
should overflow, and the bitter waters of anarchy swell in rolling floods from
our great cities, . . . the 'storm centers' of our civilization."[112]

Whether agrarian America could, in fact, continue to function as a breakwater
or safety valve for urban pressures was seriously in doubt.[113] Thus, although
Nation editor Edwin L. Godkin might lament the "steady stream of rustics into
all large cities" and support plans for the colonization of the urban poor in farm
areas, he was forced to concede that the "search of the society, the amusements,
and the chances—above all the chances—which city life affords" made the lure
of the city compelling.[114] The rural ideal became increasingly less serviceable
as a motivating philosophy, in other words, because more and more country
dwellers were rejecting rural living. An analysis of population trends in Massachusetts for the years 1850 to 1890, for example, concluded with the judgment
that it was "the young, strong, enterprising, and ambitious who migrate. The
best vitality of the country goes to large towns and cities."[115]

The tone of most of the literature on rural migration was deprecatory to the
rural ideal. "We may talk all we please of the beauties of farm life," advised
economist Edward W. Bemis, "but people are sure to follow in large degree
their pecuniary and gregarious instincts, and to settle in the city or its extensive
suburbs, where, among other advantages, life will be easier for the wife, and
where they may benefit society more than they could on the farm."[116] Rural

migrants came to cities, another observer noted, in order "to escape the bovine monotony of farm life"; they came to an urban center, "where, as in a beehive, sociability supplants the dull hut of the lonely agriculturalist, with whom new thoughts are as rare as 'roses in January.' "[117] *Charities* editor Edward T. Devine suggested that it "was useless to dissipate valuable energy in an attempt to prevent a movement of population which has shown itself to be world-wide and to rest upon necessary economic changes." Like it or not, Devine asserted, his generation had to recognize that an "agricultural revolution" had taken place and that the farm had a new and subservient place in American life.[118] A spirited challenge to proponents of the rural ideal was put forward by the editors of *The Social Economist*, who questioned "if such writers ever really think of what they are saying? . . . Are they still of the notion that country life is anything like the idyls of Theocritus and other city writers? We could wish for one of these scribes nothing worse than that he should be compelled to pass a summer and a winter in farmers' hard work on the vast shoulder of a New Hampshire hill, or the bitter fields of an English fen. It would completely cure him."[119]

The motive force behind rural migration to urban centers, most observers agreed, was escape from the crippling economic poverty and cultural stagnation of agricultural life. "North and South," the editors of *Open Church* asserted, "facts prove that one of the hardest problems we have to face at the present time is the deplorable and degenerate conditions that exist among multitudes in the rural sections."[120] C. E. Emerick of Columbia University interpreted the "agrarian problem" as a necessary consequence of world urbanization, a forward step in human evolution. According to Emerick, the farmer had no alternative but to recognize the primacy of an urban culture.[121] Other theorists were advancing, at the same time, the view that the agricultural environment itself should be examined in a new light. For too long, Frank W. Blackmar suggested, it had been assumed that "the tendency of social life in a large city is downward, and that of country life is upward"; in fact, isolation had as much of a conditioning influence upon the individual as did crowding. "The isolated life, bad economic conditions, and the morbid states that arise therefrom bring about insanity and immorality. . . . The crowd that gathers at the corner grocery may be of a different type from the city hoodlum, and less dangerous in some ways, but as a type of social degeneration it is little above imbecility itself."[122] Blackmar's "Smoky Pilgrims," in short, were closely related to Dugdale's earlier and more famous "Jukes." Dr. Lucy M. Hall advanced the environmental argument one step further and declared that sanitary conditions in large cities, although seriously inadequate, were superior to those in country districts "where new ideas are at best but slowly disseminated." "Stygian gloom" was the atmosphere that pervaded most of the sixty-five farmhouses visited by Dr. Hall in New England, the Midwest, and Far West. The great majority of them were poorly ventilated, situated too close to surrounding out-buildings, and permeated by dankness and dampness. "The house of which the poet sings, the artist raves, and which the novelist weaves into his romances, is, in real life, the most unhygienic of abodes.

Pass beyond the 'noble old elms, the vine-covered porches, and the mossy door-stone,' and fill in the further details of damp cellar, mouldy little bedrooms, and the complicated horrors which go to make the rear premises, and the picture seems to have lost its attractiveness.'' To this medical authority, city dwelling was demonstrably healthier than country life: ''The doctor who advised his patient to throw her sick child out of a fourth-story window, as offering a better chance of its life than a sojourn in the country, held extreme views, I confess; but his prognosis could easily be verified if a little margin for selection of locality were allowed.''[123]

In rejecting the rural ideal, urban theorists concentrated less upon the past contributions of rural life than they did upon the contemporary and future implications of the new balance between city and country. The good roads movement, for example, was promoted as an urbanizing force: ''Open the country neighborhoods to the visits of mail carriers and to the free exit and interchange of produce and personality,'' the editors of *The Commons* proposed, ''and the isolation which makes the village lad flee to the city and shuts the farmer in to his own thoughts and his family away from human company, and the problem of the country will be well on the way to solution.''[124] The advancement of the movement, the editors of *Public Improvements* suggested, was the duty not of the country district, but of the city, because the latter was the natural leader in transportation improvements, ''suburban homes ideas,'' and ''the spread of economic knowledge among the people.''[125] The city, in sum, was an energizing force: its trolley lines would link together a new urban-rural network;[126] its support of rural free delivery would provide the extension of ''urban privileges'' of communication.[127] The urbanization of society was regarded, then, as a basic and positive socializing force.[128]

One essential tenet of the rural ideal was, nevertheless, firmly adhered to: that home ownership was necessary in a democratic society. Political economist Simon N. Patten, in an address before the American Academy of Political and Social Science, challenged this doctrine and argued, to the contrary, that traditional American ''space instincts'' had led to the building of urban ''residence regions [that] might be called condensed farms,'' neighborhoods in which ''the peculiarities of farmlife show themselves in every home both in the form of the house and the habits of its occupants.'' In order to correct this condition, he urged, ''home feelings'' had to be balanced with ''civic feelings,'' and people had to learn to live together in communities as well as in families.[129] Patten's bold call for new neighborhood patterns of organization was decidedly the minority viewpoint, since most observers expressed concern about rising national rates of tenancy. Their anxiety over apparent declines in the rate of home ownership was the result of two well-publicized processes: the closing of the frontier and new patterns of urban living.

At the beginning of the period, the editors of *Banker's Magazine* gave witness to the cherished American belief that ''nothing adds more to the perpetuity and security of our country than the permanent settlement of the land." The land-owning, tax-paying folk had, the argument ran, a clear stake in society, one not shared by their urban brethren who were, on the contrary, "eager for a different state of things."[130] Another representative editorial from this same journal, a year later, repeated the same appeals and urged that "the Government act speedily in . . . enlarging the public domain, and securing for it the largest number of persons or settlers"; the balance between urban and rural populations, *Banker's Magazine* concluded, must be maintained.[131] In 1887 historian Albert Bushnell Hart argued that since Independence, "the nearness, accessibility, and cheapness of government land" had shaped America. "The population of the country has at last overtaken our unsettled domain. Henceforth, our conditions must be more like those of old and crowded countries."[132] In a word, the frontier had closed.

This glorification of frontiering and a consequent pessimism about the future were incorporated into Frederick Jackson Turner's frontier hypothesis to become a part of the conventional wisdom. Without access to large tracts of cheap public lands, it was held, the lower classes of the great cities would become further concentrated in space and would experience more sharply the pressures of an urban-industrial civilization. The closing of the frontier and the problems of downtown urban life were thus seen as related parts of a single national trend.

"Home sentiment," J. A. Collins declared, was the key to democracy: "A man without a home is a creature robbed of manhood, of all that delicate and ennobling sentiment that binds him by the strongest ties of affection to the land of his childhood and the scenes of his happiest recollections." America's tragedy, he concluded, was that its "percentage of . . . dependent population" exceeded that of "the monarchies of Europe."[133] In his reply to Collins's article, Gilbert L. Eberhartt berated the pessimism and defeatism of this point of view. "Many of our best citizens are tenants," he declared, "and are such from deliberate choice. And for the reason, they say, that it is much cheaper to rent than own a home." Not "landlordism," Eberhartt continued, but new patterns of living and of investment were responsible for the increase in tenantry: new types of homes were increasingly available in large towns and great cities, apartment houses and flats that were more attractive and functional than the private home of the past; new opportunities for profit in business and in real estate made the urbanite less willing to invest large amounts of capital for a domicile only.[134] Land use patterns—central city, suburban, and farm—were undergoing, as George K. Holmes recognized, a major "readjustment." Americans were, he continued, "a restless, unsettled people" who were not willing "to be tied to land. The ownership of a home hinders migration, and civilization has not yet proceeded far enough to do away with migration as a means of bettering one's condition." The migration about which Holmes wrote was primarily to the core city and its suburban rings: in the former, tenancy would expand in proportion to the city's size and property value; in the latter, home ownership would be increasingly opened to larger numbers of citizens; in both instances, "landlord-

ism'' was not a threat, since few properties were held by large interests. The
"urbanward'' movement of population, Holmes concluded, posed no threat of
either despotism or moral degeneration.[135]

Tenancy, despite intelligent explanations as to its causes and socioeconomic
significance, continued to be classified as a "problem.'' The vast majority of
urbanites, both ordinary residents and expert analysts, while ready to accept and
adapt to revolutionary modes of transportation and commercial building, were,
nevertheless, uneasy about the rapid proliferation of apartment houses, flats, and
tenements. Traditionally, "home'' had meant a free-standing residence for the
independent family, a domicile detached from other buildings, which isolated
and protected its occupants from outside forces. To the American, then, a
"home'' was more than a mere shelter: it was—and would remain—a symbol
of family and, indeed, of national unity. Since the United States has "always
lacked a native *home*'' or homeland, Earl H. Rovit has suggested, "it has always
been obsessively concerned with the urge to create homes or to find some transient
substitute for them''; hence the American "need to create and even sanctify
homes—the most natural symbolic containers of value and meaning.''[136] The
migration to the suburbs over the past century has drawn upon this concept of
home; in fact, the American version of suburban living, its search for environment, may be interpreted as a compromise between the giantism of a metropolitan
age and the localism of an age of towns and villages. Significantly, it is not a
rural but an urban solution.

The shape of the city, all of its chroniclers agreed, was changing radically.
Its central and neighborhood parks—those "acres of abstract greensward''—
were comforting reminders of an earlier municipality, of a colonial town set
in the midst of a sparsely settled countryside, of a commercial city in a new
nation of prosperous farms.[137] The abstract greensward became (and remains
today) an accepted urban amenity. But the popularity of the urban park and
the residues of bucolic imagery in the magazine literature of the period should
not be taken as evidence of a powerful anti-city tradition in the heart of urban
America. "Although the anti-urban philosophers and novelists of the nineteenth century intrigue the contemporary mind,'' historians Charles Glaab and
A. Theodore Brown have advised, "the defenders and prophets of the material city perhaps reflect more exactly the early popular view of the city.''[138] In
the magazine literature of the period, the latter outnumbered and overwhelmed
the former.

PLANNING THE IDEAL METROPOLIS

> I walked on a smooth laid sidewalk,
>   The streets were noiseless and clean;
> Though New York was busy as ever
>   This bristling city had been.

I rubbed my eyes in amazement,
    That all should so perfect seem,
And awoke to the roar of the traffic
    From future perfection's dream.[139]

Until the closing years of the century, the concept of the ideal city was little
more than a dream or, at the very most, a feverently expressed wish. Scattered
throughout the urban literature of the period, one may find occasional outbursts
of indignation at the despoliation of the physical city, as when Grace Peckham
lashed out at "the avariciousness of men in regard to city space" and at the
mindless greed which led them to build "lofty towers-of-Babel structures . . .
piled skyward[,] and these crowded together."[140] Protests of this order described,
but did not solve the physical problems of the central city. The use of every
possible foot of ground and air space by the landlords of urban America was,
in fact, transforming skylines into craggy canyons of skyscrapers, lesser buildings
into lightless and airless caverns, and the streets below into swarming and shad-
owed crevasses. Because this building boom was immensely profitable, it promised—or threatened—to expand even more in the years ahead. Its advance could
be checked or redirected only—if at all—by some vital countervailing force and,
until the late 1890s, no such power existed. The profit motive alone dictated
land uses and building practices.

At the beginning of the decade a writer for *The Social Economist* proposed
the creation of such a countervailing force, at least for New York City, through
the establishment of a specialized voluntary association, "a society for effecting
improvements and beautifying." Such a group, the proposal continued, should
begin with improvements that "will add, at once, to the comfort and pleasure
of the present generation, and after we have made those, we can attend to further
improvements and beautifying likely to benefit those who succeed us." The
major physical problems of the city—unclean streets and bad paving, a poor
lighting system, and a shortage of shade trees—should determine the organization
of the society: it ought to be divided into two major committees, one to oversee
the care of the streets, the other to attend to trees and lighting; both committees
should be organized at the neighborhood level, with at least two members of
each in every ward or district of the city; finally, a central coordinating committee
ought to serve as liaison and lobbyist with official municipal agencies. Once the
immediate problems were under control, the "society for affecting improvements
and beautifying" New York could turn to projects for the future: a uniform
building code, regulations governing the ventilation of all public structures for
meetings and amusement, the construction of glass and steel business arcades,
the introduction into the downtown areas of ornamental kiosks, and a "good
and reasonable cab system."[141] Citizen participation in such improvement associations, the tone of the article implied, was the key to a beautiful city. In
fact, voluntary associations of concerned citizens or, more accurately, dedicated
amateurs, were to play a significant supporting role in the city planning movement

of the 1890s and after. Municipal improvement associations were founded in most large cities and in many small towns, with an initial mission of popularizing and promoting the planning ideas of professionals in the new field.

Planning did not become fully accepted as a professional vocation until the early twentieth century. The calling of the first National Conference on City Planning and the Problems of Congestion in 1909 marked the real birth of a profession with its roots in the park crusade of the 1850s, the World's Columbian Exposition of 1893, various nineteenth-century humanitarian reform movements, and the development of municipal engineering. To this hodge-podge of influences—with its mixture of the romantic and the classical treatments of form, its combination of the social and the technical—still another shaping force must be added: the introduction of systematic urban theory in the age of associationalism. Thus, although the profession was not officially institutionalized until after the turn of the century, the initial formulation of modern planning norms took place during the 1890s, often in the name of the City Beautiful.

In the late 1890s, it became increasingly clear to a growing number of urbanists that there were no ready answers, no neat patterns for the shaping of the ideal city. To plan a city, architect Julius F. Harder warned, constituted a "problem of staggering proportions. Were it a fact that the deliberate purpose of building a city, let alone a great city, presented itself more frequently, or even occasionally," he explained, "no doubt the opportunities thus afforded would result in the recognition and establishment of a definite base, principles and records of experiment, those of good result to be emulated, those of failure to be avoided." There were, however, no base principles and records of experiment, since the builders of American cities had been men whose interests were those of "to-day and not of to-morrow, only of themselves and not of their neighbors." American cities were not poorly planned; they were planless: "No one will ever be accused, least of all our own municipalities," Harder declared, "of ever having had a deliberate intention of dealing comprehensively with the matter."[142] But the wasteful laissez-faire operations of the past would not suffice for the future: urban leaders had to substitute for the impromptu, short-sighted patterns of the old, Harder asserted, a new order of city building, one founded upon comprehensive, long-range planning. Planners of the future had to anticipate all needs of metropolitan America, both suburban extensions beyond the central cities and the physical renewal of core areas. The total city, Harder urged, should be "planned, or at least re-planned, by simply proceeding to make general provisions for its inevitable improvements for a hundred years to come. . . . Practically the entire city, by localities, will be rebuilt from two to eight times within a century, and the most radical changes can thus be accomplished with the slightest hardship to individuals or the public." The renewal of the downtown district, the core or "the nucleus of the city," presented the greatest challenge to the planner. Here, Harder continued, was "the field upon which the cunning of men is to be exercised"; downtown planning was "an heroic task," one that demanded "heroic treatment."[143]

Harder offered in place of the organic metaphor a designer's analogy, one that might be classified as structural and one that he applied specifically to New York:

A city may be likened to a house; its waterways, bridges, railroads and highways are entrances, vestibules, and exits; its public buildings are the drawing rooms, its streets the halls and corridors, the manufacturing districts the kitchens and workshops; tunnels and subways are its cellars, and its rookeries the attic; the parks and recreation places are its gardens, and its system for communication, lighting and drainage are the furniture. The city is a house of many chambers, and the first condition of forming its ideal plan is the shortest route from each to each. Thoroughfares and the tide of travel pouring through them have been compared to streams, where a narrowing of the way occurs, the current runs the swifter, whereas the human current of street traffic is retarded by contraction or its equivalent, congestion.

The gridiron plan of New York City, with its long and narrow system of identical blocks, presented the first planning problem. Where possible, Harder recommended, the gridiron configuration should be altered: by introducing a series of radial avenues across the existing pattern of north-south avenues and east-west streets; by widening most of the already existing streets and avenues; and by cutting the long north-south blocks in two and using the added street space for local traffic. The radial avenues were more than merely functional: "Their main advantage, still aesthetically considered, consists in quite the reverse from the picturesque: namely, the impressiveness arising out of the repose and dignity of the greater masses which they impel." The new shortened blocks would provide for an improvement in building practices: on the east, north, and west sides of the upper half of the original block, houses would be built around an open court that faced on the new east-west secondary street; on the east, south, and west sides of the lower half of the old block, the building pattern of the upper half would be duplicated to create, in place of the heavily congested row of solid structures, two horseshoe-shaped sets of buildings, each enclosing its own open courtyard and each facing upon a secondary street zoned for local traffic only.[144] For those areas in which buildings were already so dense as to preclude the introduction of radial avenues, street widening, or block bisection, Harder suggested that "a street may be floored over. An elevated platform of ample height above the roadway admitting light and air below, giving entrance to the buildings, as well above as at the level of the ground, and perhaps itself, arcaded with glass, would appear to be the inevitable fate" of much of lower Manhattan island.[145] Interspersed among the new open spaces of Harder's renewed Gotham would be small parks, children's playgrounds, and sports fields; on the city's fringes, to complete his plan, Harder recommended that New York's numerous smaller islands—Blackwell's, Ward's, Randall's, and so on—be designated as recreation areas. This ambitious prospectus for a greater Greater New York was guided by Harder's injunction—prefiguring Daniel H. Burnham's famous dictum of "make no little plans": "Utility is economy, but artistic utility is greater economy."[146]

The influential architect H. K. Bush-Brown introduced a series of papers on "The Planning of Cities," presented by members of the Architectural League of New York in 1899, with the explanation that although it might seem "surprising that the study of the planning of cities has received so little attention," students of urban America should recognize that "the utilitarian and commercial spirit has so dominated our national life that it has moulded our cities along with everything else." The time had arrived, however, for planners to begin a "remodeling of our unpicturesque American cities," a concerted effort that should start with the nation's major metropolis.[147] Fittingly, Julius F. Harder wrote the first paper in the series, an essay that enlarged upon his earlier study in *Municipal Affairs* and that supplemented his recommendations for relief from traffic congestion. To his earlier proposals, Harder added the idea of making Union Square (at the intersection of Fourteenth Street and Park Avenue and Broadway) the central terminus for all intown and suburban surface and underground transportation; of making Union Square, in other words, the planning node of the entire metropolitan area.[148] The plans of Edward P. North in the second paper in the series were also metropolitan in scope. In agreement with Harder that congestion was New York's most serious problem, North urged that its solution was to be found in the provision of "quick access to cheap lands" where New Yorkers might build "comfortable homes of their own." The erection of bridges across the East River would open to the city's tenement dwellers suburban communities in the Bronx and Queens and, at the same time, free intown land from residential use.[149] Architect George B. Post, in the third paper, expanded upon the ideas of his two colleagues. He accepted Harder's reservations about the adaptability of the gridiron street pattern and the latter's designation of Union Square as the planning node for Greater New York; he agreed with North's proposal for the settlement of the overflow of Manhattan's population into the adjacent boroughs. Then he advanced several steps beyond both Harder and North. Metropolitan New York's great problem, Post asserted, was that it was "an aggregation of villages, the villages themselves laid out on the old lanes and cowpaths, joined together without particular system." Moreover, the city was "long and narrow, with inadequate means of communication in a northerly and southerly direction, and its area has lately been increased by the addition of other cities, making the great city of Greater New York." The historical expansion of the metropolitan community had resulted, Post concluded, in a communications breakdown. To counteract the city's localisms, Post recommended concentrated municipal action, the creation of a true urban imperium: the opening of great triumphal avenues leading into monumental circles; the leveling of tenement areas by the municipal government and the erection, in their place, of great and imposing buildings; and the building of a new and magnificent City Hall to serve as a symbolic link between the residents of the diverse New York "villages." Post's imperial metropolis represented, clearly, the classical extreme in the City Beautiful tradition.[150]

The final pair of papers in the series focused upon New York's singular geographic feature, the fact that it was an island city. Milton See proposed the construction of "a terrace extending out in the [North or Hudson] river from the present shore line the entire distance [from Seventy-Second Street to Spuyten Duyvil], or about seven and one-fifth miles, the width of the terrace being from three to four hundred feet, or as wide as the federal or municipal authorities would allow, roofing over the present railroad tracks, the westerly wall enclosing which would be arcaded and balustraded, have sculptural ornamentations, etc." This North River terrace would provide the city's residents with the beauty of an Italian garden, the pleasures of a recreation area, the civic pride in a monumental municipal undertaking, and the economic gain of new lands to be developed.[151] The concluding paper in the series, by Municipal Art Society spokesman Frederick S. Lamb, extended the planning province of Greater New York beyond its borders into the adjacent state of New Jersey. The steady building of New York's waterfront had resulted in a scarcity of riverside lands for public use; the remedy for this unhealthy condition, Lamb urged, was in a metropolitan plan that would provide for recreation areas and preserve the Palisades along the Jersey coast from Fort Lee to Piermont.[152]

"The Planning of Cities" series was significant not because of the specific programs that it detailed, but by reason of the conceptual framework within which they were organized. The ordering of ideas along the lines laid down in this series marked a significant departure in the attempt to control an urban environment. In the first place, the contributors had broken with tradition by extending their influence beyond the boundaries of the historical city to include in their designs much of the developing metropolitan region. Second, they anticipated a wide use of such new technical skills as statistical evaluations for long-range planning, traffic-control measures, and new building techniques. Although many of their design standards were classical—radial avenues, monumental civic centers, river terraces, and the like—their seemingly shallow historicism and sometimes absurd neoclassical borrowings must be balanced against often creative modern adaptations of social science method and technological skills. Overattention to the urban imperium of a George B. Post slights the more functional planning of a Julius F. Harder. In their very act of producing a cooperative series on planning, these proponents of a New York Beautiful acknowledged that comprehensive plans had to be, because of the complexities of the metropolitan configuration and requisite planning skills, group endeavors.[153] And finally, the general norms that they laid down were intended to be applicable to other cities.[154]

In the urban literature of the period, planning was generally equated with progress. Opposition to programs for the improvement of the physical city came from a variety of municipal interest groups and individuals; however, in the urban journals these opponents to planning were dismissed as Philistines, knock-ers, or "mossbacks" and were seldom given the opportunity to argue their case.[155] The defenders of planning, as a result, presented a united front against criticism of the profession, its ideals, and its methods.

James H. Hamilton of Syracuse University was one in a handful of represen-tatives of the loyal opposition to professional planning. Most programs for civic betterment, he noted, were marked by "an excess of utilitarianism," a concen-tration upon the pecuniary and the quantitative, to the exclusion of the humanistic and the aesthetic. The weakness of the American urban renascence was not one of effort but of emphasis: "However practical and level-headed have been the designers of municipal programs, and with however much of cautious deliber-ation they have been worked out," he complained, "it may be said that the results of their endeavors are almost despairingly meager. . . . It may be that a wholesome sentiment for recreative and . . . [cultural amenities] will need to be joined to the more material considerations to give the reform movements the impulse requisite to their complete success." The utilitarian or reformist ideal had to be humanized, and this could be done only by enriching the spiritual or moral structure of the community. Specifically, Hamilton urged, what urban America required was the "growth of a fuller community" which, in turn, depended "upon a closer interrelation of the lives of the members of the com-munity, a larger stock of common utilities and common enjoyments." Although he admitted to the usefulness of such municipal enterprises as the formation of public clubs, the expansion of park facilities, the provision of public lecture series, and the establishment of museums, Hamilton maintained that each would have an appeal for the middle and upper classes only. What was needed, instead, was a municipal program that reached the working classes as well. Such a program, he concluded, was to be found in the formation of "a purified and elevated municipal theater and opera," which would "educate the people" and impress upon them "the consciousness of civicism." Their influence would be felt by all classes, and the urban community would be recast: "With the growth of a delight in good acting and good music, which would not be satisfied with anything inferior, a keen demand for quality would be established. The people would begin to look to the city for excellence."[156] Although the mechanics of Hamilton's plan for the creation of community may seem naive or impractical, his basic insight was a sound one. His desire to achieve "excellence" and "civicism" arose from his recognition that a great city transcends the purely physical; that it is, in large part, a cultural force. The great city, Hamilton recognized, possessed, in addition to its material aspects, spiritual qualities singularly its own: planning for its future must be more than disinterested ex-pertise; it had also to be an act of faith that testified to what Frederick Gutheim has called "the will to urban life."[157] Planning had to be concerned with the people.

Planners, it seemed to *The Public*, were more concerned with programs than with people. The editors of this single-tax magazine were suspicious of mere "municipal beautification," which seemed to them a way of looking at life "like a reflection in a mirror—everything is in reverse. . . . Life cannot be beautiful until it is complete, rational and righteous." Planning, they argued, had to begin with human beings, not things: "Let your boards of beauty require the closest observance of all the canons of art, and yet, if your city be inhabited by drudging women and slaving children and hopeless men, made so by unjust laws, artistic architecture will lend no beauty to it; it will rather emphasize its ugliness." "Before our public life can be beautiful," *The Public* advised, "our communal life must be righteous."[158] The debate between physical and social planners had begun.

The indictment against the planning profession was valid on several counts. First, the City Beautiful movement developed an American Beaux Arts style which, with its monumental proportions, was often oblivious to a truly human scale. Second, the uncritical adoption of planning—its unquestioned acceptance by urbanists as progressive in and of itself—fostered a narrowness of outlook within the profession. The planner as professional propounded an elitist ethic, one characterized by, as Lewis Mumford has noted, "the assumptions—and superstitions of unqualified power"; planning has "promised definite results, swift, visible, even striking."[159] There has been, in sum, a powerful strain of Nietzschean elitism in planning theory. Finally, planners were constitutionally incapable of bridging the gap between ideas and practice; that is, planning theory never quite caught up with the changing times.

This final caveat, however, may serve to place the preceding criticisms in proper historical perspective. Turn-of-the-century planning theory, although envisioning a new urban order, at the same time held fast to the traditional and the proven—specifically to classical form and the leadership of an accepted elite: it could not have been reasonably expected to have done otherwise. Essentially, the evolving profession of planning was progressive, not revolutionary. It reflected its times, a period during which the social conscience was informed by middle-class ideals and ideas. Lacking though it often seemed in human understanding and sympathy, it still succeeded in establishing a new conceptual framework for the rational ordering of major aspects of the urban environment. Planning proponents recognized the new dimension of urbanization, the metropolitan construct, and sketched out the outlines of their plans for its control and its development. Theirs was a necessary first step.

TOWARD VITAL CITIES

The challenges to a self-proclaimed "Land of Great Cities" seemed many and wide-ranging by the turn of the century.[160] Mass migrations into urban centers, the tearing down of the restricting walls of the historic municipality by an urban transportation revolution, and technological innovations that fostered growth—in short, the creation of a metropolitan complex—all made obsolete the traditional concepts of the good city. In their place, this generation offered, first of all, an idea of order, according to which the dream of its model city could be materialized into blueprints. Its urban spokesmen faced up to the reality of suburban growth, studied it as an integral part of the urbanization process and, overwhelmingly, accepted and planned for it as a stage in municipal betterment. What they misjudged about suburbanization was, of course, its accelerated pace; what they were unable to anticipate was the massive dislocation that eventually produced the sprawling "slurb." Yet, such an oversight, inasmuch as it preceded the automobile revolution, may readily be accounted for and understood. On the other hand, these urbanists recognized clearly the new relationships that were forming between *urbs* and *rus*, town and country, and self-confidently welcomed them. Most significantly, late-century urbanists developed and expounded a positive viewpoint on the dynamics of urban living. Although they were unable to reach a consensus on the exact direction for the shaping of the twentieth-century city, they did define the terms of debate for future generations on the nature and challenges of the urbanization process.

Late-century analyses of urban life served to clarify the possible alternatives to urban form, since they focused mainly upon the quality of city life. "Only under the conditions of city life," Leo S. Rowe advised the members of the National Municipal League in May 1897, "can the possibilities of human development be realized." The modern city, he continued, need not remain "a monotonous succession of narrow and depressing thoroughfares" with "every available open space . . . covered with flaring signs" and "at every street corner . . . a saloon . . . [where] every individual . . . [was] permitted to give free range to his fancy in the erection of dwellings." Rowe offered a more urbane future: "Through the ruralization of the city, through the erection of imposing and inspiring public buildings, through a change in the immediate environment of the poorer classes, and finally, through the acceptance of the social standard in the performance of municipal services, a new conception of municipal activity, and with it of city life, will be attained."[161]

The modern city, in brief, had to be comprehended not as a mere physical artifact, but as a complex and unified social construct. The urbanist had to experience the city, understand its forms and rhythms, provide plans for its systematic development, and thereby transform a land of great cities into a modern metropolitan commonwealth.

NOTES

1. Francis H. McLean, Review of *The City Wilderness* by Robert A. Woods, *The Twentieth Century City* by Josiah Strong, and *Social Settlements* by C. R. Henderson, *Annals of the American Academy of Political and Social Science* 14 (September 1899): 258.

2. "Editorials," *The Public* 2, no. 93 (January 13, 1900): 6. New York was even "the financial keystone of the baseball arch. A successful season at the Polo Grounds means prosperity all over the circuit, and the reverse in this city entails hardship on all

the other members of the League" (George M. Steele, "Our National Game," *Metropolitan Magazine* 11 [May 1900]: 526).

3. Bird S. Coler, "The Future Metropolis" [Address to the Cornell University Alumni Association, New York City, January 26, 1900], *Public Improvements* 2 (February 1, 1900): 146. Gross pretensions to grandeur seemed to be as frequent in this period as in the postwar era, when New York was the subject; for example, *The Public* reprinted this item from an advertisement published by the Cass Real Estate Company: "Every altruistic thought, every religious emotion, every good impulse of mind or of soul, adds to the value of Manhattan Island real estate" ("Miscellany," 1, no. 28 [October 15, 1898]: 16).

4. "Col. Waring's Prophecy," *Public Improvements* 2 (March 15, 1900): 222. His record as seer was marred only by his prediction that New York City's municipal government would be made up of "men anxious only for the welfare of the people, and who strive for their betterment."

An earlier version of this essay may be found in George E. Waring, Jr., "Greater New York a Century Hence" [reprinted from the New York *Herald*, October 24, 1897], *Municipal Affairs* 1 (December 1897): 713–17. Here, Waring predicted that "twenty years will not elapse before the horse will be unknown in New York. . . . Heavens! What a relief this will be to the Department of Street Cleaning." (p. 715)

5. The possible future use of the automobile was of wide interest by the turn of the century: the first six motorized "stages" in New York City are described in "Automobile Stages for Fifth Avenue," *Public Improvements* 3 (May 15, 1900): 320; another item in the same issue, "Automobile Stable," pp. 321–22, was concerned with the plans for a projected municipal garage; a final note, "Automobiles to Tow Boats," p. 324, dealt with the use of the new machines on the Delaware and Raritan Canal. Again, Henry Jackson Howard, in "American Progress in Automobilism," *Metropolitan Magazine* 11 (January 1900): 3–10, also predicted that "self-propelled vehicles" would come into general use; however, unlike Waring, his emphasis was upon its acceptance by society and the adaptability of the electric auto to the central city. That Waring was, on the other hand, able to anticipate a more important use for the automobile and the coming transportation revolution was, indeed, noteworthy.

6. "Notes on the Population of Cities," *California Municipalities* 3 (November 1900): 105.

7. J. H. [Joseph Hutchinson], "The Song of the Cities," *California Municipalities* 1 (January 1900): 200.

8. "Notes on the Population."

9. Leo S. Rowe, "The City in History," *American Journal of Sociology* 5 (May 1900): 721, 722, 745.

10. William Coleman, "Science and Symbol in the Turner Frontier Hypothesis," *American Historical Review* 72 (October 1966): 25–26. For its wide-ranging (and often conservative) applications, see Raymond Williams, *Keywords: A Vocabulary of Culture and Society* (New York: Oxford University Press, 1976), pp. 189–92, "organic."

11. Thomas E. Will, "The Problem of the City," *American Magazine of Civics* 7 (September 1895): 239. In this article, Will was proposing immigration restriction and argued that urban America's heterogeneity of peoples made her cities "the 'dumping-ground of Europe's filth.' "

12. John R. Commons, "The Church and the Problem of Poverty in Cities," *Charities Review* 2 (May 1893): 347.

13. "Address of Mrs. Cornelius Stevenson" [Before the Civic Club of Philadelphia, March 3, 1894], *Good Government* 13 (April 15, 1894): 123.

14. [Editorial], *American Federationist* 2 (November 1895): 165.

15. Joseph Loeb, "Motives of Municipalization," *Municipality* 1, no. 2 (June 1900): 23–30.

16. "The Suburban City," *California Municipalities*, III (Aug., 1900), 4.

17. Frederick L. Hoffman, "The Practical Use of Vital Statistics" [A Paper read before the New Jersey Sanitary Association], *Publications of the American Statistical Association* 7, n.s. 52 (December 1900): 56.

18. Gideon Sjoberg, *The Preindustrial City: Past and Present* (Glencoe, Ill.: The Free Press of Glencoe, 1960), pp. 25–51, 80–144; Lewis Mumford, *The City in History: Its Origins, Its Transformations, and Its Prospects* (New York: Harcourt, Brace & World, Inc., 1961), pp. 482–524.

19. Adna Ferrin Weber, "Suburban Annexations," *North American Review* 166 (May 1898): 616, 614.

20. Franklin H. Giddings, Review of *National Life and Character: A Forecast* by Charles H. Pearson, *Political Science Quarterly* 10 (March 1895): 161, 162.

21. Levi Gilbert, "The Down-Town Church Again," *Open Church* 2 (April 1898): 289.

22. Edwin W. Sanborn, "Social Changes in New England in the Past Fifty Years," *Journal of Social Science* 38 (December 1900): 148–49. See also, "Life and Education," *The Citizen* 1 (October 1895): 177–78.

23. "A Fearful Threat," *Yellow Kid* 1 (June 15, 1897): 31.

24. "Miseries of Suburban Life," *Yellow Kid* 1 (June 19, 1897): 8.

25. Richard Duffy, "My Suburban Sweetheart," *Yellow Kid* 1 (May 22, 1897): 8.

26. The Rev. Amory H. Bradford, "The Suburbs and the Cities," *Open Church* 2 (October 1898): 351, 352, 353.

27. "Sociological Notes. Improved Housing," Conducted by Samuel M. Lindsay, *Annals of the American Academy of Political and Social Science* 12 (July 1898): 163, 164.

28. Grace Goodwin, "Manhattan's Suburbanites," *Metropolitan Magazine* 10 (September 1899): 316.

29. Leonora B. Halstead thought it possible "that Europe and the United States shall become entirely urban or suburban, with portions set apart, as parks are now, for the raising of perishable food" ("Advantages of City Life," *The Social Economist* 4 [April 1893]: 221).

Suburbanization would be encouraged, it was generally agreed, by improved methods of transportation. The expansion of commuter services in the suburban belts between Philadelphia and New York was applauded in "Trolleys for Pennsylvania R.R.," *Public Improvements* 1 (September 1, 1899): 173–74, an article that described the Pennsy's building of trolley tracks parallel to its regular New York–to–Philadelphia line. E. R. Weeks, in "Conveyance of the Future," *Public Improvements* 3 (June 1, 1900): 337–38, celebrated the extension of community facilities through the development of low-fare electric trolleys, the improvement of roads, and the increased use of the bicycle for suburban traffic. That the bicycle still fascinated Americans during the late 1890s may be seen from Josiah Strong's proposal that young cyclists be encouraged to spread The

Word among suburban dwellers ("A New and Important Movement," *Open Church*, 2 [January 1898]: 218) and from an editorial comment in the same journal that encouraged suburban pastors to court the attendance at Sunday services of their "wheelmen" ("Editorial Table: Bicycles and Church-Going" by J. P. P., *Open Church*, 1 [October 1897]: 200–02).

30. The most frequently cited statistical analysis of American urbanization, before Weber's study, was Carl Boyd's "Growth of Cities in the United States During the Decade, 1880–1890," *Publications of the American Statistical Association* 3 (September 1893): 416–25, which argued that the largest cities were "not of such paramount importance in the growth of urban population as has been supposed" (p. 416). Boyd's hypothesis was challenged by Matthew Brown Hammond in "The Distribution of Our Urban Population," *Publications of the American Statistical Association* 4 (December 1894; March 1895): 113–16, and by Edmund J. James in "The Growth of Great Cities," *Annals of the American Academy of Political and Social Science* 13 (January 1899): 1–30.

31. William Z. Ripley, Review of *The Growth of Cities in the Nineteenth Century* by Adna F. Weber, *Journal of Political Economy* 8 (March 1900): 262, 263.

32. Samuel T. Dutton, "Educational Resources of the Community," *Journal of Social Science* 38 (December 1900): 118.

33. George E. Bissel, "Enrichment of Cities," *Public Improvements* 2 (January 1, 1900): 101.

34. Albion W. Small, "The Scope of Sociology. VI. Some Incidents of Association," *American Journal of Sociology* 6 (November 1900): 353–54, 376–77.

35. Grace Peckham, "Influence of City Life on Health and Development," *Journal of Social Science* 21 (September 1886): 81, 85, 87, 88.

36. Walter B. Platt, "Certain Injurious Influences of City Life and Their Removal," *Journal of Social Science* 24 (April 1888): 24–25, 26, 28. That noise was a pressing problem that demanded immediate attention in major cities is apparent from the antinoise ordinance drawn up by Chicago's corporation counsel and described in "Editorials," *The Public* 3 (July 14, 1900): 209 and from the demand for the formation of a civic group to encourage noise abatement in the editorial "An Anti-Noise Society," *Public Improvements* 1 (September 15, 1899): 198. The latter also labeled New York "The City of Needless Noise."

37. Platt, "Certain Injurious Influences," pp. 28–29.

38. Thomas E. Will, "The Problem of Cities," *American Magazine of Civics* 7 (September 1895): 232, 231, 233, 237.

39. Frederick J. Kingsbury, "The Tendency of Men to Live in Cities," *Journal of Social Science* 33 (November 1895): 2, 8, 17–19.

40. "Civics and Education: What Shall the City Do?" Review of *Municipal Functions* by Milo Ray Maltbie, *Gunton's Magazine* 16 (May 1899): 350–51.

41. "Cities Healthier Than the Country," *Public Improvements* 2 (March 1, 1900): 202.

42. A. E. Winship, "Does City Life Enervate?" *World's Work* 1 (November 1900): 109. In his sample, Dr. Winship reported 392 city-born, 492 country-born, and 130 foreign-born. "When it is remembered," he added, "that forty or fifty years ago—the time when most of these men were growing up—the population of the large cities was only about 12 per cent of the whole population of the nation, it becomes evident that the cities have supplied a very much larger percentage of successful men than the country."

The classification country-born, moreover, included all communities with populations under 50,000 and was, therefore, doubly misleading.

43. "Qualified," *Yellow Book*, 1 (August 1897): 7.

44. The Tourist, "A Study of Boston Streets," *Yellow Book*, 1 (September 1897): 36–37. The reference is to Sir Joseph Paxton's Crystal Palace (1851) and its numberless English and American imitations.

45. J. Walton McMillar, "The Whirlpools of New York," *Metropolitan Magazine* 11 (May 1900): 481. The major nodes of Manhattan were "at the Brooklyn Bridge entrance; at Broadway and Union Square, erstwhile known as 'Dead-Man's Curve'; at Twenty-third street at the intersection of Broadway and Fifth avenue; at Thirty-fourth street where Sixth avenue crosses Broadway; at the Circle, Fifty-ninth street; and at Fifty-ninth street and Columbus avenue."

46. Ibid., pp. 481–82. Gotham's "smart set" adopted the fad of coaching, Charles Ogden Card reported, because of its desire for status and its love of speed ("Coaching in New York. One of the Most Popular Recreations of Society," *Metropolitan Magazine* 1 [June 1895]: 363–67). In crowded cities, according to S. H. Meserve, a six m.p.h. law was strictly enforced, and fast-moving trotters were harassed by the police. In New York, citizens with speedy horses were men with money and influence, and "the pressure [that they] brought to bear was so great that a stretch of land along the eastern side of Manhattan Island was assigned for the use of the trotters" ("New York's Great Speedway," *Metropolitan Magazine* 11 [June 1900]: 631). The Harlem Speedway, which extended from 155th Street to Fort George, was wide enough for a dozen teams to ride abreast, cost nearly $1,500,000 a mile to build, and was, R. H. Hicks exulted, a "stretch of costly roadway the like of which can be duplicated nowhere else in the world" ("A Speedway Costing Millions," *Metropolitan Magazine* 8 [September 1898]: 330–31).

47. "Rapid Transit Subways in Metropolitan Cities," *Municipal Affairs* 4 (September 1900): 458, 459–80.

48. S. C. Stevens, "Mid-Air New York," *Metropolitan Magazine* 8 (July 1898): 65–66. A similar judgment on the advantages of open-air transit, both surface and elevated, may be found in M. G. Darling, "City Hall to Fort George," *Metropolitan Magazine* 11 (April 1900): 402–06.

49. James Argyle Robinson, "New York's Great Underground Road," *Metropolitan Magazine* 11 (April 1900): 360, 361–67. As the "fathers of Rapid Transit," Robinson nominated Abram S. Hewitt and the entire New York Chamber of Commerce.

50. J. Herbert Welch, "The Greatest Bridge on Earth," *Everybody's Magazine* 2 (January 1900): 46.

51. "The Great Metropolitan Bridge," *The Social Economist* (December 1895): 329–30.

52. John DeWitt Warner, "Bridges and Art" [Address before the National Sculpture Society], *Public Improvements* 2 (January 1, 1900): 97.

53. John DeWitt Warner, "The City of Bridges," *Municipal Affairs* 3 (December 1899): 651, 663.

54. "Lifts in New York," *Public Improvements* 2 (April 16, 1900): 268, 269.

55. Montgomery Schuyler, "The 'Sky-scraper' Up to Date," *Architectural Record* 8 (January–March 1899): 231–32.

56. Louis De Coppet Berg, "Iron Construction in New York City," *Architectural Record* 1 (April–June 1892): 448–68.

57. "A Picturesque Sky-scraper," *Architectural Record* 5 (January–March 1896):

299. An analysis of existing New York building codes may be found in William J. Fryer, Jr., "The New York Building Law," *Architectural Record* 1 (July–September 1891): 69–82. The Architectural League of New York, which had been founded by George B. Post in 1894 and which was later to propose the comprehensive planning program described later in this chapter, drew up a bill that demanded the outlawing of skyscrapers. Post "had the support of New York newspapers, the Brooklyn and Buffalo chapters of the American Institute of Architects, the City Club of New York and many art societies. Post felt he had the backing of the state Senate and Assembly as well as the governor, but on the last day of the legislative session his bill was left in the speaker's basket. Post attributed his failure to a strong lobby of the state's real estate men" (Eugene Rachlis and John E. Marqusee, *The Landlords* [New York: Random House, 1963], p. 197).

58. Schuyler, "The 'Sky-scraper'," pp. 231–57.

59. Louis Curtin, "First Glimpses of Gotham," *Metropolitan Magazine* 11 (June 1900): 608.

60. Carroll Knowlton, "Looking Down on Humanity," *Metropolitan Magazine* 12 (October 1900): 477, 478, 480.

61. Asa Briggs, *Victorian Cities* (London: Odhams Books Limited, 1963), p. 53.

62. Frank Leroy Blanchard, "From the World's Tallest Buildings," *Metropolitan Magazine* 10 (July 1899): 45. The image of the Tower of Babel was frequently employed by writers in popular magazines: see, for example, Arthur L. Sackett, "A Skyscraper from Cellar to Cornice," *Metropolitan Magazine* 6 (September 1897): 145–46.

63. Blanchard, "World's Tallest Buildings," pp. 45–46. The viewpoint of this observer was different from but analogous to that of Knowlton in "Looking Down on Humanity": "Men and women walking on Broadway look like ants, and horses and wagons appear to be playthings drawn by mice. It is a great lesson to the egotistical man, a view of his fellow-man from this dizzy height, if he will only reflect that he appears to others at the same range in the same proportion to his real size. It gives any man a new impression of things" (p. 49). Although the philosophical outlook is in sharp contrast to Knowlton's, the distortion of view is identical.

64. Ibid., p. 45.

65. Anselm Strauss, *Images of the American City* (New York: The Free Press of Glencoe, 1961), pp. 3–81, esp. p. 8.

66. Rupert Hughes in "Mushrooms in Steel," *Everybody's Magazine* 2 (June 1900), for example, likened skyscraper construction to warfare: "Like other warfare, it has its humdrum routine and its unpoetic features; but it has also its romance, its thrills, and its splendid rewards for him who can manipulate as a unit a host of varied forces, and snatch victory from impending defeat" (p. 520).

67. Montgomery Schuyler, "The Small City House in New York," *Architectural Record* 8 (April–June 1899): 357–62.

68. Montgomery Schuyler, "The Romanesque Revival in New York," *Architectural Record* 1 (July–September 1891): 38.

69. Montgomery Schuyler, "The Works of the Late Richard M. Hunt," *Architectural Record* 5 (October–December 1895): 97–98.

70. Schuyler, "The Small City House." 368–69.

71. Carl Schorske, "The Idea of the City in European Thought," in *The Historian and the City*, ed. Oscar Handlin and John Burchard (Cambridge: MIT Press and Harvard University Press, 1963), pp. 104, 105.

72. Hubert, Pirsson, and Hoddick, "New York Flats and French Flats," *Architectural Record* 2 (July–September 1892): 55, 55–64. The influence of the Romantic concept of "home sentiment" upon this subject is discussed later in this chapter.

73. "Diplomatic Christmas Presents," *Yellow Book* 1 (December 1897): 7.

74. "Our Janitor's Scale of Prices," *Yellow Book* 1 (August 1897): 22.

75. "Too Crowded," *Yellow Book* 1 (December 1897): 55.

76. Henry W. Desmond, "Modern Architecture—A Conversation," *Architectural Record* 1 (January–March 1892): 276. Whether this crude account of the Chicago School was intended to be totally damning is difficult to determine. The *Record* did evidence a large degree of local prejudice that was especially noticeable in its series "Architectural Aberrations." The second article in this series, for example, proclaimed that "Philadelphia, in respect of its commercial architecture, is undoubtedly the most backward and provincial of American cities" and "that Philadelphia is architecturally far more Western than the West" ("Architectural Aberrations. No. 2—The Record Building, Philadelphia," *Architectural Record* 1 [January–March 1892]: 261–62.) Again, the attack upon "Western architecture" was repeated in "Architectural Aberrations. No. 7—The Fagin Building, St. Louis," *Architectural Record* 2 (April–June 1893): 470–72, in which this mode of building was linked more with an individual life-style than with geography. At the same time, it should be noted, the buildings of New York were subject to equally intense scrutiny, and in "Architectural Aberrations—No. 16. 585–87 Broadway, New York," *Architectural Record* 7 (October–December 1897): 219–24, the threat was held out that Philadelphia's abysmal record was being "loudly challenged by what used to be the pride of New York" (p. 219); in addition, perhaps in an attempt to create a sense of objectivity, critiques on western building by western architects, such as Dankmar Adler's appraisal of his own and Louis Sullivan's "The Chicago Auditorium," *Architectural Record* 1 (April–June 1892): 415–34, were also included. In the end, however, one suspects that this journal was guilty of a large measure of local boosting; for when the series was terminated, it was replaced with one on "Provincial Architecture." The preface to this series explained: "By 'Provincial Architecture' is meant all architecture that originates outside Boston and New York in the East, and a few of the largest cities in other parts of the country" (E. C. Gardner, "Some Handicaps of Provincial Architecture," *Architectural Record* 9 [April 1900]: 405). By the turn of the century, Chicago deserved at least equal mention with these eastern cities; that it did not receive such, that it suffered by comparison, indicates the sectional prejudices of the eastern architectural fraternity.

77. Desmond, "Modern Architecture," pp. 278, 280.

78. A. D. F. Hamlin, "Architecture and Citizenship," *Public Improvements* 2 (April 16, 1900): 265–66, 266–68.

79. A. D. F. Hamlin, "The Difficulties of Modern Architecture," *Architectural Record* 1 (October–December 1891): 147–48.

80. Leopold Eidlitz, "The Architect of Fashion," *Architectural Record* 3 (April–June 1894): 351.

81. Ernest Flagg, "Influence of the French School of Architecture in the United States," *Architectural Record* 4 (October–December 1894): 218, 226–28. The successful completion of New York's Dewey Arch by a team of resident artists, who drew upon and managed authorized municipal funds (the first such experiment in the city's history), demonstrated, according to lawyer J. Wilton Brooks, that civic officials ought regularly to employ professional artists as consultants on all future projects for municipal beautification ("The Dewey Arch," *Public Improvements* 1 [September 15, 1899]: 189–91).

82. Charles Rollinson Lamb, "Civic Architecture from Its Constructive Side," *Mu-*

nicipal Affairs 2 (March 1898): 72, 68–69, 72. The Charterists referred to here were the proponents of the creation of the five-borough union of Greater New York. The City Beautiful movement in planning is the subject of a later section of this chapter.

83. Ibid., p. 50.

84. William Nelson Black, "Various Causes for Bad Architecture," *Architectural Record* 2 (October–December 1892): 163.

85. Walter L. Creese, *The Search for Environment; The Garden City: Before and After* (New Haven, Conn., and London: Yale University Press, 1966), p. 131.

86. Thomas Tryon, "Municipal Art," *Public Improvements* 1 (July 15, 1899): 98, 99.

87. Charles Rollinson Lamb, "New York—The City Beautiful," *Metropolitan Magazine* 12 (November 1900): 598–99.

88. Edwin Howland Blashfield, "A Word for Municipal Art," *Municipal Affairs* 3 (December 1899): 582.

89. Frederick Lamb, "Municipal Art," *Municipal Affairs* 1 (December 1897): 681, 674, 687–88.

90. Frederick Lamb, "Civic Treatment of Color," *Municipal Affairs* 2 (March 1898): 111, 111–16, 117.

91. Edwin Howland Blashfield, "A Word for Municipal Art," *Municipal Affairs*, 3 (December 1899): 590–91, 591–92, 592–93.

92. E. R. L. Gould, "Park Areas and Open Spaces in Cities" [Read before the American Statistical Association, May 26, 1888], *Publications of the American Statistical Association* 1 (June–September 1888): 51, 60–61. In this article, Gould rated the cities of the world as to their provision of small parks. His rankings included Washington in first place, Prague in third, Boston fourth, San Francisco eleventh, Berlin thirteenth, New York twenty-third, Paris twenty-fourth, Chicago twenty-eighth, Brooklyn thirty-third, and Philadelphia thirty-sixth. He also ranked cities as to population per acre of open space. His findings placed Minneapolis first, San Francisco fourth, Edinburgh fifth, Chicago sixth, Boston ninth, Philadelphia eleventh, Washington twelfth, London twentieth, and New York twenty-sixth.

93. Galen Cranz, *The Politics of Park Design: A History of Urban Parks in America* (Cambridge, Mass., and London, England: MIT Press, 1982), pp. 61–99. Her dates for this stage are 1900–1930; however, the park features and goals that she outlines are identical with those proposed by late-century urbanists.

94. "The Standard of Taste for Parks," *The Social Economist* 8 (June 1895): 321–23, 326.

95. Ibid., pp. 324, 325. "Gigmanity" is a slang expression, the first syllable of which refers to the popular two-wheeled one-horse carriages sported by trotting enthusiasts of the day.

96. Charles Zueblin, "Municipal Playgrounds in Chicago," *American Journal of Sociology* 4 (September 1898): 145, 146–58.

97. "Parks and Reading," *Public Improvements* 1 (June 1, 1899): 44–45.

98. Cornelius B. Mitchell, "Trees in City Streets," *Municipal Affairs* 3 (December 1899): 692.

99. Morris Loeb, "Small Gardens for Tenement Dwellers in Copenhagen," *Charities Review* 10 (December 1900): 450. The Copenhagen experiment was somewhat similar to the Hazen Pingree plan for the cultivation of vacant lots in urban centers, a program that was enacted in Pingree's Detroit and in Josiah Quincy's Boston; however, this latter

experiment was started as a depression measure and was promoted more as a relief program than as an amenity. E. Ray Stevens's "Some Present Day Municipal Problems," *Municipality* 1, no. 2 (June 1900): 15–22, was especially appreciative of this urban adaptation to "the Anglo-Saxon . . . passion for the soil" (pp. 19–20).

100. Henry Leslie Osborn, "A Mission of the Public Park," *American Magazine of Civics* 9 (August–September 1896): 190.

101. Mrs. McVean-Adams, "Children in Summer," *The Commons* 3, no. 28 (August 1898): 6.

102. Nixon Waterman, "God Help the Boy," *The Commons* 2, no. 24 (April 1898): 13.

103. Virginia Woodward Cloud, "Alien," *Bookman* 10 (October 1899): 154.

104. Frank Norman Dexter, "August Days," *The Commons* 3, no. 28 (August 1898): 5. "Oliver Wendell Holmes," Asa Briggs relates, "tired of hearing Cowper's line, 'God made the country and man made the town,' offered his version—'God made the cavern and man made the house' " (*Victorian Cities*, p. 75).

105. Robert H. Walker, *The Poet and the Gilded Age: Social Themes in Late 19th Century American Verse* (Philadelphia: University of Pennsylvania Press, 1963), p. 295; see also his chapter 3, "Gotham and Gomorrah," pp. 37–61.

106. Why the rural ideal was so consistently propounded in late-century verse is also a subject for conjecture only. The most obvious answer is that the bucolic theme had become securely established as a respectable literary convention, one to which the beginning poet would turn, as might the neophyte painter to still life. It is probable, too, that most of the magazine verse was unsolicited and therefore economical to publish; at the same time, although a minute portion of the prose writers in these periodicals were women, a vast majority of the poets were females; for them, the sentimental pull of nature was on a plane with motherhood itself.

107. For the derivations of these and other anti-rural words, see the *Dictionary of American Slang*, compiled and edited by Harold Wentworth and Stuart Berg Flexner (New York: Thomas Y. Crowell Company, 1960).

108. "The Lighter Side of Things," *Metropolitan Magazine* 10 (July 1899): 109.

109. "Encouraging," *Yellow Kid* 1 (May 8, 1897): 12.

110. Harry Thurston Peck, "A Confident To-Morrow," *Bookman* 10 (December 1899): 327.

111. William R. Lighton, "The Riches of a Rural State," *World's Work* 1 (November 1900): 99, 93. Yet, this article concluded, urbanization had left its mark upon this pastoral Eden, since nearly one-half the state's population resided in towns and villages. "The average prairie town," moreover, was "an incubus rather than an aid to progress." The towns were "unproductive" centers where one witnessed "the process of sucking the middleman's profit from the commodities which pass through their hands." The prairie towns, finally, were the residues of urban booming, the abodes of railroad men, store keepers, saloon proprietors, gang members, and the "listless sons of Micawber" (p. 103).

112. Marriott Brosius, "The Farmers and the State," *American Journal of Politics* 2 (January 1893): 108, 112.

113. Alfred H. Peters in "The Depreciation of Farming Land," *Quarterly Journal of Economics* 4 (October 1889): 18–33, simultaneously preached the rural ideal while he proved that the economic, social, and cultural conditions of the farmer were declining rapidly and inevitably.

114. Edwin L. Godkin, "The Problems of Municipal Government," *Annals of the American Academy of Political and Social Science* 4 (May 1894): 877–78.

115. F. S. Crum, "The Birth Rate in Massachusetts, 1850–90," *Quarterly Journal of Economics* 11 (April 1897): 260.

116. Edward W. Bemis, "The Discontent of the Farmer," *Journal of Political Economy* 1 (March 1893): 195.

117. Henry Powers, "How the Other Half Lives," *The Social Economist* 1 (April 1891): 106.

118. Edward T. Devine, "The Shiftless and Floating City Population," *Annals of the American Academy of Political and Social Science* 10 (September 1897): 158–59.

119. "The Social Question. As Seen in Magazine Literature," *The Social Economist* 1 (March 1891): 29–30.

120. "Editorial Notes," *Open Church* 1 (October 1897): 203.

121. C. F. Emerick, "An Analysis of Agricultural Discontent in the United States," *Political Science Quarterly* 11 (September, December 1896): 433–63, 601–39; 12 (March 1897): 93–127.

122. Frank W. Blackmar, "The Smoky Pilgrims," *American Journal of Sociology* 2 (January 1897): 485–86, 488–89.

123. Dr. Lucy M. Hall, "Unsanitary Conditions in Country Homes," *Journal of Social Science* 25 (December 1888): 59, 60–69, 70–71.

124. [Editorial], *The Commons* 2, no. 23 (March 1898): 9.

125. [Editorial], *Public Improvements* 1 (August 1899): 148.

126. Charles Barnard, "What Is He Going to Do About It?" *The Social Economist* 5 (September 1893): 152.

127. Charles Burr Todd, "Rural Free Delivery," *Gunton's Magazine* 19 (September 1900): 232.

128. In "Civics and Education: City Advantages in Education," *Gunton's Magazine* 16 (June 1899): 430–40, it was suggested that urbanization would advance to the point where "farmers, some day, will be able voluntarily to locate in town centers and go out to their fields, just as thousands of city workers now live in suburban localities and go in town every day to follow their various tasks" (p. 432).

129. Simon N. Patten, "Minutes of the Proceedings. Twenty-First Session," *Annals of the American Academy of Political and Social Science* 4 (May 1894): 963.

130. "The Public Domain," *Banker's Magazine* 39 (January 1885): 481–82.

131. "The Public Lands," *Banker's Magazine* 40 (June 1886): 887.

132. Albert Bushnell Hart, "The Disposition of Our Public Lands," *Quarterly Journal of Economics* 1 (January 1887): 169. By 1898, the editors of *The Public* were to lament, there was "little land left in the United States which may be had for nothing; and such as there is, is just about worth its price—nothing" ("Editorials," *The Public* 1, no. 30 [October 29, 1898]: 5).

133. J. A. Collins, "The Decadence of Home-Ownership in the United States," *American Magazine of Civics* 6 (January 1895): 56, 64.

134. Gilbert L. Eberhartt, "Are American Homes Decreasing? A Reply to J. A. Collins," *American Magazine of Civics* 6 (March 1895): 292–97.

135. George K. Holmes, "Tenancy in the United States," *Quarterly Journal of Economics* 10 (October 1895): 43–44, 44–48, 49.

136. Earl H. Rovit, "The American Concept of Home," *American Scholar* 29 (Autumn 1960): 522, 525.

137. The phrase "acres of abstract greensward" is taken from William H. Whyte, Jr., "Are Cities Un-American?" *The Exploding Metropolis*, The Editors of *Fortune* (Garden City, N.Y.: Doubleday & Company, 1958), p. 25.

138. Charles Glaab and A. Theodore Brown, *A History of Urban America* (New York: Macmillan Company, 1967), p. 72. Morton and Lucia White, in *The Intellectual Versus the City: From Thomas Jefferson to Frank Lloyd Wright* (Cambridge: Harvard University Press and MIT Press, 1962), provided the standard account of the anti-urban tradition, based, as the subtitle indicates, upon a star system approach to intellectual history.

139. "Ex." [poem], *Public Improvements* 1 (May 15, 1899): 25.

140. Grace Peckham, "Influence of City Life on Health and Development," *Journal of Social Science* 21 (September 1886): 89.

141. J. D., "A Plan to Improve and Beautify New York City," *The Social Economist* 2 (December 1891): 65, 66–67, 68.

142. Julius F. Harder, "The City's Plan," *Municipal Affairs* 2 (March 1898): 25. On the three major occasions when it might have been possible to institute comprehensive planning, Harder explained, the challenge had been met only once, with the adoption of the L'Enfant-Ellicott plan for Washington; after the Boston and Chicago fires, however, the occasion had been irretrievably lost.

143. Ibid., pp. 29–30, 31, 33–34.

144. Ibid., pp. 33–34, 39, 44–45. Although Harder proposed that primary east-west streets be expanded from sixty to seventy feet wide, he insisted that the secondary streets be no more than fifty feet wide, in order to keep through traffic off them.

145. Ibid., pp. 33–34. This idea was also expounded in J. Walton McMillar's "The Whirlpools of New York," in which he notes that in 1883 a pedestrian bridge had been erected at Broadway and Fulton: "This bridge was hailed with favor at the time, and it was predicted that before long an upper deck might be built the entire length of Broadway, and to this deck the sidewalks would be elevated." However, the original bridge soon became a gathering point for pick-pockets, fell into disuse, and was torn down (*Metropolitan Magazine* 11 [May 1900]: 482–83).

146. Harder, "The City's Plan," pp. 43–45, 30. Burnham is the subject of "Packaging a Plan," below.

147. H. K. Rush-Brown, "The Planning of Cities: Introduction," *Public Improvements* 1 (October 15, 1899): 297.

148. Julius F. Harder, "The Planning of Cities: Paper No. 1," *Public Improvements* 1 (October 15, 1899): 297–300.

149. Edward P. North, "The Planning of Cities: Paper No. 2," *Public Improvements* 2 (November 1, 1899): 5–6. Harder was also open to the suburban ideal: "Let methods be discovered that annihilate the condition of distances and the day of cities will be past. Man will return to live closer to nature, following his natural inclination, to escape from the crushing artificiality which hems him in" ("The City's Plan," p. 29).

150. George B. Post, "The Planning of Cities: Paper No. 3," *Public Improvements* 2 (November 15, 1899): 26–27.

151. Milton See, "The Planning of Cities: Paper No. 4. Synopsis of Scheme for the Embellishment of Water Front of the City on its Western Side, from 72nd Street North to Spuyten Duyvil," *Public Improvements* 2 (December 1, 1899): 51. Not only has See's general plan been enacted, but his recommendation for "filling in this space with the ashes that are now collected separate from garbage and other objectionable matter" has also been largely carried out.

A description of two "Recreation Piers" already in operation in Manhattan (one at the foot of East 3rd Street, the other at the end of East 24th) and a prospectus for a third (at East 112th) may be found in A. H. Paine's "New York's Recreation Piers," *Metropolitan Magazine* 6 (November 1897): 345–47.

152. Frederick S. Lamb, "Planning of Cities: Paper No. 5. On the Embellishment of New York City Water Fronts," *Public Improvements* 2 (December 15, 1899): 75–77. C. L. Marston in "The Passing of the Palisades," *Metropolitan Magazine* 7 (February 1898), lamented that the "American Rhine was being ruthlessly shorn of its beauty" (p. 181). Eighteen hundred feet of the eighteen-mile-long cliffside had already been blasted apart by New Jersey quarry interests; at the present rate of decline, Marston warned, the Palisades would be destroyed within another 1,200 years. Something, he concluded, should be done; exactly what that something was, he did not say. In later years, much of the Palisades was converted into a state reservation.

153. For the consequences of the movement in New York City, see Harvey A. Kantor, "The City Beautiful in New York," *New-York Historical Society Quarterly* 57 (April 1973): 149–71.

154. In California, for example, George Hansen complained about the "decidedly troublesome fact that every land holder who divided his area into town lots and streets has, up to this date, been permitted to do such in a manner entirely to his personal liking." As a result, urban California was chaotic. The only answer, Hansen asserted, was a general recognition of "the absolute necessity of subjecting the settlement of any community to a preconceived plan." Such plans, he concluded, should be instituted by official municipal planning agencies ("The Laying Out of Cities," *California Municipalities* 1 [November 1899]: 114–15).

155. The untenable position of Kansas City's "moss-backs" is described in William H. Wilson's *The City Beautiful Movement in Kansas City* (Columbia: University of Missouri Press, 1964), pp. 69–90; it was, very probably, typical of the national pattern.

156. James H. Hamilton, "A Neglected Principle of Civic Reform," *American Journal of Sociology* 5 (May 1900): 746, 749–50, 753, 756, 757.

157. Frederick Gutheim, "Cities and Their People," The Canadian Institute on Public Affairs, Report on the 12th Winter Conference, "The People Are the City," Toronto, January 1966 (Mimeographed.)

158. "Editorials. Municipal Beautification," *The Public* 2, no. 59 (May 20, 1899): 7.

159. Mumford, *City in History*, pp. 401–02.

160. *World's Work* 1 (December 1900): 138–39.

161. Leo S. Rowe, "American Political Ideas and Institutions in Their Relation to the Problem of City Government" [Address before the National Municipal League, Louisville, Ky., May 6, 1897], *Municipal Affairs* 1 (June 1897): 327–28.

Concept for a Plan

Did Raymond Unwin, Lewis Mumford wrote to Frederic J. Osborn in 1963, "know anything of Olmsted's work? Probably not." And yet, Mumford continued, "Unwin re-invented some of Olmsted's best tricks."[1] In this letter to Great Britain's foremost proponent of the new towns movement, America's most influential urbanist of this century proposed, however tentatively, an intriguing connection between the nineteenth-century American designer of parks and the turn-of-the-century British builder of garden cities. The possibility of such a transatlantic linkage between the men and their movements suggests an international context for reviewing Frederick Law Olmsted's contributions as an urbanist: that of a shared metropolitan vision.

It is especially fitting that Mumford should suggest the possibility of such a comparative framework, for he was the first unbiased authority to recognize Olmsted's special place in American urban history. Until the publication of Mumford's *Brown Decades* in 1931, the only sources readily available on Olmsted's design contributions were a contemporary portrait by Mariana Griswold van Rensselaer in an 1893 number of *Century*, for which Olmsted himself provided both information and theme; the first two of a projected (but stillborn) multivolume series of Olmsted papers, for which his son and namesake served as senior editor; and a pair of Menckenesque attacks on the Olmsted tradition in landscape design by Elbert Peets in the Sage of Baltimore's own *American Mercury*.[2] In *The Brown Decades* Mumford, who could claim critical distance from both the man and the tradition within which he worked, hailed Olmsted as the designer "who almost single-handed laid the foundations for a better order in city building." "As man learns to control his environment," Mumford explained, "his relationship with the land becomes more complicated. . . . City life does not diminish these relations: it rather adds new ones." And with his park designs Olmsted introduced a necessary "idea—the idea of using the landscape creatively. By making nature urbane he naturalized the city." As early as 1870, Mumford continued, "less than twenty years after the notion of a public landscape park had been introduced in this country, Olmsted had imaginatively grasped and defined all the related elements in a full park programme [for] . . . comprehensive city development."[3] He accomplished all this, according to Mumford, in a notable address on "Public Parks and the Enlargement of Towns" before the American Social Science Association, meeting in Boston on February 25, 1870.[4]

"After 1870," Mumford would inform Frederic Osborn, Olmsted "wrote almost nothing about his activities or his plans or his ideas."[5] At the time of his 1870 address, however, Olmsted could boast of a considerable readership in what he called the "Literary Republic." His first book, *Walks and Talks of an*

American Farmer in England (1852) had been a critical success. His next three—
A Journey in the Seaboard Slave States (1856), *A Journey through Texas* (1857),
and *A Journey in the Back Country* (1860)—had become national sensations.
And his summary volume of this "Our Slave States" series, *The Cotton Kingdom*
(1861), would eventually develop into an international best seller. For a time,
he also served as managing editor of *Putnam's Monthly Magazine* (1855–56)
and coeditor of *The Nation* (1865–66). But recognition in the "Literary Republic" was only one among many of Olmsted's achievements at this point in his
life. Scientific farmer, organizing genius of the wartime Sanitary Commission,
founding member of the American Social Science Association, manager of a
California mining empire, park administrator and designer: such were the early
career paths marked out by the versatile Frederick Law Olmsted.[6]

Ralph Waldo Emerson's "Vistas" for post–Civil War America, for "reconstructing and uplifting Society,"[7] opened up as well for Frederick Law Olmsted
when, in 1866, he completed the transition from polymath to practitioner by
reconstituting his partnership with Calvert Vaux, the codesigner of Central Park.
In short order, the firm of Olmsted and Vaux would project and develop the
basic components of what Mumford recognized as a "comprehensive city development" program: the central city park, the parkway, and the satellite suburb.
In 1870 Olmsted integrated all three elements in an innovative design scheme
that could have served as a model for the later Anglo-American garden city/new
towns movement, a concept for a plan of metropolitan development.

"Public Parks and the Enlargement of Towns" opens with a celebration of
what Olmsted identified as "a strong drift townward" in the United States, Great
Britain, Europe, and indeed everywhere except "where men number their women
with their horses, and where labor-saving inventions are as inventions of the
enemy." This advance of "modern civilization," he continued, demonstrated
"the intimate connection which is evident between the growth of towns and the
dying out of slavery and feudal customs, of priestcraft and government by divine
right."[8]

A utilitarian ideal of efficiency, practicality, and order drew the mobile American family townward. The female of the household, Olmsted suggested, provided the impetus: "The tastes and dispositions of women are more and more
potent in shaping the course of civilized progress," he taught, "and we may
see that women are even more susceptible to this townward drift than men."
To the modern woman, Olmsted claimed, country life seemed dull, drab, monotonous, and, most of all, dirty. "The civilized woman," on the other hand,
"is above all things a tidy woman"; hence, "the strong tendency of women to
town life, even though it involves great privations and dangers" was logical.
His civilized women were concerned with "the amount of time and labor, and
wear and tear of nerves and mind, which is saved to them by the organization
of labor in those forms, more especially, by which the menial service of house-
holds is simplified and reduced" in urban areas: "by the butcher, baker, fish-
monger, grocer, by the provision venders of all sorts, by the ice-man, dust-man,

scavenger, by the postman, carrier, expressmen, and messengers, all serving you at your house when required; by the sewers, gutters, pavements, crossings, sidewalks, public conveyances, and gas and water works."[9]

Utility made possible amenity, which Olmsted called "public recreation" and which he "conveniently arranged under two general heads," both of them urban in character. The first and more obvious he labeled the "*exertive.*" It included activities in which "the predominating influence is to stimulate exertion," such as "games chiefly of mental skill, as chess, or athletic sports, as baseball." These activities could be conducted on "numerous small grounds so distributed through a large town that some one of them could be easily reached by a short walk from every house," with all of them "connected and supplemented by a series of trunk-roads or boulevards." Their extent, then, would be citywide. The second and more important form of public recreation Olmsted termed the "*receptive.*" It happened on occasions "which cause us to receive pleasure without conscious exertion," as when enjoying "music and the fine arts." These aesthetic occurrences were based on the "gregarious inclination" of civilized society. An experience on this level had to be spontaneous (even instinctive) because, Olmsted theorized, "there is so little of what we call intellectual gratification in it." Where he himself "experienced the most complete gratification of this instinct in public and out of doors, among trees," Olmsted instructed, was along European promenades and in "our own . . . New York parks. I have studiously watched the latter for several years," he maintained, "and the more I have seen of them, the more highly have I been led to estimate their value as means of counteracting the evils of town life."[10] Urban open spaces of this order, both parks and promenades, Olmsted continued, provided "the greatest possible contrast with the restraining and confining conditions of the town, those conditions which compel us to walk circumspectly, watchfully, jealously, which compel us to look closely upon others without sympathy."[11] Green and ordered urban spaces, conversely, opened up the city and at the same time gave it a point of focus. Their extent, then, could be projected metro-wide.

"A park fairly well managed," Olmsted promised further, "will surely become a new centre of that town. With the determination of location, size, and boundaries should therefore be associated the duty of arranging new trunk routes of communication between it and the distant parts of the town existing and forecasted." A comprehensive system of interconnected landscaped roadways constituted, then, the second element in Olmsted's concept for an ordered metropolitan environment. For underdeveloped areas, they "may be either narrow informal elongations of the park, varying say from two hundred to five hundred feet in width, and radiating irregularly from it"; or, for the more developed sections of cities, "we must probably adopt formal Park-ways," which "should be so planned and constructed as never to be noisy and seldom crowded" and so arranged "that no part of the town should be many minutes' walk from some one of them." These Olmstedian parkways "should be made interesting by the process of planting and decoration, so that in necessarily passing through them, whether in going to or from the park, or to and from business, some substantial recreative advantage may be incidentally gained."[12] That "recreative advantage" drew, of course, upon the "*receptive*" division of public recreation, which joined amenity to utility to induce "gratification."

A vital part of Frederick Law Olmsted's concept for a plan—at some distance from a central city park and approachable along a parkway and by train—was the third critical element in his metropolitan scheme, the satellite or, his term, the "open town suburb." Here was the real magnet for the mobile American family as it ventured townward. "It should be observed that possession of all the various advantages of the town to which we have referred . . . does not," he cautioned, "by any means involve an unhealthy density of population." Quite the contrary, in fact: "Probably the advantages of civilization can be found illustrated and demonstrated under no circumstances so completely as in some suburban neighborhoods where each family abode stands fifty or a hundred feet or more apart from all others, and at some distance from the public road." The promise of the future included, he foretold, "suburban advantages . . . almost indefinitely extended." With commuter lines in place, Olmsted confidently predicted, "all the important stations will become centres or sub-centres of towns, and all of the minor stations suburbs."[13] Utility and amenity would lure the mobile American family to the metropolitan edges, but the connections would hold: central city parks linked to satellite suburbs along landscaped parkways. Thus did Frederick Law Olmsted conceive of an ordered metropolis.

Olmsted's concept had its British counterpart in Ebenezer Howard's turn-of-the-century vision of the garden city. That there was any direct connection between the men or their works—American and British planned suburbs of the period—remains to be demonstrated. However, as Walter L. Creese has shown, Howard lived in Chicago during the 1870s, was almost certainly aware of Olmsted's nearby "open town suburb" of Riverside. He probably visited there and apparently incorporated many of its finest features—what Mumford would call Olmsted's "best tricks"—into his garden city ideal.[14] Although the direct connections remain problematic, the essential correspondences between the planning ideals propounded by Olmsted and those of Howard are inescapable. Each sought utility and amenity, projected a long-range strategy for land use controls, and addressed directly the central question of the parts to the whole. Neither concept was carried out fully during its creator's lifetime, but both planning ideals remain alive today.

Ebenezer Howard lived long enough to see two prototype garden cities founded, and his disciples brought about the formulation of a national new towns policy for all Great Britain during the aftermath of World War II.[15] Frederick Law Olmsted carried out two comprehensive park-parkway schemes on his own, and his sons extended a packaged version of his metropolitan park systems from coast to coast.[16]

For Buffalo, Olmsted created between 1868 and 1876 the essential components of a comprehensive park-parkway system (Figure 1). It encompassed the 350-

Figure 1

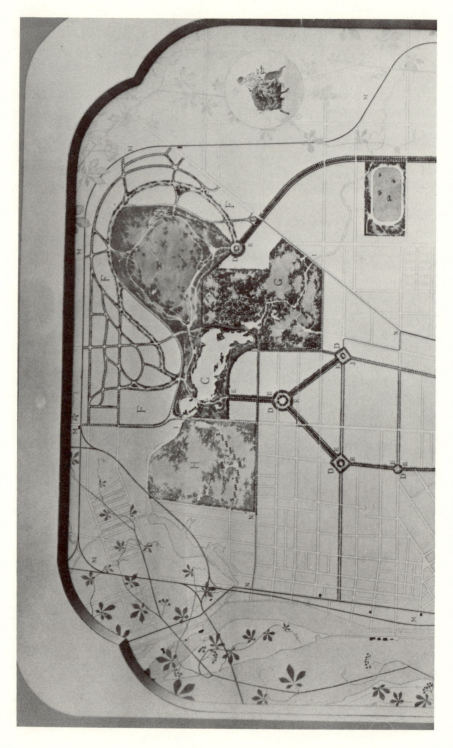

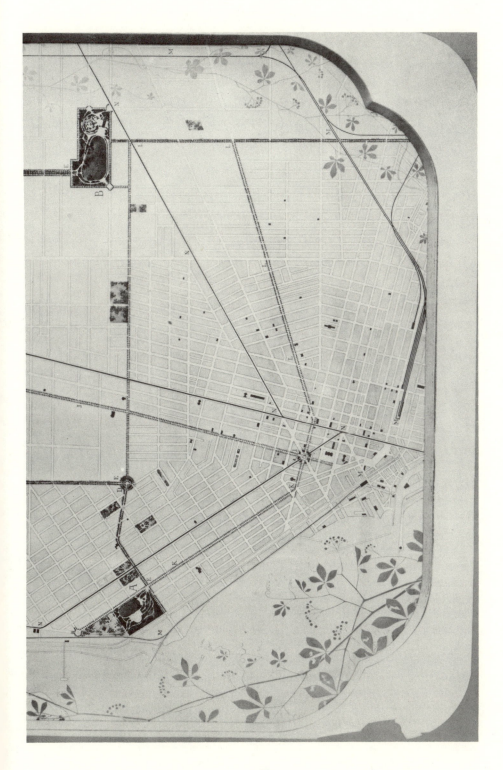

Figure 2

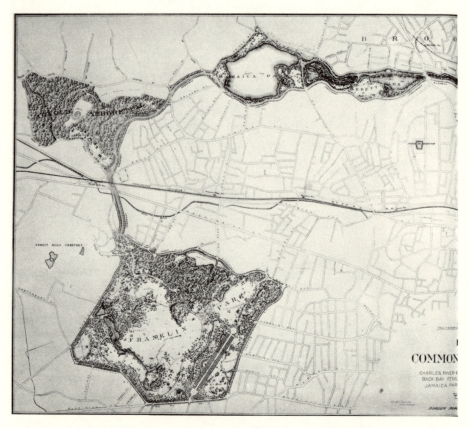

acre Delaware Park at the city's north central edge (''C'' in Figure 1); the grounds for Buffalo State Hospital (''H''), in collaboration with architect H. H. Richardson, on the central park's western border; the 32-acre Front (''A''), on the city's lower west side; the 56-acre Parade (''B''), on the east side; and, although it had been established prior to his own work in Buffalo, the rural cemetery of Forest Lawn (''G''; c. 1850). All of these open spaces were linked together by an ambitious system of parkways and boulevards (marked variously by small capital letters). Missing from the Buffalo configuration was the third element in Olmsted's concept for a plan, the open town suburb; in its place, he provided Parkside (''F''), which encircled the upper reaches of Delaware Park. In contrast with the outlying satellite suburb that he described in ''Public Parks and the Enlargement of Towns'' and shaped at Riverside (1868–69), Olmsted's Parkside was an effort at ring development according to the pattern projected by Sir Joseph Paxton during the 1840s for peripheral housing on the lots, terraces, and crescents bordering his prototype central city park at Birkenhead, outside Liverpool.[17] In advancing from the theoretical to the practical, from the ideal to the real, in

Figure 2 (Continued)

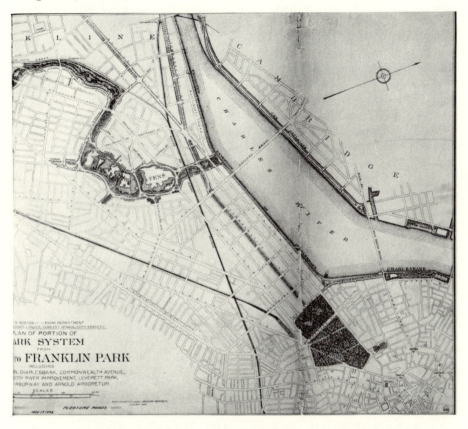

sum, Olmsted scaled down the ambitious satellite suburb from his concept for a plan to a more modest close-in housing project in his actual design.

For Boston, Olmsted fashioned between 1878 and 1895 that city's famed "emerald necklace," a park-parkway system of over 2,000 acres. From the Back Bay to West Roxbury, its five parks (Figure 2: The Fens, Muddy River Improvement, Jamaica Park, Arnold Arboretum, and Franklin Park) were linked together by a system of parkways (Fenway, Riverway, Jamaicaway, and Arborway). Again as in Buffalo, park and parkway predominated. In this final phase of his planning career, in fact, the suburban component in Olmsted's scheme for metropolitan development, which had been scaled down in Buffalo, never appeared at all.

"After 1870," as Lewis Mumford observed, "Olmsted wrote almost nothing about his activities or his plans or his ideas"; perhaps, Mumford speculated, Olmsted was silent "because he could hope to have no readers."[18] Perhaps, but it is more likely that in the quarter-century following 1870 until his retirement in 1895, Frederick Law Olmsted narrowed his readership to a select audience—

actual or potential clients. Over the years, then, he turned to other methods of communication, particularly the visual. His increasing control over this medium of expression is evident in the progression from "Public Parks" in 1870, which contained no supplementary illustrations, to the sketch map of Buffalo (Figure 1), which is almost cartoon-like in its simplicity, to the graceful curves of the Boston plan (Figure 2), which is art, as well as artifact.

After 1870 Olmsted's urban America transformed itself radically, and the evolution of his ideas reflected that transformation. In "Public Parks," by including suburbs with parks and parkways, Olmsted had meshed the private and public spheres. In Buffalo, where Parkside developed piecemeal, Olmsted witnessed the frequent gap between a concept for a plan, no matter its logic and power, and that plan's implementation. In Buffalo, where a sympathetic park commission cooperated with him in creating a park-parkway system for the public sector, there was no like authority to control landowners and builders in the private sector. Consequently, in Boston Olmsted applied the lessons learned in Buffalo, limited himself to the public sector, and planned only parks and parkways.

Thus by the mid–1890s, at the close of his career, Frederick Law Olmsted had transformed himself from man of letters to expert, municipal gardener to landscape architect, generalist to specialist, proponent to practitioner. His career, then, bridged the gap between the periods defined in these pages. And his scheme for comprehensive city development would reassert itself within a decade in the garden-city movement and, again, a half-century later in new town programs worldwide. Olmsted's concept for plan, in sum, was nothing if not viable.

NOTES

1. Michael J. Hughes, ed., *The Letters of Lewis Mumford and Frederic J. Osborn: A Transatlantic Dialogue, 1938–70* (New York and Washington: Praeger, 1972), p. 350.

2. Lewis Mumford, *The Brown Decades: A Study of the Arts in America, 1865–1895* (New York: Dover, 1931 & 1955); M. G. van Rensselaer, "Frederick Law Olmsted," *The Century Illustrated Monthly Magazine* 46 (October 1893): 860–67; Frederick Law Olmsted, Jr., and Theodora Kimball, eds., *Forty Years of Landscape Architecture: Being the Professional Papers of Frederick Law Olmsted, Sr.*, 2 vols. (New York: G. P. Putnam's Sons, 1922 and 1928); Elbert Peets, "Central Park," *American Mercury* 4 (March 1925): 339–41, and "The Landscape Priesthood," ibid. 10 (January 1927): 94–100.

3. Mumford, *Brown Decades*, pp. 82, 59, 88, 91–92.

4. Published initially for the American Social Science Association (A.S.S.A.) (Cambridge, Mass.: Riverside Press, 1870), the pamphlet was reprinted a century later in "The Rise of Urban America" series, Richard C. Wade, advisory editor (New York: Arno, 1970). It also appeared in the *Journal of Social Science* 3 (1871): 1–36. The local chapter of the A.S.S.A. sponsored Olmsted's talk to boost park development in Boston; as will be demonstrated below, nearly a quarter-century would pass before their expectations were met.

5. Hughes, *Letters*, p. 330.

6. For a more detailed account of this phase of his life, see Dana F. White, "A Connecticut Yankee in Cotton's Kingdom," in White and Victor A. Kramer, eds., *Olmsted South: Old South Critic / New South Planner* (Westport, Conn.: Greenwood Press, 1979), pp. 11–19.

7. Letter to Thomas Carlyle, September 26, 1864, *The Correspondence of Emerson and Carlyle*, ed Joseph Slater (New York: Columbia University Press, 1964), p. 542.

8. *Journal of Social Science*, p. 4.

9. Ibid., pp. 5, 6, 76.

10. Ibid., pp. 17–18.

11. Ibid., p. 22.

12. Ibid., pp. 24–25.

13. Ibid., pp. 8, 9.

14. Walter L. Creese, *The Search for Environment; The Garden City: Before and After* (New Haven and London: Yale University Press, 1966), pp. 150–57.

15. Frederic J. Osborn and Arnold Whittick, *The New Towns: The Answer to Megalopolis*, with an Introduction by Lewis Mumford (New York: McGraw-Hill Book Company, 1963), is the standard history. Letchworth (1903) and Welwyn (1920) were built with private funds as model suburbs. The New Town Act of 1946 established long-term plans and procedures, along the lines suggested by Howard, as official government policy.

16. See Dana F. White, "Frederick Law Olmsted, The Placemaker," in *Two Centuries of American Planning*, ed. by Daniel Schaffer (London: Mansell Publishing Limited, 1988), pp. 87–112, upon which the following descriptions are based, for a more detailed analysis of the plans, politics, and progress of the Buffalo and Boston projects. The metropolitan park schemes of the successor firm, the Olmsted Brothers, are examined below in "Packaging a Plan" following Chapter 3.

17. See Clifford E. Thornton, *The People's Garden: A History of Birkenhead Park* (Birkenhead: Williamson Art Gallery & Museum, n.d.), p. 5, and Jean McInniss, *Birkenhead Park* (Birkenhead: Countryvise Limited, 1984), pp. 20–21, about the provisions for peripheral housing, only a portion of which was ever actually constructed. For FLO's first visit to Birkenhead, his initial encounter with a public park in the picturesque tradition, see *Walks and Talks of an American Farmer in England*, 2 vols. (New York: G. P. Putnam and Company, 1852), 1:79.

18. Hughes, *Letters*, pp. 330, 350.

3

Governing Great Cities, 1885–1900

THE THREAT OF TWEED, A CHALLENGE BY BRYCE

The specter of Boss Tweed haunted the city halls of late-century urban America. Gross incompetence in the management of public business, crass self-interest in the performance of official duties, and a cynical disregard for cherished American values seemed to sum up the heritage of Tweed and his ilk. The classic statement of this viewpoint was Lord Bryce's familiar dictum of 1888 that "the government of cities is the one conspicuous failure of the United States." Any extant deficiencies or inadequacies at the federal or state levels, Bryce concluded, were "insignificant compared with the extravagance, corruption, and mismanagement which mark the administrations of most of the great cities."[1] That municipal government since the postwar era had become inherently rotten was an article of faith for most late-century Americans—whether they were ordinary citizens, involved reformers, or experienced observers of the civic scene. To a large extent, magazine writing about urban politics remained moralistic and thereby obscured the processes and problems of governing urban America.

The Manichean view of municipal politics—with the vigilant Good in eternal conflict with relentless Evil—held its own, both in volume and intensity, in the periodical literature after 1885. The reporter, sensationalist, and moralist outlined plots of dramatic political pillage, sketched in the profiles of its actors, and visualized the advent of heroic champions for projected happy endings. In many cases, judgment preceded analysis because as Boston settlement house pioneer Robert A. Woods noted, municipal government seemed "so corrupt as often to leave the honest citizen with a sense of public duty no recourse but that of outright and determined hostility."[2]

To this honest citizen, according to economist John R. Commons, it should be obvious that "the ignorant, foreign, unpropertied and corrupt elements are as yet too powerful in America to be trusted with unrestricted home rule."[3] Some control over urban democracy had to be exerted. An extreme answer was to eliminate democratic institutions altogether and substitute an authoritarian centralization of control: specifically, C. E. Pickard recommended, by strengthening the office of the mayor and by building army posts directly outside major cities. With the closing of the frontier, he explained, "the growing scarcity of land is forcing a constantly greater number of men into our large cities, creating a rapidly enlarging and dangerous proletariat." Consequent class antagonisms, he theorized, would lead to a final struggle to produce a "socialistic" or a "highly centralized and monarchical" government.[4] Whether that inevitable struggle would prove to be violent or gradual depended upon the initiative of honest citizens in assuming control immediately; to the friends of the "ignorant, foreign, unpropertied," it seemed that the so-called better classes were wasting no time in organizing to meet this challenge. Henry George, Jr., son and namesake of the founder of the Single Tax movement, asked, "Are We Arming Coming Masters?" and answered his own question in the affirmative. He reported examining a Gatling gun during a visit to the War Department, where he was informed by an "orderly in regulation uniform" that " 'it would be very effective in a street riot.' I had not said anything about street riots—had not thought of such a thing," George asserted. "How should a matter of such purely local concern as a riot come first in the thoughts of a soldier who does not belong to a municipality, . . . but to the nation at large as represented by the federal government?"[5] The question, obviously, was rhetorical. Thus did post–Civil War fears about the rebellion of the dangerous classes carry over into the closing decades of the century.

Reactionary fears of class warfare within the great cities were kept alive and fed by bogus parallels between political machines and the tyranny of ancient Rome. Tammany's "well trained phalanx which now holds us in political subjection had recreated, the founder of New York's City Club Edmond Kelly accused, the relationship between the Roman emperor and his Praetorian Guard: "the servant is stronger than the master."[6] The machine had produced, political commentator Thomas E. Will argued, the Man on Horseback: "One of these self-chosen despots systematically plundered the public treasury, purchased immunity with a fraction of the spoils, bought and terrorized the regular organs of public expression, and insolently asked the people "what they were going to do about it.' "[7] The same pattern had developed in Rome, advised a third foe, where "Caesar and Pompey were for some years allied bosses and ruled the city and empire with despotic sway." "Finally, Caesar did away with pretension of self-rule and was recognized as the sole master of Rome, ruling not as a king, but as a boss in the American sense, governing absolutely in the name and through the constitutional machinery of the dead democracy which still shammed life." There could be little doubt that "the symptoms of the moral, social, and political diseases which put an end to democracy" in ancient Rome "are present in abundance and in aggravated forms in our own country, and fill every patriotic heart with grave fears as to the future of government by the people in the United States."[8]

If the Rome of the Caesars served as a historical object lesson, the Rome of the popes constituted a contemporary power menace. According to L. Elseffer, American politicians, especially the minions of municipal machines, had broken faith with the Puritan acknowledgment of "Israel's God alone to be head and source of all power and authority and justice"; they had made a mockery of the national "prayer at Valley Forge"; they had chosen "the flesh-pots of Egypt to the Land of Promise"; and their sins would meet with "the ruin of Rome and the desolation of Babylon [that] await the American Republic."[9] The "desolation of Babylon" was the price to be paid for flirtation with the Whore of Babylon. Already in New York, claimed the editors of *Gunton's Magazine*, the "extraordinary power" of the Roman Catholic Church was behind Tammany. It was the church of "the poor, especially the very poor"; it pretended to champion the cause of labor, a stance that, of course, was "largely demagogy."[10] Clearly, the sides were being marked off preparatory to erection of street barricades. Certainly, warned Thomas E. Will, the cities, as "the 'dumping ground of Europe's filth,' " were courting disaster.[11]

These doleful jeremiads against the two Romes were admittedly expressions of a minority viewpoint; nevertheless, these same paranoid expressions were significant as caricatures of traditional political values. The honest citizen, holding steadfastly to the ideal of a just, impersonal, and impartial government, could not understand the "foreign" political ways of the masses. The standard genteel view of this clash of cultures was that "the poorer classes in the cities are as a rule indifferent to good and honest municipal government."[12] Their unconcern might even have been understandable had it not been combined with the "jocularity" of the masses concerning the conduct of politics.[13] Professor Jesse Macy of Grinnell College reported that "a member of the Irish race" had informed him that "the reason the Irish govern our cities as they now do is because they are a humorous people. They see a vast, intelligent, and money-making class offering themselves as victims; and they go in, and occupy the field from a feeling of irrepressible humor."[14] In answer to the "jocularity" of this "humorous people" came the regal patrician pronouncement, "We are not amused"; implied in their fears was the admission, "We do not comprehend."

Indicative of, and possibly contributing to, this lack of understanding was the marked neglect of this subject on the part of the artist. "The manner in which the machinery of politics has been ignored in the attempts of fiction to portray American life as it is," lamented *Bookman* editor Arthur Bartlett Maurice at the turn of the century, "is certainly one of the most curious anomalies of our national literature." The story of New York City politics during the past thirty-five years alone, he argued, contained "dramatic elements for a series of novels which, one might say without the slightest exaggeration, might be made to surpass anything which Balzac gave us in his *Scenes from Political Life*. "Where is the romancer," Maurice challenged, "who would dare to build out of sheer imagination anything to compare with the tremendous complications of the Tweed ring, the trials of the arch boss and his escape, his concealment in the woods near Weehawken, his flight to Spain and his final capture? . . . And yet,'' he lamented, ''of the books which have in recent years enjoyed wide popularity, we can recall but one, Mr. Ford's *The Honourable Peter Stirling*, which has made use of this side of American life.'' Maurice's question provided its own answer in what he alleged was the novelist's preference for the ''applause of high-school sentimentalists or the cackling of the 'Culture Clubs' '' to exploration into this ''very vital phase of life which has hitherto been deemed beneath literary treatment.''[15]

While the novelist ignored urban politics, the essayist endowed it with all of the drama of a morality play. About New York, for example, the founding editor of *The Nation*, Edwin L. Godkin, wrote: ''That city is governed to-day by three or four men of foreign birth, who are very illiterate, are sprung from the dregs of the foreign population, have never pursued any regular calling, were entirely unknown to the bulk of the residents five years ago, and who now set the criticism of the intelligent and educated classes at defiance.''[16] The typical machine politician, ''a selfish and jealous creature,'' according to the editors of *Good Government*, had but one purpose in life, and that was ''to obtain honors and emoluments which he has not earned, for which he is consciously unfit, but which he grasps at because he sees other men, quite as undeserving as himself, procuring such things by importunity or blandishment, purchase or threat.''[17] Tammany Hall, the archetypal machine, was ''the most powerful coterie of organized criminals that ever dominated the life of any civilization. . . . With merciless iron heel it crushes the weak, intimidates the half-hearted and defies the strong.''[18] Honest citizens, reported *City and State* editor Herbert Welsh, had had revealed to them ''the true nature of the machine.'' ''Quickly,'' he charged, ''the disguise is being thrown off—or torn off—and that well drilled and compact organization for public plunder . . . stands with increasing nakedness before the community.'' Assorted disguises, ''which peeped over the bulwarks of our pirate ship,'' were giving way to the reality of ''the swart visage, the brawny arm and warlike accoutrement of a predatory crew.''[19]

This simplistic dichotomy of Good versus Evil would be challenged increasingly during the last fifteen years of the century, for the determinism of its logic, its doctrine of the inevitability of political and social conflict seemed increasingly self-defeating, the antithesis of the reform impulse. An articulate minority of magazine contributors in the final fifteen years of the century argued persuasively that reform was not only possible, but probable. Civilization, proclaimed Leonora B. Halstead, was a state in which ''there is no longer independence, but interdependence.'' Modern urban-industrial interdependence necessitated organization, and ''in all life,'' she continued, ''the organized is higher than the unorganized.'' Social commentators and pseudohistorians were in error, she taught, when they drew analogies between the decline of Rome and the contemporary growth pains of the United States.[20] Increasing American wealth and its

concomitant development, a progressively complex social order, were not indicative of decadence but, *The Social Economist* asserted, were quite the opposite: signs "of the very essence of prosperity and civilization." For, while it
was still "the fashion to decry this increasing complexity, to attribute greater
virtue and value to simpler communities, . . . enlarge upon the beauty, strength
and worth of rural societies, . . . speak of cities as hot beds of vice and sweltering
nests of corruption," in "rural districts" were found, instead, "narrowness of
mind, vacant rudeness, undeveloped natures. . . . One does not go to a western
border to look up the fugitive virtue of New York and Chicago. He knows that
it has not gone into the wilderness."[21]

With the Rome of the Caesars confined to its appropriate historical nook, the
Rome of the popes had next to be put into proper perspective. Fear of the foreign
masses was, counseled the Reverend W. G. Puddefoot, "an old one (as old as
the nation)" and was "unworthy of the descendants of the Puritans, and was
no credit to them." "We must never forget," he urged, "that we are the first
modern nation of continental proportions with latitudes of prodigious extent; that
the nation has become what it is by European occupancy; that the invasion has
been relatively a peaceful one." The hypothesis that the immigrant was "a good
subject on the farms" but "a menace to our cities" was illogical; so, too, was
the argument that municipal problems were created by the foreign-born. "We
have cities in Wisconsin of ten thousand inhabitants, 90 per cent of whom are
German, 8 per cent Irish, and 2 per cent American, and yet are essentially
American." The problems of nineteenth-century cities stemmed from rapid
growth, and they would be solved only with time and the effort of united citizens.
"Bad as our cities are to-day," Puddefoot observed, "they are much better in
every way than eighty years ago, before the great stream of Europeans set in."[22]
Moreover, even the Whore of Babylon could be found, at times, on the side of
the angels, as was proved in Chicago when the Roman Catholic clergy defied
the machine by endorsing and supporting civil service reform.[23] When guided
by the right principles and united with native stock, immigrants and their churches
could be, some observers recognized, of service to urban America.

Such were the extremes of opinion concerning municipal politics—from the
paranoid at one end, to the pollyanna-like at the other. That the governing of
great cities aroused such strong emotions in contemporary observers fits the
general pattern of what Robert H. Walker has identified as the "reform spirit in
America." Its "important meaning" has been, Walker suggests, "the pursuit
of economic equity through the extension of political democracy; the quest for
full citizenship for all groups outside the dominant culture; and the conceptualization of models for a better society—*in that order*."[24] Such, in capsule, were
the challenges of governing great American cities at the end of the nineteenth
century. That the responses to that challenge were so strong and so varied in
the periodical press, the polar opposites of opinion sometimes appearing in a
single issue of one journal, was inevitable. For the stakes were the highest: the
future of an urbanized republic.

TOWARD A CIVIC RELIGION

For many late-century urbanists, in keeping with the ideals of American individualism and the basic tenets of Protestant thought, the problem of governing cities was moral; therefore, its solution had also to be moral. After all, prominent New York reformer Edmond Kelly asserted, those who truly desired "bad government for dishonest ends must in the very nature of things constitute a very small minority of the citizens of any city."[25] The situation, a contributor to the *Charities Review* agreed, was obvious enough: "The character of the government of a city depends upon the people who cast the ballots and hold the offices. The great problem," it followed, was "not so much to improve the form of government as to improve the character of the individual citizens and to secure better men for public office."[26] From this perspective, then, there was a sharp and undeniable distinction between the common weal and corruption, the good and the bad: there existed *a* public interest, never competing sets of interests.

The requisite virtues for good citizenship, preached William D. Maxon, D.D., were inherent in Christianity: "The Christian is a good citizen, and a good citizen cares for the good estate of his city. The city is the citizen's larger home."[27] From its beginnings, argued social-gospel theoretician Washington Gladden, the city had been part of human religious experience: "The sites of many cities were fixed by the use of distinctly religious rites; the founding of the city was a religious solemnity." Moreover, especially in pre-Christian cities, religion continued to play an "integral part" in everyday life. "It was not merely harbored and protected by the city; the administration of religion was just as much a municipal function as was the administration of law; religion was regarded as the very heart of the municipal organism." In modern times, people had been too willing to divorce religion from municipal life. Disestablishment of official churches, the withdrawing of state financial support from religious institutions, and the elimination of purely sectarian forms and ceremonies from municipal life had been to the good; nevertheless, the subsequent loss of the religious impulse, that vision of the Heavenly City, was serious. In the older order, "the society below was in constant contact and communication with a perfect society above, and the guiding lights of that upper world were unveiled to faithful watchers here below." To reestablish communication with the City of God, it would be necessary, Gladden taught, to develop a "municipal patriotism"; the foundation for this urban loyalty would be a "civic religion," which he defined as the "recognition of the fact that for every society there is an ideal—that is to say, a divine, social order; it is the attempt to discern and to realize that—to bring the life of the city below into harmony with the law of the perfect city not made with hands which hangs above it in the sky." These higher ideals had to take precedence over the purely business considerations that had led urban leaders "to get just as much as possible for themselves out of the city and give just as little as possible in return for it—of time, of money, of sacrifice."[28] A civic religion would purify the real with the ideal.

The leadership in this moral reformation of urban government, Thomas R. Slicer suggested, had to come from "among the ministers of religion and the representative laymen of the churches." "Thoughtful people" now recognized that "the struggle in municipal politics is a struggle simply of good and evil, of virtue against vice, and that therefore the balance of power must either be held in the hands of men of righteous ideals, or else committed to the hands of those whose self-interest and appetite for spoils makes the city the prey of their cupidity." The "church and its ministers," he warned, could no longer ignore the claims of citizenship "without losing power." "If the Kingdom of Heaven is to be made out of the commonwealths of earth," Slicer counseled, the church would have to provide leadership through "the virility of its ministry and the practical character of its teachings." The minister ought to provide "the inspiration of manliness." He "is permitted to be a mystic, but a mystic who is effective in this period is one who can answer a large proportion of his own prayers." Thus, he ought to be "as carefully trained in sociology as he is in theology. . . . It becomes the minister to set an example of decent living and knowledge of men which shall show him still in command of the brute forces of life in the interest of righteousness."[29]

A secular counterpart to this clerical muscular Christianity was preached strenuously by the official national patron of the Ten Commandments, Theodore Roosevelt, in his "doctrine of good citizenship, of active civic virtue." "His appeal to the educated man to do his full civic duty" was applauded lustily by *The Citizen* in its review of Roosevelt's *American Ideals and Other Essays, Social and Political*.[30] This doctrine of good citizenship was an article of faith for those acolytes of genteel reform who called themselves "mugwumps." *Good Government* regularly attempted to define, and also reprinted descriptions of, the character of the mugwump and the political phenomenon of mugwumpery, until it had finally elevated the man and the movement to the political and moral sublime.[31] According to William Dudley Foulke, a member of the National Civil Service Reform League: "Every new dissent from the old order of things is a kind of mugwumpery." Consequently, "the chorus against the mugwumps has been long and loud but it is inharmonious and unimpressive. The heelers of Tammany Hall despise a mugwump," Foulke agreed. "The policemen who levy blackmail upon the vices of great cities have infinite contempt for mugwump principles. . . . Those who give over the insane to brutal attendants to carry the ward for the straight party ticket are filled with indignation at the mugwumpery of the men who expose their iniquities. Yet still," he rejoiced, "the Mugwump survives and increases and multiplies. Advocacy is hardly necessary when so much of the world is turning mugwump without it."[32]

Yet, while mugwumps were applying themselves philosophically to the biblical injunction "increase and multiply," many of their contemporaries were skeptical both as to the depth of mugwump convictions and the adequacy of their negative, civic-watchdog creed. "Mugwump," according to editors of *Gunton's Magazine*, "is the name given to a small group of people who are eminently respectable, but who are very much impressed with their own superiority, and who imagine they have a monopoly of political virtue." Because they were "constitutionally distrusters of human nature," they were "nearly always found on the negative side of all really wholesome, flesh-and-blood movements in public affairs."[33] Because he was unwilling or unable to marshal the forces necessary to achieve his ends, the mugwump "frequently turns sour and rails like a second Timon on the corruption of the times, and the depravity of mankind, and dies broken-hearted in the midst of acrid and gloomy thoughts. Better for him to remain in his elevation, shaking the torch of his illumination in public view visible to all men, and wait for the slow-footed legions of well-meaning citizens to march up to the foot of this high tower."[34] Should he decide to descend into the arena of municipal politics after all, counseled a friendlier critic, he had to learn that it was no "pleasant thing to stand for office in a great city and bear the criticism of a hostile press and the more vicious slanders of secret opponents, to have your whole life laid bare and even the sanctity of your home invaded."[35] He had also to understand, Duane Mowry cautioned him, that "reform is indeed a disagreeable word to the American ear"; that even his social equals regarded the reformer as "an unsafe, if not a positively dangerous man; that the public is justly wary of him; that his honesty of purpose is not above suspicion; that his constructive ability is not beyond question"; and that, finally, "the majority of so-called reformers are looked upon as obnoxious individuals."[36] From the other end of the social spectrum, Louis Post's single-tax journal *The Public*, arose an even more critical voice against the argument that "the intelligent and respectable ought to govern." For, while Andrew Carnegie "would probably pass as both intelligent and respectable," he was, in actuality, "utterly unfit for even so slight an exercise of governmental functions as those which are vested in a common juryman in a criminal case." Indeed, "if the suffrage were limited to the intelligent and respectable, Carnegie could not claim more than half a vote. His respectability might give him that."[37]

The stance of the mugwump, the doctrines of civic religion, were weighed against their increasingly obvious shortcomings. First of all, they had failed the pragmatic test of power, in that, although their opposition to rings and machines had been vigorous and continuous throughout the latter half of the century, the big-city political organizations seemed more powerful by the turn of the century than they had in the postwar era. Then, too, in a positive and confident age, mugwumps seemed to be negative and pessimistic; in a nation of boosters, they were the knockers. In much of their writings, as Lorin Peterson observed, there was an annoying tone of petulance and a pharisaic self-righteousness. Too often, they scolded but failed, at the same time, to persuade.[38] Finally and most important, their critics would reject the mugwumps' simplistic account of urban affairs; in its place, from coast to coast, they announced the complexity and the challenge of an emerging metropolitan order. Mayor James D. Phelan of San Francisco maintained that "the city of to-day is a new type of human activity and organization,"[39] and Mayor Seth Low of Brooklyn (and later of Greater

New York) argued that size alone was a revolutionizing factor in the new order: "What is no problem at all on a very small scale, becomes a problem of the first magnitude by the process of enlargement."[40] Change was so rapid and so extensive, a contributor to *The Public* noted, that "city growth produces conditions faster than fitting solutions; these latter follow slowly and not without friction."[41] Clearly, many observers suggested, urban America needed more for its regeneration than the moral suasion of civic religion or mugwumpery.

The shame of the cities was neither basically a moral problem, nor a separate, localized condition of American life. Increasingly, urbanists recognized it as a constituent part of the national transformation wrought by the combined forces of urbanization and industrialization. In an especially acute, but nonetheless representative, analysis of this evolutionary process, the Chicago banker and later secretary of the treasury under Taft, Franklin MacVeagh, linked the post–Civil War "deterioration of city government in America . . . with several marked phenomena of the nation which may be taken as explanation of this deterioration." First came "the sudden vast growth of city populations"; second, "the greatly increased diversity of American city populations," through native de-ruralization and foreign immigration, both; and third, "the almost wild scramble for wealth-producing occupations, which set in before the war was quite over, and quickly grew into a great national movement as the new and varied business opportunities opened wide." Increasingly, MacVeagh explained, as "public interest became centered in private fortunes, all government deteriorated and the average man in all spheres of public life gradually lowered, and the standards of public life of course went down." When municipal life was examined from this perspective, he continued, it became clear "that, while it is only one feature of a general political deterioration, it is, in fact, perhaps the least hopeless of our political problems; for the reason that its direful state has come to be almost fully and quite generally realized, and is giving rise to the most earnest, eager, and patriotic political movements of the time."[42] Modernization, from this perspective, had created new opportunities, revealed new problems, and demanded new answers. Traditional reforms such as civic religion and mugwumpery would not meet the challenge of governing the modern city.

CORRUPTION AND THE CORRUPT

"That typical reform beginning, the exposé," as Robert Walker has described it, was as much a part of magazine writing on urban politics after 1885 as it had been in the two decades before.[43] " 'What is there in it for me?' " claimed the editors of *The Commons*, "is the key word these days." They found urban politics and municipal administration "poisoned by wide-spread suspicion and corruption": "Because the blasting, polluting blight of commercialism is upon them."[44] Corruption in American politics, whether at the federal or municipal level, was "an exact reflection, counterpart, and largely a result, of the corruption which characterizes other aspects of life, especially 'business.' " The trail from "the boodle alderman's vote to the dividend check of the street railroad stock-holder" was a clear one, in "a direct line of progress, of cause and effect." The conclusion was equally clear: "It is 'business' that corrupts politics, not politics that corrupts 'business.' " The situation was so serious, *The Commons* concluded, that the country was "in a sorry plight, and in these days it is hard to find even the 'remnant' that has not bowed the knee to Baal. It is timely for this nation to talk of sackcloth and ashes."[45] The problem of a "nation of cities," argued Oakland's Mayor R. W. Snow, was that "heroes and martyrs built the State and nation, but the building of cities has been left to a money-making people."[46] Commercialism had indeed become so pervasive, claimed Professor John H. Gray of Northwestern University, that the power of corporations and the inadequacies of municipal government, "these two great products of our social and political life, together with many of their minor offspring and con-nections, indicate that there is something radically wrong, not only with mu-nicipal government, but also with our boasted civilization, and more especially with our traditional claim to superior adaptability to new conditions and of superior capacity in regard to government."[47] Just how much was "radically wrong" with the commercial and utilitarian spirit of the age was specified in the poem, "Practical":

> There was a man made a fortune in steel,
>   Sensible man! Sensible man!
> Another one, he made a fortune in "steal."
>   Reprehensible man! Reprehensible man!
>   Steel is so strong.
>   To steal is so wrong.
> Which man would you rather be—granting you can?
>
> This question I asked of my Sunday-school class,
> Eleven dull boys and a bright little lass.
> The boys were as dumb as an old cedar post.
> The girl asked me quietly
> "Which made the most?"[48]

Specific instances of an unholy alliance, "formed between the corrupt political machine, which regards public affairs only as a money-making concern, and unscrupulous capital, which finds in the machine a convenient tool for the ad-vancement of its financial schemes," reform editor Herbert Welsh asserted, were readily at hand in almost every American city.[49] " 'Napoleons of finance,' " even when they were basically honest or at least had found it unnecessary to adopt dishonest methods, Charles E. Monroe lamented, had proved themselves especially adroit in their handling of public franchises for profit. "With their long-headed penetration they have looked far into the future, have realized exactly what would best promote their own interests, and have themselves drawn with the greatest skill the ordinances containing the coveted grants of franchises. On

the other side, the representatives of the public have too often been unable to
see any further than the immediate present; and because of this inability have
generally found the other party to the bargain to have been about five times their
match.''[50] Conversely, when public representatives had shown themselves capable of taking a "long-headed" view of the city's interest, as in the case of
the awarding of the franchise for the Philadelphia Gas Works, the Robber-Baron
element, in the corporate person of the United Gas Improvement Company, had
ignored public opinion as expressed in local political meetings, in the votes of
labor unions, and by resolutions on the subject by municipal reform associations
and patriotic societies; had been able to secure the overriding of a previous
rejection of their bid by the common council; and had managed to win the
backing of Mayor Charles F. Warwick. Their victory against the city was,
according to political commentator Clinton Rogers Woodruff, "an illustration
of how rich and powerful corporations are able in legislative bodies to defy
public sentiment and overcome official judgment. Surrounding the committee
rooms and council chambers, at all the meetings when the United Gas Improvement Company's ordinance was under consideration, was a band of the shrewdest
and most skillful lobbyists, and at one time some of them even had the audacity
to enter upon the floor of councils and direct their fight for the ordinance from
that point of vantage.''[51] By marshaling sufficient forces for their campaign, by
surrounding reluctant legislators, by out-generalling the opposition, and by seiz-
ing strategic ground, the special interests were thus able to win their battle in
Philadelphia.

If the struggle in Philadelphia resembled a conventional military campaign,
in Chicago it was more like guerrilla warfare; while the mayor and council in
Philadelphia might be attacked together, the aldermen of Chicago had to be
pacified separately. In his analysis of "The Gray Wolves and Their Flock,"
historian Ray Ginger described the aldermen of the Windy City as "independent
entrepreneurs. They paid no heed to party discipline or to anything else. It was
strictly each man for himself.''[52] In New York, Tammany Hall controlled its
municipal empire and maintained a semblance of order. In Chicago, Michael
"Hinky Dink" Kenna, "Bathhouse" John Coughlin, and Johnny "The Chief
Mourner" Powers ruled as warlords and exacted tribute from every enterprise
within their separate wards. This political anarchy, far from offering any protection against corruption in franchise dealings, encouraged it; political decentralization of this variety merely served to make it more difficult to isolate both
responsibility and culpability. The free-booting ward heeler, Chicago-style, typically remained faceless and anonymous, as in the story, "The Alderman's
Bride." In this updating of the Cinderella tale, Sniderella, a "second cook in
the palatial home of a pork-packer," was rescued from servitude by a nameless
alderman who had, nevertheless, "a salary and a pull." The future of this
charming couple seemed assured, for "there are lots of franchises to be put
through the council."[53]

The individual who often manipulated such deals, Charles T. Yerkes, the traction magnate, was to Chicago what Boss Tweed had been before him to New York—the personification of corruption. *The Public* regarded him as the representative of the "private monopoly" of the streetcar interests and "a man of great bravery, not to say effrontery, in asserting the claims of franchise grabbers."[54] When men like Yerkes were not cheating the city in a semilegal manner, private corporations were stealing from it in a criminal fashion. *The Public* regularly reported on corruption and venality in the Windy City. Chicago packing houses, for example, had tapped city water pipes and drawn off "thousands of cubic feet daily without [it] being registered."[55] Legal responsibility for this crime against the public was vested in the minor employees of the firms caught in this practice, but the "thrifty and cautious heads of the establishment" seemed beyond the law because of the limited liability of their charters of incorporation. The "shielding of moneyed criminals" was the real civic crime in Chicago; indeed, *The Public* accused, there seemed to be a conspiracy of the plutocracy, in which the newspapers took part.[56] "So complex are financial ramifications in Chicago, and so intimately do they blend with public corruption, that no great piece of public corruption can be run to its hole without disturbing financial interests which connect with and control the governing proprietors of every newspaper in the city."[57]

The running to its hole of public corruption could, however, prove embarrassing in a sister city. The *Social Economist* (later, *Gunton's Magazine*) greeted the 1894 Lexow investigation of the New York City police force as "the most important political event of the year and probably of the decade."[58] Its uncovering of scandals "so revolting" and "so despicable" would guarantee that "the world for a while will smell nothing but the New York police."[59] However, when the same commission investigated industrial trusts three years later, *Gunton's* accused it of becoming "Bryanized" and "catering to the most inflamed anticapital class feeling."[60] "To be up in arms against something or somebody is coming to be regarded as a national characteristic of this country," *Gunton's* warned. "The Bryan campaign and its sequel in this state, the Lexow commission, are largely the creatures of this kind of demoralizing and degrading journalism."[61] The uncovering of the fraud of the American Ice Company three years later was, however, beneficial. This "conspiracy against the community" was, *Gunton's* reported, a "quasi-political scheme. The American Ice Company is not merely in league with Tammany Hall but all the leading spirits of Tammany are heavy stockholders in the concern, and have manifestly acquired their stock for political aid rendered"—thereby giving a bad name to trusts in general.[62]

"Inquisitional reform" along such lines, master bibliographer Robert Clarkson Brooks observed, employed "specialists in parano/ea."[63] Still, such was to be expected from the genre exposé which, as Walker has noted, while "candidly one-sided in its selection of detail, . . . does not usually offer a remedy for the problem it describes. Rather, it builds toward a sense of outrage through the compilation of detail."[64] And for exposé of an heroic order, a larger-than-life target, such as Tweed had been during the 1870s, was required. Again, Tammany Hall filled the bill with a replica figurehead, Richard "Boss" Croker.

Tammany Hall had managed to survive the debacle of the Tweed exposures of 1871, to be reshaped by "Honest John" Kelly during the subsequent fifteen years. The first Irish-American head of the New York Democracy, himself a member of the middle class, Kelly prescribed a new regimen for Tammany: under his strict leadership, the conspicuous consumption of the Tweed Ring gave way to a calculated austerity. Power was centralized in the office of the county chairman (popularly, the "Boss"), party funds were channeled through the upper echelons of the organization, and close relationships were maintained between the party and community and church leaders. The *ring* was transformed into a *machine*, a functioning bureaucracy with a leadership less conspicuous than it had been during the Tweed era. This, then, was the organization over which Richard Croker took control after the mayorality campaign of 1886. One of the most dramatic and hard-fought campaigns in the history of the Empire City, the election was marked by the mass desertion of staunch party regulars to the banner of Single-Tax champion Henry George. The Democracy won a close election with the active support of members of the Roman Catholic clergy, by employing armies of repeaters, and by outright fraud and force at the polls. Because of its near defeat, the party was faced in 1886, as it had been in 1871, with a crisis of organization. Once again it had to reshape itself, redirect its energies, and turn to a strong leader.[65]

As the late-century machine bore a surface resemblance to the postwar ring, so, too, Boss Richard Croker seemed somewhat like a latter-day Tweed. Both men were bearded and bulky, carried reputations as brawlers, favored fast horses, and served terms in prison. Critics of Tammany, quick to note these similarities, resurrected the lexicon of abuse previously heaped on Tweed. The editors of *The Public* described a manner of doing things "Tammany fashion, Croker fashion, highwayman fashion."[66] "The truth is," confessed the editors of *Gunton's Magazine*, "that imagination pales before the facts in Croker's case. . . . That this coarse low creature is the literal czar of the metropolis is a stinging fact which everybody at all informed well knows." Because of his great power, they concluded, the actions of "the presiding genius of the Tammany organization" were newsworthy: "Personally nobody would regard his opinion on public affairs as having any significance, yet when he speaks the nation listens and New York trembles."[67] To the editors of *The Public*, the sole grace of Croker's public statements was that they were "full of native candor." "Being the boss of Tammany Hall and speaking for that organization, he can afford to be candid, boldly and cheerfully so. . . . In politics for 'what there is in it,' " *The Public* maintained, "Tammany men are undisturbed by moral considerations or political principles." Tammany-style principles "never rise above the rules of the game." All the same, *The Public* admitted grudgingly, "Tammany scorns to indulge in the homage which well-mannered vice is supposed to pay to virtue.

She is no hypocrite.'' And yet, ''she'' had seen a change in leadership style: ''Tweed was a crude rascal. Croker is a shrewd rascal.''[68]

Unlike the crude Tweed, the shrewd Croker had his defenders, the most admiring of whom was Alfred Henry Lewis, the editor of the New York Democratic weekly *The Verdict*, who proclaimed Croker ''the man uncommon.'' After having examined the barrage of ''slanders and libels'' issued against the party leader, Lewis concluded that Croker was ''the inspiration of honesty. He never plots—he fights. There is nothing indirect in his nature. . . . He hunts his foe at noon, and goes to battle with bugle and banner.'' His leadership was characterized by fair play and loyalty: ''No one ever knew him to break his word; no man ever saw him desert a friend.'' Lewis recognized in Croker the natural spokesman for the urban masses—a leader open to all and who protected all, the American version of ''a chief of some Highland clan.'' He embodied ''the force dominant in New York politics. In him was lodged the natural leadership of hundreds of thousands. . . . His place as leader of a great party,'' Lewis urged, ''was the honest, lawful sequence of his genius for control. The man was born a master; the baton of command belonged to him.'' Should it eventually become his honor to write Croker's epitaph—a task eagerly anticipated by many political observers a full twenty years before the Boss's death—Alfred Henry Lewis felt certain that he could capture ''his story in one characteristic line— *He never failed.*''[69] This uncritical admirer did, in fact, write a full biography of his hero. Croker, according to legend, began to read Lewis's idealized version of his own ''success story'' while at sea; after reading several saccharine paragraphs, the story goes, he threw the book overboard.[70]

The most spirited defense of Richard Croker and Tammany Hall came, naturally enough, from the Boss himself—either from his own pen or, more likely, from that of a ghost writer; to the surprise of many no doubt, it appeared in the *North American Review*, a magazine once noted for its mugwumpery.[71] To call Croker's article a defense is somewhat misleading, for he immediately assumed the offensive. ''No political party can with reason expect to obtain power, or maintain itself in power,'' he began, ''unless it be efficiently organized.'' Organization was the major element for achieving victory in any cause and, Croker warned, ''between the aggressive forces of two similar groups of ideas, one entertained by a knot of theorists, the other enunciated by a well-compacted organization, there is such a difference as exists between a mob and a military battalion.'' Change was effected, quite simply, not by wishful thinking, but by concerted group action. Local political organizations could prove to be harmful, of course, whenever ''depraved men of revolutionary tendencies'' took command, as had happened during the ''ghastly turmoil of the French Revolution.'' Even here, Croker continued, ''we cannot fail to admire the success, the influence, the resistless power of the Jacobin Club, not because the club was praiseworthy, since its actions were abhorrent, but because it was skillfully organized and handled.'' Organized power was, for Croker, a positive good; for the natural condition of mankind, he argued, was struggle. Politics was war. ''Chess is war;

business is war; the rivalry of students and of athletes is war. Everything is war in which men strive for mastery and power as against other men, and this is one of the essential conditions of progress.'' Progress in the Empire City, on the other hand, had remained steady because its affairs were managed expertly by a great, nonrevolutionary, forward-looking civic institution: ''I mean the *Tammany Democracy*,'' Croker proclaimed. ''I do not propose to defend the Tammany organization; neither do I propose to defend sunrise as an exhibition of celestial mechanics, nor a democratic form of government as an illustration of human liberty at its best.''[72] Each was, in a word, self-evident.

Like any other complex institution, Tammany Hall made its share of mistakes; however, it had ''no time or place for apologies or excuses; and to indulge in them would hazard its existence and certainly destroy its usefulness.'' The test for the Democracy was a pragmatic one: ''We assert, to begin with, that its system is admirable in theory and works excellently in practice.'' When the party discovered ''a diseased growth in her organism,'' she did not ''hesitate at its extirpation.'' As a tightly organized, self-governing, and carefully policed municipal institution, Tammany Hall represented, Croker concluded, the wave of the future for urban America. It ruled efficiently, governed well, and directed confidently the fortunes of the nation's greatest city. It was time for every ''knot of theorists,'' for ''closet reformers,'' to recognize this.[73]

With his *North American* article, Croker attained a semblance of respectability denied Tweed, and even John Kelly. While erecting his defenses, moreover, he had also succeeded in issuing an ultimatum to would-be reformers of municipal government. Thus, although Robert Clarkson Brooks might scoff at Croker's ''time-worn platitudes'' about Tammany being ''the only real reform party and himself the only spotless reformer within the limits of Greater New York,'' the machine was, in fact, being examined seriously in a new light.[74]

That staunch mugwump, Dorman B. Eaton, sensed the apostasy of good-government advocates—citizens of his class, gentlemen with similar educational backgrounds—when he noted that a new breed of reformer had appeared upon the scene. To this heretic, Eaton lamented, institutions and not morals were the matter for reform: ''Even the boss himself—the great embodiment of all that is worst in the mere politician—is extolled as hardly less than a saint, a martyr.''[75] And, indeed, a number of urban observers were in the process of reexamining the boss and machine in functional terms, not as pirate and predatory crew, but as leader and organization. Francis C. Lowell, for example, wrote in *Atlantic Monthly* that ''no boss [was] so bad but that he has the support of good men''; indeed, there were ''good men who believe even in Tammany.''[76] One of these good men, Bostonian Henry Childs Merwin, advanced an almost sympathetic interpretation of the organization and operations of the machine in that same influential journal. Tammany Hall was, Merwin reminded his readers, ''almost as old as a political club in this country could be. It is enriched by traditions of patriotism and good fellowship; it touches its members and adherents upon many sides. It is wonderfully organized and disciplined.''[77] The first task was to determine why Tammany had survived and would probably continue to flourish, and the initial answer had to be that it provided its membership with "personal leadership," the friendship and counsel of men who cared for them and did not distrust them, which reformers, "as a rule," did. Tammany served also as a "totem" for group loyalty, a club in which the member enjoyed the sense of identification that was experienced by the baseball fan rooting for the home team.[78] The Hall, then, was not to be damned, but to be studied. "Tammany furnishes the best object lesson in city government which this generation has seen," Merwin suggested, "and it would be wiser to take a leaf out of her book than to content ourselves with condemning her course. The rank and file of Tammany are, in the main, honest men, good citizens. They do not share the plunder. . . . What, then, holds Tammany together?" he asked; "what but the power of personal leadership and the power of the totem," he answered.[79] What held Tammany down, Merwin concluded, what would hold the Hall back from ever leading in an urban renascence, was the concentration of unlimited powers in the hands of "a few men,—nay, . . . one man,—answerable to nobody."[80] This personalization of power resulted in a certain efficiency, but the major force that it generated served to perpetuate the status quo and to prevent development; in short, the major weakness of the big-city machine was that it was intrinsically a conservative force in an expanding society, a union of caretakers—not entrepreneurs. It was, *The Public* suggested, "an office brokerage association."[81]

In order to understand party leadership, an anonymous reviewer for *Gunton's* suggested, one might look for its prototype in the streetcorner gang. The pecking order of the adolescent gang was carried over into adult life, since political clubs were created most often from the nucleus of boyhood associations. Most important, early leadership in the gang often was perpetuated in the club for, the same critic noted, the youth "who can most successfully bully the gang becomes the political boss of the ward." Each local leader operated his club as the center for political action where patronage was distributed, favors were performed, and candidates created.[82] The ward heeler, civil service reform leader A. C. Bernheim lamented, did "not enter public life inspired by a patriot's devotion to his country; he finds in it an opportunity of earning a livelihood with little effort. He often respects the commandments, and loves his family; but politics to him is a business."[83] His vision, therefore, was a narrow one. It seemed likely to *Banker's Magazine*, moreover, that "the system of bosses in politics so much inveighed against has its usefulness and reason for being, and that these associations of voters, which the bosses handle for their own purposes and alleged individual profit, are institutions arising from actual necessities and wants of the masses of our citizens, resulting from defects in our government and laws." It was most probably, this journal concluded, "a realization of the powerlessness of the individual citizen" that prompted him to join with others for "mutual protection."[84] *The Social Economist* carried the argument one step further when it asserted that "a machine in politics or anywhere else is simply an organization to reach certain ends. In so far as it is an organization, [it] is certainly better than disorganization, since no political action in communities is possible in a state of anarchy.'' For too long the rallying cry of the critics of municipal government had been ''Smash the machine,'' a program for action that involved nothing more than noise and sentiment.[85] Rather than attempt to break up the machine, advised *Banker's Magazine*, it would be better to ''subject the bosses to a process of higher education, by which they might be enabled to instruct their followers in all the amenities of life and teach them that to vote for the highest good of the whole community would most greatly benefit themselves.''[86]

That the political power structure was not immutable, and both the electorate and the party organization could change for the better, was the radical doctrine that urbanists were advancing. ''The people support Tammany not because they love the vices of Tammany, not because they love the demagogy and hypocrisy and debauchery of Tammany methods, but because to them,'' suggested *Gunton's Magazine*, ''Tammany appears to be their only ever-present and constant friend.''[87] Had the people other friends, their loyalties would change for the better; indeed, advised sanitary engineer Colonel George E. Waring, Jr., the machine was most sensitive to public opinion: ''These Tammany gentlemen are not hankering after public obloquy and disgrace. The voice of the people is the controlling power with them.''[88] Were pressure increased on the bosses, he declared, their conduct in office would change for the better. If, on the other hand, the bosses and their machines did not meet the increasing demands of their constituencies, if they remained conservative and unimaginative, John H. Pryor speculated, ''perhaps in time'' the people themselves would ''learn the power of organization in politics and fight for a safe, healthful home, where decent surroundings will make manhood and womanhood possible, and the life of a child pure, wholesome, and sweet.'' If the people could not ''succeed without a leader,'' Pryor promised, ''he will appear, to tell the story of 'the ebbing sea of weary life,' and teach that every man should have the right and a chance to do his best.''[89] Such a leader might resemble, perhaps, Toledo's Samuel ''Golden Rule'' Jones, who was capable even ''of tearing a leaf from the wisdom book of the bosses, and taken advantage in his way and for moral purposes, as they take advantage in their way and for immoral purposes, of party association.''[90] Reform thought had come full circle: from ''break up the machine'' to a call for the election of ''reform bosses.''

This reexamination of machine government along functional lines signaled the beginning of a major transition in urban thought. For the viability of machine or ring politics had become increasingly obvious since the immediate postwar years. If the mugwump press had accomplished little else, it had managed to inform urban dwellers that the big-city machine represented a continuing challenge to traditional democratic values. The machine's talents for survival, its success in winning elections, its capacity for governing cities were also inescapable. Finally, when the party leadership did occasionally speak out, as in the case of Boss Croker, it was inclined to be aggressive and hostile to traditional notions of reform. Croker's message was clear: Tammany was not to be ignored;

if the classes hoped to accomplish anything in New York, they had to deal with the masses. His reference to Jacobin excesses, the threat of "depraved men of revolutionary tendencies," may have been gratuitous, merely a historical allusion; more likely, it was a direct and conscious analogy, an ultimatum to Tammany's enemies that if the strong hand of the organization were removed, a new and more radical force might well replace it.

Increasingly, urbanists rejected the standard mugwump dichotomy between Good and Evil, attempted to comprehend the workings of the machine, and intended to institute a new and more efficient order. They planned to end the beadledom of a Tammany Hall by substituting merit for preferment; they hoped to expand the limited horizons of machine politics by introducing higher standards and sounder values. Municipal government would be transformed not by any moral revival, but by a fundamental restructuring of municipal institutions.

STRATEGIES FOR STRUCTURAL REFORM

During the final years of the century, as urbanists shifted increasingly from moral to structural reform, they sought a deeper understanding of municipal polity. They began, logically enough, at the beginning, with the history of town government and concentrated initially upon the New England colonial town. Historian Charles M. Andrews, giving voice to the eternal scholarly lament over the paucity of official records in print, expressed concern that "theories of municipal origin and development" had been based on the published town records of Massachusetts alone and had been "for this reason incomplete and unsatisfactory." Andrews chided Rhode Island and Connecticut cities for their crimes against history and challenged them to emulate the example of counterparts in their fellow colony-state by publishing their own town records: "It is a disgrace to them that they do not."[91] Yet, even with this meagerness of printed sources, Clarence Deming felt confident in proclaiming the dominance of the town in colonial Connecticut: "The main stem of Connecticut's historical tree is rooted in the three towns [Wethersfield, Hartford, and Windsor] which are still fitly symbolized by the three vines cut in the state seal." The incorporation of these and later towns and cities by the fledgling Nutmeg state "gave popular consent and formal certification to an antecedent fact." The New England town, not the colony or state, represented from its beginnings the true Yankee, and therefore American, spirit.[92] Economist Simon N. Patten took this interpretation one step further by arguing that colonial town formation (or "hiving") had been a "process of natural development" that had guaranteed the creation of effective communities centered around "a group of families having common aims and interests which bound them together in a real unit." When the national government, first under the Articles of Confederation and then under the federal Constitution, substituted for the traditional procedure of town settlement the orderly but artificial continental checkerboard pattern of settlement, a land policy more adaptable to maps than to people, "groups of settlers having common interests were no longer allowed to form local governments suited to their needs." The towns, cities, and states created on the squares of the national checkerboard were unnatural, unmanageable, and virtually un-American: "Had the fathers of our nation recognized the true function of the states and not sought to make empires of them," Patten suggested, "the present evils of our political world could have been avoided." The next logical step in this search for the legal roots of urban America, once town precedence had been established and state decadence determined, was the demand for a return to first principles through the establishment of a new relationship between city and state. "It might be well to imitate the example of the free cities of Germany," Patten concluded, "and give an autonomy to our great cities equal or nearly so to that of the states."[93]

Carefully avoiding these tortuous paths of historical revisionism, other urban theorists proposed realignments of the state-city power balance on strictly pragmatic grounds. William Draper Lewis, for example, anxious to preserve as well as to innovate, defended the traditional concept of local government with appeals to nationalism. "Cosmopolitan ideas of civilization," incorporated in world-state philosophies from Caesar to Charlemagne, he argued, had been invalidated by the "evolution of democracy": "We no longer doubt that the civilized world develops by and through the development of its great nations." Lewis, although ready to grant it greater independence, at the same time seemed fearful that the city might, in its new-found freedom, separate itself completely from traditional national institutions. In order to protect the nation against potential city-states, he proposed a compromise "local municipal state," which would be attained "by practically reconstructing our state lines, though we may not alter a word of our Constitution. Our great cities, and afterwards our agricultural and mining districts, should take the place of the irrationally defined states of today."[94]

Less concerned with the preservation of the letter of the law, historian Ellis Paxson Oberholtzer argued for state-city separation, with mutual benefits acruing to each, along the lines proposed by Simon Patten. Municipal interests, he urged, were "totally diverse" from those "of the remaining sections of the States in which they were placed by our artificial arrangement of boundaries." The solution was obvious: "For the good of cities themselves, and likewise for the good of the States, it is necessary that our large cities should be free cities."[95] And it seemed equally necessary and logical that the largest city in the land become the first "free city." The creation of a "new member of the Federal Union to be known as the city and state of Manhattan or Mannahatta," Alfred H. Peters maintained, would indeed benefit the two New Yorks by settling once and for all the upstate-downstate rivalry, by reducing the disproportionate national power of the existing state, and by inducing a needed realignment in New York politics. It would serve, moreover, to provide a "crucial test" for the body politic. "Many observers hold that the evils of democratic municipal government arise principally from the neglect of the duties of citizenship on the part of the so-called better class,'' Peters allowed. "Be this as it may, nothing would cause this class to better itself politically so much as to force it into a position where it must act in order to protect itself.''[96]

The proposals of an Ellis Paxon Oberholtzer or a Simon Patten for "free cities'' and of a William Draper Lewis for "local municipal states''—their historical logic, democratic rhetoric, appeals to efficiency, and scholarly vocabularies notwithstanding—represented the radical position on the readjustment of the state-city balance of power. It is also possible that these proposals were offered as debating resolutions, initial positions for eventual compromises, since these urbanists almost certainly understood that there was little hope for such revolutionary changes. An entrenched state bureaucracy could hardly be expected to limit its own powers, destroy political jobs, and deprive itself of major tax revenues.

A more likely approach to the problem of redressing the imbalance between city and state was outlined by George H. Haynes of Worcester Polytechnic Institute in his series on "Representation in State Legislatures.''[97] The allocation of political power within most state legislatures was markedly disadvantageous to their urban centers, Haynes began; therefore, legislative reapportionment should be the first step toward municipal reform. Intentional political discrimination against cities existed in states that set apportionment ratios requiring a disproportionate increase in population for a district before it became eligible for additional members, the fixing of maximum representation for any single political unit regardless of its population, and the guarantee of minimum representation for each political unit. "Accidental'' or "hereditary'' restraints also operated against the possibility of an urban political ascendancy through slavish attachment to traditional forms of government. The preservation of equal legal status and power among political units, which had been once homogeneous but were now often heterogeneous, primarily because of the dictates of custom, was a form of civic ancestor worship that resulted in a system under which "all is fossilized''—an unfortunate condition that was prevalent, Haynes judged, in many of the older states and even in the Senate of the United States.[98] In fact, only the newer states of the West were entirely "free from the trammels of tradition, which often upholds the pretentions [sic] of rotten boroughs''; "these communities are all young, and youth is often the period of most eager experimenting in matters political.'' Significantly, and in direct contrast with their tradition-bound senior fellow states, "the western states have as yet shown no desire to curb the proportionate influence of urban populations.''[99] If their spirit of enterprising innovation were emulated nationally, Haynes maintained, revolutionary and impracticable constitutional surgery would be unnecessary and the existing framework of government could be preserved intact. By the reapportionment of state legislatures solely on the basis of population, municipal reform would become practicable and the imperatives of democracy met squarely.

Increasingly, late-century urbanists recognized, the governing of great cities demanded innovative and extensive structural reforms. In the large city, as sociologist Philip M. Hauser has noted, " 'bureaucracy' becomes the ubiquitous form of organization. It is a rational-formal-legal organization which is an inevitable and indispensable concomitant of populations of large size and density and high levels of interaction."[100] Complexity created bureaucracy, which in turn created demands for professionalism. Urban administration, Frank P. Richard observed, seemed increasingly to be developing into "a science by itself"— but an applied science, like that of war. Both administration and war demanded organization, strategy, and the effective execution of commands; both called for leadership, training, and the will to win. The governing of the metropolis required the training of an officer corps of urban experts, Richard declared, because its operations were too specialized and intricate for the merely "honest man of ordinary experience and capacity"; eventually administrative academies, modeled on the national service schools, would probably prove necessary.[101] An *esprit de corps* had to be developed in order to overcome the prevailing pessimism about municipal government that had been fostered by those "civic prophets" who constantly predicted "only increasing corruption and ultimate ruin." The urban public, Dr. M. Mc'G. Dana warned, was "wearied with the despairing indictment of American municipalities that has hitherto been the stock in trade of a certain school of critics."[102] Professor John H. Gray promised that this past generation of urban nay-sayers, given to a self-limiting defeatism, would be replaced by "scientists" who faced urban problems squarely, intelligently, and optimistically.[103]

Critics with "pessimistic tendencies" chose to disregard the forward spirit of the times and warned instead that a "materialistic wave creeps upon the shores of our civilization with ever-increasing volume and surge, and that what Emerson calls the age of 'Tammany Hall, the omnibus, and the third person plural' waxes grosser with the waning centuries." Nevertheless, claimed Frederick Stanley Root, such carpers ignored "the wonderful growth of learned societies in our country, both in membership and in influence," a growth that promised "a brighter future for humanitarian and scholastic ideals." Root, the general secretary for the American Association of Social Science, counted "no fewer than forty such societies, ranging in numbers from two hundred to two thousand," many of which were "offshoots" of his own organization and were similarly dedicated to the practical study of human society.[104] The associative impulse, always powerful in the United States, seemed to be gathering momentum as people joined business, social, charitable, and political groups, making it "almost impossible," the editors of *Banker's Magazine* noted approvingly, "to meet an American citizen of voting age, and many who have not yet reached it, who does not belong to some organization."[105] This miscellany of groups was expected to furnish the rolls for and encourage the activities of the even more specialized national, state, and local associations.

"The historian of American political institutions," Dr. Leo S. Rowe predicted, "will probably designate the last quarter of the nineteenth century as the period of municipal experimentation."[106] The formal recognition of this climate of experimentation may be dated from *Good Government*'s announcement of "A National Conference of Municipal Reformers," which was to meet in late January 1894 at Philadelphia. This conference, it was hoped, would mark the beginning of a "great movement for the purification and improvement" of municipal government in the United States. A consensus for such a movement seemed already apparent in the "great development of popular feeling in favor of the purification of our politics, and an honest, intelligent, non-partisan and businesslike management of public affairs."[107] Its primary function would be instructional rather than educational: it would be concerned not with what reforms were needed, but with the initiation of reform movements. Unfortunately, once the conference was convened, it soon became apparent that there was a consensus on ends but not on means, that the delegates were unprepared to agree upon a coherent national program. Nevertheless, a major municipal educational organization did grow out of the conference—the National Municipal League, and it became "the leading information center among promoters of big-city reform."[108] What had thus been intended as a national political force became instead an institution of education with a nationwide membership. A precedent had also been set for similar organizations at the state level.

The League of Wisconsin Municipalities called itself a "combination for mutual protection." It, too, was an institution of civic education, composed of men of affairs and scholars who shared an interest in the "modern city."[109] The League of California Municipalities, a parallel organization, presented itself as a union or fraternity of municipalities that, "while differing in matters of population, situation and other details . . . are yet alike in all essential particulars. . . . And yet they are, for the most part, isolated." While they "are creatures of the State, . . . they are not, except in a few cases, called upon to render any service for the State." Consequently, not only was there "no necessary connection between one city and another . . . in this State, there is no official way by which one city may become aware of another's existence."[110] A state league bridged this legal gap in municipal communications by operating as a center for the exchange of information on civic concerns, by publishing a journal devoted to urban matters, and by serving as a meeting place for municipal officials and experts.

Whereas the National Municipal League and the state associations were concerned solely with information gathering and exchange, civic clubs, in addition to performing similar functions, also participated actively in local municipal politics. The Philadelphia Municipal League, perhaps the outstanding civic club in the nation, had successfully challenged the machine, distributed pamphlets at election time, established a reform network throughout the city—from the ward up to the division, and cooperated closely with existing political, labor, religious, and social societies.[111] Independent organizations in Chicago had been transformed from a "constellation of groups, made up of intense individualists," according to Albion W. Small, the founding chairman of the University of Chicago's sociology department, into a working amalgam through the administrative machinery of the Civic Federation of Chicago, which was "not the center and circumference of the new civic spirit in Chicago; it is rather the rallying point around which the civic patriotism of Chicago citizens has gathered." Organized along federative lines, like the Philadelphia Municipal League, its roots were in precinct and ward membership and extended up to a citywide central council that maintained political, municipal, philanthropic, industrial, educational, and moral departments. Its dual functions of political activism and information gathering made it, according to its supporters, a viable urban institution, "not a creature of speculative theory."[112] Democratic regular Abram S. Hewitt called the City Club of New York "a disorganized mob, . . . an independent body of free lances and free thinkers. And you undertake to fight a compact organization [Tammany] with a general at the head and a leader in every district, all fighting for a livelihood, all knowing that they will receive their pay if they are faithful." *Good Government* admitted that his argument had "much force," but it argued that he went too far in his assertion that the Civic Club had not "the ghost of a show" in its fight against Tammany. "As a rule, a mob stands a poor chance opposed to regular troops, but mobs gathered for a righteous purpose have been known to win a fight even against such odds." The editors of *Good Government* drew an analogy between the urban patriots of the civic clubs and the Minute Men of the American Revolution; the former would hold the line, as did the latter, until an army of the whole people could be organized in the war for municipal independence.[113] This spirit, far from being unique to the major urban centers, ought to be extended to the smallest of American municipalities; indeed, this journal argued, there was "nothing . . . to prevent the establishment of one Good Government Club in every city of ten or fifteen thousand inhabitants."[114]

Grass-roots—or, to be still more literal, cement-bottomed—organization might also be achieved through the social settlement movement. In defining "Our Purpose and Scope," the founders of *The Commons* admitted that the Chicago Commons was, like other settlements, "non-political"; however, it had soon become "a rallying point and moral force for civic patriotism."[115] Robert A. Woods, a movement theorist, speculated that residents, by virtue of their intimate relationship with and direct influence within the community, might be able to organize a united front within the ward and fulfil their "distinct mission,—to stand for a form of municipal government which will be not merely negatively incorrupt, in accordance with past traditions, but judiciously progressive in such a way as to serve actual public needs as they exist among the city population of the present."[116] The "settler," always the "possibilist," recognized that the municipal machine itself would be forced to accept change, for "the boss is compelled, whatever his own inclinations may be, to become a supporter of such a progressive policy. As the policy becomes more firmly established we may reasonably expect to see a better type of local political leader, a man who endeavors to supply local public needs rather than merely to 'fix' a certain number of influential citizens." The settlement, Woods hoped, would transform the machine organization into a vehicle for attaining the "protective state." Its political goals were to "lift local issues to the level of common, honest, local needs; to instill into the mind of the local voter, by actual experience on his part, a conception of the city as a co-operative enterprise based on mutual aid, instead of either an oligarchy whose favor is gained by truculence, or an efficient despotism under some commercial Cincinnatus; not to attempt the destruction of the boss, but to develop out of him a type of local leader who shall . . . stand for a distinctively local kind of public spirit," one which would appeal to "larger and larger numbers of progressive citizens, living in different sections of the city."[117] The realism of the settlement, Woods and like-minded settlers insisted, grew out of its scientific viewpoint, its methodology of controlled observation: the settler—working, studying, and observing in a clearly-defined urban community—lived out fully the ideal life-pattern of the "practical expert."[118] His answer to the demand for "social service," in any event, came closer than did the organized attempts of most of his contemporaries toward achieving a pragmatic amalgam of traditional and modern politics.

Still other apolitical but well-established organizations were urged to join the forces of specialization in urban reform. Business associations were reminded that "a city is a municipal corporation in which every voter is in reality a shareholder"; moreover, in most cities, "the business men hold the majority of the stock." The Merchants' Association of San Francisco, for one, had met its civic responsibilities by serving as *ex-officio* board of directors for the citizenry in lobbying for a new charter, promoting more efficient street maintenance and an improved outdoor lighting system, and offering expert advice to municipal officials on public finance. "Let any municipality be swayed by the level-headed men of business, trained in the solution of difficult problems and known for their sterling integrity, and you can rest assured, that the government of such a city will be conspicuous for its discretion, economy and progress."[119] But the "level-headed men of business" were not called upon to do the work alone; laboring men, reform editor Herbert Welsh urged, had to share equally in the task for, as inveterate central-city dwellers, they were the first to suffer from the mismanagement of municipal services.[120] It was time, declared economist John R. Commons, for workingmen to abandon "remote reforms" and turn to "the important opportunities of their own locality, where they have three-fourths of the votes." They had to recognize, he maintained, that "if American politics is ever cleaned, the cities will be the first. And if workingmen ever get the state and national legislation they want, it will be when they have shown that they control the cities." In order to achieve these goals they had first to organize the unorganized, educate the ignorant, and concentrate upon urban politics.[121]

The reform crusade might also be furthered at the local level by the formation of ad hoc groups sponsoring the candidacy of independent reformers and by the creation of municipal parties. That romantic skeptic and notable man of letters John Jay Chapman favored the former because it ensured the "mobility and light-armed activity of the reformers"; however, he rejected the latter because "you cannot get public confidence till you abandon formal organization." Parties were a threat to democratic institutions, for "all organizations have been creatures of their leaders and . . . they have been kept in existence because they were necessary as a means of promulgating the will of a clique."[122] Brooklyn *Eagle* editor St. Clair McKelway was ready to grant that municipal parties in themselves would not cure all political ills, since "parties are but fallible men bunched in agreements." Nevertheless, he argued, such organizations might lead to the eventual strengthening of the party system and, ultimately, to more efficient urban administration. "Such a basis provided, the superstructure of government by consent can be trusted to the vigilance of the conscience and of the interest of city communities, on the whole, the most upright communities of the land."[123] Reformers had learned "the difficulty of expecting a reform habit from a reform spurt"; therefore, they had institutionalized it. "There are so many kinds of it," McKelway explained of reform effort, "that they perplex the mind. . . . They affect every department of life. They relate to economic as well as moral problems. They comprehend home and household interests quite as much as national and international matters." In fact, McKelway urged, "This is an age of reform, and this is a nation of reformers. It is impossible to keep abreast with all the reforms or supposed reforms which appeal to mankind. It is well to be patient with all of them, and cynical toward none."[124] The crusade for a scientific and efficient system of municipal government reflected this very catholicism of endeavor, for its organization by levels truly reflected the federative principle: from the nation-wide National Municipal League, to the leagues of municipalities in the separate states, to the civic clubs in individual cities; on down to the settlements, business groups, labor unions, and municipal parties with their roots in distinct neighborhoods, among separate classes, and within previously opposed political factions.

In attempting to determine what reforms should be sought, what governmental machinery ought to be introduced, and what administrative techniques were worthy of adoption, the urbanist often employed advanced research methods and referred repeatedly to the valuable experiences of European colleagues in municipal affairs. As historians were urging that individual cities preserve the records of the past, statisticians and economists were demanding that like attention be paid to the records of the present. "There has been far too little method in American municipal experiments, and far too little scientific recording of their results," E. Dana Durand complained, "for us to hope to gain much information from our municipal history."[125] "In other countries," John Archibald Fairlie pointed out, "the importance of municipal government and the value of comparative statistics of their operations have been more fully recognized, and in several countries special publications on municipal statistics are regularly prepared."[126] Certainly, the government of the United States could afford similar projects; or, in the compiling of available statistics on municipal finance, responsibility might be entrusted to a major university or to the National Municipal League.[127] In both cases, the European example was worthy of emulation.

Clinton Rogers Woodruff expressed the hope that he would "not be deemed unpatriotic in these days when so much of cheap and tinsel jingoism passes for love of country if I admit what every candid observer must admit, that in most matters municipal many of our European sister cities have outstripped us.'' Civic progress in Europe could be turned to the advantage of American cities, nevertheless, by illustrating for them ''what good city government really is''; indeed, it involved a condition so complex ''that it cannot be defined, but rather must be described.''[128] The governments of English cities, Albert Shaw argued shortly before he was appointed editor of the American version of London's prestigious *Review of Reviews*, although they might be ''far from ideal perfection,'' were of special significance to American municipalities. The power of the city council and the high regard in which it was held by the citizenry, the relative nonpartisanship of local elections, the rejection of the concept of rotation in office, and the ready employment of experts from outside the immediate community by the municipality were among the many lessons to be learned.[129] Perhaps the noblest example set by British municipalities was their high order of civic pride, an urban virtue that thrilled many an American visitor. Toledo's reform mayor ''Golden Rule'' Jones, for one, described his first visit to the public parks of Glasgow with their ''Citizen, protect your property'' signs on the lawns, ''and when my eyes first fell upon that inscription I confess to such a feeling of delight as I never before experienced through looking at a dumb signboard. It was in such striking contrast to the boss idea expressed in the order: 'Keep off the Grass.' ''[130] Possibly, it was hoped, Americans might be persuaded to exchange their negative philosophy of municipal government for the positive creed of their European contemporaries.

A step in this direction, economist Edmund J. James suggested, would be to extend the powers of the central city into contiguous and even outlying suburbs. The growth of large urban agglomerations made it imperative to shift attention from separate central cities to entire metropolitan areas. Both the core city and its suburban rings ought to share both the benefits and the expenses of urban growth, and this could be assured by annexation. The main advantages for the suburbs would include early technical assistance and financial aid in the provision of basic public services; the primary gains for the city would consist of immediate political hegemony and the ultimate protection of the tax base.[131] The most noted and debated late-century instance of large-scale annexation—or, more properly, consolidation—was the creation of Greater New York in 1898. To statistician-historian Adna F. Weber, the merger mania approached the absurd. ''Chicago was the target of every journalistic joke-maker in New York up to two years ago, when the 'Greater New York' idea came to the front. But Chicago with all her annexations has only 189 square mile of territory,'' he noted, ''while New York now covers 360 square miles of land,'' giving it, thereby, first place worldwide, with London ''only 118 square miles, Paris 30, Berlin 24, Philadelphia 129.'' Weber wryly predicted that the time would come when ''the cities of New York and Chicago go to war to decide which shall annex Texas!''[132]

A supporter of consolidation, James W. Pryor, noted that it marked the first time in American history that an attempt had been made "to deal with the government of a great metropolitan city with a population of over three millions. . . . Its success or failure will strongly influence the development of institutions in other parts of the country." An experiment on so grand a scale and with such far-reaching influence logically demanded "scientific formulation"; however, Pryor claimed, "probably never before was an attempt made to formulate within so short a time a piece of legislation so difficult and complicated as this charter." "The view that it was more important to have Greater New York as soon as possible, rather than bring the city into being under conditions as favorable as time and deliberation could make them," Pryor lamented, "has prevailed."[133] The planning and the politicking for consolidation were likened by the editors of *Gunton's Magazine* to "a haste and an informal rush and crush . . . which are more suggestive of a crowd trying to get across Brooklyn Bridge, than of two vast populations merging into one municipality."[134] On another occasion, this same journal claimed that the consolidation was "pushed at Albany and elsewhere solely on the ground that unless consolidation is effected by 1898 the census of 1900 will show Chicago to be the leading city of the Western world in population." "It would be far more dignified to admit," *Gunton's* urged, "a desire to rival London than to confess of fear of being outstripped by Chicago." This greater challenge might be met by annexing *all* suburbs, both in New York State and New Jersey, within fifteen miles of the city proper. The resulting "Greater City" would, then possess "a political and legislative interest in both States, and an influence in both legislatures . . . which might," in turn, "pave the way for ultimately expanding this port and population into that absolutely Free City, which by the Dongan Charter it was solemnly covenanted by the British Crown that this city should be."[135] Such visions of grandeur were at the root of the drive for the chartering of Greater New York, M. N. Baker argued, feeling that urban imperialism of this variety, a mere thirst for size and power, was an unconscious substitute for overseas expansion.[136] Municipal annexation and consolidation were judged then either as necessary extensions of municipal authority or as visceral urgings toward urban giantism; in either case, emotion seemed to outweigh logic.[137]

Plans for retooling the administrative machinery of the municipality were usually presented in a less emotional manner. The streamlining of urban government, the argument ran, would result in a more business-like management of civic affairs; indeed, the example of the well-organized business corporation was a favorite model. Partisanship in municipal government—or politics itself—should be abandoned immediately, Clinton Rogers Woodruff asserted, in favor of the recognition that the management of a city was strictly a business proposition.[138] The editors of *California Municipalities* lamented the "unbusinesslike" provincialism of a five-year residency provision for prospective city officials in the San Francisco charter. "The public," they maintained, "has not yet been identified to a higher plane than to think that public office is a sinecure, a sort of makeshift occupation for a person to take up until he has nothing better to do.'' Private firms did not take such a view, nor would they ever restrict their choice of executives by such arbitrary rules.[139]

Direction of the management of urban business had to be centralized, but disputes arose as to whether it should be vested in the office of the mayor or in the council. Stanford University president David Starr Jordan opted for the strong-mayor system by asserting that, while ''Principles, not men'' might be a serviceable philosophy for national politics, ''Men, and not principles'' should be the rule for municipal administration.[140] This centralization of authority under a single executive, the popularly elected mayor, which had gained support initially in the late 1870s and early 1880s and which was still to have its advocates a century later, met with increasing opposition toward the turn of the century. The consolidation of Greater New York had been resisted, in part, *Gunton's* suggested, because it seemed ''likely to carry out the programme of still further eviscerating the City Councils and Caesarizing the Mayor in all cities.''[141] E. Dana Durand asserted that ''the most striking tendency in the recent history of American municipal government'' had been the augmenting of mayoral power, a trend that boasted the blessings of such distinguished urbanists as Seth Low, Gamaliel Bradford, Edmund J. James, Frank J. Goodnow, and the National Municipal League itself; nevertheless, the record of history did not bear out their advocacy of strong-mayor government. ''Nowhere, in fact, can the advocate of mayor domination, if he be candid, point to anything like thoroughly and continuously good administration where that system has prevailed.'' The record showed, Durand asserted, that ''temporary improvement has often followed a change in mayor rule; permanent improvement even has resulted in certain cases from doing away with the anomalies and complexities of earlier charters; but the actual success of the centralization of power has fallen very short of fulfilling the promises which were held out to us.'' The example of European cities, on the other hand, demonstrated that ''thorough-going council rule'' and administrative efficiency were all but synonymous.[142] The council system was, Durand concluded, both democratic and efficient; its strong-mayor alternative was, on the contrary, monarchical and ''un-American.''[143]

The efficient and seemingly disinterested administrative management of the semiautonomous municipal service department was often advocated as a desirable reform, and George E. Waring, Jr., was customarily singled out as the ideal professional department executive. Writer, farmer, sanitary engineer (with a specialization in sewage), Colonel Waring had come into his own in New York as ''the city's scavenger. That he made the title scavenger a term of honor was the sufficient justification of his life.'' His labors for a more sanitary New York were compared to the cleaning out of the Augean stables; however, this ''modern Hercules'' achieved his goal not in solitary splendor but by reorganizing the city's sanitation facilities. He formed voluntary inspection committees of civic leaders and reformers, organized boys' and girls' clubs to help keep the city clean, introduced the merit system and set up a board of labor arbitration within his Sanitation Department, pioneered in new methods of snow removal and waste disposal. His forceful leadership as commissioner, indeed his showmanship, was never more evident than in his success in introducing an *esprit de corps* into the ranks of Gotham's garbage brigade. "To the utter bewilderment of more than the slouches and the ne'er-do-wells," William Potts reported, "the whole department was put into uniform, and, most astounding of all, into a uniform of white duck. The city stood aghast." But Waring surprised his critics, as his men "became the 'white angels,' or 'white wings' of a renovated city, and proudly wore the much-ridiculed badge of the calling as an evidence of its dignity." Unfortunately for Waring and for the city of New York, the professional politicians were soon able to remove him from office; semi-independent department heads had yet to learn the intricacies of dynastic self-preservation later formulated by such bureaucratic czars as Robert Moses. Nevertheless, Waring's efficient administration of the Sanitation Department and its continued high standards after his departure were irrefutable proof of the effectiveness of nonpolitical municipal service departments; and even when "at the end of three years he was turned into the street" by jealous Tammany hacks, he no doubt took solace in the fact the it was a clean and sanitary street into which he had been turned.[144]

Greater efficiency at all levels of municipal government might be achieved even without the dynamic leadership of a Colonel Waring through the extension of civil service reform. Chicago, for one, was reported to have "hustled" for reform and organized a citizens' crusade against spoils and spoilsmen, but not without opposition. "Every man who held a 'soft job' in the city's employ and who had spent more time in drawing his pay than in working, and every man who wanted a full day's pay for a full hour's work was 'agin' the proposition. These gentry fought it tooth and nail." But, reported special correspondent Edward J. Phelps, "the handwriting was on the wall"; "the sheer force of public opinion" defeated the spoils system.[145] Civil service, in addition to its being a "moral" system, had the more pragmatic advantage of opening public office to more competent people. "The business of a city is not as simple as many suppose it to be," veteran politician Seth Low reminded his contemporaries, "and it is useless to expect more than barely tolerable results from an administration that aims to govern by the spoils system." The very nature of this type of government was "fatal" to superior work, for, under machine rule, even capable career officials were unable to perform effectively.[146] Increasingly, such appeals for the extension of civil service reform were directed to its most consistent foe—after the machine politician himself—the urban worker. To the engineer of the shovel and his hod-carrying colleagues, for whom the day labor jobs dispensed by the machine were often a secure livelihood, the civil service system, with its bureaucracy and examinations, seemed to be a class and a personal challenge. To allay these proletarian fears of job displacement and to shift the emphasis to the positive benefits that might be expected from civil service reform, Herbert Welsh apprised the "laboring man" of not only "what direct losses he suffers through dishonest or inefficient management of city affairs, but also those which he suffers through failure to receive the fruits of widely expended revenues, a thousand privileges and opportunities of nobler and richer living which might be his were the coming higher ideals of municipal life and municipal functions realized, and were the now squandered city resources wisely husbanded to obtain them.'' Such reform work, he continued, would mean the ''driving out from this great civic house of ours, with its many mansions, the foul and dangerous occupants which infest it, and . . . [make] these cities of ours more like the city of God.''[147] How persuasive such millennial appeals were with common laborers can only be guessed at; it is significant that even Carl Schurz, the veteran campaigner for civil service reform, was prepared, some thirty years after the movement had begun, to admit that ''the mere formal introduction of the system'' would not be ''a panacea for all the ills in municipal government that afflict us. No system, however wisely devised, will work automatically.''[148] Although civil service reform continued to be a major program for many municipal reformers, it had lost, in its first quarter-century of testing, its initial appeal of originality and suffered by comparison with newer and therefore more exciting reform measures; indeed, it was the victim of its own success, and the degree of its acceptance in city after city was never fully realized by its champions.

A far more radical, and therefore more hotly debated, governmental innovation was that of municipal ownership, also known as municipalization and municipal socialism. Civil service reform, argued New York Charity Organization Society president R. Fulton Cutting, was little more than a negative reaction to the spoils system, and its inadequacy was demonstrated by the survival and health of the machine; municipal ownership, on the other hand, was a positive, ''vivifying force,'' one which fostered a ''consciousness of personal relation'' on the part of the citizen for his government. The reformer was ''only negative; he is anti-Tammany, anti-Platt, with no positive platform, no progressive policy, no promise of continuance. . . . 'Reform' is indefinite, inadequate, and the word has lost its inspiration.'' ''Public ownership,'' Cutting promised, would revivify the body politic: ''government will draw near; an electric spark will pass; the co-operative activities of the new citizenship will disclose a mutuality of interests, and mitigate the bitterness of class antagonism.'' This civic ''spark'' would pass through the people of the city and enable them ''to apprehend the privilege of public service''; moreover, Cutting concluded, this new sense of civic patriotism and responsibility ''would penetrate and permanently occupy the executive chamber.''[149]

Milo Ray Maltbie's prognosis of the probable extension and evolution of municipal socialism in American cities, based on his comprehensive research both in this country and in Europe, was less mystical and more concrete in its analysis.[150] ''The extension of municipal functions in the direction in which the city is to act as the servant of the individual has barely begun,'' he maintained, ''and its scope, certainly to be indefinitely increased in a comparatively near future, is to be measured only by the resources of developing invention and enterprise, so rapidly developing of late that their early realization will be such as to be unthinkable now.'' Specifically, Maltbie predicted widespread improvements in transportation and communication; a more adequate water supply and artificial lighting for all urban communities; "highway facilities (including power supply as well as a clear path)," the elimination of turnpikes and toll roads, and increasingly lower fares on common carriers for workers and students; and, finally, improved public educational and recreational facilities for all. These changes, he warned would not be "necessarily beneficient." "There are some problems too deep and many forces too strong for the individual to contend with, and whether the tides in which the world's currents now run are those of actual progress, the centuries alone can determine." Nevertheless, despite his reservations about the feasibility of predicting specific changes, Maltbie was confident enough to proclaim that the general tenor of the future would be shaped by municipalization: "Urban development, in realization of the capacity of the public to serve the individual while leaving him more free instead of less so, is to be the characteristic of the century before us."[151]

Joseph Loeb was more interested in the break with the past, inherent in municipal socialism, than with the possibilities for the future. "The dogmas that govern competition, the laws of social and industrial endeavor," he argued, "are being more and more questioned as to their validity. Men are questioning rights to privileges." Men were beginning, at least, to question the basic tenets of Social Darwinism, for "the survival of the fittest . . . [seemed] now materially hindered by an inequality of start''; as a result, it was recognized "that privileged conditions which admit of monopoly should not be granted in control to any person or set of persons, but should belong to and be used for the community." This "socializing impulse" was bound to further the cause of municipalization "since it appeals to a love of equality of opportunity which is inherent in all men."[152]

Municipal ownership, its proponents generally agreed, ought to be extended into the fields of the basic utilities, transportation, and communication; while in this last category they frequently included the telephone and telegraph, they seldom called for the municipalization of the newspaper. But a wide-ranging authority on urban affairs, Delos F. Wilcox, did for "the function of the newspaper" was, he argued, "so predominantly public and its service so universally requisite, that many government undertakings are far less truly political." Since newspaper publishing was essentially a "public function," and "if the people trusted their chosen governors and were themselves united in their support of the public welfare, they would undoubtedly be willing to put the newspaper business, like education, into government hands, though not as a monopoly." Once the people were ready to accept the truth that government was not "a necessary evil" but was instead "the co-operative organization of all for the benefit of all, . . . a necessary good," the municipalization of newspapers might follow.[153]

There was no telling, however, what other revered national institutions would be subject to drastic innovations. Those skeptical of municipalization, which seemed to promise "a sort of paternal municipal republic," like *Gunton's*, demanded both more research into the philosophy of the movement and a more conservative administration of its expansion.[154] The "propaganda" for municipal ownership, John H. Gray argued, was difficult to evaluate because it was written, not to examine the system, but to promote its adoption.[155] Its proponents had failed to prove, Gray maintained, that private management of public facilities was not working well and that public management would be equally or more efficient and economical.[156] That the "socializing impulse" might not stop with municipal ownership but might extend beyond the walls of the city to the nation at large, must have been readily apparent to its adversaries. Herbert Miller, writing in the journal of the American Federation of Labor, hardly representing in itself the voice of radical unionism, predicted eventual and necessary advances from municipal to federal socialism: "When each city owns its light, as well as its water, then will each wage-earner have light cheaper and better than now; when each city owns its street railways, he can ride more cheaply to and from his work; when the whole country owns its railroads, his food and the manufactures of the world will be brought more cheaply to his door; when the people own the machinery, the wage-worker will get the full fruit of his toil; when the people own the land, there will be none idle by compulsion—no strikes, no monopolies—there will be enough for all, and all will have enough." Socialism, Miller insisted, was but another name for "economic equality," the principle on which "the whole structure of our government rests"; therefore, it could scarcely be termed "un-American."[157]

Many of his contemporaries disagreed, some of them passionately. Municipal socialism, its adversaries argued, might be practicable for the European system of a limited electorate, in which suffrage was restricted to ratepayers only. Whereas, as a result of this system of government, "English and German cities are organized under a general law, upon general principles, with a minimum of legislative centralization or interference, and a maximum of administrative decentralization or power of self-government," John G. Agar argued, American cities continued to suffer "from adoration of the false god of the federal constitution."[158] American municipalities, that is to say, were organized as republics in miniature; they functioned under a variety of charters, were subject to interference by state legislatures, and were hampered by unrestricted suffrage. *Nation* editor Edwin L. Godkin maintained that "our modern experiment in democratic government is really an experiment in the government of rich communities by poor men." Since this experiment in democracy had been an abysmal failure, it was necessary to turn for guidance to the records of classical, medieval, and eighteenth-century European cities—before the vicious leveling of the French Revolution had been forced upon civilization; in those earlier excellent societies "the great landholders ruled the country; the great merchants ruled the town." The American municipality had, then, to be ruled "like a bank or an insurance company or a railroad company."[159] "We have universal suffrage without universal taxation," Rabbi Adolph Moses pointed out; the logical solution to this contradiction in representative government was the restriction of the municipal electorate to taxpayers alone.[160]

A much-noted centralization of municipal control, in a most "business-like" manner but managed by a noncommercial bureaucratic elite, had been instituted in the federal city of Washington. Its admirers judged its government by independent federally appointed commissioners as "a laboratory of political science in which the democratic ideal of the equality of men in choosing their rulers has been tested and found wanting." "By law, the system is a benevolent despotism; in practice, it is a representative aristocracy."[161] Nevertheless, this "representative aristocracy" was not without its critics. John R. Commons argued that efficiency was not enough: "Washington furnishes a bright contrast to the gloom of American city politics; its government is strong, efficient, honest and progressive, but it is also irresponsible, undemocratic, and paternal. It cannot be contemplated for other cities."[162] But of course it was contemplated, despite its undemocratic philosophy of government and its paternalistic administration of civic affairs; moreover, some urban theorists turned in their quest for centralized efficiency to even more authoritarian models. Perhaps the most extreme example uncovered in this search was the "municipal theocracy" of Ocean Grove, New Jersey. It was based on the proposition that, as James T. Young of the University of Pennsylvania asserted, "the active part played by the people in municipal government must be reduced to a minimum. Municipal government," instead, "must be a government of concentrated power." The Ocean Grove example, Young granted, "violates the cardinal maxims of political and religious liberty in America, a union between Church and State, a theocracy, a government whose subjects have, as against itself, no political rights whatsoever"; nevertheless, its efficiency guaranteed the well-being of its citizens. Representative democracy, according to this line of thought, was out-of-date in nineteenth-century urban America: "The circumstances of to-day demand an efficient government which will occupy as little of the voter's time as possible."[163]

Thus was the extreme reached: from the good to the efficient city; from moral to structural reform. Across this spectrum late-century urbanists ranged, but they were increasingly closer to the latter *modern* goal than they were to the former *traditional* ideal.

TOWARD A NEW METROPOLITAN ORDER

Although municipal politics and government increasingly became matters for study after 1885, the major difference between the literature of urban awareness in those final fifteen years of the century and the previous two decades was more qualitative than quantitative. Whereas social critics of the earlier period had recognized that the governments of great cities were often incompetent and wasteful, their observations were more reportorial than analytical. Adhering tenaciously to the traditional American ideal that public office was a privilege and a duty, that it demanded impersonal and impartial conduct on the part of the public servant, and that its major reward was the satisfaction of serving one's

community, these observers of the city were unprepared to recognize the significance of modernization and bureaucratization.

After 1885, the simple gave way to the complex as urbanists increasingly
came to look upon the promised inevitable triumph of virtue through exposure
of wickedness as mere wishful thinking. The steady shift from mugwump righteousness to a fascination with questions of power, from investigations of individuals to examinations of institutions, from a normative vocabulary of moral
imperatives to a functional one of political alternatives did not signify total
rejection of the traditional value system; instead, it marked an adjustment of that
set of values to the realities of governing the metropolis. By destroying the
machine and controlling the masses, earlier proponents of moral reform had
hoped to serve *the* public interest, which turned out to be, in effect, the interests
of their own class—low taxes and government by the educated. With time,
however, it became ever more apparent that urban America was divided into a
variety of *competing* interests—class, ethnic, and locational. Their new perspective on municipal government, urbanists argued, called not for platitudes
but for practicality; not for tender-minded preachments, but for tough-minded
plans.

The much-excoriated but often victorious machine provided, in a sense, a
takeoff point for structural reform. Convinced as they were that a new and greater
city was the promise of their age, urbanists regarded municipal corruption as a
historical aberration in the processes of growth, not as an indictment against
American society. Their major concern was with the shaping of the institutions
of the greater city that industrialization and urbanization seemed to promise
them; therefore, although they were concerned with the public crimes of machine
politics, as had been their predecessors, the new urbanists looked beyond present
problems to future promises. Since their reexamination of municipal politics had
convinced them of the need for organization, the discipline of the archetypal
machine, Tammany Hall, served almost as an inspiration.

Innovating urbanists promoted organization through federations of voluntary
associations: from the National Municipal League, to the state leagues of municipalities, to good government clubs, to reform parties; from the settlement
movement, to business associations, to labor unions. Their ideal was an early
version of the City Efficient—an administrative reflection of the City Beautiful;
and in their attempt to achieve it, urbanists proposed a variety of institutional
innovations. They envisioned a new relationship between city and state that
would be brought about by increased state services, the annexation of suburban
rings by core cities, or by experiments in metropolitanism; they demanded the
streamlining of municipal government along business lines by increasing the
executive powers of the mayor, by establishing independent councils, by extending the powers of semiautonomous department heads, or by improving municipal civil service; they speculated about the reordering of the urban economy
by the introduction of municipal ownership or by the imposition of a suffrage
limited primarily, even solely, to property owners. Individual ideas were intro-

duced, propounded, criticized, debated, amended, rejected, reintroduced. The governing ideal of order through organization remained essentially unchallenged.

The public interest could always be advanced, the American democratic faith had taught, through the enlargement of democratic participation; yet, the increasing political power of the urban masses seemed to have frustrated the advancement of the metropolis. Here was an irony of urban democracy. Coupled with the organizational advantages of machine politics were, observers discovered, inherent disadvantages of unenlightened leadership, a severely limited concept of urban development, a traditional and conservative value system. The machine was still constricted by the walls of the historic city: its organization, membership, and energies were shaped by the composition and interests of the ward. It represented a *competing* interest, one not even fully urban, but parochial. Urbanists, conversely, voiced metropolitan goals: ranging far beyond the old inner city, their vision included the developing suburban rings; their field was broadly metropolitan. The programs they espoused and the problems they attempted to solve were too complex to be managed by the machine; the ward heeler, even more than the mugwump reformer, was an amateur in metropolitan leadership. The traditional politics of the big-city machine, Samuel P. Hays has observed in his classic depiction of the competing forces, "enabled local and particularistic interests to dominate." Structural reformers, he continued, were thus less concerned with the evils of corruption than they were with the frustrations of decentralization. They proposed "to change the occupational and class origins of decision makers. Toward this end they sought innovations in the formal machinery of government which would concentrate political power by sharply centralizing the processes of decision-making rather than distribute it through more popular participation in public affairs."[164]

By the turn of the century, then, the outlines of a new metropolitan order had been drawn clearly and broadcast widely. A precursor to the City Efficient of the early twentieth century, the municipal embodiment of the Progressive ideal, the new metropolis of late-century urbanists would be as carefully structured as a Tammany Hall, as business-like as a giant trust, as disciplined as an army. Much like a giant puzzle, all its pieces were on the board and had only to be set in place. Order through organization would be the governing principle for completing this challenging puzzle of and for urban America.

NOTES

1. James Bryce, *The American Commonwealth* (London and New York: Macmillan Company, 1888), 1: 608.

2. Robert A. Woods, "Settlement Houses and City Politics," *Municipal Affairs*, 4 (June 1900): 395.

3. John R. Commons, "State Supervision for Cities," *Annals of the American Academy of Political and Social Science* 5 (May 1895): 866–67.

4. C. E. Pickard, "Great Cities and Democratic Institutions," *American Journal of Politics* 4 (April 1894): 388, 390.

5. Henry George, Jr., "Are We Arming Coming Masters?" [reprinted from the *Philadelphia North American*], *The Public* 3, no. 93 (January 13, 1900): 12.

6. Edmond Kelly, "Philanthropy and Politics," *Charities Review* 2 (May 1893): 362, 359.

7. Thomas E. Will, "The Problem of the City," *American Magazine of Civics* 7 (September 1895): 236. The despot was William Marcy Tweed.

8. Rabbi Adolph Moses, "Democracy and Despotism," *American Magazine of Civics* 9 (October 1896): 266, 268. In his Presidential Address to the American Association of Social Sciences, Frederick John Kingsbury turned to still another fallen civilization and instructed the membership to investigate whether some "Babylonian Tammany Society" had brought about the destruction of that failed city ("The Reign of Law," *Journal of Social Science*, 33 [November 1894]: xiii).

9. L. Elseffer, "A Return to the Basic Principles of Self-Government," *American Magazine of Civics*, 7 (November 1895): 491, 494–95.

10. "Economics and Public Affairs: The Secret of Croker's Influence," *Gunton's Magazine* 17 (September 1899): 163.

11. Thomas E. Will, "The Problem of the City," *American Magazine of Civics* 7 (September 1895): 239.

12. Rabbi Adolph Moses, "Democracy and Despotism," *American Magazine of Civics* 9 (October 1896): 272.

13. L. P. Gratacap, "The Political Mission of Reform," *American Magazine of Civics* 7 (September 1895): 303.

14. Jesse Macy, "Practical Instruction in Civics," *Journal of Social Science* 32 (November 1894): 151–52.

15. Arthur Bartlett Maurice, "The Politician as Literary Material," *Bookman* 11 (April 1900): 120, 121. The reference is to Paul Leicester Ford's 1894 novel.

16. Edwin L. Godkin, "The Problem of Municipal Government," *Annals of the American Academy of Political and Social Science* 4 (May 1894): 858.

17. "The Month," *Good Government* 13 (November 15, 1893): 51.

18. [Editorial], *Good Government* 12 (August 15, 1892): 19.

19. Herbert Welsh, "A Danger and An Opportunity," *Good Government* 14 (January 15, 1895): 95.

20. Leonora B. Halstead, "Advantages of City Life," *The Social Economist* 4 (April 1893): 223, 220.

21. Leonora B. Halstead, "The Decline of Rome," *The Social Economist* 2 (May 1892): 385–86.

22. W. G. Puddefoot, "Is the Foreigner a Menace to the Nation?" *American Magazine of Civics* 9 (July 1896): 1, 6–7. Historian John Bach MacMaster came to a similar conclusion in his survey of "A Century of Social Betterment," *Atlantic Monthly* 79 (January 1897): 20–27.

23. Edward J. Phelps, "How Chicago 'Hustled' for Reform," *Good Government* 14 (April 15, 1895): 137–38.

24. Robert H. Walker, ed., *The Reform Spirit in America: A Documentation of the Pattern of Reform in the American Republic* (New York: G. P. Putnam's Sons, 1976), p. xx.

25. Edmond Kelly, "Philanthropy and Politics," *Charities Review* 2 (May 1893): 363–64.

26. E. Ray Stevens, "Some Present Day Municipal Problems," *Municipality* 1, no. 2 (June 1900): 15–16.

27. William D. Maxon, "The Christian Citizen and the Municipality," *American Magazine of Civics* 7 (November 1895): 543.

28. Washington Gladden, "Civic Religion" [Read before the National Conference for Good City Government, Cleveland, May 1895], *American Magazine of Civics* 7 (December 1895): 624, 625, 626, 629, 627, 631.

29. Thomas R. Slicer, "Relation of the Church to Municipal Politics," *Municipal Affairs* 4 (June 1900): 386, 393.

30. Review . . . ,*The Citizen* 3 (December 1897): 240–41.

31. [Mugwump defined], *Good Government* 12 (August 15, 1892): 15; (September 15, 1892): 30; (October 15, 1892), 49; 14 (July 15, 1894): 3–4; (March 15, 1895): 125.

32. "Independence in Politics. From an Address on 'The Mugwump,' by Hon. William Dudley Foulke," *Good Government* 15 (February 15, 1896): 23. Almost any essay by E. L. Godkin reflected the mugwump view; see, for example, his "Peculiarities of American Municipal Government," *Atlantic Monthly* 80 (November 1897): 620–34.

33. "Institute Work," *Gunton's Magazine* 13 (November 1897): 389–90.

34. "Machine Politics," *The Social Economist* 2 (November 1891): 9.

35. C. P. Walbridge, "Citizenship and the Civil Service," *Good Government* 14 (February 15, 1895): 110.

36. Duane Mowry, "Reform and Reformers," *American Magazine of Civics* 7 (November 1895): 465, 462.

37. "Editorials," *The Public* 1, no. 34 (November 26, 1898): 3.

38. Lorin Peterson, *The Day of the Mugwump* (New York: Random House, 1961), pp. 13–20, 30–32.

39. James D. Phelan, "The League of California Municipalities," *California Municipalities* 1 (August 1899): 3–4.

40. Seth Low, "Civil Service Reform in Cities" [originally, "Civil Service Reform from the Point of View of City Government," an address delivered August 8, 1893], *Good Government* 13 (September 15, 1893): 29.

41. Benjamin Doblin, "The Problem of the Great Unwashed," *The Public* 1, no. 49 (March 11, 1899): 13.

42. Franklin MacVeagh, "A Programme of Municipal Reform," *American Journal of Sociology* 1 (March 1896): 551.

43. Walker, *Reform Spirit*, p. 270.

44. "Service Its Own Reward," *The Commons* 2, no. 22 (February 1898): 8–9.

45. [Editorial], *The Commons* 2, no. 23 (March 1898): 8–9.

46. R. W. Snow, "The Higher Municipality" [synopsis of a speech to the Oakland Board of Trade], *California Municipalities* 2 (May 1900): 111.

47. John H. Gray, "Some Preliminary Problems and Their Possible Solution," *Journal of Social Science* 34 (November 1896): 176.

48. "The Teacher," "Practical," *Yellow Book* 1 (December 1897): 46.

49. Herbert Welsh, "Civil Service Reform and Labor" [Address before the School of Ethics, Plymouth, Mass., July 1895], *Good Government* 14 (August 15, 1895): 195.

50. Charles E. Monroe, "The Time to Deal With Corporations Asking Public Fran-

chises'' [Paper to the League of Wisconsin Municipalities], *Municipality* 1, no. 3 (August 1900): 7.

51. Clinton Rogers Woodruff, ''The Philadelphia Gas Works: A Modern Instance,'' *American Journal of Sociology* 3 (March 1898): 613.

52. Ray Ginger, *Altgeld's America: The Lincoln Ideal Versus Changing Realities* (New York: Funk & Wagnalls Company, 1958), pp. 89–112; the sentences quoted are on p. 93.

53. William Wallace Cook, ''Fairy Tales Up to Date. The Alderman's Bride,'' *Yellow Book* 1 (October 1897): 21.

54. ''Editorials: The Street Car Question,'' *The Public* 1, no. 45 (February 11, 1899): 5.

55. ''Editorials,'' *The Public* 3 (September 22, 1900): 369.

56. ''Editorials,'' *The Public* 3 (October 6, 1900): 404.

57. ''Editorials: Triumph of the Countingroom,'' *The Public* 1, no. 16 (July 23, 1898): 7–8.

58. ''A Putrid Police,'' *The Social Economist* 7 (July 1894): 9.

59. Ibid., p. 11.

60. ''Editorial Crucible,'' *Gunton's Magazine* 12 (February 1897): 126.

61. ''Editorial Crucible,'' *Gunton's Magazine* 12 (March 1897): 203.

62. ''The Ice Trust Outrage,'' *Gunton's Magazine* 18 (June 1900): 516–17.

63. Robert Clarkson Brooks, Review of *Satan's Invisible World Displayed, or Despairing Democracy*, by W. T. Stead, *Municipal Affairs* 2 (June 1898): 305.

64. Walker, *Reform Spirit*, pp. 276–77.

65. For background information on the Kelly and Croker regimes, see Alfred Connable and Edward Silberfarb, *Tigers of Tammany: Ten Men Who Ran New York* (New York: Holt, Rinehart and Winston, 1967) and, for the 1886 election, see Charles Albro Barker, *Henry George* (New York: Oxford University Press, 1955), pp. 48–81.

66. ''Editorials,'' *The Public* 1, no. 20 (August 20, 1898): 2.

67. ''Economics and Public Affairs: The Secret of Croker's Influence,'' *Gunton's Magazine* 17 (September 1899): 162, 161.

68. ''Editorials,'' *The Public* 1, no. 20 (August 20, 1898): 2; 2, no. 55 (April 22, 1899): 4.

69. Alfred Henry Lewis, ''Richard Croker: The Man as He Really Is,'' *Metropolitan Magazine* 7 (February 1898): 129, 130, 131, 129–30, 134.

70. Connable and Silberfarb, *Tigers of Tammany*, p. 227.

71. Richard Croker, ''Tammany Hall and the Democracy,'' *North American Review* 154 (February 1892): 225–30.

72. Ibid., pp. 225, 226, 227.

73. Ibid., pp. 228, 229.

74. Robert Clarkson Brooks, Review of *Satan's Invisible World Displayed, or Despairing Democracy*, by W. T. Stead, *Municipal Affairs* 2 (June 1898): 306.

75. Dorman B. Eaton, ''A New Variety of Mugwump,'' *North American Review* 153 (July 1891): 50. A champion of mugwumpery since the early 1870s, Eaton's anti-majoritarian biases are examined in Chapter 1.

76. Francis C. Lowell, ''The Boss,'' *Atlantic Monthly* 86 (September 1900): 295. Lowell believed that ''the principal causes of the existence of the American boss are the universal need of elaborate and expensive political machinery, the undue importance

given by the American system to those who operate it, and the confusion caused by conducting local elections upon the national party lines'' (p. 298).

77. Henry Childs Merwin, ''Tammany Hall,'' *Atlantic Monthly* 73 (February 1894): 251.

78. Merwin, ''Tammany Points the Way,'' *Atlantic Monthly* 74 (November 1894): 685, 682, 685. ''Five thousand men will go out to witness the contest,'' Merwin reported, ''and will shriek themselves hoarse if *their* nine wins, or will strive to mob the umpire if *their* nine is in danger of being beaten,'' ''*their* nine'' being, of course, ''nine hirelings.''

79. Ibid., p. 688. Merwin proposed the establishment of ''a big political club in every large city, taking in all ranks and conditions of men, holding out rewards and honors, and opportunities for friendship and society with club-houses in every part of the city; a club in which the rich should help the poor, and in which rich and poor should be united by ties of self-interest, of fellowship, of loyalty to common leaders, of devotion to a common purpose'' (pp. 686–87).

80. Merwin, ''Tammany Hall,'' *Atlantic Monthly* 73 (February 1894): 251. Edward M. Shepard in the ''Political Inauguration of the Greater New York,'' *Atlantic Monthly* 81 (January 1898): 104–20, also admitted that the New York Democracy regularly provided more than adequate municipal services at reasonable costs; its major drawback, he felt, was its constituency—an unlettered and unskilled immigrant proletariat. Dr. Lewis G. James in ''The Municipal Problem in America,'' *The Social Economist* 2 (May 1892): 395–405, was so impressed by the Hall's efficient operation that he, too, recommended it as a model for political action groups. L. P. Gratacap lamented that ''this stalwart and ancient house,'' with its membership that included ''strong men of common sense, good men of virtuous purposes, enthusiasts in the imaginative creation of a beautiful metropolis,'' had lacked the ''moral fiber'' to reform itself and lead New York in its quest for betterment (''The Political Mission of Reform,'' *American Magazine of Civics* 7 [September 1895]: 303).

81. ''Editorials,'' *The Public* 2, no. 55 (April 22, 1899): 4.

82. ''Current Literature: The City Wilderness,'' Review of *The City Wilderness*, ed. by Robert A. Woods, *Gunton's Magazine* 16 (February 1899): 136–37.

83. A. C. Bernheim, ''Party Organizations and Their Nominations to Public Office in New York City,'' *Political Science Quarterly* 3 (March 1888): 122.

84. ''Editorial Comment: Political Bosses—Are They a Necessary Evil,'' *Banker's Magazine* 52 (June 1896): 712, 713.

85. ''Machine Politics,'' *The Social Economist* 2 (November 1891): 1.

86. ''Editorial Comment: Political Bosses,'' pp. 714–15.

87. ''Economics and Public Affairs,'' p. 167.

88. George E. Waring, Jr., ''Greater New York a Century Hence'' [reprinted from the New York *Herald*, October 24, 1897], *Municipal Affairs* 1 (December 1897): 717.

89. John H. Pryor, ''The Tenement and Tuberculosis: Apropos of the Movement for Better Housing Conditions in New York,'' *Charities Review* 10 (December 1900): 446.

90. ''Editorials. Mayor Jones,'' *The Public* 2, no. 60 (May 27, 1899): 6–7.

91. Charles M. Andrews, Review of *The Early Records of the Town of Providence*, printed under the Authority of the City Council of Providence, *Annals of the American Academy of Political and Social Science* 4 (March 1894): 825, 826.

92. Clarence Deming, ''Town Rule in Connecticut,'' *Political Science Quarterly* 4 (September 1889): 409, 411.

93. Simon N. Patten, "The Decay of State and Local Governments," *Annals of the American Academy of Political and Social Science* 1 (July 1890): 29, 36, 41.

94. William Draper Lewis, "The Political Organization of a Modern Municipality, or Local Municipal State," *Annals of the American Academy of Political and Social Science* 2 (January 1892): 460, 464.

95. Ellis Paxson Oberholtzer, "Home Rule for our American Cities," *Annals of the American Academy of Political and Social Science* 3 (May 1893): 763.

96. Alfred H. Peters, "Manhattan: A Proposed New State," *American Journal of Politics* 2 (March 1893): 266–69, 269–70. See also the proposals of Lucien Saniel for "Two New York States," *North American Review* 148 (January 1889): 86–96.

97. The four-part series was published in the *Annals of the American Academy of Political and Social Science*: "Representation in State Legislatures" ["North Atlantic"], 15 (March 1900): 204–35; "Representation in the Legislatures of the North Central States," 15 (May 1900): 405–25; "Representation in State Legislatures. The Southern States," 16 (July 1900): 93–119; "Representation in State Legislatures. The Western States," 16 (September 1900): 243–72.

98. Ibid., 15: 231.

99. Ibid., 16: 259–60, 243.

100. Philip M. Hauser, "Urbanization: An Overview," *The Study of Urbanization*, ed. Hauser and Leo F. Schnore (New York: John Wiley & Sons, 1965), p. 28.

101. Frank P. Richard, "The Study of the Science of Municipal Government," *California Municipalities* 1 (October 1899): 74, 75. Such schools were also proposed by both Richard T. Ely and Lester Frank Ward; see Sidney Fine, *Laissez Faire and the General-Welfare State: A Study of Conflict in American Thought, 1865–1901* (Ann Arbor: University of Michigan Press; London: Oxford University Press, 1956), pp. 235, 258.

102. M. McG. Dana, "The American City," *Gunton's Magazine* 11 (August 1896): 136.

103. John H. Gray, "Some Preliminary Problems and Their Possible Solutions," *Journal of Social Science* 24 (November 1896): 174–75.

104. "Annual Report of the General Secretary, Rev. Frederick Stanley Root, M.A., of New York," *Journal of Social Science* 36 (December 1898): 57.

105. "Editorial Comment: Political Bosses," p. 712.

106. Leo S. Rowe, "American Political Ideas and Institutions in Their Relation to the Problem of City Government" [address before the National Municipal League, Louisville, May 6, 1897], *Municipal Affairs* 1 (June 1897): 317.

107. Charles Richardson, "A National Conference of Municipal Reformers. Reasons for Calling It, and Subjects for Discussion," *Good Government* 13 (December 15, 1893): 65.

108. Peterson, *Day of the Mugwump*, p. 26. The conference results are covered in Blake McKelvey, *The Urbanization of America, 1860–1915* (New Brunswick, N.J.: Rutgers University Press, 1963), pp. 101–04; the model charter of the League is examined in Clifford Patton, *The Battle for Municipal Reform: Mobilization and Attack, 1875 to 1900* (Washington, D.C.: American Council on Public Affairs, 1940), Chapters 4 & 7.

109. Charles E. Monroe, "The Time to Deal with Corporations Asking Public Franchises," *Municipality* 1, no. 3 (August 1900): 5–6.

110. Phelan, "The League of California Municipalities," p. 3–4.

111. Clinton Rogers Woodruff, "The Philadelphia Municipal League," *American Journal of Politics* [*American Magazine of Civics*] 5 (September 1894): 287–94.

112. "The Civic Federation of Chicago," *American Journal of Sociology* 1 (July 1895): 79–80, 93. Daniel Levine examined the initial organization, structure, and activities of the Federation in "Reform and the Status Quo: The Civic Federation of Chicago," *Varieties of Reform Thought* (Madison: The State Historical Society of Wisconsin, 1964), pp. 48–63. For the progress of other voluntary associations in Chicago, see Henry B. Fuller, "The Upward Movement in Chicago," *Atlantic Monthly* 80 (October 1897): 534–49, and Edward Burritt Smith, "The Municipal Voters' League of Chicago," *Atlantic Monthly* 85 (June 1900): 834–39.

113. "The Month," *Good Government* 12 (February 15, 1892): 90.

114. "The Month," *Good Government* 12 (May 15, 1893): 127. An interesting proposal for the formation of independent leagues of citizens—societies to be modeled on the American Copyright League, the Civil Service Reform Association, and the Indian Rights Association—with the intention that these leagues serve as permanent pressure groups in municipalities, very much in the manner of citizen rights organizations, was fostered in "The League as a Political Instrument," *Atlantic Monthly* 69 (February 1892): 258–60. Less activistic groups were also called for, such as city and village improvement associations; see, "Value of Improvement Clubs," *California Municipalities* 2 (May 1900); 109–10.

115. "Our Purpose and Scope," *Chicago Commons* [*The Commons*] 1, no. 1 (April 1896): 1.

116. Robert A. Woods, "University Settlements: Their Point and Drift," *Quarterly Journal of Economics* 14 (November 1899): 77.

117. Robert A. Woods, "Settlement Houses and City Politics," *Municipal Affairs* 4 (June 1900): 396, 398. The concept of the "protective state," the "democratic service state," or the "general-welfare state" is developed in Fine, *Laissez Faire and the General Welfare State*, Chapters 6–10.

118. Robert A. Woods, "University Settlements: Their Point and Drift," *Quarterly Journal of Economics* 14 (November 1899): 79–86; the applied skills of the practiced resident are examined in Chapter 5.

119. J. Richard Freud, "Relation of the Business Man to the Municipality," *California Municipalities* 1 (August 1899): 15, 17.

120. Herbert Welsh, "A Danger and an Opportunity," *Good Government* 14 (January 15, 1895): 195–96.

121. John R. Commons, "Workingmen and City Government," *American Federationist* 2 (March 1895): 1.

122. John Jay Chapman, "Is a Third Party Necessary in Municipal Reform Work?" *Municipal Affairs* 4 (June 1900): 336, 332, 333.

123. St. Clair McKelway, "The Need of Municipal Parties" [from a Paper read before the American Social Science Association, September 3, 1896], *Good Government* 15 (September 15, 1896): 121.

124. St. Clair McKelway, "Modern Municipal Reform," *Journal of Social Science* 34 (November 1896): 131, 126.

125. E. Dana Durand, "Council Government *Versus* Mayor Government," *Political Science Quarterly* 15 (September 1900): 433.

126. John Archibald Fairlie, "Comparative Municipal Statistics," *Quarterly Journal of Economics* 13 (April 1899): 343.

127. Frederick R. Clow, "Suggestions for the Study of Municipal Finance," *Quarterly Journal of Economics* 10 (July 1896): 455–66.

128. Clinton Rogers Woodruff, "The Problem of the City," *American Magazine of Civics* 9 (November 1896): 382.

129. Albert Shaw, "Municipal Government in Great Britain," *Political Science Quarterly* 4 (June 1889): 229, 216–29.

130. Samuel M. Jones, "Improving Our Citizenship," *The Public* 1, no. 34 (November 26, 1898): 12.

131. Edmund J. James, "The Growth of Great Cities in Area and Population," *Annals of the American Academy of Political and Social Science* 13 (January 1899): 8–15.

132. Adna F. Weber, "Suburban Annexations," *North American Review* 166 (May 1898): 612. The editors of *Public Improvements* also found the "strife between some of the larger cities of this country for supremacy" to be "a source of considerable amusement": "first Chicago enlarges its boundaries and takes in some of the state of Illinois, so that it will be the largest city in this country[;] this is immediately followed by the establishment of the Greater New York, a movement which is as ridiculous and unsatisfactory as it was unnecessary" ("Municipal Rivalry" 1 [July 1, 1899]: 81).

133. John W. Pryor, "The Greater New York Charter. The Formation of the Charter," *Annals of the American Academy of Political and Social Science* 10 (July 1897): 20, 25, 32.

134. "Politics of Greater New York," *Gunton's Magazine* 10 (March 1896): 172.

135. "Greater New York," *Gunton's Magazine* 10 (May 1896): 341, 342.

136. M. N. Baker, "Municipal Co-operation *vs.* Municipal Consolidation," *Municipal Affairs* 3 (March 1899): 18–32.

137. A third interpretation, the mugwump view that constitutional changes were futile without a moral reawakening in the municipality, was offered by Albert Shaw in "The Municipal Problem and Greater New York," *Atlantic Monthly* 79 (June 1897): 733–48.

138. Clinton Rogers Woodruff, "The Philadelphia Municipal League," *American Journal of Politics* 5 (September 1894): 287–94.

139. "Discouraging Expert Officials," *California Municipalities* 2 (June 1900): 141.

140. David Starr Jordan, "A Continuing City" [Address before the Convention of the League of California Municipalities, December 14, 1899], *California Municipalities* 1 (February 1900): 232.

141. David Starr Jordan, "Politics of Greater New York," p. 170.

142. Durand, "Council Government *Versus* Mayor Government," pp. 426, 436.

143. Ibid., (December 1900): 708.

144. William Potts, "George Edwin Waring, Jr.," *Charities Review* 8 (December 1898): 464, 468.

145. Edward J. Phelps, "How Chicago 'Hustled' for Reform," *Good Government* 14 (April 15, 1895): 137–38.

146. Seth Low, "Civil Service Reform in Cities," *Good Government* 13 (September 15, 1893): 29.

147. Herbert Welsh, "Civil Service Reform and Labor," *Good Government* 14 (August 15, 1895): 196–97.

148. Carl Schurz, "Civil Service Reform in Municipalities" [from an Address to the National Conference for Good City Government, January 25, 1894], *Good Government* 13 (February 15, 1894): 95. Schurz did believe, nevertheless, that a properly administered civil service system would exert an influence powerful enough to overthrow and destroy Tammany Hall.

149. R. Fulton Cutting, "Public Ownership and the Social Conscience," *Municipal Affairs* 4 (March 1900): 4–5, 7, 11, 6.

150. Milo Ray Maltbie, "Municipal Functions: A Study of the Development, Scope and Tendency of Municipal Socialism," *Municipal Affairs* 2 (December 1898): 577–799. His analysis, which made up an entire number of this journal, was based on questionnaires from 150 American and 350 foreign cities, consultations with experts, consular reports, city documents, standard texts, pamphlets, and magazine articles.

151. Ibid., pp. 784–85, 787.

152. Joseph Loeb, "Motives of Municipalization," *Municipality* 1, no. 2 (June 1900): 28–29.

153. Delos F. Wilcox, "The American Newspaper: A Study in Social Psychology," *Annals of the American Academy of Political and Social Science* 16 (July 1900): 89–90.

154. "Institute Work: Practical Municipal Reforms," *Gunton's Magazine* 16 (May 1899): 389.

155. John H. Gray, Review of *Municipal Monopolies: A Collection of Papers by American Economists and Specialists*, ed. Edward W. Bemis, *Journal of Political Economy*, 7 (September 1899): 564–65.

156. John H. Gray, "Some Preliminary Problems and Their Possible Solution," *Journal of Social Science* 34 (November 1896): 176–81.

157. Herbert Miller, "Socialism in the United States," *American Federationist* 2 (August 1895): 98, 97.

158. John G. Agar, "Shall American Cities Municipalize? Value of Foreign Experience As a Guide," *Municipal Affairs* 4 (March 1900): 20, 23.

159. Edwin L. Godkin, "The Problems of Municipal Government," *Annals of the American Academy of Political and Social Science* 4 (May 1894): 865, 866, 881.

160. Adolph Moses, "Democracy and Despotism," *American Magazine of Civics* 9 (October 1896): 272. An obvious alternative that would protect the interests of the taxpaying minority was the adoption of proportional representation. This electoral device was described by Edmund J. James in "An Early Essay on Proportional Representation" [read before the Political Science Association of the Central States, Indianapolis, January 1, 1896], *Annals of the American Academy of Political and Social Science* 7 (March 1896): 233–52; the essay to which James referred was written in 1844 by Thomas Gilpin. For a lucid explanation of the intricacies of this system see Peterson, *Day of the Mugwump*, p. 332.

161. C. Meriwether, "Washington City Government," *Political Science Quarterly* 12 (September 1897): 407, 419.

162. Commons, "State Supervision for Cities," p. 867.

163. James T. Young, "Notes: A Municipal Theocracy," *Municipal Affairs* 2 (September 1898): 538, 535, 537.

164. Samuel P. Hays, "The Politics of Reform in Municipal Government in the Progressive Era," *Pacific Northwest Quarterly* 55 (October 1964): 161, 163.

PACKAGING A PLAN

By the turn of the century, comprehensive park planning expanded from coast to coast but, paradoxically, contracted as a design ideal and influence. Following Frederick Law Olmsted's retirement in 1895 and death in 1903, for example, his sons completed a number of ambitious park-parkway schemes including those for Seattle, Washington, and Portland, Oregon, in 1903–1904. Comparable in scope with the senior Olmsted's earlier and long-term efforts in Buffalo and Boston, the Olmsted Brothers' plans in content ran from seventy to ninety pages, included either no illustrations at all or only a modest selection of maps and photographs, and demonstrated throughout a self-confident technical virtuosity together with a sure grasp of site characteristics, the potential directions for real estate development, and the tastes and values of client-readers—the commission or board members who paid the bills.[1] Thus, during a brief two-year period, the Olmsted Brothers extended across the continent the park-parkway configuration that their father had spent a quarter-century in perfecting. Yet, as the Olmstedian concept for controlled metropolitan development was being packaged and marketed nationwide, it was also losing force as a design ideal to a new, vital, more ambitious construct: one that was articulated vividly and persuasively in the 1902 plan for *The Improvement of the Park System of the District of Columbia*.[2]

The McMillan Plan, as it came to be called, was a remarkable fabrication. A weighty tome, 9 1/4 inches high and 6 across, its 123 pages of text, 48 of appendices, plus various maps and illustrations were bound handsomely between maroon cloth-covered boards with gold lettering on cover and spine. Especially noteworthy were its hundred-odd numbered illustrations and baker's dozen maps and plans: while most were page-size, sixteen views and photographs folded out as far as 15 1/4 inches, one plan to 25 inches, and three five-color end maps opened up to 26 1/2 by 28 1/2 inches; what is more, seven matching-scale maps on translucent paper provided overlay views of the extant and planned park systems of Washington with those of London, New York City, Paris, and Boston. This visually rich—indeed, splendid—production promoted a planning ideal that would dominate the profession throughout the first half of the twentieth century.

The visions of a City Beautiful and a Garden City combined harmoniously in the McMillan Plan.[3] In coverage and content, it was a team effort of architects Daniel H. Burnham and Charles F. McKim, sculptor Augustus St. Gaudens, and landscape architect Frederick Law Olmsted, Jr. But in scope and spirit, it was singularly Burnhamesque.

Of maligned urbanists, only Robert Moses would ever match Daniel Hudson Burnham as a target for villification. "Elephantine, tackless, and blurting," as portrayed by fellow Chicago architect (and competitor) Louis Sullivan, "Burnham's megalomania concerning the largest, the tallest, the most costly and sensational, moved on in its sure orbit, as he painfully learned to use the jargon of big business." As the central figure in planning the 1893 World's Columbia Exposition in Chicago—the "Columbian Ecstasy," according to Sullivan—Burnham had set loose upon the land "the virus of the World's Fair."

The market was ripe [Sullivan complained], made so through the hebetude of the populace, big business men, and eminent educators alike. By the time the market had been saturated, all sense of reality was gone. In its place had come deep-seated illusions, hallucinations, absence of pupillary reaction to light, absence of knee-reaction—symptoms all of progressive cerebral meningitis: The blanketing of the brain. Thus Architecture died in the land of the free and the home of the brave,—in a land declaring its fervid democracy, its inventiveness, its resourcefulness, its unique daring, enterprise and progress. . . .

The damage wrought by the World's Fair will last for half a century from its date, if not longer. It has penetrated deep into the constitution of the American mind, effecting there lesions significant of dementia.[4]

In these characteristically purple passages, Sullivan prepared a place for Burnham, after his eventual fall from the planning Pantheon, in a devil-rid Pandemonium.

Seemingly few design professionals, conversely, ever elicited such loyalty among their associates and admiration from their clients as did Louis Sullivan's arch villain. "Daniel Hudson Burnham was one of the handsomest men I ever saw," wrote Paul Starrett, once a lowly employee in the great man's office and later, after establishing himself as a top executive in the nation's most successful building firm, a working associate. The architect-planner "had a beautifully molded head, a great crown of dark-brown hair that curved low over his broad forehead, a thick, reddish mustache above his powerful jaw, a quick, direct glance out of his deep-blue eyes." What is more, Starrett added, this paragon among planners possessed "a magnetic personality. That, combined with his magnificent physique, was a big factor in his success." Indeed, his admirer continued: "It was easy to see how he got commissions. His very bearing and looks were half the battle. He had only to assert the most commonplace thing and it sounded important and convincing." Most significantly, for Starrett, "Burnham saw the temper of the time and seized on it to his advantage, as no other architect had done."[5]

Born in Upstate New York in 1846, Burnham moved with his family to Chicago in 1854 where, as in a New England prep school later, he compiled a dismal academic record, then subsequently failed the entrance examinations to both Harvard and Yale. Following a brief venture in 1869–1870 into silver mining in Nevada, he returned to Chicago where he established himself as an architect in the year following the Great Fire of 1871. Two subsequent partnerships opened exciting new vistas for this almost archetypal late bloomer. In 1873 Burnham and John Wellborn Root established the architectural offices of Burnham and Root, which over the next eighteen years would build, according to his modern biographer Thomas S. Hines, "over $40,000,000.00 worth of buildings, including residences, office buildings, railroad stations, hotels, schools, churches, warehouses, stores, hospitals, and miscellaneous structures from barns and convents to casinos and ceremonial monuments.'' In 1874 Burnham married Margaret Sherman, the daughter of stockyards magnate John B. Sherman. ''Daniel and Margaret rose socially as Burnham and Root rose professionally,'' Hines has observed, ''the movement of both inevitably and inextricably entwined.''[6] By the late 1880s, then, Burnham had become a force in Chicago.

The competition among American cities for the privilege of hosting a fifteenth world's fair was won by Chicago on April 25, 1890, when President Benjamin Harrison signed an act providing for an ''international exhibition of arts, industries, manufactures, and the products of the soil, mine, and sea'' to be held there. At the outset, Burnham served as unofficial adviser to the ad hoc corporation that was established to plan and manage the fair, then collaborated with Frederick Law Olmsted in selecting its site, and later acted as its director of works. The World's Columbia Exposition of 1893, which evolved out of these efforts, overwhelmed urban America. As Henry Adams, who devoted a full chapter in *The Education* to what Sullivan had derided as the ''Columbian Ecstacy,'' proclaimed: ''Chicago was the first expression of American thought as a unity; one must start there.''[7] American city planning would.

Fame and honor followed the fair. In 1894 both Yale and Harvard awarded Burnham honorary master of arts degrees and Northwestern his first honorary doctorate. In 1893 and 1894 his professional peers elected him president of the American Institute of Architects. And, with the death of his business partner in 1891, the firm of D. H. Burnham and Company succeeded Burnham and Root, expanding its influence far beyond Chicago and the Midwest. Subsequently, on travels in southern Europe, the Middle East, and northern Africa during 1896, Burnham gained a vision that transcended even the national. ''The trip,'' Hines has written, ''opened new worlds to Burnham and made real for him what had formerly existed only in a world of dreams and picture books.'' For the remainder of his professional life, ''Burnham sought to bring to American soil much of the power, grandeur, mystery, and monumentality he saw and imbibed in his Old World travels. Somehow, he thought, there must be in America the same sense of wonder for Americans who would never be able to travel abroad.''[8] He found it in the nation's capital, that City of Magnificent Intentions.

Other urbanists, too, found a sense of wonder in *The Improvement of the Park System of the District of Columbia*. The McMillan Plan embodied much of the American urban experience: its historical roots, in that it represented ''generally a reinstatement, reiteration, and enlargement of the L'Enfant Plan of 1791'';[9] municipal rivalry, by setting a standard for emulation or transcendence;[10] an operative style, in its expression of aggressive nationalism;[11] and, most of all, linkage. The McMillan Plan reached back to the postwar sanitary movement and parkite crusade, linked them with late-century concepts of civic art and the City Beautiful, and hinted at even more elaborate manifestations of the Burnhamesque for the future.[12] In essence, it fleshed out the skeleton of the Olmstedian park-parkway configuration.

It was Burnham's "boldness," his "sheer presumptuousness," planning historian Jon A. Peterson has argued recently, that accounted for "the unique comprehensiveness of the McMillan Plan": "the fact that it was no little plan that had emerged in Washington. 'Big' enough and 'noble' enough to stir 'men's blood,' " the historian parodies the planner, "it became in the words of the planning motto so often identified with Daniel H. Burnham, 'a living thing, asserting itself with ever-growing insistency'—capable indeed of shaping the nation's capital and inspiring a national planning movement."[13] That capability for inspiration was an essential and purposeful component of the plan itself.

"Selling the plan," Washington historian Frederick Gutheim has noted, "was an important aspect of the McMillan Commission's work and would prove immeasurably important in the plan's reception." Commission Secretary Charles Moore, himself a former journalist, managed news releases "to keep the interest of the press and public whetted." Architect Charles F. McKim's "concern about the layman's ability to appreciate plans and drawings led him to ask leading illustrators of the nation's magazines to do renderings of the designs and landscaping for public buildings and monuments in relation to the over-all scheme." A brilliantly staged and skillfully orchestrated exhibition opened on January 15, 1902, to mark the submission of the commission's official report "in the hemicycle of the still-new Corcoran Gallery of Art. . . . The place of honor," Gutheim sums up, "was held by two models: one of the city as it existed in 1901 and the other showing proposed changes."[14] These gallery-filling models (Figures 3, 4, and 5) drew for their accuracy on over 5,000 photographs and were produced at a cost of approximately $24,500 or nearly 2 1/2 times the initial estimated appropriation for *all* Commission expenditures.[15] They reflected the "confidence and panache" of the commission.[16] Their style was the monumental, their vision the epic.

The selling of the plan involved, quite simply, a sophisticated advertising campaign; as such, it was typical of the communications revolution of the period. Even the title of the published report, *The Improvement of the Park System of the District of Columbia*, recalled that of Charles Mulford Robinson's recent *The Improvement of Towns and Cities*, published in 1901 and reissued in eleven editions by 1916, becoming in the process the bible of the civic art movement.[17] Still, even though it drew upon and pulled together many of the best ideas and expressions of the period, the McMillan Plan stood as more than the sum of its parts. Summary and forecast both, it was also urban theater at its most effective.

Figure 3

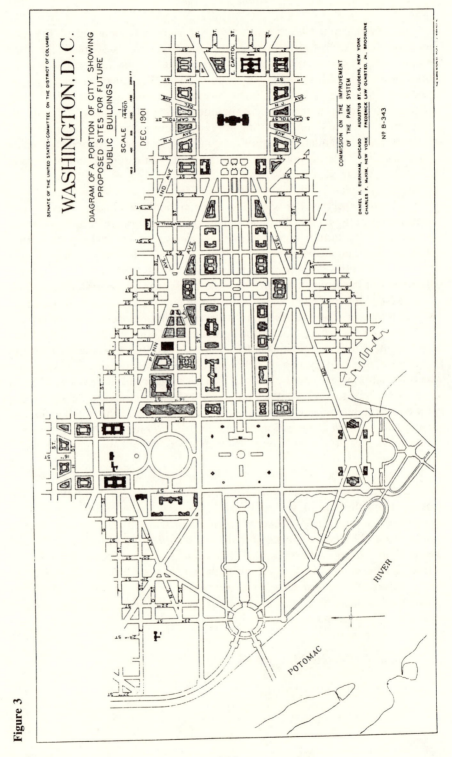

146

Figure 4

NO. 34.—MODEL OF THE MALL, SHOWING PRESENT CONDITIONS. LOOKING WEST.

Figure 5

Washington Common.

Lincoln Memorial.

Executive group of buildings.

Legislative group of buildings.

NO. 35.—MODEL OF THE MALL, SHOWING TREATMENT PROPOSED. LOOKING WEST.

NOTES

1. *Report of the Park Board: Portland, Oregon, 1903: With the Report of Messrs. OLMSTED BROS., Landscape Architects, Outlining a System of Parkways, Boulevards and Parks for the City of Portland* (reprinted by supporters of the 40 Mile Loop, c. 1978), esp. pp. 13–75; and the *First Annual Report of the Board of Park Commissioners, Seattle, Wash., 1884–1904* (Seattle: Lowman & Hanford Stationery and Printing Co., 1905; reprinted by Friends of Seattle's Olmsted Parks, 1984).

2. U.S. Congress, Senate, 57th Congress, First Session, Senate Report No. 166, *The Improvement of the Park System of the District of Columbia*. I. *Report of the Senate Committee on the District of Columbia*. II. *Report of the Park Commission*, ed. Charles Moore (Washington, d.C.: Government Printing Office, 1902).

3. See Chapter 2 for the city beautiful movement; see Chapter 1, the second interlude, and Chapter 2 for parks, comprehensive park planning, and garden cities/new towns.

4. Louis Sullivan, *The Autobiography of an Idea*, with a Foreward by Claude Bragdon (New York: Dover Publications, Inc., 1924 & 1956), pp. 288, 324–25.

5. Paul Starrett, *Changing the Skyline, An Autobiography*, With the Collaboration of Webb Waldron and a Foreword by Bob Davis (New York & London: Whittlesley House, McGraw-Hill Book Company, 1938), pp. 29, 30.

6. Thomas S. Hines, *Burnham of Chicago: Architect and Planner* (New York: Oxford University Press, 1974), pp. 16, 21.

7. Ibid., Chapters 4 and 5; Adams's quotation, p. 73.

8. Ibid., p. 137.

9. Ibid., Chapter 7, "The New Capital," p. 151.

10. Harvey A. Kantor, "The City Beautiful in New York," *New-York Historical Society Quarterly* 57 (April 1973): esp. 153, 155, 167, concerning the impact of the McMillan Plan upon the New York City Improvement Plan of 1907.

11. Michael T. Klare, "The Architecture of Imperial America," *Science & Society: An Independent Journal of Marxism* 33 (Summer-Fall 1969): esp. 278–81.

12. Burnham's 1909 Plan for Chicago, his most ambitious effort in comprehensive planning, will be examined in the concluding Interlude.

13. Jon A. Peterson, "The Hidden Origins of the McMillan Plan for Washington, D.C., 1900–1902," in Antoinette J. Lee, ed., *Historical Perspectives on Urban Design: Washington, D.C. 1890–1910*, Occasional Paper No. 1, Center for Washington Area Studies (Washington: George Washington University, 1984), pp. 10, 13. The "planning motto" parodied here by Peterson is the famous: "Make no Little Plans; They have no magic to stir men's blood and probably themselves will not be realized. Make big plans." For the provenance of this quotation, see Henry H. Saylor, " 'Make No Little Plans,' Daniel Burnham Thought It, But Did He Say It?" *Journal of the American Institute of Planners* 27 (March 1957): 95–99.

14. Frederick Gutheim, *Worthy of the Nation: The History of Planning for the National Capital* (Washington: The Smithsonian Institution Press, 1977), p. 122.

15. See Peterson, "Hidden Origins," pp. 9, 11, for commission expenses. See John W. Reps, *Monumental Washington: The Planning and Development of the Capital Center* (Princeton, N.J.: Princeton University Press, 1967), pp. 105–08, for a vivid description of the staging of the Corcoran Exhibition.

16. Gutheim, *Worthy of the Nation*, p. 133.

17. See Donald A. Krueckeberg, ed., "Introduction" to *The American Planner: Biographies and Recollections* (New York and London: Methuen, 1983), pp. 13–14, and Jon A. Peterson, "The City Beautiful Movement: Forgotten Origins and Lost Meanings," in Krueckeberg, ed., *Introduction to Planning History in the United States* (New Brunswick, N.J.: The Center for Urban Policy Research, Rutgers University, 1983), pp. 51–53.

4

Cities of Extremes, 1885–1900

"The booming, bustling Downtown Age," as novelist William Kennedy has characterized it, was born toward the close of the century.[1] Changes in the business and living patterns of commercial districts were obvious to the most casual observer of urban America. Its skyscrapers and slums were visible indications of change, signs of a remarkable dual process of concentration in both commercial activity and population. The new downtown seemed to epitomize the modern city.

The mixed-class, multiuse, sprawling market center of the preindustrial town was giving way to the single-class, one-function, compact central business district of the modern metropolis. The city's center was becoming clearly separate and easily distinguishable from other urban districts. It was being turned over, almost entirely, to commercial activities, developing into a working zone, not a living area. Its daytime population—from financial and industrial titans, to corporate officials, to merchants, office workers, and clerks, to skilled and unskilled laborers—still made up a cross section of urban America; however, its nocturnal population—workers, both native and immigrant, the alienated, social outcasts—represented only the lowest orders of society. The upper and middle classes, while fully exploiting the economic potentials of the inner city, were simultaneously deserting its confines for more desirable living areas uptown and in the suburbs. With them they took their traditional support for necessary urban institutions—church, school, service organization—and their leadership. Whether in their drive for profits and for improved living conditions for themselves and their own, they had also torn the vitals out of the central city and thereby imprisoned the lower classes who were packed into its slums, both scattered within and massed on the edges of the business districts, was the major socioeconomic question of the day.

This marked cleavage between the classes, then, posed the threat of creating an Americal social system similar to England's "two nations," with a triumphant and overbearing plutocracy on the one side and a repressed and defiant proletariat on the other, the two divided sharply by physical distance and economic barriers. Urban America faced the mounting challenge of class stratification in an avowedly open society.

"BUSINESS BLOCKS SHOOTING UPWARD"

"Business blocks shooting upward to the fifteenth and twentieth stories," proclaimed the editors of *The Social Economist*, "give architectural expression to the growth in wealth now going on, as perfectly as the castles and cathedrals of the middle ages expressed the power of the church and the baron." The "architectural transition" that was taking place in New York "and to some extent Chicago and other American cities," this journal boasted, was "not unlike that which occurred to the ancient city of Rome when a single ruler could say of it that he found it of brick and left it of marble." The contemporary boom in urban construction was, however, judged to be no mere repetition or extension of past advances. It was singular, indeed revolutionary: expanded office facilities and the introduction of elevators, telephones, and typewriters had resulted in a "fifty-fold" rise in efficiency.[2] The celebration of this commercial triumph ought to be, argued muralist Edwin Howland Blashfield, a primary function of public art: for example, "the history of the development of finance, the story of how money grew into being as a means of exchange, then how that exchange was made easier and easier to handle as an instrument; all this, I say, would look . . . well on the walls of an American Clearing House."[3]

The challenge of the revolution in building was clear enough, especially to the New Yorker whose dreams of urban imperialism were unbounded: "Upon us," urged New York City Congressman John DeWitt Warner, "is the responsibility never before laid on a people—of building the world's capital for all time to come. What we do well will serve mankind forever; what we do ill will be a stumbling block until it is remedied. To none before us have been given such opportunities—to be used or wasted." To meet this responsibility, to face up to this challenge, to achieve growth and enterprise and greatness, the citizens of New York—and, for that matter, of every great commercial center—had the right "to ask and expect" the capitalist to "contribute to the city's adornment" by securing "the utmost of beauty and public utility consistent with the greatest profit on his investment." In "building here the greatest financial and trade center the world has seen," Warner proposed, New Yorkers had the opportunity to "stir the pride of every dweller and the wonder of every stranger in our gates" by shaping a city "compared with which the business structures of other cities will seem dolls' houses."[4] This Brobdingnabian projection of a mercantile metropolis reflected the confidence of many economic observers throughout the period that the uneven business fluctuations of prosperity and panic, which had prevailed from the early 1870s into the mid–1890s, would be overcome. By the mid–1880s, in fact, this bullish spirit had begun increasingly to manifest itself.

No late-nineteenth-century periodical could match the expansive optimism of *The Social Economist* (later, *Gunton's Magazine*) about the future of the American economy. An initial prospectus proclaimed that the journal "represents a departure in economic discussion. Not that," it was quick to add, "it has any scheme to propose for bringing in a social millenium at short notice."[5] Despite this ready disclaimer, a distinct philosophy for a new social and economic order pervaded its pages, one that called for a concentration or centralization of both population and industrial power. "Not the rustic but the citizen is favorably situated and carries the future in his hands, and the people are beginning to know this, and to endeavor to share the life of the town. And they are wise and well-advised to do so." Even life in a tenement was preferable to life in "a birch wigwam." In order to improve conditions in the teeming cities, "let the rich not give more, but spend more, set on foot larger enterprises and more of them, employ this wealth."[6] The "centralists" had to be trusted with the health and growth of the economy, for "the centralist party has always been composed of the more intelligent portion of the body politic; and furthermore, we notice that the centralists do the most to prevent their principle from being carried to an extreme."[7] In defending editor George Gunton's lecture on "Society and the Coming Billionaire" against the attacks of the New York *World*, *The Social Economist* not only welcomed the nascent billionaire, but also advised society concerning the necessary order of public affairs: "The real function of capitalists in the community is to devise new means for creating profit; and the duty of the community is to take these profits in higher wages, reduced prices, and public improvements."[8] The function of centralization, then, might be summarized as the "Doom of the Small," the precondition to "a higher phase of emancipation."[9]

Social and economic concentration, centralization, or organization was indicative of "the product of centuries of evolution towards the most perfect form of representative institutions" and the trust was one such "perfect form."[10] The happpy transformation of the American economy through "trustification" was always a favorite theme of *Gunton's*; therefore, when it printed an article by C. D. Chamberlin that was mildly critical of, but generally sympathetic to, this process, and when that same article was followed immediately by a soothing and correcting editorial comment, one is tempted to suspect that the piece was planted as a propagandistic straw man. Thus, while Chamberlin was ready to grant that the trust was an indigenous American (as opposed to European) institution and that it promised greater efficiency and economy, he feared that "the trust necessarily seeks a commercial and financial center, a large and wealthy city where it is daily in touch with the pulse of trade and finance." This process led inevitably, then, to the "abandonment of the smaller factories in the rural towns and withdrawal of the employees who are the tenants of the houses of which the town is built, patrons of the local stores, and consumers of the products of the local farms, leaving the thrifty manufacturing village an empty distributing point for rural necessities which are obviously sold to the farmers at a higher price, while their product is bought at a much lower price on account of the transportation charges anticipated to get it to the customer.'' The end results of this complex of events meant the elimination of middlemen and jobbers, the decline of the local merchants and banking interests, and a drop in general property values. The ''Editorial Note'' appended to this article praised Chamberlin's judgment about the advantages of the trust, and gently corrected his errors. The major problem was in his misreading of urban growth statistics that showed, when properly interpreted, that medium-sized cities were eclipsing the larger population centers in their expansion, that regional variations in population movements favored the booming West—the area of agricultural discontent that was uppermost in the national mind, and that the enterprisers in the newer areas would naturally benefit from expansion and trustification. Nevertheless, it had to be recognized that many hamlets and villages would go under in this very process. ''From a sentimental or local standpoint it may perhaps be deplored, but the nation's interest is not in the mere preservation of little cross-roads hamlets but in the increase and distribution of communities sufficiently large and complex to exert a genuine socializing influence on its inhabitants and the surrounding country.''[11] This heady urban imperialism was given even more extreme expression in an editorial several years later in which corporations were urged to encourage rural out-migration among ''at least the young—putting them into the strait-jacket of active industry, and thereby sharpening their wits, stimulating their interest in healthy activities and pursuits, and reviving their sense of moral duties and obligations.''[12] These were the standard claims for a business state; yet, *Gunton's* glorification of industrial and urban centralization signified a sharp break with postwar socioeconomic thought of a similar cast. Gilded Age proponents of the business state were basically backward-looking in their championing of a monied plutocracy: wealth and the stability associated with aristocratic order were their aims, ends that must be characterized as being essentially reactionary. *Gunton's*, on the other hand, was forward-looking; it conceived of society as an ongoing process; its aims were power and expert direction. ''Centralists'' were not reactionary, not even conservative, but vigorously progressive.

Traditionally, bankers have been more inclined to hold their ground with the bears than to charge with the bulls; the editorial tone of *Banker's Magazine* seldom made exceptions to this rule. Excessive optimism and the temptations of speculative gain had led many ''shrewd business men'' into ruin in the past, A. F. Sears told members of a convention of the American Society of Civil Engineers at the beginning of the period. Convinced as they were that ''the location of capital at a given point [was] by far the most important factor in determining the location of towns and ports,'' ''intelligent men of enterprise'' had often been ruined in their town-building ventures. Money and enterprise were not sufficient to guarantee success; the virtue of restraint was also necessary.[13] ''We are growing too rapidly in wealth and population to grow healthfully," *Banker's Magazine* cautioned five years later. "The increase in both directions means decay in true national power and greatness. A long period elapsed in Roman living before the marks of decay were apparent to the unthinking, but the more thoughtful could clearly see them."[14] Simultaneously, however, bankers were dissociating themselves from the constricting pessimism of classical economics. Their journal pointed out that "in Wall Street the Bears, as they are called, or the fearful and desponding class, have control of the market"; nevertheless, although "Wall Street prefers to live under a cloud, let no one imagine that it extends further, for it does not."[15] Moreover, within another five years, this same journal was prepared to accept trustification as the mark of a new era: "The trust is really the result of the distrust of men in their individual capacity to struggle against the circumstances that surround them. . . . The pioneer may have been all-sufficient to himself, but his descendants are obliged to combine for the opportunity to live." The trust was "the natural outgrowth and development of a free business society. There will, of course, always be men who look backward and hold back, but they will not retard the natural progress of society."[16] At this point, the bankers seemed ready to charge into the future in a bullish fashion.

By the end of the period, the editors of *Banker's Magazine* were prepared to admit that prosperity was "more marked than ever before"; moreover, "if this condition of affairs continues to manifest itself for a few years longer, it is very possible . . . that New York will supersede London as the financial centre of the world. The great banks and banking firms of New York City are already alive to these possibilities, and are preparing themselves for the requirements of this high financial position." This preparation, of course, was being made in a seemly and conservative fashion.[17]

This transition of the financial spokesman from bear to bull was most obvious in his own version of urban commercial imperialism. The national financial system necessitated, the editors of *Banker's Magazine* argued, a new relationship between city and parent state: "It is impossible to separate entirely the spirit and life of a system from the material environment, but while locality must to some extent control bank statistics, the rigid adherence to State lines encourages many fallacies and defeats a clear understanding of banking methods."[18] Banking was now urban and national, perhaps even metropolitan and international. Charles A. Conant opted for the latter probability in an address to the American Bankers' Association in October 1900. The end of the domestic slump and the recent emergence of the United States as a great colonial power "have contributed," he asserted, "to bring New York into the circle of international markets and have raised the question whether the star of financial supremacy was not to move westward from the precincts of Lombard street to our own chief city." Every improvement in the national economy tended "to broaden the pedestal of wealth and national prosperity, upon which New York must have her firm footing if she is not to slip and fall in the struggle for financial supremacy with her great rivals in the Old World. . . . Every step forward which New York makes, on the other hand, in the struggle for supremacy in the many markets of the world is a step which lifts up and benefits the whole country.''[19] Walking boldly, then, hand in hand into the bright future, the United States and its Wall Street imperium were assured the greatest of expectations.

Writing in a vein perhaps more suitable to the organization-inclined *Gunton's Magazine* than to the more conservative *Banker's Magazine*, Lindley M. Keasbey foresaw international economic interaction leading inevitably to world political union. ''The industrial organism of the modern national state,'' he asserted, ''is the fairest flower of economic evolution. But the tree of industrial development still tends heavenward and gives promise of perhaps more perfect blossoms.''[20] This verdant offering to the bullish spirit of the times is presented as the final fruition of an expansive economic mood—shared simultaneously, if unevenly, by American industrial and financial spokesmen—a mood that may best be described as the full flowering of Victorian optimism.

That this sunny optimism was not necessarily held to by the community at large was apparent from the flippant criticisms of *Yellow Kid*, a popular comic weekly. ''Mr. Hayseed (who reads the papers)'' warned his wife upon their arrival at Wall Street: ''Ooo! Hold on t' y'r pocketbook, Mirander.''[21] Again, in a parody of Shakespeare's Hamlet soliloquy, the institutions of ''Waltz Street'' were gently burlesqued:

> To sell or not to sell? That is the question.
> Whether 'tis wiser in a chump to suffer the chills
>   and fevers of a crazy market
> Or put up stuff against a sea of losses
> And, by a closing, end them? To sell—to close—
>   no more—
>
> . . . .
>
>   Thus Waltz Street does make asses of us all,
> And thus the native hue of speculation
> Is sicklied o'er with a bull cast of thought
> And enterprises of great point and margin,
> With this regard, their profits turn to rye
> And lose the game in action. Soft you now!—
>   The ticker works![22]

This ''bull cast of thought'' was subjected generally to harsher analysis by its many critics. The social costs of the building boom in urban America had been, according to New York City Municipal Art Society official Frederick S. Lamb, extremely high: ''Streets are rendered almost lightless, buildings tower to the skies, and the poor foot-passenger is left sunless and cheerless.'' Urban imperialism, ''the so-called utilitarian spirit, the so-called progress, the so-called practical citizen have much to answer for.''[23] The ''term 'modern office buidling,' " itself, argued George Hill, "is used to describe the mammoth structure, of many stories, that the conditions of our present business life require us to erect in all centres of population where the fever of money getting is permitted to have full swing, unhampered by any traditions that involve avoidable loss of time."[24] A contributor to *Architectural Record* bemoaned the impersonalism of the commercial world: "To whom it may concern! What better motto can we inscribe on the banner of our Progress!" Indeed, that very word "represents one of our modern fetiches, as repulsive as a barbarian's totem, suggestive of ignorance, superstition and inhumanity" to the point that "we have come to regard tons of coal, miles of rail and other physical quantities as an end and a good in themselves. Poor Humanity!," the *Record* lamented: "Quite one-quarter of the people of New York pass their lives in squalid streets and crowded tenements, where the savor is hardly that of anything one dare call Civilization."[25]

That general dissatisfaction with the status quo was on the rise was recognized by many. C. F. Emerick of Columbia University indicated moderate optimism in his interpretation that such unrest was the natural result of inevitable and largely beneficial social change. "The process of redefining the rights of individuals in their new relationships, of adjusting the legal framework of society to corporations, trusts and all the complex phenomena of modern life, is necessarily slow."[26] To the editors of *Gunton's Magazine*, on the other hand, discontent had been "propogated with a semi-religious zeal" by "opportunist politicians and sentimental reformers." Their propaganda was not to be confused with the rational and ordered European brand of socialism; on the contrary, it was "not demagogical but painfully superficial and sentimental." Preferring always organization to disunity, *Gunton's* pointed out that: "It is not the organized socialists, who believe and preach a consistent economic doctrine, who are sowing the seeds of social disruption that may some day menace the safety of property and threaten free government itself."[27]

Centralists who sought an organized, orthodox opposition were able to find it readily enough in the ranks of the followers of Henry George, those highly vocal advocates of that uniquely urban-oriented doctrine of the single tax. Even *Banker's Magazine* felt compelled to publish an article that defended the single tax, "not because we adopt or endorse the views contained in it, but because it is a temperate statement of a doctrine in respect to the taxation and ownership of land, which is more or less agitated at the present time."[28] Other defenders of the established order were content to dismiss Henry George's panacea for a tax on the so-called "unearned increment" of land as being too absurd to merit serious attention; still others attempted to meet it squarely by demonstrating, for example, that "the logical outcome of his doctrines, so far from impoverishing property owners to enrich society, would impoverish society, by depriving it of the part-ownership which it now holds in every form of wealth, and enrich property owners by relieving them of the public duties now recognized as binding upon them.''[29] Although the areas of the counteroffensive might vary, the critical barrage had necessarily to be maintained against the onslaughts of the single-tax forces.

A major single-tax journal, Louis Post's *The Public*, sought constantly to expose "the exceptional power of landlordism in large cities."[30] Landlordism was, it maintained, the root cause of most domestic and international political, economic, and social problems. "When it is remembered that the entire population of the United States could be located in the single state of Texas, with over two acres of land to every man, woman and child; when it is known that more than half the area of the city of New York is vacant; when we look over the spreading area of Chicago and see that even a smaller portion is used . . . and when we supplement these considerations with a reflection upon the unemployed, the unhoused, the unclothed, the hungry, and those who fear loss of employment and hunger and rage and homelessness . . . how can we for a moment assume that we must force our way into other countries to find the resources of nature and the energies of man still dormant? They are dormant here! at our very doors! in New York, in Chicago, throughout the whole land."[31] Cities, *The Public* argued, suffered most from the existing system of property taxation which, as an example, was driving "rich men away from New York. That would be no great loss, for rich men, merely as rich men, are useless. . . . But," this journal continued, "these New York rich men, though they continue to draw unearned incomes from New York, will escape the payment of personal taxes here. . . . In its final results, therefore, the more stringently personal property taxation is enforced, the greater the inducement for rich men to get beyond the jurisdiction and leave the other fellows . . . to bear the burdens they thus escape."[32]

The single-tax apprehension about the urban-industrial order are conveniently summarized in the dystopian tale "Spero Meliora."[33] During the late twentieth century, the narrator, Dick Norris, returned to the United States from England only to find his homeland under the harsh domination of a landlord elite. His first encounter with a member of this ruling clique, the Hon. Robber-van-Rent, and his personal entourage convinced Norris that the professional classes—especially the architectural, legal, and clerical—had betrayed society in their complicity by supporting the new caste system. The new order was landed, not dissimilar to the corrupt feudalism of medieval Europe. The ravages of landlordism were particularly visible in New York City; here, stores and offices and even saloons had been deserted. "There was a certain melancholy charm about that quiet big desolate city, as I now recall it," the narrator mused. "The view from the window of my room embraced the harbor, and what had apparently once been the busiest section; and it seemed incredible that but few generations had elapsed since an enormous export and import trade thronged the harbors with vessels, and that the streets, now almost deserted, were once filled with busy crowds."[34] This metropolitan and national catastrophe had been brought about by ever-increasing taxes, the consequent bleeding of industrial and union treasuries to pay them, and the resulting enrichment of landlords who, of course, benefited from the unjust system of distribution of the national wealth; in addition, the wealthy had established or taken over large universities and professional schools, thereby providing the trained elite for their economic *coup d'état*. A postscript to this tale warned readers that these revolutionary forces of reaction were dangerously present in contemporary society. Americans had now to recognize "the influences constantly at work for evil—a press whose ill-concealed purpose was to promulgate falsehood in order to perpetuate economic wrong; the church, a relic of medievalism, fearful of raising its voice for the truth; and the few with honesty to accept and courage to fight for that truth, subjected to ridicule, persecution, and social ostracism."[35]

The opposition to the established order expressed by single-tax advocates represented only one of many voices of general unrest during the closing years of the century. Although industrial and financial spokesmen looked on optimistically at "business blocks shooting upward," those harbingers of "growth and enterprise and progress," many of their more skeptical contemporaries were more likely to view them as signs of a "furious decay." "It is mockery," *The Public* proclaimed, "to tell the people in times like these that they are prosperous. With employment agencies overrun with applicants vainly hunting for work; . . . with underpaid women displacing men, and men going into private kitchens as household servants; with hosts of small merchants passing out of independent business and into the overcrowded ranks of hired clerks . . . ; with vice-spreading slums in every city and sturdy tramps upon every highway; with a thousand other manifestations of social maladjustment and misery, the whole culminating in a universal fear of loss of employment or business, a paralyzing dread of poverty—with such thrusting themselves hourly upon public attention, thoughtful men are in no mood to listen patiently to silly jabber about our 'wonderful prosperity' "[36]

"NOR EKE DEPARTMENT STORES"

Parodying Rudyard Kipling, Ernest Crosby reminded those expansionists who sought to introduce "the American Way" to their "little brown brothers" in distant lands: "And don't forget the factories,/ On those benighted shores,/ They have no cheerful iron-mills,/ Nor eke department stores." The department store, introduced first in the United States during the war years but still regarded as a novelty, was the object of a great deal of attention in the closing years of the century.[37] At times, it served as a stage for lighthearted burlesque, as in the tale "One Afternoon." This story, set in the middle of the twentieth century, took place entirely within "Soandso's" department store. "At that date the institution known as the department store had reached its fullest development. There was not a single article of any kind on the market which could not be purchased at one of these mammoth emporiums." There, hero Charlie Hussel and heroine Mildred Uptodate had met, courted, and been joined in holy matrimony by the "department store clergyman"; there, they purchased their clothing and furniture and had their honeymoon arranged for them by the store's "transportation department." A happy ending, unfortunately, was not their fate. "A moment later the proud husband was watching his wife, as, with the ease born of long practice and perfect training, she fought her way though [sic] the crowd and reaches the counter. Soon she returned waving triumphantly a folded paper." It read: "Divorces marked down from $2.75 to $1.69. This Day Only."[38]

The editors of *The Social Economist* were inclined to take these great "bazaars" far more seriously, to evaluate them, in fact, as but one more sign of the "Doom of the Small." A new department store that was to be built in Chicago by Cooper, Siegel & Company would, *The Social Economist* reported, be able "to furnish absolutely everything, from a ton of coal to a refracting telescope, from a servant or a situation free of charge to a loan of any sum familiar to bankers, from a locomotive to a lamp; they will furnish a house complete, or build it new; they will sell you a suit ready-made or have it made to order; they will accommodate you at a hotel for an hour or sell you a residence in fee; take your telegram for transmission to any point, or manage your estate while you go to Europe; give you a shave and a bath or introduce you to a wife; sell you a horse from Kentucky with a record of 2.15 or Bourbon whiskey from the same state with edge like the scimeter of a Saracen—in short, it is common repute that they will give you fifty dollars to order anything with which they will not supply you." Never was the bullish optimism of this journal higher— nor, it should be added, more gullible—than it was in the contemplation of this one stop-and-shop institution of its vaunted "higher phase of emancipation."[39]

The editors of *The Public*, however, were less optimistic and more concerned with the "department store question" that had been raised in political contests in Chicago and its suburbs. "The great department stores of the city were denounced as giant monopolies, which had already driven thousands of small storekeepers out of business, and were steadily and surely concentrating in a few hands all the retail business of the community." In retaliation, the small retailers demanded "the obstruction, and if possible the suppression, of the business of department stores, by legislation."[40] *The Public* judged such action to be unwarranted and ill advised. "It is not the department stores," it asserted, "but retail buyers that are closing the small stores. All that the department stores do is to offer goods at low prices. Buyers do the rest." The "department store question" was, it continued, a part of the national evil of monopolistic control; on this occasion, however, its effects were being felt by the middle as well as the lower classes. "The cry of pain which the small shopkeeper emits merely shows that the labor problem is now pinching him for a solution, and that the problem is by no means funny nor its solution so simple as he thought when it only pinched 'workingmen.' "[41]

Annie Marion MacLean's decision to complete her research for the National Consumer's League on working conditions in Chicago department stores by obtaining employment in two of them during the Christmas "rush" was indicative of the pragmatic idealism of her generation of social scientists; moreover, it prefigured the methodology of many later, more celebrated Muckrakers.[42] "It seemed evident that valuable information could be obtained," she asserted, "if someone were willing to endure the hardships of the saleswoman's life, and from personal experience be able to pass judgment upon observed conditions." In her first position, although she had been promised three dollars a week, she was actually paid only two dollars, plus a five percent commission on her sales. Immediately, she learned that salesmanship was of a higher value than was honesty: "One of the difficult things at first was keeping track of the prices, for they were frequently changed during the day, and the penalty for selling under price was immediate discharge, while selling above price met with no disapproval."[43] Work began at 8:00 A.M. and continued until 10:00 P.M., with short breaks for lunch and supper—the second meal, paid for by the store, might run up to fifteen cents. Salesgirls worked under constant and even degrading pressures: they were threatened with dismissal for poor sales totals; they were subjected to harassment by crude and unthinking shoppers; and they were under constant surveillance by management—even in the squalid ladies' rest rooms, those previously inviolate female sanctuaries. MacLean's second position, while it was in a more fashionable store, was little better than the first; although the sanitary conditions were adequate, her hours were extended to 11:00 P.M. each evening, and to 12:00 P.M. on Christmas Eve. The wages were "woefully insufficient." "It was an openly acknowledged fact among the girls there that the paths of dishonor were traversed to supplement their small incomes. . . . They viewed the matter solely from a commercial standpoint, and justified their conduct by the urgency of the need. The girls themselves said that more than a third of them were leading lives of shame." To the author, this involuntary recruitment into prostitution was the most serious social problem of the city. To combat this moral pestilence, she recommended the economic devices of unionization and the adoption of the fair employment practices of the Consumers' League.[44]

The sales instinct was obviously on the rise in urban America. "We are a race of hustlers, keen only for the chance of grasping the elusive dollar," a contributor to the pleasure-oriented *Metropolitan Magazine* lamented; "we take our pleasures reluctantly, and chiefly with regret that even our business pursuits must be abandoned for holiday-making. . . . The slaves of trade are numerous indeed in the metropolis."[45] Salesmanship was especially noticeable at Christmas time in downtown New York, with a jolly Saint Nick on every corner; yet, "the modern Santa Claus is only a clever salesman and is in the employ of the merchant."[46]

What may be labeled an urban retail revolution was a part of what historian David M. Potter classified as "The Institution of Abundance: Advertising."[47] Sidney A. Sherman's detailed analysis of the media employed in advertising, the products promoted, and the organization of advertising agencies confirmed that such a revolution had taken place.[48] The periodical, particularly the weekly magazine or newspaper, was the initial medium of the advertising industry; then almanacs, calendars, handbills, and circulars were used extensively. These ventures were followed quickly by the use of posters on street railways and local trains, and finally, downtown itself became an advertising medium.[49] First, tradition was consulted and hawkers invaded the streets: "Sandwich men, or 'banner packers,' as they are known to the craft, were common in London fifty years ago, and doubtless had existed much earlier. From one to fifty men parade the streets and form a conspicuous advertisement. There are estimated to be from 1000 to 1200 sandwich men in the city of New York alone." The face of downtown was also altered with the increasing use of store-window displays: "Window decorating has seen a phenomenal development within a decade or two, especially in the large stores of the cities. It has become a vocation, recognized and well paid by merchants."[50]

Those engaged in advertising ranged from the hawker to the "executive of [the] great corporation . . . who calls to his aid a dozen different agencies directly or indirectly connected with the desired end. The latter is the modern type." Significantly, according to Sherman's estimates, the "modern type" were strategically located: 63 percent in New England, 33 1/3 percent in New York State, 92 percent north of the Mason-Dixon Line and east of the Mississippi, and 48 percent in the cities of New York, Boston, and Chicago; indeed, "nothing could more strikingly show the concentration of business in great centers." The earliest agencies had been organized in New York. "New York has always been the center, and in 1871 one-half the agents were in the *Times* building in that city and did nine-tenths of the annual business of the country." In all, advertising expenses ran between $200 to $5 million a year, or about 5 percent of the value of all goods sold nationally.[51]

Even in its adolescence, this booming industry was organized much in the manner of present-day Madison Avenue: specialization was the rule; a manager planned the "campaign"; and status and emotional appeals predominated: "The advertiser cultivates wants."[52] Moreover, much as today, this glamour industry was under heavy attack, as critics like politician John DeWitt Warner characterized the age as one marked by "the increasing anxiety of the individual to attract public attention, and his unscrupulous ingenuity to secure this. . . . Today, however—when business competition in every line includes whole countries and frequently the world, and when one's individuality is as lost in the crowd of the well-to-do as ever was that of the peasant in the mob of his fellows—we see combined two of the strongest possible impulses—business policy and personal vanity." In short, the dynamic drive of commercialism had been combined with aggressive status seeking to produce "the advertising curse."[53]

Fortunately, Warner observed, the American advertising industry had yet to match the vulgar audacity of its English counterpart, and there remained American municipal landmarks that were unsullied by gigantic billboards; however, as the case of the Dewey Arch in Madison Square illustrated, this situation threatened to be short-lived. Here, "in a blaze of color by day and a glare of electric flash-lights by night, the sculpture and the lines of the Arch . . . stand out against and are contrasted with what is probably the most offensive advertisement that now challenges our brick-bats.'' This turn-of-the-century op art featured a "thirty-foot cucumber, in bright green on an orange background, above a field of scarlet, lettered in white, . . . [which was] incapable of description in words printable here. In the evening the dancing flash-lights of the '57 varieties' of beans, pickles, etc., thrown in the faces of all who throng Madison Square—the real center of the life and art of New York—are unimaginable except in nightmare.'' This bizarre Heinz extravaganza was matched only by the display at the very gates of the Empire City where "on the Newark Meadows such monstrosities as the 40 foot plaster and blue balls[,] each 18 feet in diameter, flank the 'Big Store' advertisement . . . and harmonize well with their surroundings—the rank stretch of marsh with its foul water curdling green and its corruption shimmering in the sun . . . the rot and reek of the salt meadows, that man has wholly wrecked and but partially conquered.'' Such abominations ought not, obviously, be permitted to proliferate. Americans should, Warner urged, organize "societies for the preservation of scenic beauty,'' much as the English had done in their Society for Checking the Abuses of Public Advertising. Should such groups gain power, "even New Yorkers may hope for a millennium when the city shall give the elevated roads and street cars the choice of not using the streets or using them for transport alone—except to the extent that under heavy license taxes a limited number of advertisements shall be permitted under such strict regulation as shall clear away offensive boardings and prohibit the worst of their present sins against good taste.''[54] Good taste, Warner maintained, was a civic responsibility.

Although a national advertising industry was already in an advanced stage of development, contemporary observers were more likely to regard the "mammoth emporiums'' as characterizing the retail revolution. As the department store, that colossus of commerce, raised its giant's head among the "building blocks shooting upward'' in downtown urban America, many, although mindful of its might, were more concerned with its scabby front.

PATRICIANS OR PARASITES?

Many contemporary observers would have agreed with Robert N. Reeves that "we are rapidly drifting away from our old social democracy and becoming worshipers at the shrine of wealth and titles. This fact is more noticeable in our large cities, where the greatest wealth is concentrated and where the wealthiest and oldest families reside.'' It was equally obvious, Reeves continued, that the spirit if not the fact of aristocracy was spreading rapidly: "The only explanation that can be given for this un-American spirit is the rapid accumulation of enormous private fortunes—fortunes which dwarf the magnificent incomes of the wealthiest European kings, princes, or emperors.''[55] The "accumulation of enormous private fortunes'' was not, of course, a peculiarly late-century phenomenon, inasmuch as postwar periodicals had vividly recounted the rise of the new rich. Yet, there was a difference. In part, late-century magazines, as in planning and politics, were better equipped to comprehend the complexities of the class structure; what is more, an "American metropolitan upper class" that began to assert itself during the mid–1880s seemed determined to establish its identity before the nation and the world. Conspicuous consumption and equally noticeable philanthropy, the establishment of a system of exclusive schools and colleges, and the "Europeanization of the leisured classes" all made the metropolitan upper class distinctive and highly visible.[56] This last characteristic, moreover, was especially galling to the American democrat. The visiting titled foreigner had become, Robert Reeves chided, "an object of idolatry. . . . He cannot take a walk or a drive unless he becomes the center of a fawning crowd, who eagerly watch his movements and then run off to practice them upon the first acquaintance they chance to meet." The deference paid by the American upper class to the European nobility seemed, what is more, to be coupled with a complete disregard for the welfare of their fellow citizens, most pointedly for the lower classes.

> Think of the grand ball given recently in one of our large cities for the entertainment of a visiting duke; of the coats of arms, the flashing diamonds, the dazzling costumes, the costly fountain playing in the center of the grand ballroom; think of all the pageantry of those who without thought or care of the poor and the wretched spent a fortune that night for the entertainment of one man, and then think of all the unknown dead in our great cities, of the shivering poor who beg to live, of all the suffering and sorrow and misery, and then let us stop and ask if such conditions are not conditions that are dangerous to the future prosperity of our country. And if they continue, just as surely as the prodigal expenditures caused by the profuse magnificence of Louis le Grand plunged France into revolution, just as surely will our country have cause to regret in the future the present leaning of our wealthy toward luxury and aristocracy.

This "hothouse aristocracy" would certainly breed "another and more fiery element in American society—anarchy."[57]

Such angry sentiments were not, obviously, voiced by all observers of American urban life; in any society, but most especially in a money-oriented one, there were defenders of the upper classes. These champions of the established order could have based their judgments upon reasoned convictions or upon reasons of base self-interest; in any case, it is difficult to distinguish between the true believer and the sycophant, and the case of *Metropolitan Magazine* is no exception to this generalization.

Metropolitan heralded the nuptials of the Hon. Lord John Spencer Churchill, the ninth duke of Marlborough, and Miss Consuelo Vanderbilt, the fourth "daughter of the house of the railroad king," as being the marriage of the century; a more recent chronicler of the era has called it the "first form of the Marshall Plan."[58] The English nobility had, *Metropolitan* maintained, more to gain from this union than did the American aristocracy. First, the financial health of the House of Marlborough was somewhat delicate, a condition that would be cured immediately by vital and substantial transfusions from the Vanderbilt vaults. Second, although the Vanderbilt family history contained "no Oudenarde or Ramillies on which it bases its claims to prestige,'' it had triumphed in enough ''hard-fought campaigns in Wall street'' to assure its right ''to enter the nobility of Croesus.'' Finally, whereas the groom's appearance was, at best, unprepossessing, the bride's was regal—although she was no ''scorcher,'' Miss Vanderbilt, who stood a good head taller than her duke, was a handsome woman. A coat of arms appended to this article—two hearts entwined, one crowned with a coronet, the other with a dollar sign—seemed appropriate both for the marriage of the century and for the tone of its sympathetic critics.[59]

The triumphs and glories of the ''nobility of Croesus'' were celebrated regularly and breathlessly by *Metropolitan*; thus, that arch-toady, Ward McAllister, was eulogized as a ''remarkable figure in contemporaneous history'': ''Count D'Orsay and Beau Brummel each represented an era in English social life, and McAllister represented an era in the social history of New York City.''[60] An even more remarkable manifestation of this ''era in the social history of New York City,'' however, was the plutocracy's contemporary version of urban renewal. ''It is an almost incomprehensible fact that there are enough actual millionaires on Manhattan Island to cover a mile of space on a closely-built avenue, but New York has enough and to spare. In fact, they are crowded off Fifth avenue.'' Cornelius Vanderbilt's late Gothic or early Renaissance (or both) mansion had been piled onto Fifth Avenue, a building of such grandeur that most observers were ''overpowered by the thought of the vast millions that are at the control of its owner; but if one can divorce himself from the selfish point of view and look at the building with an artistic eye, he is wont to say, 'Who has the means to gratify such an exceptional taste?' '' Clearly, American ducal palaces were first in the world: ''Here the aristocracy of money—more powerful, if not so historic as that of birth—indulges itself in the erection of houses which kings would be proud—and lucky—to own.''[61] Indeed, ''of late years there has been considerable rivalry in the building of these mansions, until they have come to be looked upon as the most expensive form of advertising the extent of one's bank account.''[62] This rivalry of the monied aristocracy, moreover, extended beyond the fashionable avenues of Manhattan high life to the ''great cities of the dead that surround New York.'' Between 1897 and 1899, over $1.5 million had been invested in more than one hundred palatial mausoleums. The Vanderbilt vault was one of the more magnificent of these monuments to plutocracy: ''It is forty feet in height, sixty in breadth, and about one hundred and fifty in depth, and contains places for two hundred sleepers.'' Situated on twenty-one acres of land and valued at between $500,000 and $1 million, this tomb (and rival sites as well) boasted of strict security measures against ''resurrectionists.''[63] Very likely, the swelling chorus of protest directed against the ''nobility of Croesus'' contributed to their paranoiac apprehensions about their property and about their persons, both in this life and the next.

The social criticisms of *Yellow Kid*, for example, ranged from good-natured jesting to biting satire. The taste of the Four Hundred was a readily available target: ''Rural Relative (in New York)—I suppose that young lady in that fine carriage belongs to the 400 doesn't she? City Host—Guess not. She's too pretty."[64] There was also the situation of the "Gotham Girl" who was unable to break into Society: "When I was abroad I wasted my time among art galleries and old ruins, instead of staying in London and picking up English slang."[65] In yet another instance, when her dressmaker informed "Society Belle" that a half yard of material was needed to complete the train on her gown, she replied: "Well, take it off the neck."[66]

Far more damning than these mild forays against fashion were *Yellow Kid*'s sharp satiric comments on the young man of leisure or the playboy—the Dude, the Chappy or Cholly, the Gayboy, or the Gilded Youth. This leisured gentleman was, in the first place, a delicate social flower; in one instance, a "Chorus of Other Chappies" gathered around a "Melancholy Chappie" to watch him commit suicide by smoking a cigar;[67] again, "Cholly Chapleigh (with chattering teeth)," upon spotting some murderous looking tramps, asked his female companion to "T-t-t-try to talk real g-g-g-gruff to them and make them think y-y-y-you're a man."[68] The Gilded Youth was not only light-hearted but also feather-headed; thus, "Chappie" observed that it was fortunate that his set had hair on their heads because "if we didn't how could any one tell the backs of our heads from our faces?"[69] Again, "Chapleigh" asked "Satira" to explain why "the character 0" had been chosen to stand "for naught," and she replied that it was "the shape of a dude's head."[70]

The absurdities of fashion and the asininities of gilded youth constituted only a part of the indictment against society. The social climbing of "The Snob" was another count against the so-called values of the new upper class, for although he "was descended from five murderers, ten horse thieves, a counterfeiter, seven robbers (and poor ones at that. Not robber barons you will observe, but barren robbers), a rogue or two, some spendthrifts, a knight of the road, and assassins, conspirators, and regicides ad lib," he had only "to adopt some ancestors and change it all."[71] The plutocracy's vulgar display of its riches and its seeming disregard for the well-being of the lower classes were criticized often; moreover, its tendency to emphasize the gulf between "the two nations" was regarded as a still more serious matter. Slumming and "hard times parties" were met with marked hostility:

The Hard Times Party given by the *creme de la creme* of New York society was, to use the expression coined for the occasion by a brilliant young newspaper man, "one of the most enjoyable events of the season." Garrets and cellars were ransacked for old and cast-off garments and the effect was ludicrous.

Mrs. Van Rentsarelow Sugar appeared in a costume that she had worn twice before. Her embarrassment wore off (her embarrassment not the costume), as the evening progressed. Mrs. "Fweddy" Wanderbuilt wore a costume decorated with point lace over three hundred years old. She appeared as a beggar girl and diamonds representing tears were tastefully sprinkled down the front of her dress. Mrs. Bogden Hills wore a placard set in rubies that read "I am starving." To carry out the effect she munched at angel cake throughout the evening. Mrs. Daring Heavens was gorgeous and glittering as Mary

Queen of Scots. She chose the character because historians refer to her as "poor Mary Stuart." Mr. Whisperhard Youart created great amusement by wearing a full dress suit with the price mark "Only $75" still on it. He said the bad fit gave him a bad fit. He was wittier than usual. Mr. Brockton Holt emphasized his appreciation of poverty by wearing a full dress necktie that was "bought tied" instead of "tied by himself," and a pair of reversible cuffs. These are but few, however, of the many amusing features. The cards to the lunch-room (refreshments by Meldonico) were labelled "Soup Tickets." Each dance had an appropriate air written for the occasion. Some of them were "Papa's Clipping Coupons All Alone," "We Dine but Thrice a Day Now, Mother," "Once a Watch, Now a Ticket," "Papa, I've Come Home to Board," "They Will Not Give Us Any Work To Do," "My Income's Only Fifty Thou. a Year," etc., etc.[72]

The "many amusing features" of the society ball, that "bacchanalian jambouree," were treated with scorn by many observers of urban America;[73] equally unwelcome was the *noblesse oblige* of the wealthy. "A rich countess has come to Chicago on her yacht," reported *The Public*, "to provide for the poor. She proposes to turn her yacht into a coffee kitchen where the hungry may be fed, and to build a factory where the unemployed may find work at low wages. We have no intention of reflecting upon the good feeling and good faith of this woman. . . . But we cannot avoid recalling in this connection Tolstoi's words, when he said that the rich are willing to do anything for the poor except get off their backs."[74] The editors of this same journal were similarly unimpressed with the news that "an entirely new fad in the way of doing good to the poor and 'regulating their lives,' is to be undertaken this summer in New York. Some of the swell women are to spend a week 'right down in the slums.' . . . To emphasize their picturesqueness, they are to dress with becoming simplicity in white muslin caps, gray print gowns and blue neckerchiefs. The great pity of all this mockery," *The Public* editorialized, "is that the rich women who engage in it sincerely imagine that they are useful."[75]

Many social critics held that, because of the great gulf that they had created between the two nations, the so-called "upper classes" suffered from an "uneasy conscience"; moreover, they maintained, this crisis of conscience had developed at too slow a pace.[76] An editor of *Open Church* regretted that his contemporaries in the business world had decided to play "the part of a Napoleon," a role distinguished by its "colossal selfishness." "Many of our best church people seem to think," he continued, "that it is right and proper for a man to use the wonderful talents of organization which God has given him to make himself a 'captain of industry,' not for the benefit of the people at large, but for his own benefit, in order to amass for himself a great fortune." A superior model for the representative man was to be found in the life of George Washington, who was "morally the greater man" and who "left behind him, not only to his nation, but also to the world, a much richer and better heritage than did Napoleon."[77] An even sharper contrast of representative men was that made by *The Public* between the man of wealth and Jesus Christ. Taking issue with Lyman Abbott's view that Christ, had he been living in the nineteenth century, would have been a capitalist, *The Public* maintained with consistent single-tax logic that: "He could not be an Astor, for instance, living in luxury upon the increment of city land, to which all contribute; nor a Rockefeller, drawing fabulous sums from the monopoly of mineral resources and rights of way for pipe lines. . . . It is unthinkable that Christ, if he were here, would, like them, be a wealthy man"; instead, he would be found "making furniture in Grand Rapids, digging coal in Pennsylvania, or hammering on some anvil, or following a plough."[78]

The concentration of wealth and power in the United States had created, Speed Mosby argued, a "piratical fraternity of multi-millionaires," who subsisted, "like the regal plunderers of Europe, upon the fruits of privilege. They are an untitled nobility. The sunshine scintillates upon their gilded palaces in every great city of our land; but in the same cities there are dens of squalid misery and want, where the sunbeams never penetrate, and where no kindly ray dispels the darkness of despair that lurks within." "We are face to face with as great a crisis as ever threatened any republic since Rome first trembled at the glance of Caesar."[79] The editors of *The Commons* also foresaw a coming revolution, one inspired, not by the proletariat, but by the plutocracy. "A good deal of exaggerated nonsense," they observed, "is talked and written about the alleged degeneration of public spirit and political character in this country, but it is no exaggeration and it is high time to say that the welfare of this country and the perpetuity of its peace and of its fundamental institutions are threatened to-day, not by wild-eyed economic fanaticism, not by erratic financial theories, not by indiscriminate immigration, nor by free trade, nor by high tariff, nor by the growth of any foreign religious dominion, but by the insidious growth and inculcation of the idea that financial success is the standard by which men's actions are to be judged, that property is more sacred than human life and liberty and honor." Anarchy was indeed to be dreaded, but "the 'anarchist' whom we need to fear in these days is the man who tramples under foot the rights of his fellow-men, who by the power of wealth forces his will upon the people in spite of their protesting helplessness." This type of anarchy had caused "the downfall of the great nations of the past," and it now threatened the United States.[80]

Defenders of the status quo were also ready to admit that "the ruin of Rome and the desolation of Babylon await the American Republic"; however, the downfall of the established order would be the result of a failure to control the lower classes. "It is patent to the most casual observer of passing events in our social history that we are on the highway to ruin, rushing thereto in delirium with frightful velocity. . . . The engineer is whistling for breaks [sic], and they must be set at once, wherever they are, or the momentum with which we are now moving down this awful incline will carry us to utter destruction."[81] To the editors of *The Public*, the defenders of the established order seemed more intent upon using force than words in the social struggle. With the outbreak of the war with Spain, 1,063 of 1,067 members of New York's Seventh Regiment voted against enlisting. "New Yorkers seem to regard this as an act of cowardice; but the real reason may be the one given by the members of the regiment, that they do not wish to mix with social inferiors." Indeed, "what the Seventh appears to be fitted for in the way of fighting is strike duty. Against unarmed workingmen it might make a warlike record. Why not detail it to the coal regions of Pennsylvania, where it could shoot fleeing coal miners in the back?"[82]

The likelihood of open conflict between the upper and lower classes of urban America, a topic fearfully alluded to in the postwar decades, was openly debated in the final years of the century; however, dire predictions of class warfare seem to have had the primary purpose of warding off such a calamity by reforming, not revolutionizing, the existing social balance. "The history of the city, her past, may be summed up in a word," sociologist Franklin H. Giddings instructed: "it has been the attempt of the elite to evict the crowd. Is her future to be the attempt of the crowd to evict the elite?" The challenge, he concluded, was "to establish an equilibrium of justice between the elite and the crowd," in which both would "undergo the psychological evolution and develop the social consciousness that association should create."[83] Not confrontation, then, but an accommodation between the two halves of urban society seemed to be the pressing need.

THE OTHER HALF

"The other half" was more than a convenient catch phrase coined to describe slum and skid-row inhabitants: the city's center housed not only this "submerged tenth"; it also contained, Levi Gilbert, D.D., asserted, "the five-tenths still struggling to keep from degenerating."[84] Sharp increases in the highest and lowest orders of urban society had been readily discernible since the postwar decades; however, by late century, a radically new pattern of social stratification seemed apparent for, as the upper and lower expanded, the middle class seemed to have diminished in both size and power. "The supposed 'middle class' of wealth owners," George K. Holmes asserted, "exists perhaps as much in appearance as in reality." Contemporary observers had mistaken material display for financial security; in fact, Holmes concluded, the wealthy were closing in on the middle class from one end of the social spectrum, while the lower orders, which already seemed to outnumber the middle, were moving in from the other end.[85] Such expressions of fear were common during this period of social change. To contemporary observers, the patterns of social change remained unclear and, often, they tended to misjudge the direction and degree of class realignments. Moreover, so complex was this restratification that even today scholars continue to debate the extent of social mobility and the nature of changing class relationships in nineteenth-century American society.

Threats of class conflict raised the question of whether a reorganization of society was in order. Two basic principles, University of Chicago sociologist Albion W. Small pointed out, would determine the answer. The first was the essential similarity of all men in their capacity for happiness: although individuals differed, "there is no principle of desire potent in the prince or plutocrat that is

not latent in pauper or peasant." Yet, upper- and lower-class standards of living
were in sharp contrast. While plutocrats reveled in their great palaces, "residents
in every large city know that thousands of children are growing up in their
vicinity in a physical environment unfit for cattle." Small's second principle,
which was based directly upon Jean-Jacques Rousseau's concept of the social
contract, was that whenever a group began "to resolve itself into a society, the
process involves a tacit agreement that some of the persons in the collection will
attend to certain work needed by the society, while others will look after the
remainder." Although "it has been the fashion for a long time to pour indiscriminate ridicule upon" this doctrine, Small asserted, the nation still reserved
the right to punish the ruling class for its evasion of its duties to the lower orders.
Since both of his basic principles had been challenged by a "successful and
arrogant individualism" that had defied "the law of mutualism that must reign
in the right society," Small answered his initial question in the affirmative: a
reorganization of society was necessary. The alternative was social revolution:
"The unrest of our society today is due, in large measure, to suspicion that men
are falling more and more into the position of toilers for other men who are
evading the law of reciprocal service."[86]

"Toil, toil, toil from early morn until late at night; when home they swarm,
tumble into their wretched beds, snatch a few hours of disturbed sleep battling
with vermin in a polluted atmosphere, and then up again to work; and so on and
on in [an] endless, mirthless, hopeless round, until in a few years, consumed
with diseases, mere rotten masses of painful wretchedness, they die. Such,"
lamented the official organ of the American Federation of Labor, "is the situation
today." Instead of "a few hundred palaces . . . supported by the wretchedness
of a million hovels," the nation should be one of "millions of modest but
contented homes."[87] Yet, the "professor" and the "brainy" newspaper editor
and "Sir Bullionaire" blamed mass unemployment, low wages, and poor working conditions on the laborer himself, pointing specifically to the working man's
attachment to city living. "A very popular fad is to advise the workless to 'go
to farming.' Even if capital (of which the workers are minus) was not absolutely
necessary in farming as well as in other ventures, when the would-be farmer
runs up against a few crop failures, battles with the festive potato bug, and falls
into the clutches of the pluck-me store run by the country commission merchant,
he is liable to breed discontent even there." Discontent seemed, inevitably, to
be a characteristic of the age; for, with the threatened disappearance of the
middle class, the nation would be faced with a confrontation between the elite
and the masses. "Revenge cannot bring back the lustre tarnished, but the re-
membrance of a toilsome childhood, a life of dirt, debt and misery, may be in
some degree blotted out in the shadow of a Caesar's Column."[88]

The editors of *The Public* joined vigorously in attacking the "curious superstition . . . that the cities are full of men" and that the agricultural regions might
serve as a safety-valve for urban unrest.[89] It was "one of the vicious tricks of
the prosperity claque . . . to pretend to city workingmen that work at high wages

on farms is abundant. Perhaps it is abundant, but how long will the abundance last? For three weeks or a month," after which such men became "promising candidates for admission to the order of tramps." Then, warned *The Public*, "doleful tales of the tramp pest in farming districts . . . will be circulated . . . by the very prosperity claque to which they will be indebted for having become tramps."[90] Nor was the urban labor problem one of overcrowding. "The very power of city industry consists in minimizing space, working close together. Moreover, there is no lack of space in any city. In no city in all this country is the space half utilized." The problems of labor extended beyond the city's walls to include the entire nation: "It is not overpopulation either in city or country that makes work scarce; it is over-monopoly and consequent under-use of working opportunities."[91]

The abject condition of the toiling masses was recognized, moreover, as the price paid for "progress," the achievement of rapid urbanization and industrialization. The late-century industrial city differed immeasurably from early Lowell, recollected nostalgically by a reviewer in the *Journal of Political Economy* as "a city and a people living in almost Arcadian simplicity, at a time which, in view of the greatly changed conditions of factory labor, may well be called a lost Eden for . . . our working men and working women."[92] This industrial paradise lost had been replaced by an often inhumane economic order, wrote E. D. M'Creary, that exacted "great sacrifices of human life . . . in carrying on the great industrial system of modern civilization." The abuses of the new economic order were at their worst "in what are called the 'sweat shops' in our great cities"; here were found "the most inhuman disregard of the health, comfort, and even life of . . . employees. In one of these dens where the roof was like a sieve, exposing the workmen to rain and storm, the employer, on being asked why he did not repair the roof, churlishly replied, 'Because men are cheaper than shingles.' In another, where a large number of women and girls were engaged in sewing on machines, the employer, on being interrogated as to why he did not have the machines run by steam-power, brutally replied, 'Legs are cheaper than steam.' "[93]

Those very symbols of commercial progress, the "business blocks shooting upward" in downtown urban America, exacted an incredibly heavy tribute in human life. "Travelers from the United States of Africa will stand in the twenty-fifth century with awe and curiosity beside the monster buildings of lower Broadway, and wonder what sort of people planned such structures with their hundreds of little windows and pigeon-hole rooms." These future tourists would indeed be shocked to learn "that the men who were the actual builders of those skyscrapers and bridges were worked ten hours a day, paid less for a day's wages than would buy a front seat to see 'Zaza,' and were either killed or disabled in ten years"; they would be appalled to hear that, in New York State alone, twelve hundred of these workers had been killed or maimed in the year 1900; "it is not likely that a very high opinion will be formed of present-day civilization."[94]

The degrading working conditions in urban America contributed significantly to lower-class unrest, and this unrest led to disorder and violence. Chicago's Chief of Police McClaughry, at a session of the Pinkerton Investigating Committee of the United States Senate, "expressed his opinion that 'the reason the police do not deal more successfully with labor troubles is that they are so intimately entwined in political deals, and therefore cannot be so impartial as they might be.' " A politically independent police force would be able "to protect the peace and property of the city."[95] Spokesmen for labor, on the other hand, felt that the police had dealt too "successfully" with labor disputes and that Chief McClaughry's version of safeguarding "the peace and property" of the community might degenerate into "the Homestead-Chicago method" of dealing with the labor question.

> The process seems to be first to oppress or cheat the workmen; then to insult their representatives or repudiate their unions and refuse to consider all overtures for arbitration, leaving the laborers no alternative but to strike. Then, at an enormous cost to the community, to call out an extra police force to give encouragement and protection to a few incompetent ne'er-do-we'els temporarily to take the place of strikers to bluff the public into the belief that there are multitudes of competent men ready and willing to accept the conditions against which the strikers are protesting; and when, by this series of unfair tactics, the laborers or their sympathizers are goaded into a breach of the peace, the strike is terminated in favor of the corporations by bayonet and bullets.[96]

The "Haymarket-Chicago method" had been developed, according to *The Public*, by "plutocratic interests": "What the plutocratic press of Chicago called a riot, and worked up so sensationally to justify President Cleveland's invasion of a state with federal troops for local police purposes, had no other basis than a conspiracy of railroad magnates. They caused some of their own rolling stock to be destroyed, by their own employees, for the purpose of making out the appearance of a case of riot against the strikers."[97] A "shrewd entrepreneur," moreover, might even create a strike situation for quick financial gain. A Chicago builder, S. V. Lindholm reported, faced with rising prices for construction materials, once he could be certain that "feverish prices have reached a climax or are near it, . . . will endeavor to postpone his business operations until he can make his calculations on a reduced price level. If he can precipitate this crisis by causing a shock to the market, his reputation for sagacity does not suffer. No better way to attain these ends could be found than to paralyze the business altogether by a general labor blockade."[98]

The workingman, pitted openly against these Machiavellian lions and foxes of the business arena, had also to contend with a different breed of labor exploiter. The "sweater," often portrayed as a ruthless and brutal capitalist, was in many cases a hard-pressed Jewish immigrant who earned less than his best-paid workers. "This meek little man" was guilty, explained social work authority Joseph Lee, primarily of having taken the gospel of success too seriously. He saw himself "not as a laborer but as a future capitalist. He has the courage and the capacity for looking toward the future to begin saving even then, calculating

how long it will take him, by a judicious use of these savings, to become a
Rothschild or a Seligman.''[99]

For his struggle against economic exploitation, from without and within,
contemporary spokesmen for the worker recommended governmental inspection
and regulation of specified working conditions, stronger and more effective
unions, and a shorter work week. As was to be expected, *American Federationist*
concerned itself primarily with unionization; but it was left to that champion of
organization, *Gunton's Magazine*, to propose a national "Labor Senate," which
would consist of a joint board of management and labor to be organized for the
attainment of the legal rights of workers.[100] Other friends of labor were more
concerned with an immediate shortening of working hours. For example, since
his first visit to industrial England in 1865, the brutalizing impact of overwork
had been apparent to Dr. U. M. Weideman: "I stood one summer day in 1865
on old London bridge and made an attempt to count the hunchbacks, the cripples,
the palsied, and others of the unmistakable victims of the iron hand of bad pay
and overwork. The task was beyond my ability to perform." Now, he continued,
this same ruthlessness of industrialization was "rapidly honeycombing the cities
and towns of our own land with a population of the same kind." Only higher
pay and shorter working hours could bring an end to this mass martyrdom.[101]
The alternative was the continued brutalization of the working masses, a situation
summed up in "The Dialogue of the Spirits," a poem in which the conscience
of History asked the voice of Progress to " 'Tell us, how about your men?/
Shall they,' " despite the great scientific and advantages of the age, " 'like live
automatons, still drudge their lives away . . . ?' " History cautioned Progress
" 'in this climax of the years:/Make no machine of man.' ''[102]

If the machine was not adopted to symbolize the fate of the lower classes,
the jungle was; if the masses were not to be manipulated into automatons, they
might be transformed into animals. "The 'dark city' and the 'dark continent'
were alike mysterious" for British writers on urban themes, historian Asa Briggs
has observed, "and it is remarkable how often the exploration of the unknown
city was compared with the exploration of Africa and Asia."[103] There remained,
nonetheless, an alternative to a full recognition of the brutalizing impact of
industrialization on the proletariat: urban America was able to face the existence
of the slum and, simultaneously, ease its social conscience by romanticizing
poverty. This might be accomplished by the author, often a poet, assuming the
Whitmanesque posture of the classless comrade: "Here's to my brother, the
broken bum,/And here's to the girl gone wrong,/And here's to all the refuse of
men,/The miserable, destitute throng."[104] More frequently, the lower classes
were transformed into colorful, serio-comic characters: to complement the fashionable dude, Gilded Youth, and Chappy, the slums offered their own gamin,
street urchin, and Chimmie Fadden. Chimmie, created by Edward W. Townsend,
was New York's answer to Chicago's Mr. Dooley; the humor of his situation,
Bookman editor Arthur Bartlett Maurice observed, stemmed from "the fact that
Mr. Townsend forces us to look upon life, while reading, with Chimmie's eyes

and from Chimmie's point of view."[105] Literature of this order, according to a contemporary critic, promised not only a "change of subject-matter" in its desertion of "the groves of Daphne," but it also held out "a new angle of vision." "Doubly difficult is the portrayal of the child of the slums, so different in his careworn precocity, his brute-like adaptability to harsh conditions, from the little ones in the homes of wealth. . . . Those who have eyes to see must recognize that in the child of the slums we have the saddest, the most threatening product of our modern civilisation."[106] Nonetheless, critics who were able to portray Boss Croker as a highland chief were equally capable of picturing children of the streets as elfin blithe spirits: "Their ready wit, tact and pluck is truly wonderful, and so thoroughly American that it savors of Yankeeism. . . . Nurtured under the very stamp of horses' hoofs, they seem to grow like weeds in a country garden patch; and dart and glide through the labyrinth of cable cars, wagons and carts like a bird that flashes through the tangled wildwood."[107]

The romantic characterization of the gamin, like that of the dude, more often contained at least a touch of social criticism. Thus, Johnny Looney, with his knees on roller-skates and a tin can in hand, explained to Swipes the Bootblack: "I'm goin' up de avenoo t' do de creepin' game and beg. Dere's no use tryin' to make a honest livin' no longer. D' yez know any mug wot's got a dawg to lend?"[108] In another instance, when an "Old Lady" asked a "Street Urchin" why he was crying, he answered that he was " 'Fraid." "Old Lady—Afraid? . . . I didn't know you street gamins were ever afraid of anything, seen or unseen, in this world or the next. Street Urchin—Y-e-s, we're 'fraid of—of each other."[109] A comment on a sketch of the Yellow Kid, the prototype of the gamin, in the first issue of the magazine so named, pointed out his "bald head (on a boy), the two teeth, the abnormal feet, the formless shirt of yellow—color of decay—covering a multitude of other abnormalities. Every street gamin possesses the same characteristics in a less exaggerated degree, and that is why the Yellow Kid cannot die while degeneracy exists and degerates."[110]

The substandard residential district or "slum," that breeding ground of urban ills, was more often described in realistic than romantic terms. In many poems, for example, the narrator, as he guided his readers through slum areas, seemed intent upon overwhelming his audience with a surfeit of appalling detail—of "vile human smells," of the "moist, pallid faces" of exhausted workingmen, of children "screaming in dirt as they play," of "woe-begone women, with babes at the breast," of conditions that would "make angels despair."[111] Another poet described "Black, slimy passages [that] worm through the block/Like roots, and midway burst in hideous flower/Of fetid courts—foul, formless, vague, that shock/Like some abortion born to make an hour."[112]

Perhaps the most singular quality of the slum was the contrast it presented with every other aspect of urban living. The contrast with the "nobility of Croesus" was immediate and inevitable: while the plutocracy amused itself by weekending at such "little summer and winter villa" cities as Lakewood, New Jersey; while it retreated from the summer's heat to such vacation palaces as

George J. Gould's "Georgian Court" with its polo grounds, tennis courts, skating rink, private theater, swimming pool, and gymnasium grouped around the two-block long main building with its 116 bedroom suites; while it was closing the $500, gold-inlaid door of the villa to the problems of the teeming cities, "700 babies died in the city of Brooklyn alone" during one week.[113] A still more basic contrast in the central city was between the liveliness of fashionable society and business and the pervasiveness of death among the poor. The slum seemed to place the lowest possible value on human life. "In any great city of the world you can buy a first-class baby for less money than will buy a second-class dog. Usually you can get a first-class baby for nothing. You can never get a fairly good dog on such terms. . . . The joke seems to be on poor old mother Nature."[114] As a final contrast, "the joke" seemed also to be on basic American traditions: although loyal citizens decorated "with lavish hand/The 'graves of the blue and gray,' " they ignored the fallen of more recent battles, "The heroes of toil and pain,/Who always have to yield,/Of love and hope and of courage slain,/In . . . dismal Potters' Field."[115]

Almost without exception, misery was accepted as the basic condition of slum living, and descriptions of life among the "submerged tenth" differed more in degree than in kind. The editors of the settlement house journal *The Commons*, for example, attacked "the popular notion that among those known as 'the poor,' the real suffering is limited to the winter time. Those who live and observe in the underprivileged sections of the great cities know that there scarcely could be greater suffering for human beings than in those breathless noons and nights when the thermometer's sluggish variations were between 95 and 105 degrees. . . . A tour at night through the streets of Chicago's crowded quarters exhibited conditions of suffering almost incredible."[116] Significantly, *The Commons* did not deem it necessary to preface this description (or others) with even the briefest of arguments about suffering being endemic to slum life: the general condition of substandard living areas was almost universally accepted in the final fifteen years of the century, and only the particulars demanded extended comment. Increasingly then, moralistic lamentations over the plight of the urban poor gave way to detailed analyses of specific locales. A representative example of this type of study was that done by *The Commons* of the Kansas City "Patch," a two-block area that bore "the poetical pseudonym of 'Armourdale.' The land is owned partly by corporations and partly by an individual. Altho the occupancy looks as if it might be by right of 'squatter sovereignty,' the site of each shanty is leased by its owner for two dollars per month. There are almost one hundred of what, by poetic license, may be dignified as 'houses.' " Only two of these buildings were of more than one story, and all contained no more than "three small, low, ill-ventilated and poorly lighted rooms. None of these habitations is connected with either the sewer or the water system. . . . Water is supplied by 'driven wells'—driven thro the low, marshy 'bottom' land, polluted by the neighboring packing house and stock yard drainage and by the outhouses which are shared with the inhabitants by their cows, horses and pigs. No provision has been made for streets, in place of which are irregular, unpaved, winding alleys, from eight to ten feet wide, which reek with filth, are rank with noisome stenches and swarm with children.'' The Patch boasted a population of nearly 1,200 Austrian, Polish, Italian, German, Afro-American men, and one Irishman. They were, for the most part, unmarried; and they either lived in boarding houses or established ''clubs'' for themselves, hiring women to do their housework. There were on the ''Kansas side of 'The Bottoms' twenty-two saloons, more than half of which flank 'the Patch,' besides which, on Saturday nights, wagons from rival breweries unload kegs and half-barrels at nearly every door, and then 'the very dances of death begin, lasting till early Monday morning.' There is said to be no need of 'bad houses.' Criminals from both cities of the two states are said to flee to this City of Refuge to lose themselves in its safe hiding.''[117] From such an environment, society could expect only a criminal and pauper class; in fact, Clare de Graffenreid, a pioneer investigator of working conditions for women and children, claimed that such environments had transformed ''the ethnic type'' into ''a misshapen being. The form is stoop-shouldered, the legs bowed, the gait shambling, the eye dim and the skin pallid.''[118]

To many observers, the ''ethnic type'' seemed to personify the crisis of urban America; such people not only inhabited, but also created the sprawling slums. (For the most part, native rural immigrants, though numerous, seemed less visible and were, consequently, largely overlooked.) There was the increasing danger, political economist Thomas E. Will warned, that the central city would become unmanageable—''the 'dumping ground of Europe's filth' ''; that the municipality ''composed of a congeries of nationalities, representing all Europe and much of the world, each holding aloof as far as possible from all the others,'' would foster social anarchy.[119] There was an equal threat that each urban center would come under the control of a single ethnic group. The Public reprinted predictions from the French scientific journal Cosmos that ''the capital of the German kingdom . . . will be in Chicago; that of the French, New Orleans; while New York will be at the head of the United States, now including only New England and the middle states, San Francisco is to remain as a sort of free city in her Chinese environment. 'Thus,' comments Cosmos, 'will end a great and beautiful experience in democracy.' '' This account, The Public editorialized, ''is not from a humorous journal, but is put forth as a genuine deduction from sociological premises.''[120] That many contemporary observers took such predictions with the utmost of seriousness must have been at least apparent, if not understandable, to the enlightened editors of The Public. To J. F. Bartlett, D.D., it was obvious that ''America is no longer Americanizing Europe, but Europe is DE-Americanizing America. The flag is not secure to-day,'' he warned. ''It trembles on its standard. . . . America is not what she was fifty years ago, and there are not many of the native stock who do not feel that there are some elements present in the body politic which are a menace to prosperity and peace, and not ministers of blessing and prophets of hope.''[121] Indeed, America was not ''what she was fifty years ago,'' and recognition of her changed condition had been sharpening throughout the latter part of the century.

Bridget and Paddy were still the targets of occasional satire. An Irish lass "fresh from Castle Garden,'' after having informed her mistress of the variety of groceries on hand, confessed that she was unable to prepare dinner: "Oi do not see ony pot down there big enough to howld thim all, mum.''[122] In another instance, the "knight Terence of Hoolihan'' offered himself to the "Countess Irene'' of Harlem—all that's left of me after scrappin' wid a nagur.''[123] Nevertheless, Bridget and Paddy, representing the "old'' immigration, were rapidly giving way to a new ethnic comic character—Einstein or Moses Swipestein, the money-grubbing Jew, embodying the "new.'' A crass materialism was presented as the distinguishing characteristic of the Jewish immigrant: "Einstein—Vas you on vriendly terms mid him? Issacstein—Cerdainly; ninety tays!''[124] "Bowery Bill—(threateningly)—Say, was youse d mug wot give me de laff jes' now? Einstein—(indignantly)—Did you efer know me to kiff away somedings for noddings?''[125] What is more, the assorted "Steins'' seemed readily identifiable by their physiognomies: "Nodd—Einstein is always sticking his nose into my business. Todd—Your business must be very extensive.''[126] The substitution of the grasping Shylock for the ape-like son of Erin reflected significant population changes; in addition, this shift from one stereotype to another followed changes in the political balance of power within the large cities. Jews and other new immigrants made more convenient—and safer—targets than the descendants of the old immigration. Native politicians were able, as a result of this shift in emphasis, to court established ethnic power groups, play upon deep-seated prejudices, and discriminate against powerless immigrants. In this manner, nativist spokesmen were able to advocate "racial'' superiority and, by adopting tactics of divide and conquer, adjust their teachings to the reality of the ethnic power structure.[127]

The new nativism relied upon the so-called lessons of history for intellectual support and respectability. The mass invasion by "beggarly, law-despising, God-hating hordes which sweep over our land from Continental Europe, to the jeopardy of our liberties and of our national peace and prosperity'' invited, predictably, comparisons with the fall of ancient Rome.[128] "Unlike the ancient pagan, we invite the 'stranger' and 'barbarian' to the midst of us, offering to them as rights our dearly-bought, and, theoretically, highly-prized privileges.'' Not only did the strangers and barbarians accept the invitation, but they came "in hordes,'' many from that "class which took refuge with David at the cave of Adullam. Some have written their names in blood in Chicago; and we are told, taken their children to hear the theory propounded that no man's property is his own, and that death is the penalty for possession.''[129] To such pseudohistorical arguments against the new immigration were added those of pseudoscience. The lengths to which racial theorists were prepared to go in order to attain intellectual respectability may be seen in the following late-century analysis: anthropo-sociology, the science of the "ethnic factor," divided the races into the *Homo Europaeus* (the dolichocephalic or Aryan), *Homo Alpinus* (the bracycephalic), and the Mediterranean type. *Homo Europaeus* surpassed *Homo Alpinus* in wealth, inventiveness, and adaptability to urban living: "*Important cities are almost always located in the dolichocephalic regions or in the least brachycephalic parts of brachycephalic regions.*" The pressures of city living created, thereby, a "Law of Urban Elimination": "*Urban life acts as an agency of selection in favor of the dolichoids and destroys or rejects the most brachycephalic elements.*" The lower orders, the Mediterranean types, this analysis concluded, were totally unfit for urban environments.[130] Translated into standard English, this pseudoscientific gobbledegook meant that the native American (*Homo Europaeus*) naturally took precedence over the old immigrant (*Homo Alpinus*), and that the new immigrant (the Mediterranean) had no place in American society. This was science. Opposition to it was rank emotionalism. Those who argued that the inferior races had been and could be assimilated into the mainstream of American society, economist-statistician Richard Mayo-Smith countered, "do not consider what will happen if we run in a lot of chaff, or even a little dynamite occasionally. Such idealists pay no regard to any theories of the mixture of races, either biological, sociological, or historical." Such idealists, in short, were unscientific and, therefore, anti-intellectual. Environmentalism was a part of this scientism. The nation had in the past, the argument ran, promoted "self-reliance" and a "capacity for self-government" through the conditioning of "frontier life"; now, however, first- and second-generation immigrants, although they made up 32.9 percent of the population, were concentrated "in towns and cities where these primitive influences are not felt. In this respect each succeeding generation of immigrants escapes more and more the immersion into the chilly but bracing waters of a social life where each man counted for what he was worth. It was in many respects a cruel test, yet the opportunities were great, and the reward for the survivors correspondingly great."[131] Mass immigration, according to the economic argument, made the monetary rewards for all, both native and foreign, necessarily smaller: "The struggles of the wage workers for a higher living, for more independence, for greater opportunities is rendered more desperate by the constant addition of others more helpless than themselves, having no understanding of affairs, and who, accustomed to lower standards of living, make possible the sweat-shop and the slums." This new and seemingly permanent proletariat was unlike "the hardy, independent and intelligent people who came from England, France, Ireland,"—Paddy, finally, had passed—"Scandinavia, Holland, Denmark and Belgium and settled upon the wild lands and built independent communities." It would have been far better for the new immigrants to stay at home and reform their own countries.[132] The English observer Arnold White gave this last recommendation a Machiavellian twist by reminding Americans that the "Russian Exodus" was part of the czar's plan to rid his empire of "chronic incurable paupers"; should the United States exclude these Jewish refugees, it would hasten a long overdue revolution in Russia and pit America and England against the Russian despotism. "There is," White assured his transatlantic audience, "little sentiment in this matter of immigration. It is a business matter."[133] In fact, of course, sentiment—better still, prejudice—outweighed pragmatic considerations.

The peculiar status of the black citizen in the urban community—old settler and new "problem"—took form in the final years of the century; it, too, was shaped by emotional, not logical reactions. The black migrant from the rural South was regarded often as a perennial child. " 'Following the band,' " Irene Rowland observed, "is the height of human happiness in the darky mind; the young girls dance to the music in a comical fashion all their own, the young fellows cakewalk to the tune of 'Hail Columbia,' the pickaninnies shout for very glee, and indeed, 'when the band plays,' all Darktown seems to be doing its very best to prove that, in spite of all that city life and city ways have done to make the negro the counterpart of his discontented white brethren, he is still a soul made for merriment and music, and that he still holds the secret for the ingredient in the recipe of life which makes it all happiness and sunshine." The potential of the race was clearly limited, but the well-educated and talented African-American might eventually become "a valuable assistant in business houses, as type writer, stenographer, and even secretary. He shows traces of his slave heredity in a pleasing, child-like docility that is neither servile nor officious."[134] Attempts by black urbanites to create their own social hierarchies were, however, met with ridicule. Kate Carter defined the African Methodist Episcopal Church of Harlem, West Side, as "a congregation of colored aristocracy of upper Manhattan Island, haughty unto exclusiveness, tolerant of no other creed, boastful always, and as clannish in every way as it is black." This "colored aristocracy," although it might cover itself in the trappings of wealth, was often ridiculed in the popular press.[135]

Not only words but actions, too, were directed increasingly against urban blacks. *Public Improvements*, for example, reported that "for the first time in the history of Virginia, and probably in the United States, separate cars for negroes are now being run on the street railway at Norfolk." The Virginia legislature had reacted to complaints from white passengers that their clothes had been dirtied from contact with black coal trimmers on the cars and passed this segregation ordinance. "Many of the negroes took kindly to the innovation," according to this account, "while others grumbled, although no objection was made. It is said that 'trailer' cars for negroes will be put on every line in the city."[136] In northern communities as well, Guy Carleton Lee pointed out, there was growing pressure for racial separation. The antebellum "free negro" in Carlisle had been subjected to a minimum of prejudice; however, the postwar "freed negro" threatened the stability of this Pennsylvania town. Carlisle whites generally (and predictably) respected "the older negroes, for they, as a rule, are polite, hardworking citizens"; members of the younger generation, on the other hand, were regarded as "worthless, indolent loafers, immoral, criminal, a sorrow to their parents and a curse to the community."[137] As there were "good" and "bad" immigrants, the old and the new, so too there were "good" and "bad" blacks. In both instances, the group's worthiness was determined by its place in society, that is, whether it had already established its position in the urban community.

That the settlement of southern African-Americans in northern urban centers constituted a "problem" was recognized by their friends and foes alike. Although their enemies in the South encouraged migration to the North, the editors of *The Public* warned that if large numbers of blacks decided to leave the South, "the same whites that now lynch them upon suspicion of crime would lynch them for attempting to go away. This is no unfounded suspicion. It is precisely what the whites did at the time of the negro exodus of 20 years ago."[138] Yet *The Public*, although it was genuinely sympathetic to the improvement of the black man's position in American life, maintained that "what has made negro oppression in this country possible, is a perversion of the conquering disposition of the white race and of the affectional disposition of the blacks. These qualities—the disposition to conquer and the disposition to serve—when not degraded, are not hostile but complementary."[139] This racist judgment takes on special significance, since it was pronounced by one of the most egalitarian magazines of the period. A more realistic analysis was offered by Monroe N. Work in his sociological study of the high crime rate among Chicago blacks. "Of all the peoples dwelling in Chicago's slums," Work pointed out, "The negroes are the most neglected. They are the ones that need the most done for them"; they were the ones who had been deserted by the churches and neglected by the settlements. Although he believed that there were "race characteristics peculiar" to Afro-Americans which contributed to their low state, Work concluded that black citizens would be able to transcend this present "economic phase" of their "transitional state" between slavery and freedom with improved economic opportunities.[140] W.E.B. Du Bois's study of black Philadelphia documented the economic handicaps under which the urban black labored and revealed a situation "which, on the whole," a reviewer noted, "is anything but creditable to our civilization, our Christianity, or our boasted freedom of the north." Du Bois's analysis documented "a system of industrial exclusion that is most far-reaching in its results,—tending on the one hand to poverty and crime, and on the other to the discouragement of any attempt to rise in the scale of civilization, because of the almost impossible difficulties placed in the way of securing employment."[141]

"There has been so much talk, both North and South, about the condition and progress of the American negro that it is quite time that we have some results of accurate observation laid before us as a basis for future discussions." The first such study, duly welcomed by the *Annals*, was the one-hundred-page compilation of statistics in the May 1897 *Bulletin* of the Department of Labor.[142] The second was the calling of the Atlanta Conference on Negro City Life in the same month. The major achievement of this meeting was the completion of a survey of the black populations of eighteen American cities (all but one—Cambridge, Massachusetts—in the South) by more than 300 prominent "colored men" which concluded that housing was not, on the whole, substandard; that, nevertheless, the use of a single room by one family for cooking, eating, living, and sleeping was common; that black home ownership was rare; that its birth rate, both legitimate and illegitimate, exceeded that of the white population; that black children began life with "good constitutions," a finding based on low rates of rickets; that while "malarial fever" was the most common malady, other unknown diseases were prevalent; and that although the black death rate greatly exceeded that of the whites, it had decreased markedly in the past fourteen years. The still relatively high mortality rates, the conference concluded, were due not to "environment and the sanitary condition of houses," but to "ignorance and disregard of the laws of health." This finding was of "vast importance": "since the excessive death rate is not due to these causes, there is reason for the belief that it may be reduced without regard to the present economic conditions of the colored people." The solution to the problems of the urban black was the classic one of self-help: "It appears that the negro must reform himself, and that he is not dependent upon charity or municipal regulations, but has the means in his own hand."[143]

Their well-wishers were often quick to recommend to the various ethnic and racial minorities some form of self-help. Any national threat from unrestricted immigration, Joseph H. Senner of Ellis Island argued, was "very much exaggerated in a country where suffrage is distributed with so little discrimination that millions of half-savage negroes enjoy the right of suffrage, while our intelligent and highly cultured women are precluded from availing themselves of its privilege." Senner's "lynx-eyed" colleagues in the Immigration Service would hold back the diseased, insane, and criminal; the decent immigrants would take care of themselves. "*Hic Rhodus hic salta*, here is to be found the point where the real solution of the problem follows as a natural sequence: Let each immigrant receive the proper information, enlightenment and guidance, so that he may readily find the place where he can work with best advantage to himself as well as to his adopted country."[144] The immigrant, after all, was worthy of some trust: "Are we Indians? Was not our nation with all its cities created by immigrants and their descendants?"[145] Ellen Battelle Dietrick maintained that immigration had to be viewed as a national, not a local phenomenon: while it contributed to general American wealth, arguments for its restriction came primarily from "the seaport cities, where the poor immigrant is seen in his most miserable estate. Worn out by a voyage taken under conditions which make it a foretaste of the Inferno, uncouthly clad, forlorn, bewildered, unable to make himself understood, he certainly does not have the appearance of a desirable addition to the ranks of citizenship." Nevertheless, he stayed on in the coastal city because "everything possible is done to tempt him to stay there. If he be of the pauper brood," Dietrick advised, "the freemasonry of pauperism has already acquainted him with the multiplicity of devices provided by the rich for making city life easy for non-self-supporting families." Day nurseries; "free" hospitals, dispensaries, almshouses, games; "free warm rooms with books and papers . . . all invite the shiftless to stay and be cared for. If we scatter crumbs for birds, we may be sure the birds will come"; so, too, with the "pauper brood."[146]

That there was a natural cycle of betterment for these ethnic minorities, that their condition could be improved by self-help alone, that the cities were pampering them with welfare services: all of these hypotheses were challenged repeatedly and vigorously. "There is only one thing to do," advised the Rev. W. G. Puddefoot. "Help the people who come to us as only we can help. Build better schools and more of them; have large playgrounds in our slum districts." The negative approach must give way to the positive: "We put up contagious disease hospitals instead of cleaning our streets and abolishing the slums. We sterilize our milk instead of killing the diseased cows. We are shocked at the women who could condemn the dying gladiator, and we rest while 75 per cent of the children of New York City die before they are two years old and every tenth person dies a pauper, and we propose to stop immigration instead of doing our duty and the grandest work God ever gave a nation to perform."[147]

The nation's cities were also called upon to face a special challenge in their core areas as a new social subclass manifested itself in the persons of the homeless and the alienated. The key to this new group was its transiency or mobility; indeed, as an observer in New York remarked of the loiterers in City Hall park, "You never see the same face twice."[148] "In diagnosing the situation" of downtown urban America, model housing advocate Robert Treat Paine observed, "the most salient and important fact is that people are so migratory. Streams of people pour into our cities and soon vanish away."[149] So mobile had the lower orders of the urban population become that *Review of Reviews* editor Albert Shaw joined in referring to it as "the floating population of all large modern cities. . . . It is composed of strangers seeking work; of unfortunate persons who through illness or other mishap have lost their means of livelihood and are unable to pay for a fixed habitation; of the low criminal and semi-criminal classes; of the victims of intemperance and vice; of tramps and of a countless variety of people whom we may term unclassified casuals." The "dangerous classes" of the postwar decades had become, then, the "floating population" of late century. In both periods they were suspect, but even more so in the later years. There seemed to be more of them. Most importantly, Shaw warned, members of the "floating population" threatened to invade the slums and "contaminate and disturb a population several times as numerous as they are themselves"; in order to control this alienated group, it would be necessary for the cities to isolate them by constructing municipal lodging houses, or "poor men's 'Metropoles.' "[150] Indeed, "those wonderful caravansaries" seemed to reflect "the whole tendency . . . toward the barrack plan, where every man lives under marching orders."[151] Regimentation of this sort would benefit the entire nation, *Charities* editor Edward T. Devine advised. The containment of the floating population in major urban centers was preferable to its unhindered movement about the country, because "the city is a better and less dangerous and less expensive place for the vagrant than the country. His migration to the city should be welcomed rather than discouraged. If he is in the city we shall be more conscious of his existence, but for that very reason we shall be better able to deal with him."[152]

The lowest order of the floating population of any great city consisted of "a heavy percentage of men who, to call on an overworked metaphor, are but drifting hulks on the sea of the metropolis."[153] The lowest of the low, the tramp, was sometimes portrayed in serio-comic terms: "Born with a weariness of limb / And mind, beer-soaked and / Tattered like a wind-shorn tree, / He is a sight for gods and men / To sneer at and the dogs to bite. / Merry his soul; nor rain nor snow / Can make his view of life / Less of a joke."[154] A less romantic view of the tramp was taken by Professor John J. McCook of Hartford's Trinity College who concluded that "industrial causes have but little to do with pauperism in general, or vagabondage in particular"; intemperance was the cause, he argued, of better than 60 percent of the cases of pauperism and vagabondage, and society ought to commit "drunkards and vagrants to places of detention where they must abstain from drink, must work, must keep clean, must avoid licentiousness— and that for an indefinite period."[155] Since, "labor is the life of society," a contributor to the *Charities Review* agreed, "the beggar who will not work is a social cannibal feeding on that life—a social highwayman with his hand upon the throat of that society, asking both for its money and its life, and just in proportion as society is greater than the individual, so in proportion is a beggar the highest of criminals."[156] The lowest of the low, then, while regarded as a part of the challenge for a better urban environment by some, were seen as a threat to its stability by others. To both sets of social critics, nevertheless, the lower strata of the other half were as symbolic of the condition of the urban-industrial complex as was its opposite manifestation—the very vigor of its commercial life. American cities could not afford to ignore this other half; indeed, many held, they must reorder it.

TOWARD UPLIFTING THE OTHER HALF

The central city served as the showcase for a business culture. The general agreement of industrial and financial spokesmen on the inevitability of sustained economic development, which despite periodic business upheavals began to take form during the mid–1880s and was all but completed by the late 1890s, had its roots in the increasingly visible signs of affluence in great urban centers. The "business blocks shooting upward," the magnificent department stores, and the construction of park systems and civic centers were all evidence of an improved standard of living. The philosophical foundations of laissez-faire capitalism went largely unchallenged in magazine literature; the American system seemed "triumphant"—its gospel of wealth, as historian Ralph Henry Gabriel has described it, a "fighting faith."[157]

Yet, it could not be denied that social stratification had produced class antagonisms; what was more important, it might lead to class conflict. Obviously,
something had to be done. The excesses of the plutocrats could be contained,
promises of upward mobility were held out to the middle ranges of society,
improved working conditions for skilled labor would follow from economic
expansion and unionization. These groups, in short, would be socialized in time
and, for the most part, by their own initiative. There remained the other half:
concerning them there was, if not a climate of fear, at least a mood of considerable
apprehension.

Late-century urbanists misled their readers as to the essential composition of
this disadvantaged minority. While a large percentage of the urban proletariat
was made up of native, white rural in-migrants, overwhelming attention in the
magazines of the period was centered upon recent foreign immigrants, with
increasing notice paid to native black migrants; moreover, much of this literature
was nativist and racist in tone and message. It is now generally accepted that
American policy, both national and international, became increasingly nativist
and racist during this period; unquestionably, this was the case in the urban
literature. The ethnic minorities must have seemed strange, backward, and pat-
ently un-American. To some, they seemed altogether unassimilable; to others,
they were ingredients for the American melting pot. In either case, they could
not be ignored: proposals were advanced for their exclusion, containment, assimilation. Native whites migrating from the farm to the city, it was assumed,
should become, with little difficulty, participating members of the "better element"; failures from this group, along with some members of the ethnic minorities, it would seem, fell under the vague classification of the "floating
population." Black rural in-migrants, it was generally agreed, would remain
permanently separate.

The essential precondition to uplifting the other half was to distinguish between
those who could be admitted to the greater society and those who should be
excluded. Postwar critics of the urban scene, confronted though they were by
the "dangerous classes," had offered few constructive programs for the achievement of an urban social equilibrium. Their late-century counterparts, conversely,
as in their proposals for political reform and physical planning, were to suggest
a variety of institutional innovations in their drive toward the establishment of
a new metropolitan order. The primary focus in their planning would be the
distinction between the redeemable and irredeemable elements among the lower
orders—those who could be assimilated and those who should be excluded;
hence, the importance of their analyses, with their nativist and racist overtones,
of the ethnic minorities and the floating population. The key consideration in
their process of social selection was whether the individual or group was a
member of the "potential" or "submerged" middle class. By identifying the
"worthy poor" and by providing institutionalized means for their uplift, class
antagonisms would be lessened, class conflict avoided, and the promise of American life fulfilled. The urban core might then reflect the perfection of the new

metropolitan order, one based upon aggressively middle-class values and expectations.

NOTES

1. William Kennedy, *O Albany! Improbable City of Political Wizards, Fearless Ethnics, Spectacular Aristocrats, Splendid Nobodies, and Underrated Scoundrels* (New York: Penguin, 1983), p. 8.

2. "The Rebuilding of New York," *The Social Economist* 5 (December 1893): 329, 327, 328.

3. Edwin Howland Blashfield, "A Word for Municipal Art," *Municipal Affairs* 3 (December 1899): 587.

4. John DeWitt Warner, "Matters That Suggest Themselves," *Municipal Affairs* 2 (March 1898): 123, 125.

5. "*The Social Economist*," *The Social Economist* 1 (March 1891): 1. In redefining its position six years later, this journal maintained: "We repeat, therefore, that *Gunton's Magazine* is neither a 'machine organ,' a 'trust organ,' a 'labor organ,' nor a 'protectionist organ,' but it is the advocate of an economic and political philosophy which recognizes the economic utility and social necessity of concentrated capital and organized labor, without defending the shortsighted greed of narrow capitalists or the impulsive wrongheadedness of superficial labor leaders: a philosophy which recognizes the importance of encouraging and protecting, through government aid if needs be, the development of manufactures and the diversification of industry; and emphasizes the political importance of organized parties, without either defending favoritism in legislation or corrupt bossism in politics" ("Position of *Gunton's Magazine*," ibid. 13 [November 1897]: 366). For background on this journal and its founder, see Jack Blicksilver's "George Gunton: Pioneer Spokesman for a Labor-Big Business Entente," *Business History Review* 31 (Spring 1957): 1–22, which links Gunton to Theodore Roosevelt, Herbert Croly, and the "New Nationalism" of 1912.

6. "The Social Question. As Seen in Magazine Literature," *The Social Economist* 1 (March 1891): 29–30, 31.

7. Theodore Cox, "The Corner Stone of Social Strife," *The Social Economist* 4 (January 1893): 45.

8. "Editorial Crucible," *The Social Economist* 4 (February 1893): 120.

9. "The Economy of the Large," *The Social Economist* 8 (May 1895): 267, 272.

10. "Position," p. 365. The "trust problem" and, for that matter, all aspects of national economic issues extend beyond the range of this study; however, *Gunton's* analyses, because they were concerned with the special relationship between urbanization and industrialization that had been engendered by the centralizing forces of the industrial trust, have been included as important approaches to urban theory.

11. C. D. Chamberlin, "Trusts Vs. the Town," *Gunton's Magazine* 15 (September 1898): 174, 180.

12. "Civic and Educational Notes," *Gunton's Magazine* 17 (August 1899): 134.

13. A. F. Sears, "Commercial Cities," *Banker's Magazine* 39 (June 1885): 887. The comments of social gospel leader Washington Gladden in a lecture at the Chicago Commons settlement house were representative of the contemporary distrust of speculation. Gladden, the settlement's magazine reported, "was especially unsparing in his denunciation of gamblers, 'who produce nothing, distribute nothing, but make their living

at the expense of the community.' Whether they gamble in the cheap hells of the criminal sections of the great cities, or in the more 'respectable' precincts of the stock exchange, they are all parasites, Dr. Gladden said, and so far as the social service is concerned are to be classed with sneak thieves'' (''Social Economic Conference. Earnest Men and Women Discuss the Needs and Aims of Society. Aspects of Human Progress from Many Points of View,'' *Chicago Commons* 1, no. 9 [December 1896]: 4).

14. ''Is the Country Prosperous?,'' *Banker's Magazine* 45 (July 1890): 4.

15. ''Business in Wall Street and Outside,'' *Banker's Magazine* 45 (November 1890): 321, 323.

16. ''Editorial Comment. Development of the Trust,'' *Banker's Magazine* 51 (August 1895): 141.

17. ''Editorial Comment. Prosperous Condition of Business,'' *Banker's Magazine* 58 (January 1899): 14. The very same prediction was made in ''The Course of Financial Empire'' [reprinted from the *Ohio Valley Manufacturer*], *Public Improvements* 2 (April 2, 1900): 242.

18. ''Editorial Comment. A Financial Map of the United States,'' *Banker's Magazine* 61 (September 1900): 335.

19. Charles A. Conant, ''The Financial Future of the United States,'' *Banker's Magazine* 61 (October 1900): 591, 595. Bankers argued also that a measure of social stability might be achieved in cities with established banking facilities. ''It is a singular fact that in cities like New York, Boston, and Philadelphia, where savings banks have been in operation the longest, and where the numbers of depositors is greatest, the masses of the people are the most law-abiding; and, although anarchists and socialists from abroad have lately come among the foreign-born population, to incite to riot and resistance to law, the voice of public opinion has been unanimously against them. . . . While in places like Chicago and Milwaukee, having no savings banks, this class of people, with evil designs, have influenced 'fellows of the baser sort' to riot. . . . It may not, therefore, be claiming too much to say that savings banks have demonstrated that accumulations in them of capital by the masses, whose trustees largely invest in property in the vicinity of the banks and in the bonded debts of the Commonwealths and of the United States. influence the depositors to become more useful and peaceable citizens; for they correctly reason that the safety of their deposits and the certainty of dividends depend primarily on the enforcement of law and the maintenance of order'' (John P. Townsend, ''Savings Banks in the United States,'' *Journal of Social Science* 25 [December 1888]: 106–07).

20. Lindley M. Keasbey, ''The Economic State,'' *Political Science Quarterly* 8 (December 1893): 621–22.

21. ''Slightly Mixed,'' *Yellow Kid* 1 (April 3, 1897): 38.

22. Joe Kerr, ''A Waltz Street Soliloquy,'' *Yellow Kid* 1 (June 5, 1897): 17.

23. Frederick S. Lamb, ''Municipal Art,'' *Municipal Affairs* 1 (December 1897): 674.

24. George Hill, ''Some Practical Limiting Conditions in the Design of the Modern Office Building,'' *Architectural Record* 2 (April-June 1893): 445.

25. Secundus, ''Crosscurrents,'' *Architectural Record* 1 (January-March 1892): 363–64.

26. C. F. Emerick, ''An Analysis of Agricultural Discontent in the United States,'' *Political Science Quarterly* 12 (March 1897): 120.

27. ''The Growth of Socialism,'' *Gunton's Magazine* 17 (July 1899): 6, 11, 15.

28. [Editorial Preface to] James P. Kohler, "The Industrial War," *Banker's Magazine* 41 (August 1886): 117.

29. Charles B. Spahr, "The Single Tax," *Political Science Quarterly* 6 (December 1891): 625.

30. "Editorials," *The Public* 1, no. 12 (June 25, 1898): 2. Charles E. Burton argued that the major contemporary urban problem was a sense of "alienation from the commonwealth, a feeling among the employed, non-property owning classes that they have no part, and can have no part, in the *common wealth* of the community" ("Why Municipal Reform is a Failure," *American Magazine of Civics* 6 [June 1895]: 613). Burton, too, proposed the single tax to reintroduce enlightened self-interest (pp. 614–15).

31. "Editorials," p. 3. The case has often been made that concern over land monopolies was motivated, in part, by a "populistic" xenophobia. At first glance, *The Public* seemed guilty of this nativist fear, since it maintained that the existing land system "enables foreign countries to conquer this country and subjugate its inhabitants"; nevertheless, it continued, "If America is to be owned at all, it might as well be owned by a few foreigners as by a few Americans. But little difference can it make to those who are governed by lords of the land, whether the lords be foreign or domestic" (p. 4). These statements, as do many more in this study, illustrate the not always obvious fact that the vocabulary of protest must not always be taken literally; that, moreover, the protesters turned often both to hyperbole and to stock slogans and phrases (which were often misleading in connotation) in their efforts to insure themselves a hearing.

32. "Editorials," *The Public* 1, no. 29 (October 22, 1898): 6.

33. "Spero Meliora. A Warning," *The Public* 1, Nos. 40–41 (January 4 and 17, 1899): 13–16, 13–16.

34. Ibid., no. 40, p. 15.

35. Ibid., no. 41, pp. 14–15, 16.

36. "Editorials. Prosperity," *The Public* 2, no. 78 (September 30, 1899): 6.

37. Ernest Crosby, "The White Man's Burden" [reprinted from the New York *Times*], *The Commons* 3, no. 33 (January-April 1899): 10. The department store is one of the five "new cultural expressions" examined in Gunther Barth's *City People: The Rise of Modern City Culture in Nineteenth-Century America* (New York: Oxford University Press, 1980), pp. 110–47.

38. Isaac Anderson, "One Afternoon. A Department Store Romance," *Yellow Book* 2 (January 1898): 31.

39. "The Economy of the Large," *The Social Economist* 8 (May 1895): 267, 271, 272. *The Social Economist* also reported the alleged plans of John Wanamaker and associates to erect a $100 million building between Fifth and Sixth avenues and Eighteenth and Nineteenth streets in New York City ("Editorial Crucible," 8 [February 1895]: 113–15). This "*fin de siècle* structure," which had been in the planning stages for five years, Gunton's journal reported, "will contain a city within itself with stores among the lower floors equal in dimensions to any now in use, without interfering with offices and residences, churches, libraries, schools and hotels, baths, theatres, and the like, all within the same massive structure" (pp. 114–15).

40. "Editorials. Department Stores," *The Public* 1, no. 32 (November 12, 1898): 6.

41. Ibid., p. 7.

42. The league and its operations are examined in Roy Lubove, *The Progressive and*

the Slums: Tenement House Reform in New York City, 1890–1917 (Pittsburgh: University of Pittsburgh Press, 1962), pp. 207–15.

43. Annie Marion MacLean, "Two Weeks in Department Stores," *American Journal of Sociology* 4 (May 1899): 721, 725.

44. Ibid., pp. 735, 736. The author herself earned only $11.88 for 175 hours of work.

45. Jonas Hudson, "People Who Have No Christmas," *Metropolitan Magazine* 12 (December 1900): 839.

46. Alice Nevins, "Christmas Shoppers and Sights of the Metropolis," *Metropolitan Magazine* 6 (December 1897): 455.

47. David M. Potter, *People of Plenty: Economic Abundance and the American Character* (Chicago: University of Chicago Press, 1954), Chapter 8.

48. Sidney A. Sherman, "Advertising in the United States," *Publications of the American Statistical Association* 7, n.s. 52 (December 1900): 1–44.

49. According to Sherman, streetcar advertising was heavily centralized in a few powerful agencies: "One of these companies claims to control 14,000 cars in 100 cities; another controls over 4500 cars in 40 cities" (p. 9). Railroad advertising was even more spectacular in its inventiveness: "Sometimes a special train is made up by a single large manufacturer, and the whole is made a moving advertisement whose coming is heralded in each city and town through which it is to pass."

50. Ibid., pp. 10, 9. Chauncey M. M'Govern in "Living Signs: How They Advertise in New York and Chicago," *Everybody's Magazine* 2 (March 1900): 217–22, reported that vaudeville actors were hired to play the following roles in promotional stunts: a giant on stilts gave sample cigars to residents on the second floors of apartments; a "dude" with a black valet did the same for passers-by at street level; and sidewalk Uncle Sams, between drubbings of dummies in Spanish uniforms, handed out their products to pedestrian patriots. "One prophecy that seems plausible," M'Govern suggested, was "that before long we may have free circuses, free musicals, and even free theatres, indoors as well as out, to call attention to the excellence of this or that brand of pills" (p. 222).

51. Sherman, "Advertising," pp. 23, 24, 26. Sherman listed the earliest New York agencies as those of Orlando Bourne (1828), Volney B. Palmer (1841), and John W. Hooper & Co. (1842). Arthur Brooks provided a rather breathless description of Broadway as "The World's Greatest Business Street," *Metropolitan Magazine* 8 (December 1898): 602–07. Broadway was, Brooks boasted, "a monument to the American spirit," that is, the "commercial spirit" (p. 607).

52. Sherman, "Advertising," p. 41.

53. John DeWitt Warner, "Advertising Run Mad," *Municipal Affairs* 4 (June 1900): 267–68.

54. Ibid., pp. 277, 274, 284–85.

55. Robert N. Reeves, "Our Aristocracy," *American Magazine of Civics* 8 (January 1896): 23.

56. The formation and institutionalization of a readily identifiable national upper class during the 1880s and 1890s has been covered in detail by E. Digby Baltzell in *Philadelphia Gentlemen: The Making of a National Upper Class* (Glencoe, Ill.: The Free Press, 1958), esp. pp. 17–24, 230, 291–334, 389–91.

57. Reeves, "Our Aristocracy," pp. 24, 29, 28.

58. H. M. Breen, "The Vanderbilt Marlborough Union," *Metropolitan Magazine* 2

(December 1895): 375; Leon Harris, *Only to God: The Extraordinary Life of Godfrey Lowell Cabot* (New York: Atheneum, 1967), p. 146.

59. Breen, "Vanderbilt Marlborough," pp. 377–79, 380.

60. "Men Who Have Been Talked About This Month," *Metropolitan Magazine* 1 (April 1895): 182–83.

61. F. J. James, "A Mile of Millionaires," *Metropolitan Magazine* 2 (September 1895): 156, 156–57, 159–60.

62. Ibid., pp. 155–56. H. G. Warren described the Hudson River homes of the rich, inhabited only a month or so a year, in "A River of Palaces," *Metropolitan Magazine* 8 (November 1898): 507–11. Still another example of this devotion to the monumental homes of the wealthy may be found in Paul Richmond's "Biltmore House," *Metropolitan Magazine* 3 (May 1896): 287–89, which was designed for George Washington Vanderbilt by Richard Morris Hunt and landscaped by Frederick Law Olmsted.

63. Gilson Willets, "The Last Palaces of the Rich," *Metropolitan Magazine* 10 (October 1899): 377, 378, 378–79. Hunt and Olmsted collaborated on this commission in 1881.

64. "One of the Outs," *Yellow Kid* 1 (June 5, 1897): 2.

65. "Barred Out," *Yellow Kid* 1 (June 19, 1897): 39.

66. "Economy in Dress," *Yellow Kid* 1 (June 19, 1897): 5.

67. "Call the Police," *Yellow Book* 1 (September 1897): 42.

68. "A Bright Idea," *Yellow Book* 1 (September 1897): 43.

69. "How Fortunate," *Yellow Kid* 1 (July 3, 1897): 33.

70. "The Reason," *Yellow Book* 1 (December 1897): 40.

71. "The Snob," "My Ancestry," *Yellow Book* 1 (September 1897): 4. The editors of *The Public* observed that "William Waldorf Astor does an unnecessary injustice to his family when he endeavors in the biography of his great-grandfather to trace the family lineage to French counts, seigneurs, knights, baronets, and marquises. . . . New York conveyancers credit the family with a more honorable ancestry." John Jacob Astor, it continued, had a brother named William Ashdon who came to America with Hessian mercenaries during the Revolution; later, this same brother settled down to become a butcher, then a gentleman. Although it was not certain about the accuracy of these facts, *The Public* maintained that they would do credit to the Astor name ("Editorials," 2, no. 70 [August 5, 1899]: 4).

72. The Chaffer, "Hard Times in the 400. A Hard Times Party," *Yellow Book* 1 (August 1897): 46.

73. "Bacchanalianism and Misery. We Will be Free Yet, You Bet," *American Federationist* 3 (February 1897): 260. "The '400' of New York are now bestirring themselves in preparation for a most extravagant and ridiculous event. One of our millionaire heiresses who has purchased a foreign dude is creating an unusual sensation even among her set. A fancy dress ball in the royal fashions of centuries ago, is to be given by the Bradley-Martins at the Waldorf Hotel, New York, in which it is fairly estimated that the outlay will be over $1,000,000."

74. "Editorials," *The Public* 1, no. 34 (November 26, 1898): 1.

75. "Editorials," *The Public* 1, no. 61 (June 3, 1899): 1.

76. "The 'Man With the Hoe,' " *The Commons* 4, no. 41 (January 1, 1900): 4.

77. "Editorial Table: Captains of Industry," by John J. Peters, *Open Church* 1 (July, August, September 1897): 152.

78. "Editorials, If Christ Were Here?" *The Public* 1, no. 7 (May 21, 1898): 7, 8.

79. Speed Mosby, "The New Nobility," *The Public* 3 (September 8, 1900): 343, 344. Mosby saw a social revolution as inevitable; however, he hoped that it would come about through free elections—"the bloodless guillotine of the new revolution."

80. "The American Peril," *The Commons* 2, no. 14 (June 1897): 9.

81. L. Elseffer, "A Return to the Basic Principles of Self-Government," *American Magazine of Civics* 7 (November 1895): 495, 494.

82. "Editorials," *The Public* 1, no. 5 (May 7, 1898): 3.

83. Franklin H. Giddings, Essay review of eleven books by French sociologists, *Political Science Quarterly* 11 (June 1896): 351.

84. Levi Gilbert, "The Down-Town Church Again," *Open Church* 2 (April 1898): 288.

85. George K. Holmes, "The Concentration of Wealth," *Political Science Quarterly* 8 (December 1893): 599. Holmes, a social Darwinist, approved of the contemporary concentration of wealth; since there was "a narrow diffusion of economic instincts" in society, concentration seemed inevitable and beneficial. His analysis of the process of social stratification was one of optimistic approbation: "The general appearance of comfort and well-being seen almost everywhere, except among the poor whites and blacks of the South and the poorer factory and tenement-house populations, indicates a disposition to live for the present, even if wealth in the future is delayed, rather than to sacrifice the present for the future. While the few have been getting a principal share of the new wealth, the many, on whom the progress of the nation ultimately depends, have been increasing their material comforts, their enjoyments and their knowledge." (p. 598). Since, however, 9 percent of the people owned 70 percent of the national wealth, it might eventually become necessary, he concluded, to check their power by income, gift, and inheritance taxes (pp. 599–600).

86. Albion W. Small, "Private Business is a Public Trust," *American Journal of Sociology* 1 (November 1895): 276, 277, 283, 279–80.

87. P. J. Maas, "The Situation To-day," *American Federationist* 2 (May 1895): 42–43.

88. A. S. Leitch, "The Ignorance of the Educated Class," *American Federationist* 4 (October 1897): 181, 181–82, 182. The final reference is to Ignatius Donnelly's popular dystopian novel of 1891.

89. "Editorials," *The Public* 3 (November 10, 1900): 483.

90. "Editorials," *The Public* 1, no. 18 (August 6, 1898): 3.

91. "Editorials," *The Public* 3: 483.

92. Alzina Parsons Stevens, Review of *Loom and Spindle: Or Life Among the Early Mill Girls . . .* ,by Harriet H. Robinson, *Journal of Political Economy* 7 (June 1899): 412.

93. E. D. M'Creary, "Martyrs of Industry," *American Magazine of Civics* 8 (April 1896): 352, 357–58.

94. "The Structural Iron Workers" [reprinted from the *New York Journal*], *Public Improvements* 3 (December 1900): 582. Condemnation of industrial civilization was often framed in religious terms, for example: "Calvary's woe is upon us. The cross, fashioned in cruelty and persecution and bigotry, and planted in tears and bodily anguish, lengthens its shadow over this nineteenth century. . . . The world no longer demands an eye for an eye and a tooth for a tooth. It is content with a life for a life. . . . Capital, the great high priest, condemns, and sated monopoly, the modern Pilate, washes its hands." Christ "reaches forth His nail-marked hands, not in blessing, but in denunciation." "He enters the factories and stores and sweatshops. He lays His denouncing touch upon the greedy

proprietors and they shrink; on dropsical corporations and they collapse" (Olla Perkins Toph, "The Nazarene and Labor," *American Federationist* 5 [September 1898]: 129).

95. "An Expert Opinion," *Good Government* 12 (December 15, 1892): iii.

96. "Editorial Crucible," *The Social Economist* 8 (February 1895): 11–12.

97. "Editorials," *The Public* 3 (November 3, 1900): 469.

98. S. V. Lindholm, "Analysis of the Building-Trades Conflict in Chicago, from the Trades-Union Standpoint," *Journal of Political Economy* 8 (June 1900): 342.

99. Joseph Lee, "The Sweating System," *Charities Review* 2 (December 1892): 100, 101.

100. "Recent Street-Railroad Strikes," *Gunton's Magazine* 17 (August 1899): 93. From its inception, this journal preached the natural and inevitable partnership of big business and big labor. It generally took the side of the workers in strikes, but it took them to task for their class prejudices: "If the workingmen insist upon organizing on the idea that every capitalist is their common enemy, and cling to the notion that nothing benefits them which does not reduce those above them to their own level, they will but place themselves in direct opposition to the very forces which make for their own improvement" ("Public Effect of Great Fortunes," *The Social Economist* 8 [May 1895]: 278).

101. U. M. Weideman, "The Physiology of Overwork," *American Federationist* 2 (March 1896): 46.

102. Sam Walter Foss, "The Dialogue of the Spirits," *The Commons* 3, no. 27 (July 1898): 1.

103. Asa Briggs, *Victorian Cities* (London: Odhams Books Limited, 1963), pp. 59–60.

104. W. D. McCracken, "The Glad Hand," *The Public* 2, no. 104 (March 31, 1900): 13. This particular poem combined, surprisingly and awkwardly, the theme of Walt Whitman and the style of Rudyard Kipling. Its final verse, for example, parodied the latter's "The Ballad of East and West": "For they who hunger and thirst shall know / The Lord of Creation and Birth, / So here's to the common men, / For they shall inherit the earth."

105. Arthur Bartlett Maurice, "Mr. Chimmie Fadden of New York," *Bookman* 9 (May 1899): 213.

106. Grace Isabel Colbron, "The Child of the Slums in Literature," *Bookman* 9 (April 1899): 165, 167.

107. "Types of the Metropolis," *Yellow Book* 2 (Januaray 1898): 14.

108. "A Genius," *Yellow Kid* 1 (June 5, 1897): 45.

109. "Only One Fear," *Yellow Kid* 1 (May 2, 1897): 40.

110. Dr. Nax Mordeau [pseud.], Frontispiece, *Yellow Kid* 1 (March 20, 1897). This pseudonym stands for Max Nordau, author of the controversial bestseller *Degeneration* (1895), who wrote the first extended essay in English on Friedrich Nietzsche.

111. Ernest Crosby, "Ninety-nine in the Shade," *American Federationist* 7 (August 1900): 233.

112. Perley A. Child, "Midsummer in the City. (East Side.)," *Bookman* 2 (August-September 1895): 23. This otherwise realistic poem ended with a romantic hope for the future by sentimentalizing over "A ragged child that hugs a ruined rose / With eyes of rapture innocent as prayer."

113. Henry George, Jr. "Are We Approaching the Roman Catastrophe?" [reprinted

from the *Philadelphia North American*, July 23, 1900], *The Public* 3 (September 15, 1900): 364–65.

114. "Miscellany. Babies Cheaper Than Puppies" [reprinted from the New York *Evening Journal*], *The Public* 1 no. 52 (April 1, 1899): 9.

115. Emma Playter Seabury, "The Potters' Field," *The Commons* 4, no. 34 (May 1899): 3.

116. "Summer in City Slums. Suffering in the Poor Quarters of Chicago—New York's Good Work," *Chicago Commons* 1, no. 6 (September 1896): 2.

117. "Kansas City's 'Patch.' Frightful Conditions in Which Child-Life is Being Destroyed by Wholesale," *The Commons* 2, no. 15 (July 1897): 1, 2.

118. Clare de Graffenreid, "Some Social Economic Problems," *American Journal of Sociology* 2 (September 1896): 190.

119. Thomas E. Will, "The Problem of the City," *American Magazine of Civics* 7 (September 1895): 239.

120. "Miscellany. Prophetic Geography" [reprinted from *The Literary Digest*], *The Public* 2, no. 75 (September 9, 1899): 12.

121. J. F. Bartlett, "National Perils," *American Journal of Politics* 2 (January 1893): 12–13.

122. "Lack of a Proper Utensil," *Yellow Kid* 1 (July 17, 1897): 3.

123. The Novelist, "*The Countess Irene*: a Tragedy," *Yellow Kid* 1 (July 3, 1897): 38.

124. "His Definition," *Yellow Book* 1 (August 1897): 4.

125. "A Complete Alibi," *Yellow Book* 1 (October 1897): 33.

126. "To Accommodate It," *Yellow Book* 1 (December 1897): 62.

127. In *Ancestors and Immigrants: A Changing New England Tradition*, (Cambridge: Harvard University Press, 1956), Barbara Miller Solomon has traced such a native-immigrant power struggle in Boston.

128. E. R. Donehoo, "John Chinaman," *Charities Review* 7 (January 1898): 921. On the other hand, Donehoo maintained, the immigrant from China was thrifty, generous, and the champion of his home and community; moreover, since he was a "heathen," he was a welcome potential convert to Protestant Christianity.

129. E. Carlyle, "Day Nurseries," *Charities Review* 1 (June 1892): 365. "It is safe to say that a barbarian who appeared at the gates of Rome, ignorant of its customs, its language, its laws, with but $20.29 in the pocket of his tunic, and who asked to be admitted to full citizenship, including eligibility to the Senate, might have counted himself fortunate to have escaped with his life" (John Watrous Knight, "The Working-Man and Immigration," *Charities Review*, 4 [May, 1895], 374–75).

130. Georges Vacher de Lapouge, "The Fundamental Laws of Anthropo-Sociology," trans. Carlos E. Closson, *Journal of Political Economy* 6 (December 1897): 69, 85.

131. Richard Mayo-Smith, "Assimilation of Nationalities in the United States," *Political Science Quarterly* 9 (September 1894): 428, 441. Mayo-Smith's analysis, since it was environmental and not strictly biological, was more pessimistic about immigrants than about their offspring; in fact, he maintained that the loyalties of second-generation Americans would be based upon class and not ethnic attachments.

132. Henry White, "Immigration Restriction as a Necessity," *American Federationist* 4 (June 1897): 67, 68.

133. Arnold White, "Immigration of Aliens" [reprinted from the *Proceedings* of the

International Congress of Charities and Correction], *Charities Review* 3 (December 1893): 77–78.

134. Irene Rowland, "The Negro of the City Streets," *Metropolitan Magazine* 11 (June 1900): 642, 647.

135. Kate Carter, "A Negro Baptism in the Hudson," *Metropolitan Magazine* 12 (August 1900): 225, especially 228.

136. "Separate Cars for Negroes," *Public Improvements* 2 (April 16, 1900): 277. An earlier note in *Every Saturday* about the "negro-in-the-horse-car excitement" described the racial tension in Louisville during the early 1870s as being in a "state of high feverishness" over the use of that city's transportation facilities by black citizens. "Their only alternative," editorialized this Boston magazine, "is to go afoot and congratulate themselves that pedestrianism is a thing with which no act of Congress can interfere" ("Current Topics," n.s. 2 [June 3, 1871]: 507).

137. Guy Carleton Lee, "Negroes Under Northern Conditions," *Gunton's Magazine* 10 (January 1896): 63. In an addendum to this article, the editors of *Gunton's* answered that: "If Mr. Lee's investigations prove anything, it is that the negroes cannot be helped by colonizing them in Northern cities, but, on the contrary, that their progress and improvement must be sought by the interjection of Northern enterprise and Northern economic methods of industry into the Southern States. By this means take to the negro, and for that matter, the poor whites, the influences and incentives of order, discipline, thrift and energy in his own environment" (pp. 63–64). The editors of *Gunton's* also objected to Lee's harsh judgment of Afro-American morality, since their problems were "largely traceable to the greater immoralities of the whites who have had the right to coerce them; and if we are to suppose the white people to be superior, their immorality is much the viler of the two" (p. 64).

138. "Editorials," *The Public* 2, no. 57 (May 6, 1899): 4.

139. "Editorials. The American Negro," *The Public* 2, no. 73 (August 26, 1899): 6.

140. Monroe N. Work, "Crime Among the Negroes of Chicago. A Social Study," *American Journal of Sociology* 6 (September 1900): 208, 223.

141. Henry J. Phillips, Review of *The Philadelphia Negro* by W.E.B. Du Bois, *Charities Review* 9 (February 1900): 575–76. The book is the focus of the next Interlude.

142. "Sociological Notes. Condition of the Negro in Various Cities," Conducted by Samuel M. Lindsay, *Annals of the American Academy of Political and Social Science* 10 (July 1897): 143, 143–45.

143. "Sociological Notes. Atlanta Conference on Negro City Life," Conducted by Samuel M. Lindsay, *Annals of the American Academy of Political and Social Science* 10 (September 1897): 301, 302.

144. Joseph H. Senner, "The Immigrant Question," *Annals of the American Academy of Political and Social Science* 10 (July 1897): 13, 6, 18.

145. Burton, "Why Municipal Reform Is a Failure," p. 612.

146. Ellen Battelle Dietrick, "The Restriction of Immigration," *The Social Economist* 5 (July 1893): 25–26.

147. W. G. Puddefoot, "Is the Foreigner a Menace to the Nation?" *American Magazine of Civics* 9 (July 1896): 3, 8.

148. "Types of the Metropolis," *Yellow Book* 2 (January 1898): 14.

149. Robert Treat Paine, "The Relations Between the Church and the Associated Charities," *Open Church* 1 (October 1897): 197.

150. Albert Shaw, "Municipal Lodging Houses," *Charities Review* 1 (November 1891): 20, 21.

151. "Restore the Home?" *Charities Review* 9 (November 1899): 378–79.

152. Edward T. Devine, "The Shiftless and Floating City Population," *Annals of the American Academy of Political and Social Science* 10 (September 1897): 159.

153. William Eugene Lewis, "Some of the Many Failures in Metropolitan Life," *Metropolitan Magazine* 10 (December 1899): 601.

154. P. M., "The Tramp—A Eulogy (dedicated without Permission to 'The Man With the Hoe.')," *Metropolitan Magazine* 12 (August 1900): 287.

155. John J. McCook, "Tramps," *Charities Review* 3 (December 1893): 65, 69. McCook's detailed analysis of conditions among the tramp population was far more sophisticated than his moralistic preachments would indicate. Based on a questionnaire that he administered personally to 1,349 tramps, McCook classified the pecking order of the "Bum" (a term that he preferred to "tramp") as descending from the "Ho-Bo" nobility of the "Railroad Tramp," to the "saltigrades" or train-"Jumpers," to the "Pike Bum," down to the "City" or "Mission" or "Religious Bum," and on to the lowest order, the "Gay Cat" or beggar; a corresponding order of female bums included "Magpies," "Petticoat Bums," and "Bags." Among the bums interviewed, McCook found a high percentage of Irish, English, and German extraction, but few Italians; he estimated that 90 percent were literate and "certainly not inferior" in intelligence to the average citizenry (pp. 59–69).

156. John Glenn, "Co-operation Against Beggary," *Charities Review* 1 (December 1891): 67.

157. Ralph Henry Gabriel, *The Course of American Democratic Thought*, 2d ed. (New York: The Ronald Press Company, 1956), pp. 162–63.

A SOCIAL SURVEY

The provenance of what historian James H. Cassedy termed the "statistical mind" has been traced back variously to the imperial headcount in colonial America and to the official report in Victorian England.[1] For American urbanists, however, the inevitable immediate inspiration for statistical inquiry on the grand scale was Charles Booth's massive survey of turn-of-the-century London.

"Arguably the greatest work of social research ever carried out in Britain," as historian Michael J. Cullen has claimed, Booth's survey was probably, as sociologist Ruth Glass has speculated, "more admired than read."[2] The first two volumes of Booth's *Labour and Life of the People* were published in 1889 and 1891; a second edition, retitled *Life and Labour of the People in London*, was released between 1892 and 1897 in nine volumes; and his culminating study, maintaining the revised title, was issued in 1902–1903 in seventeen volumes.[3] Admired, if not always read by American urbanists, Booth's massive work was certainly much imitated.

For Chicago, Jane Addams and colleagues produced *Hull-House Maps and Papers* in 1895 and for Boston, Robert A. Woods and associates prepared *The City Wilderness: A Settlement Study* in 1898—both surveys drawing heavily on Booth for method and format. During the opening years of the new century, what is more, almost every metropolis-on-the-make produced a massive social survey *à la* Booth to accompany its comprehensive park-parkway scheme *à la* Olmsted and its monumental city-beautiful master plan *à la* Burnham. With the Pittsburgh Survey of 1907–1908, which was published in six volumes between 1909 and 1914, the movement established its benchmark: the recently founded Russell Sage Foundation, which had supported the work in Pittsburgh, created in 1912 a separate Department of Surveys and Exhibits to promote such efforts nationwide; and the once independent journals *The Commons* and *Charities*, which had merged in 1905 to create *Charities and The Commons*, changed title again in 1909 to *The Survey*, the better to spread the gospel of the secular Booth.[4] From among these many studies—most of them, like their London progenitor, "more admired than read"—one stands out and endures: because of the stature of its author and the scope of his subject, W.E.B. Du Bois's *Philadelphia Negro* has maintained its vitality for nearly a century.[5]

When he established residence in Philadelphia during August 1896, William Edward Burghardt Du Bois was twenty-eight years old. Behind this promising young scholar, even this early in his career, there stood a record of notable achievement. The first African-American to be awarded the Ph.D. by Harvard University, a member of the pioneering generation of Americans who studied the new social sciences in Germany, Du Bois's doctoral dissertation on *The Suppression of the African Slave-Trade to the United States of America, 1638–*

1870 was published during the very year of his arrival in Philadelphia as the initial volume in the Harvard Historical Series. Ahead of him stretched nearly seven more decades of achievement at Atlanta University, with the National Association for the Advancement of Colored People (NAACP), in Africa—as teacher, scholar, editor, philosopher, novelist, poet and, by his death in 1963, symbolic figure of Third World liberation. But the Du Bois who came to Philadelphia as assistant instructor in sociology at the University of Pennsylvania, who was a resident of the Philadelphia College Settlement at Seventh and South streets through January 1898, was a less complicated composite. Historian, social scientist, settler, and would-be reformer, he would harmonize these several voices in his *Philadelphia Negro* into a veritable Greek Chorus of civic drama; in these pages, Du Bois would carry the method of the social survey to its scientific limits.

The Philadelphia study drew considerably upon the London prototype. In the first place, in the tradition of Charles Booth's early work, it was location-specific, rather than citywide. As Booth had concentrated on the problem area of East London, Du Bois focused on Philadelphia's Seventh Ward, which he described as "a typical ward for the year 1896," when it contained a population of 21,177 whites and 8,861 blacks, or slightly less than a quarter of the city's entire Afro-American populace.[6] Second came presentation. As Booth had employed "mataphor and figurative language sparingly," so as to convey "a deliberate no-nonsense quality to the prose," so also did Du Bois spare the adjectives. Third, and closely related, both men wrote in "the grand tradition of English empiricism," albeit Du Bois with a Germanic flavor, which held "that the facts speak for themselves, that they are perceived by the senses, gathered up by an impartial mind, and formed into even larger and more accurate generalizations."[7] Fourth, both Booth and Du Bois adhered to the tenets of economic liberalism, which maintained that the problem was not poverty but the poor—"a matter of the character of a segment of the population rather than a condition of society."[8] Thus, Booth classified London residents according to their "social condition," which ranged from "A. the lowest class of occasional labourers, loafers, and semi-criminals," at the bottom, to "H. upper middle class," at the top, all neatly divided between "D" and "E" by "the line of poverty."[9] Du Bois, too, established "grades" for Black Philadelphia: "1. Families of undoubted respectability earning sufficient income to live well . . ."; "2. The respectable working-class . . ."; "3. The poor . . ."; and "4. The lowest class of criminals, prostitutes and loafers; the 'submerged tenth.' "[10] Fifth and last, both men exploited fully the expanding universe of statistical data available on urban problems as beginning points for their studies; nevertheless, as Booth found that he had to rely increasingly "on his personal impressions, on what might be called qualitative descriptions,"[11] so too did Du Bois advance from the ideal of scientific detachment to the necessity of participant observation. Still, although they shared much in common, there remained significant differences between the men and their works.

Booth's magnum opus, it has been charged, emits "an aura of hodgepodge";[12] Du Bois's landmark study easily defies any such indictment. The contrast between the two social surveys emanates from the differences between the respective career directions of their authors: for the middle-aged Liverpool merchant, *Life and Labour* was a culmination, a monument to an avocation, the justification for a second career. For the youthful scholar *The Philadelphia Negro* was simply a step forward, beyond apprenticeship, a probe toward a new career. Whereas Booth's approach was one-dimensional, Du Bois's was multifaceted. His ambitions as man of letters, historian, sociologist, and race leader inspired *The Philadelphia Negro*, shaping it into a book that was not only to be admired, but also read.

Du Bois described his survey as "a huge volume of five hundred pages but not unreadable." It is, in fact, a polished work. For Du Bois, as Herbert Aptheker, the editor of his papers, has noted, scholarship was "*writing*; one who produces a book should try, thereby, to produce *literature*."[13] *The Philadelphia Negro*, consequently, has a recognizable structure, which may be divided into four parts and labeled: History as Lesson, chapters 3–4; Setting the Scene, chapters, 5–10; Life, Organization, and Disorder, chapters 11–14; and People and Places, chapters 15–17. These sections were introduced with two brief methodological chapters and concluded with "A Final Word" (Du Bois's title), appendices, and a report on domestic service. That his book's composition would be an end in itself comes as no surprise when it is recognized that Du Bois began annotating his collected papers at the age of fifteen—and would go on doing so for the next eighty years—and once, as he described it in his first autobiography, wrote a theme on "October 3, 1890 for Barrett Wendell, then the great pundit of Harvard English," which concluded, Du Bois records: "I believe foolishly perhaps, but sincerely, that I have something to say to the world, and I have taken English 12 in order to say it well."[14] As a purposeful man of letters, then, Du Bois plotted his book with the care of a novelist, wrote in a spare prose style to convey the weight of his findings, and saved his rhetorical tricks for suitable perorations.

As a published historian, Du Bois would never have been satisfied with the cursory "background information" chapters too often found in social science (and planning) reports. In their stead, he provided two chronological chapters on "The Negro in Philadelphia," from 1638 to 1820 and from 1820 to 1896. This survey, sociologist E. Digby Baltzell has written in partial justification of the 1967 reprint, is "one of the most important contributions of this book" for its recognition that "in the city where the Declaration of Independence was written and the nation founded, the Negroes also had an important history, which Du Bois carefully documented: here in Philadelphia was the first expression against the slave trade, the first organization for the abolition of slavery, the first legislative enactments for the abolition of slavery, the first attempt at Negro education, the first Negro convention, and so forth."[15] In recording these "firsts," Du Bois sought to demonstrate the national significance of the local

Figure 6

DECEMBER 1, 1896.   NO.————————   Investigator.

1	Relationship to head of family? . . . .
2	Sex? . . . .
3	Age at nearest birthday? . . . .
4	Conjugal condition? . . . .
5	Place of birth? . . . .
6	Length of residence in Philadelphia? . . . . .
7	Length of residence in this house? . . . .
8	Able to read? . . . .
9	Able to write? . . . .
10	Months in school during last school year? . . . .
11	Graduate or attendant at any time of any higher school? . . . .
12	Attendant of any industrial school? . . . .
13	Occupations since November 1, 1891? . . . . . .
14	Present occupation? . . . .
15	Place of work? . . . .
16	Average income from present occupation { weekly? monthly? yearly?
17	Weeks unemployed at above occupation during last twelve months? . . . .
18	Weeks employed at any other occupation during last twelve months? . . . .
19	Name of such other occupation? . . . .
20	Average weekly earnings at such other occupation? .
21	Number of days sick during last twelve months?
22	Nature of illness? . . . .
23	Sound and healthy in mind, sight, hearing, speech, limbs and body? . . . .
24	When and where have attempts been made to find other employment? . . . .
25	Why was application refused? . . . . .
26	Amount of real estate owned? . . . .
27	Situation of such real estate? . . . .
28	Amount of other property? . . . .
29	Member of what building, secret, beneficial or insurance societies, or labor union? . . . .
30	Average monthly dues to such societies? . . . .

31 | Budget:
Total income for one year?
Expenditure for one year?

Expenditure for	W'kly.	Monthly.	Yearly.	Expenditure for	W'kly.	Monthly.	Yearly.
Rent				Amusements .			
Food				Tobacco			
Fuel				Alcoholic drinks			
Clothing				Sick's and dt'h.			
				All other purposes			

Total expenditure for one year?
Total savings for one year?

32 | Chief form of amusement?
33 | Member or attendant of what church?
34 | Remarks.

See Instructions for Family Schedule, 1.

Figure 6 (Continued)

UNIVERSITY OF PENNSYLVANIA.

CONDITION OF THE NEGROES OF PHILADELPHIA, WARD SEVEN.

Home Schedule, 3.

DECEMBER 1, 1896.   No._____   Investigator.

1	Material of house? . . . .
2	Stories in house above basement? . . . .
3	Number of homes in house? . . . .
4	In which story is this home? . . . .
5	Number of rooms in this home? . . . .
6	Is this home rented directly of the landlord? . . . . .
7	Number of boarders in this home? . . . .
8	Number of lodgers in this home? . . . .
9	Number of servants kept? . . . .
10	Total number of persons in this home? . . . .
11	House owned by . . . .
12	Rent paid monthly? . . . .
13	Rent received from sub-letting? . . . .
14	Bath-room? . . . .
15	Water-closet? . . . .
16	Privy? . . . .
17	Yard, and size? . . . .
18	Where is washing hung to dry? . . . .
19	Light? . . . .
20	Ventilation and air? . . . .
21	Cleanliness? . . . .
22	Outside sanitary conditions? . . . .

THE HOME.

		Room No. 1.	Room No. 2.	Room No. 3.	Room No. 4.	Room No. 5.	Room No. 6.
23	Use?						
24	Dimensions?						
25	Outside windows?						
26	Furniture?						
27	Occupants at night?						
28	Additional rooms?						

29	When and where have you had difficulty in renting houses?

Figure 7

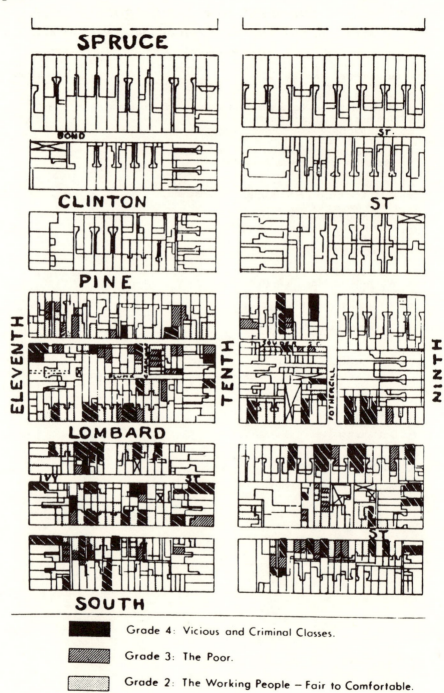

Grade 4: Vicious and Criminal Classes.

Grade 3: The Poor.

Grade 2: The Working People — Fair to Comfortable.

Figure 7 (Continued)

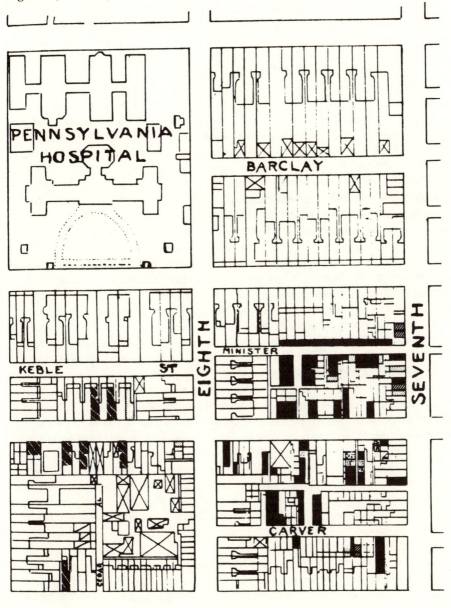

Grade 1: The "Middle Classes" and those above.

Residences of Whites, Stores, Public Buildings, etc.

record, indicate that Philadelphia was a representative or model city for the race, and establish a historical context for the survey results that followed.

"W.E.B. Du Bois went to Europe in 1892 an historian; he returned two years later," Francis L. Broderick claims, perhaps stretching the point a bit, "a sociologist." At Harvard, Du Bois had studied institutional history and taken only one social science course, Francis G. Peabody's Ethics of Social Reform; at the University of Berlin, he turned to political economy and worked under such pioneer social theorists as Heinrich von Treitschke, Rudolph von Gneist, Adolph Wagner, and Gustav von Schmoller. The last named, in whose research seminar Du Bois wrote "The Plantation Proprietorship System of Agriculture in the Southern United States" and who exerted a profound influence on the young American scholar, propounded a three-tiered approach to social change: "first, accumulation of accurate information; then, social policy based on that information; the whole suffused with the ideal of justice." The Philadelphia Negro, Broderick judges, "met Schmoller's standards almost precisely."[16]

As a working sociologist, Du Bois drew upon the proven techniques of the social survey. To begin with, he gathered his information carefully, devising detailed schedules for amassing data on the family, individual, home, house servant, street, and institution (Figure 6). Then, his findings were categorized, classified, and mapped out block by block for the entire ward (Figure 7). Finally, following the hand's-on emphasis of the movement, Du Bois took up residence in the Seventh Ward, living with his wife in a room over a cafeteria owned by the College Settlement House. From the proven techniques of the social survey, Du Bois next turned to the experimental methods of the new social sciences.

As a professionally trained sociologist, Du Bois drew precise patterns of generalization from the mass of his data. He demonstrated, for example, that black migration was no simple rural to urban movement but was, instead, a phased progression from the southern country district to the small town to a large town, on to such major cities as Norfolk and Richmond, then to Washington, and finally to Baltimore and Philadelphia; that the lines between the plantation South and metropolitan North were maintained through family lines and cultural ties; that mobility remained characteristic of Philadelphia life, as its black residents began replicating the outward suburban migration patterns of their white counterparts (Figure 8); and that all this movement had created within black Philadelphia four generations whose experiences had been shaped, in turn, by the antebellum town, the city of Civil War and Reconstruction, the municipality of the Centennial, and the new metropolis of the day.[17] He established, too, that job scarcity for men across the board, as contrasted with employment availability for women in domestic service, led to such imbalances in the black community as "a large proportion of single men," and "unusual excess of females"—many of them unmarried, widowed, or separated—and a consequent "widespread and early breaking up of family life."[18] He urged, then, that since "the proportion . . . of men to women is a rough index of the industrial opportunities of the Negro" and that since Philadelphia was a manufacturing-service

Figure 8

MIGRATION OF THE NEGRO POPULATION, 1790–1890.

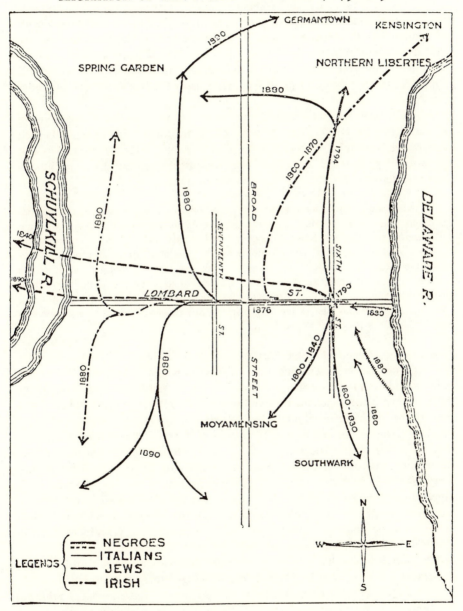

center, the economic future of its Afro-American population depended ultimately upon a new direction and a redirection in "a twin movement—the diversification of Negro industry and the serious training of domestic servants."[19] Service would provide the base, industry the ladder for upward mobility. Yet, despite the logic of his appeal, Du Bois remained skeptical about industrial America's acceptance of black workers for, as he recognized, "one of the great postulates of the science of economics—that men will seek their economic advantage—is in this case untrue, because in many cases men will not do this if it involves association, even in a casual and business way, with Negroes. And this fact," he concluded, "must be taken account of in all judgments as to the Negro's economic progress."[20]

As an African-American explicating the condition of an urbanizing segment of his race, W.E.B. Du Bois offered a closer reading of this community than could have been achieved by a Charles Booth or even a Jane Addams. His was an insider's perspective, that of the true participant observer; therefore, he discerned heterogeneity where others saw homogeneity.

There is always a strong tendency on the part of the community to consider the Negroes as composing one practically homogeneous mass. This view has of course a certain justification: the people of Negro descent in this land have had a common history, suffer to-day common disabilities, and contribute to one general set of social problems. And yet if the foregoing statistics have emphasized any one fact it is that wide variations in antecedents, wealth, intelligence and general efficiency have already been differentiated within this group. . . . And there is no surer way of misunderstanding the Negro or being misunderstood by him than by ignoring manifest differences of condition and power in the 40,000 black people of Philadelphia.[21]

These same "manifest differences of condition and power," what is more, derived from nurture, not nature. Thus did this outspoken champion of his people, who would soon take on the powerful Booker T. Washington and eventually take his own place beside the revered Frederick Douglass in the Black Pantheon, reject "the inevitable racial implications of social Darwinism." And he got away with it. "One is amazed to find," Baltzell confesses, "that the reviewers did not come out openly and criticize Du Bois's definitely environmental, rather than racial, approach to the problems of Philadelphia Negroes."[22] Perhaps this very emphasis explains Gunnar Myrdal's judgment in his own monument to applied environmentalism, *An American Dilemma*: "We cannot close this description of what a study of a Negro community should be without calling attention to the study which best meets our requirements. . . . We refer to W.E.B. Du Bois, *The Philadelphia Negro*, published in 1899."[23]

The author would likely have agreed with this particular critic. In his autobiography, in fact, W.E.B. Du Bois acknowledged that his Philadelphia book was "so thorough that it has withstood the criticism of forty years."[24] Still, he recognized its limitations, which were those of its methodology. Early in the new century, then, upon his appointment as a faculty member at Atlanta University and as editor of the "Atlanta University Publications," Du Bois took an imaginative leap beyond the social survey and proposed an effort that would dwarf even Booth's: a one-hundred-year program, organized according to decade-by-decade investigations of such topics as the family, church, business, welfare organizations, and the like in Afro-American life.[25] Twenty volumes of the AU Publications, sixteen of them supervised by Du Bois, were eventually published; however, by the time of the series's demise, Du Bois had left Atlanta for New York, the NAACP, and a new career as activist. It would remain for another social scientist to make no little plans of his own and thereby advance the study of people in cities to its next level.

NOTES

1. James H. Cassedy, *Demography in Early America: Beginnings of the Statistical Mind, 1600–1800* (Cambridge, Mass.: Harvard University Press, 1969), and Michael J. Cullen, *The Statistical Movement in Early Victorian Britain: The Foundations of Empirical Social Research* (New York: Barnes & Noble Books, 1975).

2. Ibid., p. 149. The Glass quotation is from Harold W. Pfautz's "Introduction" to *Charles Booth on the City: Physical Pattern and Social Structure; Selected Writings*, ed. H. W. Pfautz (Chicago: University of Chicago Press, 1967), p. 4.

3. Ibid., pp. 313–14, for full bibliographical references.

4. For the Pittsburgh Survey and its influence upon the Russell Sage Foundation, see Roy Lubove, *Twentieth-Century Pittsburgh: Government, Business, and Environmental Change* (New York: John Wiley & Sons, Inc., 1969), pp. 5–10; and for background to "The Survey and Related Magazines," see Frank Luther Mott, *A History of American Magazines*, Vol. 4: *1885–1905* (Cambridge, Mass.: Harvard University Press, 1957), Sketch 30, pp. 741–50. The "secular" Booth of the London survey was often compared with the religious or "General" Booth of the Salvation Army; see below, Chapter 5.

5. W.E.B. Du Bois, *The Philadelphia Negro: A Social Study*, Together with A Special Report on Domestic Service by Isabel Eaton, with an Introduction by E. Digby Baltzell (New York: Schocken Books, 1899 & 1967). Often rendered as DuBois, the preferred form of Du Bois is used throughout this text.

6. Ibid., pp. 58–65.

7. Albert Fried and Richard M. Elman, "Introduction" to *Charles Booth's London: A Portrait of the Poor at the Turn of the Century, Drawn from His "Life and Labour of the People in London,"* ed. Fried and Elman (New York: Pantheon Books, 1968), pp. xxi, xx.

8. Pfautz, ed., *Booth on the City*, p. 13.

9. Ibid., pp. 50–51.

10. Du Bois, *Philadelphia Negro*, pp. 310–11.

11. Fried & Elman, eds., *Booth's London*, p. xxxi.

12. Pfautz, ed., *Booth on the City*, p. 42.

13. W.E.B. Du Bois, *Dusk of Dawn: An Essay toward an Autobiography of a Race Concept* (New York: Harcourt, Brace, 1940), p. 269. Herbert Aptheker, "The Historian," in *W.E.B. Du Bois: A Profile*, ed. Rayford W. Logan (New York: Hill and Wang, 1971), p. 251.

14. Du Bois, *Dusk of Dawn*, pp. 38–39. His professor, Du Bois comments, "rather liked that last sentence. He read it out to the class."

15. E. Digby Baltzell, "Introduction" to Du Bois, *Philadelphia Negro*, p. xxviii.

16. Francis L. Broderick, "German Influence on the Scholarship of W.E.B. Du Bois," *Phylon*, 19 (1958): 367, 370, 369.

17. Du Bois, *Philadelphia Negro*, pp. 73–82, 299–309.

18. Ibid., pp. 66–67, 53.

19. Ibid., p. 139.

20. Ibid., p. 146.

21. Ibid., pp. 309–10.

22. Ibid., pp. xxi, xxiii. For magazine literature on racial theory, see Chapter 4.

23. Gunnar Myrdal, with the assistance of Richard Sterner and Arnold Rose, *An American Dilemma: The Negro Problem and Modern Democracy* (New York: Harper and Brothers, 1944), p. 1132.

24. Du Bois, *Dusk of Dawn*, pp. 58–59.

25. Ibid., pp. 64–65; Elliott Rudwick, "Note of a Forgotten Black Sociologist: W.E.B. Du Bois and the Sociological Profession," *American Sociologist*, 4 (November 1969): 304.

5

Toward Equilibrium, 1885–1900

The urbanist's role in the social reordering of the city was, in many respects, similar to the part that he or (in this one aspect of urban affairs, significantly enough) she played in municipal politics and government. The urbanist was faced here, too, with new challenges: first, to establish authority in the field—in some instances, create an area of expertise; next, come to an understanding of an unfamiliar lower-class community which was in many municipalities, as was the case with the big-city machine, often ethnic and premodern in its structure and values; and finally, establish and coordinate a working alliance of organizations, so as to institutionalize approaches to a new social order, and thus guarantee continuity of effort. Although late-century urbanists advocated a variety of social philosophies, institutional innovations, and organizational schemes, they all shared the same ultimate goal—the achievement of an urban social equilibrium; unlike their postwar counterparts, who had been satisfied with temporary palliatives, late-century observers sought permanent solutions to major social problems. Once more, a search for order permeated the magazine literature of the period.

THE SCIENTIFIC ORDERING OF SOCIETY

"American life," it was often noted, "is growing more tense, more strenuous, year by year. There are titanic forces at work here among us . . . —the clamorous spread of population, the pitiless laws of competition, the growing powers of the trusts, grinding and fashioning our social fabric with a power . . . steady and relentless."[1] These same "titanic forces," Dr. Henry Ling Taylor observed, included "the extreme specialization of pursuits and occupations, tending to narrow and restrict experience, and the herding together of dense masses of population in large cities, toward which the more venturesome and ambitious individuals tend to gravitate, and where large opportunities are provided, only at the cost of more strenuous competition, and in many respects less favorable hygienic conditions.'' ''The modern city served,'' Taylor suggested, as ''a kind of biological furnace. . . . If, in the course of this fiery ordeal, the individual receives a keener temper or a finer polish, he may not become stronger physically or better balanced mentally; and thousands, unable to endure the strain, are cast off or incapacitated. . . . This straining of powers till they crack, this incessant fiddling at the nerves,'' he concluded, ''is apt to make our city life restless, asymetrical, and unsatisfactory.''[2]

The pressures of an urban-industrial culture necessarily created, Frank W. Blackmar recognized, conditions that fostered pathological tendencies in the human community. ''We need,'' he maintained, ''social sanitation; which is the ultimate aim of the study of social pathology.''[3] ''Social sanitation'' might be achieved, C. M. Hubbard hoped, from what he called ''practical sociology.'' ''A great city with its various grades of people and conflicting interests is a laboratory in which the student of sociology may test and prove his conclusions derived from studies in the classroom.'' Employing a popular analogy of the period, he continued: ''What the physical laboratory is to the physicist or the chemical laboratory to the chemist, so must be experimental knowledge to the student of humanity.''[4] This same social scientist could not expect, however, to escape controversy and to go unopposed in his work. ''Representatives of two very respectable classes of the community,'' University of Chicago sociologist Charles R. Henderson warned, ''are apt to find themselves in hostile attitudes in the discussion of contemporary social questions—the scientific student of social phenomena and the 'captain of industry.' Has the student of sociology a right to discuss the central theme of his field of research? This is the matter in dispute.'' His posing of this question was a mere rhetorical device, for Henderson asserted that it was ''the duty of the ethical theorist to show that the self-interest of the manufacturer and landlord do not secure the public welfare in any city of this country, and that it is precisely this self-interest, narrowly conceived, which prevents rational legislation against child-labor and sweat shops. . . . To show these phenomena, their causes and wide results is precisely the duty of the social scholar.'' Henderson recognized and accepted, moreover, the militant dedication of the capitalist to his credo of self-interest, his equation of success with financial reward, his activism and basic anti-intellectualism, and his amoral conception of the economic order; he hoped, nevertheless, for mutual respect and cooperation between sociologist and businessman. ''The frank recognition of division of intellectual labor and of common social concern is all that is asked by the social theorist, and,'' he warned, ''in an age when the pen is mightier than sword or hammer, his claim is not likely to be permanently ignored.''[5] This new science was to serve as, what might be identified today as, a ''change agent'' in society.

A scientific study of urban America would demonstrate, John Franklin Crowell of Columbia College asserted, that social dislocation was the concomitant result of "the necessary loss of personal capacity by the transfer from rural to urban conditions of life, especially in the case of the young, but generally of all ages. It is not a collapse, but rather what geologists would call a 'fault'—community on a somewhat lower moral plane, by a let-down through absence of sustaining social conditions." The socioeconomic problems of urban America, then, extended beyond the mere assimilation or exclusion of European immigrants; they were basic to the transformation of the national culture. "It is too much the habit of the times," Crowell concluded, "to write and reason about things American much as the English tourist does—as if this country had little in it except a score of cities connected by railroads running through nowhere."[6] The urban observer had to recognize that the social as well as the political facets of city living had been transformed by urbanization and industrialization, that much was being lost in the transformation from preindustrial to modern. "The progress has been largely material," noted union official Henry White, "We have not retained the social and institutional order which prevailed prior to the substitution of steam for hand power, when master and workman were joined together by ties of intimacy and mutual welfare, and when the perplexing problems of over-production, involuntary idleness and undeserved poverty had not arisen to embarrass us. We have lost the amenities and neighborliness which so dignified and broadened life in the days of the village community and townships, and have as yet developed no substitute. How, under modern conditions, to preserve the good features of the cruder form of society, is the grave question." The problem would not be solved, this perceptive critic pointed out, by returning to a preindustrial order: not a negative, but a positive philosophy of urbanism was needed. "We are beginning to see," White concluded, "that the city is something more than an institution existing only for the purpose of doing police duty and other indispensable things, but rather it is a corporation with many co-operative features; that the municipality is a great household, primarily concerned with the affairs of the home; and that it can improve industrial conditions to a large extent and raise the standards of life of the workers."[7]

The most obvious approach to the improvement of urban society was general education, that is, the process of learning conceived of in the broadest of terms.[8] Education, like science, had a special meaning for this generation: more than instruction and training, education came to mean conditioning and even social engineering. An unsigned review in *Gunton's Magazine*, for example, declared that "the work of education goes on whether we will or no, and if it is not organized and directed in the lines of wholesome ideas and responsible conduct, it will organize itself for the destruction of all that is decent in society." It was necessary, then, to "educate the people through the methods of their social enjoyment. This is the way that educational forces must reach the under-side population of our large cities if Tammanys are to be abolished and the cities to be a strength instead of becoming a menace to the Republic."[9] Samuel T. Dutton included among the educational forces of urban America its homes, churches, schools, museums, theaters, and libraries; its newspapers, magazines, industries, and governments; and "those intellectual and ethical aptitudes of the people which make it possible for them to be quickened and influenced in the right direction." "If all these forces could be made to work in harmony," he predicted, "their power would be invincible; but the trouble is that they do not pull together. There is a force of individuality and a persistence of type that often seems to defy any attempt at unity of action." In order to counteract this fragmentation of effort, these institutions "must be federated and brought into close co-oper-ation"; in addition, "there should be an earnest effort to improve the social mind, to elevate the taste and appreciation respecting books, the drama, art, music, and such things as afford nutrition to the higher nature."[10]

"Education is beyond doubt a factor in the amelioration of evil conditions," the editors of *Citizen* claimed, "and an element of strength and comfort to the weaker members of society."[11] Formal education, as a force for social control, had obviously to be effective at its most basic levels, the urban elementary schools. That the teaching staffs and facilities of municipal grammar schools were both of higher quality than those of rural America was almost unanimously recognized.[12] Whether these same schools, however, were as effective in shaping "character" as they were in training young minds was often questioned. W. M. Beckner, a Kentuckian propagandist of the New South, granted the higher levels of intellectual training in the Yankee city school systems. "But do they produce more great men? . . . The city schools make all more intelligent, but an inferior education in the country has certainly in many instances developed individuality of character, and produced great leaders of men."[13] The children of the city, Dr. Henry Ling Taylor agreed, were often overdeveloped mentally and under-developed psychologically. "The city boy's supplemental training at school is far from perfect, but his fundamental, unstudied training by contact with Nature in the free use of his proper activities is wofully deficient." Moreover, the urban youth's "notion of such fundamental objects as the sky or horizon," Taylor punned unconsciously, "must be extremely hazy."[14]

An obvious solution to the denatured schooling of the children in municipal centers was the vacation school movement, and the lamentations of Sadie Amer-ican over the paucity of greenery in central cities were typical of this viewpoint. Not only had the city covered nature's lawns with concrete carpets of its own devising, but "what grass there is no longer invites the tripping feet, but sternly warns 'keep off!' Birds and butterflies have fled to the parks, too distant for the child to follow; and the buzz of bees is replaced by the gong of the electric-car Moloch, claiming the street for his own, and sacrificing all who may dispute his sovereignty." A recognition of this pernicious state of urban degeneration, she continued, had encouraged many major cities to inaugurate vacation schools and fresh air funds for the poor of the slums. Boston's lead in this direction in 1885 had been followed by New York in 1894, Chicago in 1896, Cleveland, Brooklyn, and Cambridge in 1897, and Philadelphia in 1898.[15] Another possible solution to this problem was to be found in the often-related movement for children's playgrounds in congested downtown areas, itself an off-shoot of the urban park movement. Miss American, in promoting the playground movement, urged, "The child is father to the man, and the street is no place of rest or refuge for one or the other in his leisure moments." It was clearly time, she urged, for "the wise [to] see to it that resorts for upbuilding recreation insure such occupation of leisure hours as shall be indeed a recreation for body and spirit, and give us a generation strong and joyous and fortified to resist and repel with a happy laugh every deteriorating temptation and tendency."[16] The city streets were, in fact, a threat to the entire urban community, to all orders of the municipality. "Among all classes," argued Stoyan Vasil Tsanoff, "the prevalent tendency is to neglect the children." The child, grown too big for the confines of a backyard, joined the society of the streets; there his enemies were the police, the storekeeper, the driver, and the pedestrian; challenged by their authority, the streetcorner youths organized to fight back. "Moved by the irresistible spirit of physical and psychical activity, they inevitably absorb and reproduce whatever meets their vision. Wherever there is quarreling or fighting, . . . wherever there is an arrest or a revolting scene, there the children flock. . . . When they have graduated from the vile school of the streets, they receive a diploma that entitles them, by depraved tastes and appetites, to enter the saloon, the gambling den, the low theatre and the dive."[17] Such street smarts, Chicago sociologist Charles Zueblin would have agreed, marked the education—or lack thereof—of the entire municipal community. "A 'return to nature' is as necessary a demand for the modern city as it was for the romanticists of the eighteenth century. There can be," Zueblin asserted, "no successful life which ignores nature."[18]

A clear majority of urban theorists would have added that there could be no successful municipal life that ignored moral uplift. Thus, a contemporary civil engineer, echoing the call of postwar sanitarians, advocated the introduction of "rain baths" in the public schools: "It is only by educating our poorer classes in cleanliness in early life that we shall make them, as a whole, love it for its own sake, and hate dirt and those habits which tend to make man lower than the beasts of the earth,—too often now arising from an acquaintance, an intimate association, with dirt and dirty homes among the poor." The lesson of "sanitary science," this observer taught, was that "poverty may be clean"; moreover, the scrubbed poor would be more amenable to social uplift. "Is it not a fact that, besides being a detriment to health, lack of cleanliness gradually leads to loss of self-respect, to bad habits, vulgarity, and vice?" School "rain baths" checked this degeneration and even helped "to reduce the sharp contrasts which exist between the laboring classes and the well-to-do people."[19] Perhaps these same baths might even be made available to adults after working hours. *Mens sana in corpore sano*.

The sound mind, as the basic object of general education, might be conditioned, it was hoped, by such "original and far-reaching" societies as the City History Club of New York, a group formed "to make the boys and girls of New York good citizens—public-spirited, unselfish, patriotic." "Almost all the ills that afflict our body politic in New York," it was argued, "arise from the

indifference or selfish love of ease of the citizens, and no little of this apathy
arises from ignorance of the city's noble and romantic history.'' The club sponsored a full program of lectures, discussions, lantern-slide shows, and local
excursions to historic shrines to fill this vacuum in civic pride: it organized the
children into five district groups and attempted to encourage their senses of group
loyalty.[20] A far more regimented drive for group awareness and solidarity was
to be found in the movement for military drills for youth and boys' brigades.
Military bearing, the editors of *Charities Review* pointed out, did not necessarily
foster a warlike frame of mind; rather, it ensured a sense of discipline and
cooperation with the group, pride in organization, the building of "good character," cleanliness and order, and control of boys. This ideal of military order
was clearly related, if often unconsciously so, to the aggressive nationalism of
the 1890s, a relationship indicated by the editors of the same journal in their
attempts to appeal to the patriotism of the young recruits: "Then there is the
flag! The flag of our country, which is free from stains of blood wantonly shed
to wreak the personal spite, or win the personal aggrandizement of a despot."
Not surprisingly, the militant youth of urban America were led by "an invisible
commander-in-chief"—A.K.A. the Prince of Peace; thus, nationalism and religious tribalism were joined neatly together. To this amalgam was added the
necessary social control of an urban-industrial order. "When the mischievous,
teasing wayward life is all gone from the corporate personality, self-surrendered
to a definite purpose, when the soldiers are as blocks of wood in the hands of
their captain and their wills so plastic that they seem not to exist—then may be
seen the stirring of a life more efficient because better regulated than the life
which knows no outlet but in idle pranks, more poignantly interesting to itself
and others than the incoherent jumble of words and actions in which untrained
exuberance of spirits finds expression."[21] A practical demonstration of this mold-
ing of the "corporate personality" was to be found in the history of the Boys'
Brigade of Baltimore, a group organized initially along informal lines.

> The experiment seemed at first nearly hopeless as to its influence on the character of
> the boys. They were for the most part employed in glass houses, factories and breweries,
> all of them poor schools of morals. Their conception of fun was noise and confusion,
> and brute force their only argument. Ingenuity they had, and it was exercised to invent
> methods of tormenting one another, and evading suggestions of those harassed young
> ladies who had them in charge.
> From almost the first, however, there was perceptible an innate chivalry that made it
> possible for these ladies to influence them as no men could do, and before the work
> closed for the summer a marked improvement of manners was seen. In the fall of '93 a
> change of plan was made; the boys were organized into companies, with a lady lieutenant
> to each company, and adopted the present brigade motto, "Christ's Faithful Soldiers".
> . . . A member of one of the Baltimore regiments gave the boys military drill one evening
> each week, and this was of great service in many ways.[22]

The philosophy behind military training for urban youth, regardless of whether
boys' brigades were drilled by local Mars or Minerva, betrayed inclinations

toward an authoritarianism that some Progressive leaders of the next generation would adhere to more tenaciously and propagate even more vociferously.[23]

The direct approach of overt regimentation most likely gained adherents because of, in part, the dilemma of employing the young people of the great city. With women replacing boys in clerical positions, with modern technology making obsolescent many of the jobs formerly held by the young and unskilled, and with immigrants monopolizing most of the manual trades (both skilled and unskilled), "The cowboy is to-day," observed one critic, "almost the only native unskilled laborer."[24] The philosophy of "trade and technical education" had itself to be modernized, Florence Kelley of Hull House maintained, in an "epoch of industrial instability, by reason of which the working boy of today needs not so much any one trade, as that combination of qualities which will enable him to turn with facility from one occupation to another as each, in turn, is supplanted in the course of the industrial evolution." Unless such training was provided, American society would continue to be faced with large numbers of unemployable adolescents, "this horde of incompetents."[25]

To some urban theorists, the problem of education in the great municipal centers was even more basic than that of simple economics. John Beverly Robinson, for one, interpreted the problems of education as those of national change: "Modern times are upon us; have come upon us, and are still rushing on, with such celerity that we can scarce keep up with them. The vast modern city—a new thing in the history of the world—grows, as a microbe colony grows, millions almost in a night, so that we strain ourselves to build schoolhouse after schoolhouse, each fitted for its thousands of children, without outstripping our needs." Even though his own generation had improved immeasurably upon the work of the past, Robinson concluded, "We ourselves probably are doing still the most inadequate things, judged by the light of the future."[26]

The pressures upon individuals and families subject to the processes of education and acculturation in the great cities were seldom noted; however, when they were, the personal tragedies caused by urbanization and industrialization were inescapable. Thus, Henry W. Thurston of the Chicago Normal School recounted an interview with a teamster who had encouraged his daughter's ambitions to become a school teacher only to find his own self-respect jeopardized: he was forced first to rent a new flat and buy new furniture; he was then expected to entertain his daughter's status-conscious, white-collar friends; as a result of his added expenses, the father was forced to send out his younger children to supplement his now inadequate wages; and finally, his teacher-daughter threatened, at every sign of opposition from her father to leave her home for more congenial surroundings. Thurston also related the case history of a bolt maker faced with the same challenge to his status, a man isolated in his own home by his own family.

How they wish I [related the bolt maker] could be happy living in my own quiet little world—the kitchen. They know my lot is unjust, but they hope I'm too stupid to know it. They know I'm not stupid. . . . No, in my young ambitious day, with the help of night schools and colleges, paid for by my hard-earned savings, I educated myself until I compare favorably with the high school graduate of to-day. All this I did for myself, it seems, only that I might appreciate how hard and unjust my lot truly is. Had my children obtained their education in the manner I did it would have been better for them.

. . . .

No education in its existing form is not for the poor. It cultivates the mind at the expense of the heart; it estranges parents from their children—their one source of happiness. It has been the cause of many a misery in the poor man's home. It has broken up families. It displaces love in the poor man's home circle.

This eloquent spokesman for the urban proletariat concluded that "my family is no worse than other families. It is their wish to be happy."[27]

BLUEPRINTS FOR BETTERMENT

> Enter this hallway; climb five flights of stairs;
> Visit the dens where the poor have their lairs,—
> Kitchen and bedroom and parlor are one,
> Cooking the life that was left by the sun,—
> Windowless cupboards where men try to sleep,
> Heedless of roaches and bugs as they creep.
> Some burn with fever, and here they must die,
> Crowded like litters of pigs in a stye.
> One narrow house, rising floor upon floor
> Holds a full hundred of mortals or more.[28]

There seemed to be little doubt that life in slum tenements represented an urban heart of darkness. Their inherent evils were never denied; on occasion, nevertheless, their total impact on urban America was questioned. A writer for *The Social Economist* doubted that Jacob Riis's investigations were, in fact, applicable to the poorer half of New York City: "If New York is, in sober truth, in anything like one-half its population, the poverty-stricken, helpless, hopeless, vicious, wicked and criminal place that this book makes it out to be, it has already passed beyond hope and chance of salvation. Its name should be Sodom, and it should be destroyed as quickly and completely as was that ancient resort." Gotham was, of course, no Sodom; instead, Riis had exaggerated his findings in his efforts to make his book more "*readable*."[29] The tenement and the slum, the editors of *Gunton's* assured their readers, were residues from a preindustrial society, not portents of an urbanized future, "a survival of barbarism which civilization must and will eliminate. . . . A slum district would be an impossibility among people entirely the product of American social, industrial and political conditions."[30]

Optimistic projections into such a visionary capitalistic utopia were, however,

rare. More often, the social observer concentrated upon detailed and vivid descriptions of existing tenement conditions and created, thereby, a distinct *genre*
of shock literature. The account of New York slum housing by Mary E. Herrick,
a medical doctor, was typical of this format. The standard jerry-built tenement
house, its dark narrow halls, its crowded rooms did not tell, she maintained, the
entire story of its degrading impact upon its tenants.

Add to this the sounds which proceed from the neighboring adjacent tenements, the sights
and sounds from neighboring opposite tenements, the atmosphere of a dirty, crowded
street or of a badly kept yard, and you may have a faint idea of a tenement-house. But
even this will hardly be enough. You should imagine the even more crowded quarters,
whose six or eight ''boarders'' are added to the ordinary household, sleeping on the floor
of the living-room. You should imagine the crawling vermin, the stifling atmosphere.
You should imagine rows and streets of such houses, the yard space in many instances
occupied by a second house, the duplicate of the first. Imagine the street itself, with its
decayed garbage, unemptied ashbarrels, and unswept walks. Imagine the courts and yards
into which the rear houses open, the choked and overflowing closets, the decaying refuse
and stench of it all,—and you will begin to have some idea of tenement-house life, the
peculiar phases of which are probably nowhere better shown than in New York City.[31]

The tenement-house problem was complicated, moreover, by the fact that
these crowded buildings served as both domiciles and miniature factories. The
sweating system turned the home into a workshop: the labor being performed
by the entire family in their own apartment, as was the case with the garment
industry; the contractor renting an entire tenement building, as was true in the
cigar-making industry. Julius M. Mayers, special counsel to the Reinhard Committee on female and child labor in New York City, maintained that ''the welfare
of the people demands that the workshop and the home shall be separate and
distinct. Their combination is contrary to the genius of American institutions.''
Mayers recorded interviews with child victims of the system: Eva Lunsky did
not know the months or seasons of the year, had attended school for only three
months of her young life and was ignorant of the significance of the Fourth of
July; Fannie Harris earned two dollars a week (from which came her allowance
of two cents), could not spell *dog*, and had paid a lawyer twenty-five cents to
notarize a false affidavit concerning her age.[32] ''The sweaters' victims are perhaps,'' Florence Kelley observed, ''the least versatile of all the indoor-trades
employes.''[33] They were also the most often exploited, medical doctor Anna S.
Daniel noted, people ''whose hours are limited only by their physical strength
and the amount of work they can obtain; who pay for the rent, light, and heating
of their work-shop; who eat, sleep, are sick, and die in the same rooms in which
they manufacture goods in whole or in part.'' ''The people working in tenement
rooms have a decided grievance against the city of New York, in that its sanitary
and health laws are not enforced; and against the greed of employers, who give
the work to the tenement-house people simply because it is cheaper.''[34] ''Property
owners and business men are,'' sanitary engineer Charles J. Wingate agreed,

"careless, selfish and indifferent in too many cases, and must be forced to do their duty. The law usually sides with the landlord against the tenant, and protects the property owner far more than is just." Because of this imbalance, Wingate concluded, the next battle "must be to enforce the first principles of the Declaration of Independence, 'The right to live,' and to insist that the poor man's child has as just a claim to enjoy sunlight and fresh air as the spoiled darling of the millionaire."[35] The problem, objected playground advocate Joseph Lee, was not class exploitation but economic efficiency: individuals and businesses were less to blame for tenement and sweating abuses than was the system itself; tenement house reform could be brought about not by exhortation, but by applied expertise.[36] The problem, in fact, was ill defined.

The experts who stepped forward to lead the struggle for tenement house reform did not, despite their intensive studies of slum life, really come to grips with the system of land use in downtown areas. To begin with, these "housers" were uninformed, or even misinformed, on basic points of housing economics: vital questions of tenement ownership, building and maintenance costs, and space priorities in the central business district and adjacent edges were unanswered, misinterpreted, and unasked. Frequently, they approached lower-income housing blinded by the narrow preconceptions of their class: "decent" housing meant middle-class housing; "slum" housing fell beneath this standard. Because of their cultural blinders, their inability to view the social organization of the urban proletariat in its own terms, they were unable to understand that slum living was, perhaps, a necessary stage in urban development and that slums possess, as architectural historian Walter L. Creese has described it, "an inner life and vitality of their own."[37] Although they instituted and advanced a systematic program both for the inspection and policing of substandard buildings and for the design and operation of improved or model tenements, their legalistic jargon of expertise did not altogether mask their naive Victorian idealism—an optimistic fatalism that might well have found expression in the banal verses of W. D. McCracken: "Holy Moses! what a rush!/See them leave the slums!/Kids a-skipping on before,/Then the drunken bums."[38]

The indignities and agonies of slum dwellers—from the "kids" to the "drunken bums" to the solid working classes—presented an inescapable challenge to the "better element" in urban America. "The people living in these sections [i.e., the tenement districts]are powerless," George E. Bissel advised, "to change or escape these conditions"; and, he counseled, it was "good business as well as good health and good morals to make the lives of the working masses as comfortable as possible and it is good politics also, for riot and revolution are born of the unbearable miseries and neglect of the laboring masses, whose only argument for redress of grievances is force."[39] The vile conditions of slum living, Dr. Arnold Eilvart asserted, resulted from the "selfishness of dirty tenants," the "rapacity and indolence of landlords," and the "neglect of [public] officials." The first requirement for tenement reform was the awakening of the civic consciousness of the slum dweller. "For the true self-interest of the clean tenant once aroused will form 'down town,' " Dr. Eilvart continued, "as it now forms 'up town,' an ever-present automatic check not only on the aggressions of landlords and officials, but ultimately on the aggressions of dirty tenants. . . . It is such manly maintenance of right that brings into life the spirit of civic pride." This same "manly maintenance of right," the militant spirit so evident in the education movement, could be achieved, in part, through the organization of tenants' associations—"not a class, not a trade, but a neighborhood."[40] The tenants themselves, Kemper Bocock agreed, were at the root of the tenement house problem: "So long as we have done nothing to make the late tenants of the bad tenement want to tenant a good tenement, we are merely scratching the surface. We will never catch up with the growth of the bad tenement population in that way, for we are simply running a never-ending race with the city's social cancer, with the cancer always ahead." The arresting of this cancerous growth could be achieved, Bocock concluded, only by "education" (that is, socialization) and by strict and enforceable housing codes. "There must be no maudlin sympathy for tenement landlords who violate the laws of physical and moral health for the sake of making forty to one hundred percent on their investments. . . . Batter down every infamously unsanitary tenement, haul the landlord into court, fine him, imprison him, or both, and he, too will soon have a wholesome desire—the desire to respect the law."[41]

The focus of the professional housers' drive for tenement reform was New York City; however, civic leaders in other major cities also joined the movement. Harold Kelsey Estabrook, an agent of the Twentieth Century Club, warned against a "self-satisfied Boston." Boston, he maintained, "in the housing of its poor . . . may be unfortunate in having been better off than other great cities, if public sentiment in favor of improvements is allayed; and other cities may be counted fortunate in that their distinctly worse conditions have roused a healthy public sentiment which demands improvements. Because Boston has never had any slums like those of Mulberry bend in New York and those of Bethnal green in London, very few persons in the city have felt the need of improving the houses of the poor."[42] Chicago, too, Frances Buckley Embree maintained, had failed to recognize its slums. "Chicago, with a vigorous faith in herself as the favored of the gods, is loth to believe that she has a housing problem; and in the absence of a tenement-house census the task of convincing her is, indeed, a difficult one." Embree predicted that documentary proof of its housing problems would lead Chicago inevitably to a civic reawakening, "for the city has every opportunity both of nature and of grace, for becoming a model city; of nature, because the prairie about her offers unlimited space; of grace, because her people are wide-awake and enterprising. The results of the unsanitary housing of the poor once understood, capitalists will vie with one another in the erection of model tenements in Chicago."[43] In San Francisco, finally, there was no problem of a general awareness of poor housing, since "Chinatown" was clearly "filthy, wretched and generally unsanitary physically and morally." The English lead in slum clearance in Manchester and Birmingham might serve, the journal of the League of California Municipalities suggested, as a model for San Francisco. "It would be a good and paying investment for the city to buy it [Chinatown] outright, tear down the old shacks and erect modern tenements."[44] The precedents for what later became the urban renewal and model cities programs were thereby projected in late-century urban America.

For most housers, however, the solution to the tenement house problem was a simpler one, "philanthropy and five per cent." The concentration of population in urban centers was, they maintained, at least a necessary evil, at best a social and economic good. Representing the latter viewpoint, the editors of *The Social Economist* predicted that "the social city, with its theatres, libraries, and cultivating influences shall be removed from the din and dirt and humdrum of the commercial and workshop city; and this advance will necessitate the replacing of the tenement rookeries by profitable business structures, and thus abolish existing tenement-house conditions, which are the great stigma upon modern city life." Indeed, this journal claimed, the transition was already under way: "Millionaire capitalists are building houses, and every one is built upon an improved plan, so that the new tenement house has more improvements than did the houses of the wealthy fifty years ago."[45]

The public could expect the cooperation of enlightened business interests in tenement and sweating-system legislation argued Henry White, secretary of the United Garment Workers of America, because of the current "recognition that business is of a social nature, that the 'captains of industry' have obligations and duties to perform toward their employees and the public." Their opposition to progressive social measures in the past had been due not to "malignant motives," but to their attachment to outmoded theories of political economy.[46] Thus, with an enlightened business leadership involved, progress in housing the poor become all but inevitable.

The writings of Lawrence Veiller, secretary of the Tenement House Committee of the New York Charity Organization Society and the leading houser of the period, reflected considerably less optimism. "Not only does New York city," he began, "suffer from density of population, from a lack of homogeneity of race, changing climatic conditions and many other influences of a similar kind, but its tenement houses have the worst conditions in regard to light and air of any city in the world." Gotham's high-rise buildings had created a unique crisis, one which had "never been dreamt of in the slums of London, where the worst buildings are seldom more than three stories high."[47] "It has been reserved for New York City, the modern Rome," Veiller observed elsewhere, "to duplicate the evils of tenement-house structure known in ancient Rome alone among all the cities of the world." In true imperial fashion, the Empire City had "not only duplicated these evils, but has intensified them to a degree beyond belief." The multiplication of these malpractices, moreover, Veiller observed, continued because, although reforms had been enacted since the earliest housing bill of 1846, substandard dwellings were still erected at a faster rate than were model tenements: during the 1890s, only two of the latter had been erected by philanthropists, whereas over 15,000 of the former had been built by "speculators." Although he believed that the tenement-house problem was "at the root of most of our social evils," Veiller saw no alternative to facing and solving it. "To set the drift back to the fields, away from the city" might be suggested, But "Let us not deceive ourselves and neglect the housing of this population, with the thought that people 'ought to live in the country.' The well-to-do classes do not live in the country, and so long as they live here there will be a large number of persons to do their work, on whom they are dependent for their very lives, 'hewers of wood and drawers of water,' or their modern equivalent."[48] Housing for them had to be provided by enlightened capitalists who were prepared to accept reasonable (but modest) profits of 5 and 6 percent per annum. Their financing of the model urban and suburban projects of the City and Suburban Homes Company and other professional housing organizations would, thereby, satisfy the requirements of both philanthropy and capitalistic dogma. To the early houser, then, reform and the profit motive were inseparable.[49]

Veiller's contemporary in the movement, statistician E.R.L. Gould, agreed with this rationale, inasmuch as "the housing problem belongs to social economics, but not to philanthropology." Housing reformers had, then, to discover "how to house the masses with financial profit and yet in such a manner that health, morality, sound family life and social stability may be subserved." Gould was quick to add, however, that "one cannot look to economic axioms to furnish invariable rules of guidance. The housing problem relates almost exclusively to the city, and the modern city is something which was not foreseen when the great fathers of political economy formulated their dicta." "The great doctrine of 'let alone,' under such [urban] circumstances, would be reduced," he maintained "either to the simple formula of 'let die' or license to degrade and brutalize." In the provision of housing for the urban masses, moreover, one had to make a "distinction between *living* and *existing*."[50] Since Gould was certain that the housing question was "the most fundamental of social problems relating to environment," he judged Veiller's widely publicized Tenement House Exhibition, which opened during February 1900 in New York, to be a "noteworthy event in metropolitan sociological history." Nevertheless, Gould's program for the housing of the urban masses was far more detailed and autocratic than was Veiller's, in that the former was more fixed and rigid in his views on character and environment than was the latter. "Strong-willed, intelligent people may create or modify environment," Gould held. "The weaker-willed, the careless, and the unreflecting are dominated by environment. Such is a fairly rough estimate of the relation. For all but the exceptionally strong and virile, home environment determines the trend of life."[51] His major concern, then, was in establishing "scientific differentiation of the various divisions" of wage earners. "The higher wage-earning element should be encouraged to become owners of suburban homes. . . . City dwellers with more moderate stipends may become clients of model housing companies." Lower down on the scale came "those who from one kind of misfortune or another have grown deeply in debt and lost heart, . . . the casual worker, the irregular rent payer and the shiftless laborer" who required minimal oversight. Those at the bottom, "which include the drunkard, the incorrigible, the criminal, the immoral and the utterly useless, must be treated in more drastic fashion. . . . Until we can find some method of rounding up such characters, possibly into public lodging-houses, the sexes separated, and the children placed in institutions where they may grow up to be useful members of society, we are not likely . . . to rid ourselves of such undesirable members of society."[52] The achievement of these ends, Gould regretted, would prove difficult, for "adult male members [of this class] possess the franchise." Democracy could thus be perceived as a barrier to reform.

Gould's "scientific differentiation" of the subclasses that made up the urban proletariat called for, in brief, a program of full segregation along economic lines. The future of the blue-collar elite seemed the most promising in a dawning "electric age." "The simple trolley, while it can hardly represent the acme of achievement, is already," Gould exulted, "an important factor in improving [the] living environment, and its future influence we are not competent to measure." The trolley and rapid transit promised an increasing movement into the suburbs, the incubator for future middle-class aspirants. The Octavia Hill method of rent collecting offered to the next highest of the lowly guidance in budgeting and, perhaps more important, the uplifting example of the "better sort." Under this plan, Gould explained that in each project "a women rent collector is in charge of what may be called the financial side of the work. Rents are collected in the apartments and her intercourse with tenants often becomes cordial and helpful in a social way."[53] For the lowest of the low, according to Gould, there were only public institutions and the promise of extinction. His class-segregated metropolitan society of the future promised a rigid stratification by caste, a dystopian compartmentalization of a nation of cities. In exaggerated form, this vision of an American urban life represented the extreme view of late-century housing reform, with its twofold emphasis upon uplift and exclusion: it provided for the upward mobility of the "potential" middle class, while it condemned the economically and culturally unfit to a life apart. It could not go unchallenged.

The main thrust of the opposition to the rigidity of the tenement reform movement was directed against the housers' tendency to seek social stability along existing lines of class stratification, their overeagerness, that is, to accept contemporary inequalities. Housers, for example, were quick to applaud the building of downtown boarding houses for working women, such as Boston's "Boffin's Bower," as expressions of enlightened philanthropy and working-class self-help.[54] Annie Marion MacLean, that perceptive critic of working conditions in Chicago's department stores, welcomed "homes which offer board at very low rates" as "veritable virtue-saving stations. Under the present economic systems," she continued, "they are of vital importance." For as long, that is, as it remained "impossible for a girl to earn enough to support herself unaided, just so long will it be necessary to make provision for the respectable housing of working women, and that, of course, outside of so-called charitable institutions.''[55] Working girls' homes were nothing more than ''so-called charitable institutions,'' and such implied reservations about ''the present economic system'' spelled out, to the editors of *The Public*, the basic problem of ''well-meaning'' but ''thoughtless philanthropy,'' inasmuch as the ''world's worst enemies'' were ''often its well meaning friends.'' ''In the long run,'' this journal observed, ''those who maintain these houses contribute to the lowering of working girls' wages.'' Their philanthropy enabled ''some girls, not all, to live in comparative comfort for less than such a living costs. . . . They are, therefore, always a factor in the labor market upon which employers can count when they want to scale wages down.'' Accusations that this was the motivation behind employer contributions to such projects might have been unjust, *The Public* admitted, ''but they have been suspected'' of the same.[56] Innovations or reforms in urban housing which aimed at the betterment of working-class living conditions ought not, then, to preserve extant class lines and environments, but break them down.

Critics of the housing movement sometimes went so far as to argue that ''tenancy and freedom are incompatible conditions,'' that urban and suburban homeowning were the only cures for the evils of the congested slums. This, however, was an extreme position.[57] The major criticism of the tenement reform movement was that it encouraged population concentration in downtown centers and that ''we are repeating the blunders of Europe, and the time will come when we will pause, and ask, 'Must a big city necessarily be made up of huge buildings, crammed with human beings who have little sunlight and air?' '' In truth, ''no city where a vast population lives in crowded tenements where the air is insufficient, foul, or tainted with disease, and where the sun never shines, can be truly great, have a decent government, or add strength to a nation.''[58] Urban America faced the threat of a ''homeless citizenship.'' ''It will be the peril of the next thirty years in our cities,'' an observer for *Open Church* lamented, ''that the majority of those who live therein will have no tradition of the home—no experience of its charms, its privacy, its culture, its love.'' Although this same writer was prepared to agree with the ''warm-hearted friends of the 'cliff dwellers' '' that there were ''evidences of virtue, sympathy and humaneness'' in tenements, he was more concerned with the pressing problems of unnecessary population concentration.[59] His judgment, therefore, was no mere sentimental manifestation of a rural ideal; rather, it was an answer to the emotional appeal of what political scientist Scott Greer described as the tradition of downtown ''hallowed ground,'' the romanticization of central city living.[60]

The spirit of the housers, with their model tenements and high-minded duties of philanthropy, seemed to some of their critics to indicate an ''aristocratic sentiment'' that smacked of a ''Roman 'bread and circus' flavor.''[61] The impracticality of their economics bothered others. The only solution to the tenement house problem, William Nelson Black asserted, was a more affluent society with a more even distribution of wealth. ''But until that time comes it is probable that the rapacious landlord will be about the best philanthropist, and, architec-

turally, the most cultivated gentleman, whom we shall meet.'' Model tenements
were not the answer, because of the shortage of investors in such enterprises
and because of the scarcity of people willing to live in the philanthropically
supported and controlled houses. Only ''cranks'' had faith in such panaceas.[62]

Improved transportation systems offered some hope to the critics of both the
downtown slums and the housers' programs for their reform. ''Doubtless rapid
transit will not solve either the housing problem or transform our cities into
utopias,'' the editors of *Municipal Affairs* admitted, ''but it will alleviate social
conditions and prevent what otherwise would be unbearable evils.''[63] ''The
development of rapid transit,'' the editors of *Gunton's Magazine* agreed, ''is
another factor that will eventually do much to relieve the slums by permitting
laborers to live in the suburbs and give their children the benefit of healthy
outdoor life.'' This was not, however, an unmixed blessing: ''Those who go
into the suburbs should not take with them less commodious and sanitary quarters
than they left in the city—a misfortune that is likely to result when men of small
incomes are encouraged to build houses of their own. . . . The most important
things for the workingmen are a good home, freedom of action and increase of
public improvements.'' Then they, too, might share in the middle-class dream
of suburban living. This search for environment, so much a feature of the age,
would best be realized ''when capital supplies the houses and carries the responsibility for them.''[64] Predictably, *Gunton's* turned to the corporate giants
for its solution to the housing problem; nonetheless, despite its narrow business
partisanship, this journal recognized the basic uncertainty of both inner-city and
suburban housing markets, the financial insecurity of the small investor, and the
resulting inevitable instability of the construction industry in the metropolis.

The drive for tenement house reform was moderately successful in the attainment of its immediate goals, but its impact on future governmental programs
was, perhaps, even more important. Its model tenements, although they provided
for only a fraction of needy slum dwellers, set basic standards—unfortunately,
rather low ones—for later public housing projects; what is more, the movement
established a precedent for single-class compounds, which often functioned as
instant ghettoes. Its influential restrictive building codes also set needed minimum
standards; at the same time, however, they encouraged the development of slum
clearance as public policy without, significantly, providing for the relocation of
the displaced—once more establishing another unfortunate precedent for later
federal, state, and municipal housing agencies. The late-century movement for
tenement reform was, according to Lawrence M. Friedman's distinction, a model
of the ''*social-cost* approach'' to housing, its energies focused upon ''the costs
imposed by the slums on society at large''; the ''*welfare* approach,'' which was
responsive to the ''costs imposed by the slums on the people who live in them,''
was, quite clearly, a minority position.[65] This social-cost approach led most
housers to an organic theory of slum eradication: by the enforcement of building
codes, by the exertion of pressure on landlords, and by the demolition of dilap-
idated dwellings, they would be able, operating within a free enterprise setting,

to cut out these cancerous growths from the body politic. Like the grand designs of their contemporaries, the early city planners, the housing programs seemed to express *the* public interest, inasmuch as they conflicted with no major interest group. Challenged ineffectively by unorganized builders and landlords, easily dismissed as "slumlords"—as "mossbacks" had been by planners—the tenement reformers promised a healthy environment within a generation or two. Yet, ultimately, their hopes faded. Eventually, the model tenements and housing projects would be inhabited by undesirables—the "ethnic type," members of the "floating population," and the "dangerous classes"—until they, too, began their ascent from the depths; in the meantime, the "potential" middle class had to find its own way up. The issues of the debate over urban housing at the turn of the century—concentration versus dispersal, group versus individual ownership, model tenement or project versus separate dwelling—all would remain undecided. The housing problem, that bane of the industrial city, would continue to challenge and confound the new metropolis.

ON THE JOB UPLIFT

If a stable urban community was to be established and if the "submerged" middle class was ever to participate fully in the greater metropolis, the gap between the "haves" and "have nots" had to be bridged by social "mediators" or "gate-keepers."[66] Such agents of socialization set up and staffed three important late-century movements: charity organization societies, which represented a new and comprehensive concept for welfare activities on a citywide basis; open and institutional churches, which modernized existing but seemingly outmoded religious institutions at the neighborhood level; and the settlement houses which, while they shared the structural originality of the former and the limited spatial range of the latter, marked a new and important departure in municipal social action. All three movements stressed voluntaryism; all three were direct responses to a felt need; all three were, at best—measured by their own standards—limited successes. Their ultimate historical significance resulted from their failure to achieve their goals. They were the last bastions of urban individualism—their walls the final barriers to the welfare state adaptations of post–New Deal America.

Observers of municipal social problems generally judged charity programs harshly as being mere expedients, at best, or as leading inevitably to economic decline. Charitable giving, *American Federationist* declared, "not only humiliates and unmans the receiver, but demoralizes and spoils the giver"; a dole, this journal argued, was no substitute for job opportunities.[67] Most social theorists, however, were more concerned with the debilitating effects of charity upon its recipients than upon its initiators. Although traditional moral imperatives were increasingly subject to new humanitarian, scientific, and bureaucratic pressures throughout the period, theories of poverty and charity were still frequently defined in terms of the accountability of individuals, possessed as they were with free will, and their culpability for surrender to sin. Had not 1,800 years of Christian giving, Bolton Hall asked, proved that charitable work was a failure? Despite public and private attempts to better the conditions of the children of the poor, for example, "still the little ones die, one in every three; and death is not the worst for children 'whose angels are always beholding the face of Our Father which is in heaven,' yet who grow up, in the natural course of events, to fill the hospitals, the prisons, and the brothel." Death for the spiritually doomed was a blessing, the charity that preserved only their physical lives was a curse. "If they were only to die!" Hall prayed. "Poor little children! Think of the mother who sees her darlings, not growing up, but getting old, diseased, unclean, depraved; who knows that life must make them so, yet cannot change it." Model tenements and suburban homes served only "to transplant the weed"; charitable "feeding interferes with legitimate business"; prison reform might make corrective institutions havens for the poor; as for hospitals, asylums, homes for the aged and the blind: "By such institutions we oppose the law of natural selection, which is almost our only law of progress, moral or physical."[68] This fervent confession of social Darwinism was, nevertheless, an expression of a dying faith, for the neat logic of the survival of the fittest betrayed an internal contradiction. Any society which chose to await the advent of a universal betterment that was to be achieved by the unfolding of natural economic laws, Edward Cummings warned the National Conference of Unitarian and Other Christian Churches, was doomed to extinction: "For the growth of civilization is but a name for the growth of sympathy. The fruits of sympathy are philanthropy, charity, sanitation, medical science, all that makes against the sufferings of our race."[69] So that society might be saved from itself, traditional optimistic fatalism had to be replaced with a vigorous professionalism, the "natural order" had to give way to "social sanitation."

"Public out-door relief," most observers agreed ought not to become the foundation for urban charity. Civic activist Homer Folks maintained that "extended experience in many cities and careful study of the subject, answer unhesitatingly in the negative, and declare that material relief given from public funds to people in their own homes causes more suffering than it relieves, undermines the desire for self-support, discourages foresight and thrift, encourages immorality and political corruption, and brings in its train a long series of evils that affect a community to its very center." The cure for the ills of poverty was to be found instead, Folks concluded, in the combined action of public and private welfare agencies: "Every opportunity that comes to a public institution of enlisting the interest of a new group, or a larger number of citizens, should be availed of, to the end that the needs of those institutions, becoming more generally known and better understood, more adequate appropriations may be made, and that the work of faithful public officials may receive its due recognition."[70] Private charity, in brief, must be allied with public agencies in this progressive war against poverty.

The danger inherent in charitable work was that it seemed inevitably to degenerate into a "science of administering gifts," that, as the editors of *The Social Economist* warned, "charity makes beggers [sic] as well as relieves them, and that there is no more hopeless idler and vagabond than the man or woman who has learned to get a living without work out of the hands of the charitable."[71] Nathan Oppenheim, attending physician to the Children's Department of Mount Sinai Hospital Dispensary, pointed to the "grotesque spectacle of charitable institutions advertising the free benefits which they thus force upon the less wealthy part of the community, and of like institutions bidding against each other for patronage; there are even instances in the writer's personal knowledge where charity has not only been forced upon the people, but also where in order to be accepted it has really gone a-begging."[72] Discipline, both observers argued, was the first requirement for urban charitable work—discipline for both Dives and Lazarus, both giver and receiver.

The institutional innovation designed to impress this social discipline upon urban America was the Charity Organization Society (COS). Modeled after an English prototype and first introduced into the United States in 1877, COS was dedicated to the creation of a "science of charity" through the systematic application of business principles and methods to the administration of all charities. Organized on a citywide basis, each local COS served as a central headquarters for all local charities, a repository for case histories, a bureau of investigation for the selection of deserving mendicants, and an institution of public information and instruction in its science of charity. "The application of business methods to charity included," historian Marvin Gettleman has noted, "the organization and rationalization of the preexisting and generally haphazard charities in a COS bailiwick (usually a city; Charity Organization was an urban movement)."[73] Its objectives were the eradication of poverty, the encouragement of voluntary participation in charitable endeavors, and a business-like efficiency on the part of all participating charities; its principles were given voice in *Charities Review*.

A basic premise of the movement, set forth in the first issue of its journal by minister and popular author Edward Everett Hale, was that the American social order was not comparable to the European: "There they are carrying their Old Man of the Sea." The United States, conversely, because it had no hereditary poor, had "no need for Lady Bountifuls, . . . no need of gracious condescension from one class to another class. All that we need is to give to everybody in America the place to subdue the world which the good God wants him to occupy." American society, Hale continued, if not quite classless, was still open. The main function of the COS had to be, then, positive, not negative; it was not so much a system for healing, as it was a force for invigorating all of urban society.[74]

A major benefit of Charity Organization, Baltimore civil service advocate Charles J. Bonaparte assured his COS colleagues meeting in New York City in February 1892, was "the 'object lesson' it affords, showing how much, under our form of government, can be done to lessen crime, vice and misery by voluntary association and with no immediate legal sanction. In this feature it is peculiarly and thoroughly America; the genius of our institutions is jealous of interference by the government.'' Voluntaryism, Bonaparte proclaimed, symbolized America's "untrammeled freedom to do good.''[75] What distinguished COS work from earlier and more primitive voluntary efforts "to do good,'' however, was its efficiency. The movement not only adopted the structure and methods of contemporary business, but it also shared its boundless ambition. "The Standard Oil Trust is perhaps the most monumental achievement of our time,'' Alfred Bishop Mason declared. "A Flesh-and-Blood Trust would be greater still.'' As "a business man trying to take a business view of the world's most important business—the manufacture of men, of men who shall be fit to woo women and so fit to be the fathers of that posterity which will certainly judge us and may bless us,'' Mason lamented that "the world too often makes a bad blotch of this business of manufacturing men. It dabbles in shoddy. Its goods are sometimes simply 'bads.' ''[76] "Misapplied and mischievous charity,'' theologian Washington Gladden warned, contributed to the preservation of the "bad'' elements in society; properly administered charity would lead, conversely and beneficially, to the "prevention of charity.'' The elimination of unnecessary and ill-advised charities, Gladden maintained, would result in "a moral change in the community, upon the whole subject of dependence.'' "There is no amount of suffering that I would not cheerfully endure sooner than sink into the mental and moral habit of mendicant. And what I thus freely and intelligently choose for myself,'' Gladden concluded confidently, "I ought to choose for my neighbor.''[77] The spirit of voluntary organization, expansive optimism in a triumphant industrial capitalism, and a self-congratulatory bourgeois tone were the identifying and lasting marks of the Charity Organization Societies.

Proponents of the COS continually stressed that the good example set by genteel volunteer workers among the lower orders was one of the chief contributions of the movement to the reform of urban America. The "friendly visitor'' gave evidence of the welcome social condition in which, in the judgment of Frederic Almy, "a man cannot hold his head erect if he is not on at least one committee where he gives his time to the public without reward.''[78] "The friendly visitor is the spark, the social light,'' Charles F. Weller explained. "If he be touched with the true flame, he will enkindle others, and possibly, those social developments which must come slowly, one by one, will seem to come at last like the enlistment of Abe Lincoln's volunteers, like a new crusade.''[79]

The fighting faith of the COS did not, however, make the movement acceptable to all contemporary social critics, and much of the energy of *Charities Review* was devoted to answering criticisms from the right and the left.[80] "Scarcely a week passes nowadays,'' medical authority Dr. Woods Hutchinson complained, "without our hearing philanthropy denounced as 'promoting the survival of the unfit.' '' Reactionary arguments of this type, he countered, misjudged the struggle for existence (in itself, good) for a war of extermination. "We venture to assert that love, with its daughter, goodness, is not only a legitimate product of evolution, but (next to hunger) the *most powerful factor* in it.''[81] More frequently, however, opposition came from more humanitarian social theorists—from church leaders, heads of public charitable institutions, and settlement workers. These critics were less concerned with the softness of COS policies than they were with the grim social philosophy propounded in *Charities Review*. "Very well, dear friends," the editors of that journal answered, "if it suits you better, call it the 'Anti-Charities Review.' So far from its being the champion and apostle of almsgiving, it is distinctly committed to the advocacy of the sound ethical and economic doctrine, that, of all forms of charity, almsgiving is the least satisfactory and the most dangerous." Moreover, they continued, "Poverty is the least of the ills which humanity has to bear, and to help others to bear."[82] Organized charity's social role would be, J. S. Menken offered, "in helping the poor without destroying their spirit." Not the poor, but the causes of poverty must be the target of the COS. "The charitable association that feeds the hungry of to-day, reforms the tenement, or gives other temporary relief, is merely patching an old garment, which really can't be permanently improved."[83] COS, its defenders challenged its critics, answered the needs of urban America—the needs "of classification, of division of labor, of co-operation, of oversight, of system and method."[84] COS was an active social force, not a "mere official-dom," never a contended bureaucracy. The movement had to counteract any charities which "by ignorance and antiquated methods are working against the very aim of organized charity! . . . Not peace, but a sword, has been and must be, at times, the means to a high end."[85] "Not peace, but a sword" was the COS response to critics, mendicants, and all urban America.[86]

Assaults from without were aggravated by struggle from within. A paradox basic to the movement could be seen in its fruitless attempt to balance the incompatible amateurism of friendly visiting with the professionalism of expert administration. Helen Bosanquet, for example, in her defense of COS training procedures, asserted that charity workers had to be "specialists" in "an age of specialization"; nevertheless, when she came to characterize effective charity workers, she designated them "artists." "I say all artists," she explained, "for there is always something of the artist about the true philanthropist, and the harmony of life which he aims at creating is hardly less important than that of the painter, the poet, or the musician."[87] Yet, a "scientific system," Bosanquet and her colleagues seemed increasingly to recognize, had little use for artists. Instead of amateur friendly visitors, it needed professional case workers. The limited success of COS did not result from a lack of will or of effort; its failure stemmed from the basic inadequacy of *noblesse oblige* in an urban-industrial order. Its halfway compromise with traditional morality and its habit of giving aid with a flatfooted gracelessness often combined to aggravate the conflict between rich and poor. The society for the "suppression of benevolence," as many contemporaries called it, was, at best, an indifferent mediator between the "two nations" in urban America.[88]

Traditionally, from the days of the Puritan theocracy to those of frontier and big-city revivalism, the churches had served as key mediators in American society. Whether decentralized denominations, based as they were essentially upon loose confederations of separate congregations, both inner-city and sub-urban, could continue to fulfil this function in the new metropolitan setting was, by late century, seriously in doubt. *The Public*, for instance, reprinted the questionings of political economist Frank Parsons as to the sincerity of Christian love in cities in which "millionaires go to church and read the Bible and pay fine ministers to preach the brotherhood of man," while, at the same time, their laboring brothers were excluded from the congregation and exploited by the economic system. Under these circumstances, the situation was obvious: "We are not brothers."[89] The editors of this same journal, after having noted that clergymen in Cleveland had advertised sermons on "subjects of popular interest" and were contemplating a season of prayer and fasting in their efforts to increase church attendance, asked: "Have they tried the experiment of making their churches religious instead of pious?"[90] Again, the pietistical preacher was char-acterized in a poem about a "parish priest of austerity" who had isolated himself in a church steeple "To be nearer to God, that he might hand/ His Word down to the people." Twice each Sabbath, this same cleric "dropped . . . down on the people's heads" sermons which he believed to be "sent from Heaven." As he finally made ready for his death, he called to his God: " 'Where art thou, Lord?' And the Lord replied:/ 'Down here, among my people!' "[91] The church, the editors of *The Public* warned, was in danger of alienating these same people, for it had avoided responsibility in its quest for "respectability," and had "really come to be little better than a weekly social club. . . . And the idea that the great object in life for every man is to save his soul has had not a little to do in promoting the corrupting process"; in fact, "this ideal of sublimated selfishness" ignored "the profound truth that he would save his soul must lose it for his brother's sake."[92] The church, *The Public* challenged, had to find a new meaning for the term "social." The church, poet Katherine Lente Stevenson taught, had to be returned to the people. "We rear vast domes unto Thy name;/ We build our church-walls broad and high,/ They hide, from us, our deepest shame." For, "Outside, the cowering people crowd."[93] These "cowering people," Emma Playter Seabury warned, could be turned into a "clamoring mob," as they stood at the doors of the church with their spokesman, Jesus Christ, who commanded their admission:

> "Behold I stand at the door and knock,
>   But no one seems to hear,
>   Will you list to the clamoring crowd?
>   The ominous, countless beat,
>   Growing louder, and yet more loud,
>   Of the people's bleeding feet?
> They will burst with an earthquake shock
>   The doors—they are coming near!

> The starving have no fear,
> *They* will not stand at the door and knock.''[94]

Urban America presented its churches with both a challenge and a threat.

The first demand that the modern city made upon the Christian church was that it adopt a new social philosophy. ''With the passing away of independent individualism,'' George Howard Gibson wrote, ''the practice of individual Christianity has also necessarily ended.''[95] The church had to recognize, economist-historian John R. Commons maintained, that any ''social problem'' had ''no significance except as it is a religious problem. Man is made in the image of God.'' The church, however, as the formal institution of Christianity, had held to dogma and ignored the lessons of scientific investigation. The church regarded Sunday labor as profane, science demonstrated that it was an economic necessity; the church blamed corrupt municipal politics on sinful officials, science determined that the governmental system itself encouraged inefficiency and peculation; the church saw intemperance as a moral fault and proposed prohibitory measures, science recognized it as a result of social pressures and suggested institutional reforms. Organized Christianity, Commons urged, had to incorporate into its collective wisdom the findings of social science; its ministers had to be trained in sociology, penology, and the methods of institutional charity. Only after it had prepared itself to face up to the complexities of the urban-industrial order could the church take an intelligent and informed public stand for Christ and His people.[96]

Most social theorists agreed that the church should play an active role in the affairs of the nation's cities. It was responsible, Thomas R. Slicer observed, for the ''business integrity of its members''; and the running of a city was a business operation. ''The city as to its administration has three functions: (1) it has common interests as to business; (2) it has mutual interests as to order; (3) it has inseparable destiny of all its people, as to the happiness and misery of its inhabitants. The public business is only an aspect of the general business carried on in that great aggregation of human life called the city.''[97] The church's leadership role in the city was inescapable, Walter Laidlaw, executive secretary of the New York City Federation of Churches, asserted: ''Originated by the Holy One from one of the least cities of Judah, commissioned in Palestine's largest city, her literature christened with the names of the ancient world's greatest cities and city, her social ideal a city let down from heaven, the church has opportunity to take the primacy, beyond all question, in altruistic movements.''[98]

One method of establishing the church's primacy in the urban order was the evangelistic. Dr. W. R. Huntington, the editors of *The Commons* reported, ''pleads for nationalism in religion as a necessary temporary expedient to lead out from home rule to the universal kingdom of the Father.'' The major missionary field for the modern church was to be its own teeming urban centers.[99] ''Never before was there a nation with so much foreign missionary work to be done within its own borders as our own,'' the Rev. J. D. Davis observed; ''and unless it is done we shall not long remain a nation.'' Missionary work still remained for the individual communicant. "Are there not,'' Davis asked, "those among the up-town Christians whom God is calling back to move back down town, to form centers of Christian love and life, *ganglia*, as it were, which shall make more living and effective the weaker and more interrupted efforts?''[100] The experience of the Tabernacle Church in Chicago's Seventeenth Ward, *Chicago Commons* reported, seemed to answer to the negative. Although this congregation had been fortunate in having "all through the years a 'remnant' of the faithful, a kind of 'Old Guard,' who always could be counted upon in the darkest hours to be on hand and to do their best,'' the Tabernacle Church, "like all other similarly situated, suffered early the effects of the exodus of the more resourceful folk to the suburban homes and churches, and of late years it has been an increasingly difficult problem how to do the work that needs to be done.''[101]

Although many of his contemporaries agreed that the work of the urban church had become "increasingly difficult'' to perform, liberal theologian Walter Rauschenbusch was among the few who wondered "if there has ever been a great city that was really religious. I do not know,'' he confessed, "but I am sure that there is no great city in which modern industrialism has set up its smoking and flaring altars of Mammon in which religion is not struggling for its life like a flower growing among the cobble stones of the street.''[102] The church, if it were to survive and have meaning within the urban-industrial order, had to draw upon untapped resources and initiate new programs. Complacency had to give way to innovation.

The militant framework of the Salvation Army was presented as one such institutional innovation, but it was immediately and almost unanimously rejected. The tactics of the Army, *Charities* editor Edward T. Devine asserted, while "presenting themselves as a semi-charity,'' served mainly to perpetuate existing evil conditions.[103] The editors of *Architectural Record* judged the new Army headquarters in downtown New York an "architectural aberration''—indeed, an inevitable one:

Consider what is the "basic principle'' of the organization in question, so far as that principle can be expressed in building. Is it not that, in order to regenerate a man's spiritual nature, you need not improve him in any other respect? He needs no more mental culture, no more social culture than is already in the possession of the humblest. He does not even need a change of linen or an application of soap and water. More specifically, the method of the society is to vulgarize religion in order to convert the vulgar. The same vulgarity and foolishness that appear in the "knee drill'' and the big drum should appear in the facade of a building devoted to the uses of the Army.[104]

The "basic principle'' of this urban Christian Army, W. J. Ashley maintained, was merely another "nostrum.'' "The new fashion of the pill no longer: 'Pass this or that piece of legislation, and society will be regenerated.' It is: 'Put your money in the slot, and the machine will work. Send in your subscriptions, and the Salvation Army will do the rest.' '' Churchmen would do better, Ashley advised, in passing over General Booth's *In Darkest England* for a careful study of Charles Booth's *East London*.[105]

While the ''vulgarity'' of the Salvation Army might have been scorned, its militancy was adopted and modified. The downtown churches enlarged considerably their activities within the community, a development that contemporary and later social observers labeled the social gospel movement. An innovation for American Protestantism, this movement also drew upon the hitherto untapped resources of traditional Christianity and, closer at hand, the examples of the Roman Catholic Church. This shift in social emphasis was due, in part, to the spirit of denominational competition; Protestantism, Walter Laidlaw remarked frankly, was ''not holding the people as compared with Roman Catholicism.''[106] Protestant ministers and their flocks, Levi Gilbert lamented, sold their ''valuable property for business sites'' and removed to the suburbs. ''How seldom do we see this ruinous policy imitated by the more astute Roman Catholic churches, under the guidance of their secular priests, long-headed men with business instincts.'' The Catholics, in fact, ''more frequently move into than away from down-town districts, and show a marvelous instinct in acquiring and holding on to large blocks of business property in the very heart of our great cities.''[107] Moreover, some of these same ''long-headed, secular priests'' were beginning to evidence a social awareness that had previously been unique to the Protestant clergy. The Rev. Thomas J. Ducey, for example, linked his ideas with those of Pope Leo XIII, Ralph Waldo Emerson, George D. Herron, and Henry Demarest Lloyd in his opposition to ''the disgrace of great wealth, the puerility of culture, the corruption that inheres in the possession of power.'' Ducey predicted the formulation of ''a new kind of conscience. . . . The physical misery of the world's disinherited is becoming the spiritual misery of the world's elect.''[108] Such pronouncements were, of course, standard among American intellectuals and reformers; however, such a statement by a ''Romanist'' spokesman gave evidence that the American Catholic establishment was coming of age and had now to be reckoned with as an active social force, one more American than Roman. No longer, as at mid-century, quite so feared as a foreign threat and, for its part, less evangelical and thus less abrasive as a competing denomination, the late-century church, like the big-city machine, was the subject of study and emulation; however, as had been true with the machine, the church's effectiveness was sometimes overestimated. Still, the importance of its parish structure as a model for neighborhood action could not be denied.

The Protestant establishment responded to the demands of the new urban order by attempting to charge the energies and redirect the actions of its central-city churches, those embattled enclaves in teeming commercial districts. It encouraged a socialization of church activities designed to transform traditional Protestant meeting houses into modern parish centers. Its new social emphasis was reflected in the formation of the Open and Institutional Church League and in the pages of its official organ, *Open Church*. This journal, according to church historian Aaron I. Abell, "was particularly significant for its excellent descriptions of the new institutions which had sprung up in the chief cities. In this way, Christians for the first time obtained an adequate picture of the changing religious scene."[109] The logic of the movement was governed by its basic premise, as enunciated by the Rev. Everett D. Burr, that the motive force behind an awakened urban Protestantism ought to be service, the sense of duty contained in the Christian injunction that the church had "*not to be ministered unto, but to minister.*" The goal of the movement was a cradle-to-grave Christianity, a religious community in which all were "found, fed, held and helped by the church, and from the very first contact of the church with the life of the family or of the individual by the subtle processes of love and of life Jesus Christ is presented, so that as every method and agency is suggested by His spirit, they all lead back to Him directly. Christ is all in all."[110] This complete Christian community would be achieved, apologists of the institutional church movement theorized, by a broadening and reordering of the social functions of the church, a process that they judged to be thoroughly modern but nevertheless marked by some traditional—indeed, medieval—influences.

The modernity of the movement was apparent in the emphasis that its proponents placed upon the virtues of efficient organization, the balancing of expert and voluntary work, and business-like methods. Although the operations of each congregation had to be determined by its own community's special needs and resources, the organization of one open and institutional church, Boston's Ruggles Street Baptist Church, was offered by *Open Church* as a representative example of effective Christian social action. Its primary distinguishing mark was its "utter simplicity of organization." The Ruggles Street Church combined the labors of professional and volunteer workers in two collateral and cooperating divisions: "departments of labor" were staffed by salaried assistants to administer dispensary, relief, and labor departments; "committees of service" were made up of lay volunteers who augmented the work of the professionals in Committees of Ministration, a Home Department, a Converts' and Inquirers' Committee, a Temperance Committee, and the like. Working in tandem, the professionals and volunteers provided the church with a "multiplied ministry." The church's "free seats" and "open doors," moreover, encouraged the maximum use of the physical plant. All told, the church's "simplicity of organization brings directness of contact and increase of power by short leverage. Put all the power you may on the end of the lever, but get the fulcrum close to the weight to be moved is good dynamics for Christian work. It must be conceded that one of the greatest problems our churches face to-day is the waste of power." The open and institutional church guaranteed "a minimum of politics and a maximum of power."[111] This same "increase of power" that "institutionalism" supplied emanated from an affluent urban milieu: "In the city a wealthy church opens its doors, lures efficient workers, musicians, physical directors, lecturers, kindergartners, cooking and sewing teachers, and with countless attractions gathers in the multitudes."[112] Institutionalism meant, then, the urbanizing of Protestantism.

Apostles of the movement as they urbanized the church's message and activities were inevitably subjected to sharp criticism by their conservative coreligionists. The institutional church, it was charged, sacrificed the gospel for social action. The response: institutional churches "are open for preaching and teaching of the gospel, not one day in seven, but seven days in seven. . . . They are campaigning churches and are constantly in the field. They are fishing for men all the time, and therefore use steadily all the means for catching men." The institutional church, it was charged, was unorthodox. Response: "the open churches . . . preach 'Christ and Him crucified,' with a fidelity and zeal the best witnesses for which are the spiritual fruits." The institutional church, it was charged, coddled people. Response: so did Christ. The institutional church, it was charged, was not a financial success. Response: "Well, what of it? Christianity is not a speculation. The Church in Jerusalem was not a financial success. . . . There should be 'whips of scorpions' for the miserable idea that church work is to be measured by financial standards."[113] Church work was to be judged, rather, by its service to the urban community.

The idea of service that was promulgated by advocates of the movement was modern in one sense, traditional in another. The Rev. Mr. Burr, for example, in his championing of "an evangel of handicraft" was proposing a return to the preindustrial value of the "dignity of labor."[114] Charles A. Dickinson recognized and warned against the temptations besetting his colleagues in the movement toward "groping wearily and darkly down to the primitive church through the ages of ecclesiastical history and tradition."[115] The progressive and modernized church clubs themselves, with their "manly" ministers and "Get-About" committees, certainly drew heavily upon military pomp and commercial boosterism in their organization and activities.[116] However, they were also throwbacks to the medieval ideal of the guild. The guild concept seemed especially appropriate for Protestant laymen because, unlike female church members, they were not organized into religious associations. "From time immemorial," the Reverend John Clark Hill advised, "there have been general and local associations for the furtherance of specific departments of Christian ministration, but these organizations, until recent years, have been confined largely to the Roman Catholic Church, and those we may class as ritualistic."[117] Their modern Protestant counterparts would be marked not by ritual, but by vitality. And, in a sense, they were both modern and vital; however, in another sense, they were conservative, for they—and the institutional church movement itself—represented the effort of Protestant urban America to achieve a compromise with the new industrial order. And that compromise was to be effected on the church's own terms.

The dominant theme of American Protestant thought had always been, and continued to be, the achievement of the Kingdom of God; however, as historian-theologian H. Richard Niebuhr has suggested, the vision of the kingdom took on a new meaning during the late nineteenth century, a meaning that was basic to the compromise made by the institutional church movement.[118] Although institutionalism adopted the organizational methods of the urban-industrial complex, it looked back to the simpler structure of a preindustrial society. "What we look for," Elias B. Sanford confessed, "are the signs that the church is the body of Christ. That it is alive to its great mission as the chief instrumentality for advancing and bringing in the Kingdom of God." The modern church, in other words, was to assume the universality of the medieval church. "Organic unity is still a dream of the future. Federation is a present possibility. The churches of a community collectively represent the body of Christ in that community."[119] The "body of Christ" was thus transformed into an immanent, not a transcendent force; the church spiritual was to become a church temporal. This urbanized church militant, with its uneasy amalgam of modernity and medievalism, its boards of experts and its guilds, its sophisticated administrative machinery and its "organic unity," awkwardly straddled two worlds. Liberal theologian Walter Rauschenbusch recognized this when he said that "the institutional church is a necessary evil. The people ought to be able to provide for themselves what the churches are trying to provide for them." Society, Rauschenbusch perceived, could not revert to organic simplicity (if such had ever existed); instead society's complexity had to be acknowledged and acted upon.[120] Compromise for the institutional church movement, as for the Charity Organization Societies, resulted ultimately in failure: a nation of cities required much more than a modified individualism or an updated medievalism for the achievement of a new social equilibrium. The modern city had to be met on its own terms and its own grounds—as a complex, not simple, socioeconomic entity. Eventually, the pressures of the market place brought home to these churches the realities of the economic order: due to financial exigencies one service after another had to be curtailed, and the ministers discovered that they, too, were disadvantaged.[121] Their secularized kingdom was not to be of this world.

The settlement movement, the most creative and effective of the three late-century municipal mediating agents, was the victim of its early successes. Many of its well-meaning sympathizers seemed ever anxious to match Toynbee Hall against Tammany Hall in an urban Armageddon. Overreacting to its novel methods of operation, Edward Cummings noted, many of its supporters held for the settlement a "central Africa conception of philanthropic work": "A great slum, reeking with vice and crime, and in its midst a sort of moral stockade, from which valiant and pure young men and women go forth to unknown dangers,— this is something like the ordinary conception of a university settlement, repeated so persistently that it is almost a wonder the university settlers are not more frequently deceived about themselves."[122] The reason for this basic misconception of the settlement idea, Cummings maintained, was twofold: the failure on the part of many to familiarize themselves with the actual workings of a settlement and also to the naturally "stimulating contrast of culture and squalor [that] inevitably excites the imagination." Although the emotional response could

scarcely be overcome by persuasion alone, a knowledge of the history of the
movement, Cummings asserted, one based on the record of the parent settlement
house, London's Toynbee Hall, might tend to promote a more realistic view of
the settlement idea. In order to achieve this balanced judgment, critics of the
movement had to recognize that it was neither an "evangel of aestheticism and
good will" nor a "sort of philanthropic picnic in a wilderness of misery and
sin"; nor, moreover, would "a multiplication of similar efforts" revolutionize
and transform urban society. Its significance stemmed from the part that it played
in "our renaissance," a supporting not a major role.[123]

Despite the mystique that had been formed about the Toynbee Hall enterprise,
Edward Cummings judged this original settlement to be a pleasant gentlemen's
club, one in which there was "not the slightest suggestion of austerity or privation
either in the men, their surroundings, or the location of the club." The young,
respectable London settlers, he suggested, failed to reach the real submerged
tenth; their impact was only upon the "remnants of slum respectability." The
very limits of their influence proved that "it is not enough to drink tea and
smoke cigarettes with the great unwashed. They cannot be teaed or even lectured
into the higher life, to any great extent." The question that leaders in the
movement had to answer was "what, in reality, is the *policy* of the settlement?"
If they failed to answer this query satisfactorily, there was little to keep the
movement "from degenerating into many of the juvenile eccentricities of college
life." "The danger here is superficiality," Cummings cautioned, "superficiality
of motive, of short-term residence, of mistaking curiosity or love of sensation
and adventure for serious purpose to help and learn." Observers of urban society,
he warned, had to abandon "the absurd notion that any large social salvation is
to be purchased by this vicarious self-ostracism of a select few." And yet,
Cummings admitted, the personal experience of settlers was of incalculable
benefit to society: "It is difficult to overestimate the value of a brief and comparatively superficial sojourn, which teaches the prospective clergyman or politician or president of associated charity organizations and anti-tenement leagues
how the other half lives,—yes, and smells."[124]

The settlement movement, its American philosopher Robert A. Woods assured
his readers, preferred skeptical to romantic opinions of its achievements; most
of all, however, it desired a suspension of judgment until the movement had
matured. Nevertheless, visions "in which the flower of the country's youth,
touched with a new chivalry, go forth to establish outposts of civilization among
the supposed barbarian hordes that threaten the modern city" were certain to
gain credence; for the settlement movement possessed an *élan* that encouraged
their creation, a vitality that was reminiscent of the vigor of primitive Christianity.
The settlement mystique might contribute, Woods admitted, to a blurring of the
aims of the movement; however, this seemed inescapable. The organization of
a settlement, he insisted, could not be fashioned after military, business, church,
or educational models. The closest approximation to its organization and methods
was to be found in the world of politics; here, too, "compromise" determined

policy. The philosophical foundations of the settlement idea were not "based upon *a priori* conclusions, but in patient experimental action, guided by an acquaintance with the facts that is both extended and minute."[125] The settlement idea was rooted in pragmatism.

Experience had taught settlers, Woods maintained, that the dislocations of industrialization and urbanization had been sharpest among the laboring masses. For the submerged tenth some physical relief was available; for the plutocracy education served as a civilizing force. The proletariat, however, was cut off from both: "It scorns charity. It is indifferent to offers of advanced education." To the working masses, then, the settlement offered "fellowship," a sense of belonging, an opportunity for community building. The settlement house that stood in the midst of the teeming big-city neighborhood, as once had stood the medieval monastery in the center of a war-torn feudal society, offered sanctuary from industrial struggles, a place for communication and sharing. "The function of a settlement as a connecting link between the two great sections of society is one that will be more appreciated as the extent of the cleavage between them comes to be realized," Woods maintained. "It is unfortunately true in large cities, at least, that the Americanizing process, remarkable as its achievements are, has had its results rather in opening up fuller intercourse within this heterogeneous immigrant mass than in relating it in any way to the original American element in the population." The pragmatism of the settlement movement, Woods asserted, gave it the best opportunity for transforming this "Americanizing process' into a "true Americanism."[126] "Settlement policy," he maintained, "is essentially a policy of compromise. In educational matters, in the labor problem, in religion, the settlement worker is always the possibilist." He was motivated "by the desire to come into fellowship with the people who happen to be about him, and not by doctrinaire standards or the abstract passion for perfection."[127] Woods agreed with Cummings that the settler himself was the chief beneficiary of the movement, for his experience provided him with "a sounder and more constraining sense of social service. The coming into touch with persons of another walk of life, who have the unexpected intellectual and moral values which go with that type of existence, leads to a sort of illumination comparable with that which comes from travel in a foreign land."[128]

The settlement idea seemed, indeed, to be based upon a fundamental paradox: community was to be achieved by personal "illumination," the collective was to develop from the individual. Christopher Lasch acknowledged this same paradox in the career of Jane Addams when he concluded that her "method was essentially autobiographical."[129] Addams herself emphasized the personalism of her program for social action in one of her major essays on the settlement idea. After having quoted approvingly from the writings of John Dewey and William James, she concluded that "the dominating interest in knowledge has become its use"; and that, finally, interested citizens had "consciously formed themselves into groups for the express purpose of effective application" of such applied knowledge. These groups were then called settlements:

The ideal and developed settlement [Jane Addams continued] would attempt to test the value of human knowledge by action, and realization, quite as the complete and ideal university would concern itself with the discovery of knowledge in all branches. The settlement stands for application as opposed to research; for emotion as opposed to abstraction, for universal interest as opposed to specialization. This certainly claims too much, absurdly too much, for a settlement, in the light of its achievements, but perhaps not in the light of its possibilities.

This, then, will be my definition of the settlement: that it is an attempt to express the meaning of life in terms of life itself, in forms of activity.[130]

Individual residents, Herman F. Hegner reported, who had removed to settlement houses, came to them as sentimentalists, as privileged individuals experiencing crises of conscience, as "methodical" students of society, as properly motivated men of the cloth who had despaired of individual salvation; they emerged as social realists, graduates of a great "educational clearing house." Their "illumination" was, as Robert A. Woods had suggested, "comparable with that which comes from travel in a foreign land"; yet, their journeys were necessarily inward ones, pilgrimages that were "essentially autobiographical."[131]

The individuality of the settler or resident was reflected in the distinctiveness of each separate settlement house; nevertheless, although the movement was distinguished by its variety of forms, three general models may be identified. The English prototype, Toynbee Hall, may be taken as the pure university settlement, the house that was run in close cooperation with an academic establishment; the second type, the church settlement, was a house sponsored and administered by either a single congregation or a larger denominational body;[132] finally, there was the independent settlement, the house organized by nonaffiliated individuals, as was Jane Addams's renowned Hull House. There were, moreover, settlements that mixed elements from all three models. The Chicago Commons, for example, combined the organization of the university and independent with the spirit of the church settlement; of more significance for this study, its official journal became, as Frank Luther Mott described it, "the leading exponent of the settlement movement."[133] The unique character of *The Commons* stemmed from its direct contact with a working settlement house in a major urban center. This was because its progress reports about the Chicago Commons made possible the type of pragmatic test for social theories that proponents of the settlement movement judged to be so necessary. At once, theory was modified by fact.

The initial challenge that faced the founders of the Commons, the journal's first publisher and editor John P. Gavit reported, was not in defining the resident's role in either house or community; it was, rather, in convincing anyone that *this* settlement would locate and remain in *this* community. Thus, Gavit continued, the reaction of the real estate broker to founder Graham Taylor's request to sign the lease for the original house was one of utter disbelief:

"Do you mean to say [the realtor asked] that you people, who could live on Ashland boulevard, are going to make your home deliberately down here among the Italians and Polacks, in this dirt and smoke?"

"That [Professor Taylor answered] is precisely what I mean."

"And not to have any home but this?"

"That exactly."

The young man looked at the Professor a long time, and then, turning to his brother, exclaimed: "Well, brother, there are such people in the world, I suppose, but this is the first one I ever saw."

And with the neighborhood it was precisely the same. . . . That any man who could live where there are good air, clean streets, green lawns, well-dressed passers-by, should voluntarily share humble surroundings and the pressure of municipal misrule and administrative discrimination, making his home, his citizenship, his neighborship and fellowship his gift to the community where he could contribute what he had and was to those to whom he chiefly owed it, was so utterly in opposition to ordinary ways of doing and ordinary human motive that it must be prompted by some sort of hypocrisy, and must cover some kind of trickery.[134]

The first call upon the new settlers was for communication, not introspection; and this challenge was met by Graham Taylor in his selection of the settlement's name. He had searched, Taylor confessed, for a name that would reflect the idea of sharing, the very concept of community itself. He finally decided upon "that good old English word *common*," in order to suggest the "ideal of social democracy" that was at the root of the settlement movement, an ideal that would be central to the mission of his Chicago Commons—the " 'clearing-house' for the commonwealth."[135]

Introspection immediately followed communication. The settlement's "initial statement" of aims and methods defined it as "a group of Christian people who choose to live where they seem to be needed, for the purpose of *being* all they can be to the people with whom they identify themselves." The Chicago Commons, the editors of its journal added, was dedicated to preserving "as little of an organization and as much of a personal relationship" as possible; indeed, they concluded, should the Chicago Commons "become institutionalized" and abandon its "corporate personality," it would lose its reason for being.[136] A concomitant danger, The Commons warned—and here it agreed with critics of the general movement—was the danger of a "settlement cult." "The social settlement is not an institution, manned by a peculiarly constituted priesthood, and divinely ordained, in the division of human labor, to do what no others can do." It was, instead, "a miserable pittance, and only a pittance, paid on account against the unspeakable obligation of Social Justice."[137] Settlers ought not "to forget the master-motive of self-spending, and . . . attempt to build up self out of the neighborhood rather than to build up the neighborhood out of self." Settlement workers had next to recognize that they themselves were not "superior persons" among a "semi-barbarous" poor, that they, as representatives from a "more privileged sphere of life," had not been chosen to introduce morality.

"In every ward of the great city," the editors of *The Commons* asserted, "there is a force of righteousness enough in existence among the people to redeem the community from corruption and filth of any kind." The true need was, again, for communication: "a means of expression, and it appears to us evident—so evident that the utterance of it smacks of platitude—that those who would be useful in settlements or in any other form of service among these crowded populations must first buckle to and give aid and direction and expression to the impulses of the people."[138] The informed resident, then, knew his community and understood his role in it; he did not dictate its values, but articulated them; he did not work *for* his neighborhood, but *with* it.

The distinguishing quality of the Chicago Commons was its concentration upon action, a characteristic expressed vividly in the poet Ernest Crosby's line "Overdoing, perhaps, but what a glorious overdoing it is."[139] The doing began within the settlement house itself: concerts were arranged for neighborhood children, since "no influence . . . [was] more potent to elevate, refine, refresh, and unify than music";[140] courses "based on the needs of a neighborhood literally wedged in between railroads, factories, and crowded street-car lines" were offered in an attempt to expand the horizons of this confined mass of humanity; "picnics and outings, club parties, bazaars, entertainments, socials to the neighborhood, free-floor discussions, the gathering together of all clubs before some special lecturer" were but part of the intense activity of the Commons.[141]

The doing, moreover, was to be shared with existing community institutions. "So far from being what many suspect the settlement to be—a proposed substitute for churches—Chicago Commons has no higher aspiration than to help the Church to become more of a social settlement in each community for the social unification, the Christian neighborliness and the spiritual fellowship of all the people in that 'righteousness, peace and joy in the Holy Ghost' in which the Kingdom of God consists."[142] In the better community of tomorrow, the preacher "will not preach less to individual men; he will preach more to the crowd."[143] For this new ministry, the Chicago Commons might serve as a training ground. The settlement house functioned also as a center for discussion, since it was "one of the few oases of self-conscious democracy in the wilderness of social confusion and industrial chaos, where distinctions of class and caste may be ignored, and mere human manhood may be the title to free speech and frank opinion."[144] Yet its main role continued to be an educative one. "By teaching its neighborhood to demand better housing, better public facilities, better conditions of industry, more educational privileges, good books, lectures, music, art, recreation, indoors and out, means of cleanliness, public and private, leisure for these things, etc., etc., and by educating its outside constituency to see the righteousness and reasonableness of these demands," *The Commons* taught, "any settlement is on a shorter road to human freedom and happiness than in fomenting demands for the raising of 'pay,' in individual cases or trades, above the 'going wage.' "[145] The educational role of the settlement extended, moreover, beyond "popular social propaganda" into the field of professional training, as "more and more students are making laboratory use of the social settlement everywhere."[146]

The settlement would serve as both school and laboratory, but its ultimate justification was as a secularized religious institution. The roots of the Commons, Robert A. Woods instructed its residents, were the three cardinal virtues. *Faith* was its "utopian" motivating force. Hope "must lead us to see in every man that interest, that possibility, which God sees, and through hope we devote ourselves to working out that man's higher destiny, as God does." *Hope* was the belief "that the far-off Utopia which faith reveals is taking shape even amid the confusion of instant, daily facts." *Charity* was expressed in "the consecration of friendship, the actual imparting of some of that love for our fellow-men which we profess to feel."[147] The actual living out of the cardinal virtues of the Judeo-Christian tradition were summed up eloquently in *The Commons's* turn-of-the-century declaration of faith, "1894—CHICAGO COMMONS—1900":

Omnipresent and unconquerable dirt and stifling smoke, ceaseless din of traffic in crowded streets and nearby railroad yards, and always the pressing and depressing atmosphere of poverty, with its inevitably attendant miseries and inexorable degradation and destruction of precious human life—these are the conditions of daily life that have been made endurable by the unstinting co-operation of those who have believed in us and in the ideal for which we have stood, enough to trust us to administer sacrificial gifts, leaving us at the same time free to develop method out of experience; and not less by the unreserving confidence and friendship of noble souls within our neighborhood, unspoiled by even hardest pressure in the merciless struggle for existence. Amid such conditions, and sustained by such co-operation and encouragement as this, we have succeeded in maintaining a home and in gaining a recognized place in the community as friends, fellow-citizens, neighbors; and our house has come, slowly but surely, to be a neighborhood center, a place of fellowship and sharing of personal values; amid the chaos of modern industrial conflict, an outpost, as it were, of human democracy and brotherhood.[148]

In essence, one of the early residents at the Chicago Commons suggested, the social settlement sought "to mediate between the alienated classes by making a sincere effort toward adding the social function to democracy."[149]

In many settlement houses, it would seem, such otherwise overworked phrases as a "sharing of personal values" and "human democracy and brotherhood" and "mediate between the alienated classes" were taken quite literally. Even now, almost a century after their first appearance in American cities, the enterprising spirit of the settlements enlivens the writings of their early settlers, to capture the imagination and win the admiration of the modern reader. Their appeal has a timeless quality about it. The settlements were, as their friends claimed, "outposts" in a physical sense, comfortable homes in run-down neighborhoods; what is more important, they were also "outposts" in a moral sense, centers of generosity in an often selfish and sometimes brutal socioeconomic order.

It is difficult to assess accurately the impact of so varied a movement on urban society. Lewis Mumford has suggested that, at its best, the settlement served as "an organizing social nucleus"; Arthur Mann has estimated that individual settlements ranged from fashionable homes in the slums to vital urban reform centers. In the most extensive survey of the movement to date, Allen F. Davis has indicated that the achievements of settlements in education were far-reaching and long-lasting; that neighborhood women and children, but seldom the men, were it most receptive clients; and that, because of class and language differences, most settlers, no matter how long their stay, remained "outsiders" to the community.[150] Residency was, for the most part, short-termed. In a way, it typified the difficulties faced by any change agent at the local level: the high geographical mobility of the slum population, a common lack of visible neighborhood boundaries; the probable side-tracking of strictly local efforts in the larger economic and social community of the metropolis; the greater cohesiveness of interest groups based upon other than geographical limits; "social dilution and functional ineffectiveness and frustration": all, as political scientist Luther H. Gulick has suggested, work against effective, long-term neighborhood action.[151] Those slum dwellers who were best able to use settlement services were, very probably, members of the "potential" middle class. Such individuals, and not the "floating population," were, as Robert A. Woods wrote, the true clients of the movement; but in what manner and just how many of these persons actually benefited from participation in settlement activities remain impossible to determine.

The essential contribution of the movement remained, in the end, the very *élan* or mystique that so concerned the magazine critics, the sense of individual service and self-giving that stirred the imagination of late-century city dwellers. The innovating settlers, more than contemporary housers or charity workers or members of institutional churches, mediated between the classes by offering sustained personal involvement as one means toward achieving their generation's search for community.

THE CITY AS SOCIAL LABORATORY

The ideal and the real stood in sharp contrast in late-century urban America. The ideal municipality would have boasted a humane and impartial democracy built upon a homogeneous and classless society. The contemporary city mocked this dream with its own style of democracy, one often misgoverned by seemingly foreign cliques or by rapacious interest groups, and its own version of a social balance, one that set plutocracy against proletariat. These tensions produced an effervescence of reform spirit on matters both political and socioeconomic, but urbanists proved themselves to be more progressive and creative in the fields of government and politics than they were in the area of everyday living. Whereas many of their administrative innovations were to stand well the test of time, their nonpolitical programs for the most part, were scarcely to survive the next generation. Any interpretation of this disparity in achievement must take into account the fact that changes in governmental organization and operation, since they touch upon matters closest to the surface of society, are the simplest to achieve; political life itself, because it generally reflects the power situation in a municipality, is far deeper and more difficult to reshape; and, finally, the socioeconomic balance of the community—its very vitals, its most zealously defended form, its least understood condition—is the last to change.

The reaching out of late-century urbanists for a science of society was an indication of their growing awareness that new theories and methods were requisite for the attainment of a tolerable social equilibrium. Earlier generations had based their programs for human betterment upon traditional historical, philosophical, and religious truths; this generation, which had begun to recognize the inadequacy of preindustrial doctrines and values in an industrial age, sought to develop a distinctively modern frame of mind about the metropolitan social structure. The contemporary urbanist relied, as he did also in matters politic, upon institutional, rather than individual changes, rejected the laissez-faire approach of an earlier generation, and substituted for it the ideal of organization for all phases of community living.

Education at all levels was looked upon increasingly in terms of socialization. Indeed, education became practically synonymous with conditioning: general education became a vehicle for the development of a civic consciousness; elementary education became part of the process of Americanization; informal education, vacation schools, and boys' brigades became centers for character building. The children of the foreign-born had to be Americanized, the offspring of rural migrants had to be urbanized, and all of the city's population had to be socialized. Too often, in contemporary reform thought, however, the subjects of these educational efforts appeared as faceless masses to be manipulated by their intellectual and moral superiors; in the process, the subjects became objects. Then, too, education could prove to be divisive between generations, as children were educated "beyond" their parents. Thus, progress became painful.

Housing and charity reform both aimed at a rationalization and reorganization of the existing socioeconomic system through the institutionalization and regulation of fair standards for shelter, on the one hand, and for poor relief, on the other. Housers, by means of such innovations as the model tenement and slum clearance, proposed a more efficient reordering of the physical environment for the lower classes. Charity workers, with increased bureaucratic efficiency and the influence of friendly visiting, sought to eliminate urban poverty. Both movements, in the end, underestimated the problem. Housing was not *sui generis*: it could not be separated from the larger issues of land use, property values, and metropolitan population densities. Housing, then and now, is basic, central, crucial, vital to civic order: it is not *an* urban problem; in a very real sense, it is *the* urban problem. Charity organization proved more immediately effective: through its promotion of centralized information clearing houses, it provided a pattern for what would evolve into the Community Chest and United Way campaigns nationwide; through it championing of friendly visiting, it inadvertently pointed up society's need *not* for amateur benevolence, *but* for professional work. Both movements, finally, represented an uneasy compromise between the old and the new: an essential problem for each was that of its distance from its client group, its patrician stance before a lower order. Each movement failed in its attempt to combine traditional noblesse oblige with modern impersonal service. In the process, the distance between provider and recipient widened, tensions increased.

The institutional church movement and, more especially, the settlement movement met this need for communication and mediation. The institutional church was less successful than the settlement, perhaps, because its freedom to experiment was limited by the formal and informal rules and traditions of Protestant Christianity and because of congregational and denominational exclusiveness and distinctiveness: each congregation was, in effect, closed to outsiders by the covenant that gave it a communion in Christ; each denomination was particularistic in its creed. Residents of the settlements, on the other hand, began their adventures with a minimum of doctrinal strictures, with, in fact, only their own personal values to be adjusted. The contribution of both movements to their communities, nevertheless, was one of communication through experience. What historian Ray Ginger has said of the settlers at Hull House may be said of many in both the institutional church and settlement movements: "If they were high-minded, they were also hardheaded."[152] Their contribution to this nation of cities was personal and intense, essentially autobiographical and unforgettably humane.

Under the best of circumstances, with the most enlightened personnel, and in the best of all possible urban worlds, the dislocations wrought by urbanization and industrialization could not have been "solved" by urbanists of the late nineteenth century. Encumbered as they were with outmoded concepts of the workings of community and limited though they were in scientific methods of social analysis, they managed, nevertheless, to move forward with new ideas and institutions. They thought, probed, and created. With confidence in the value of personal experience, they sought out answers to the problems pressing down upon their great urban centers. Their cities became, in fact, their social laboratories.

NOTES

1. Frederic Taber Cooper, "Frank Norris, Realist," *Bookman* 10 (November 1899): 238.

2. Henry Ling Taylor, "American Childhood from a Medical Standpoint," *Journal of Social Science*, 30 (October 1892): 44–45, 54.

3. Frank W. Blackmar, "The Smoky Pilgrims," *American Journal of Sociology* 2 (January 1897): 500.

4. C. M. Hubbard, "Practical Sociology," *Charities Review* 4 (December 1894):

93. *The Public* remained consistently suspicious of all "students of humanity." A "hardness of heart" was, it argued, the basic reason for the problems of the city. "Even our 'students' of social conditions who go down (?) into the 'slums' dare not, or will not, see the road of simple justice as the one and only way of undoing the evil—of relieving the sufferers." "Suffering," it pointed out, "has too long been made a subject of 'study'; and much that is going on to-day under that cover is no whit different from the unseeing curiosity of the crowd that lounged around the cross of the matchless Sufferer 1900 years ago." (L. R. N., "On a Criticism of Edwin Markham's Poem," *The Public* 2, no. 78 [September 2, 1899]: 15–16).

5. Charles R. Henderson, "Business Men and Social Theorists," *Charities Review* 1 (January 1896): 385, 393, 397. *The Public* feared this great power of the pen. It rejected the avowal of the University of Chicago's President Harper that the urban university should be "prophet, priest and philosopher" for its community; such logic encouraged the creation, the editors of *The Public* warned, of a "professsorial cult": "No one would be esteemed fit even to vote unless he held a university diploma for excellence in industrial history, economic science ('as she is taught') and modes of administration. What university, governed by professors and endowed by millionaires, could safely be entrusted with such authority?" ("Editorials," *The Public* 1, no. 41 [January 14, 1899]: 4).

6. John Franklin Crowell, Review of *American Charities*, by Amos G. Warner, *Political Science Quarterly* 10 (September 1895): 544–45.

7. Henry White, "The City's Health—Working Conditions," *Municipal Affairs* 2 (June 1898): 237, 238.

8. A somewhat different version (and interpretation) of this material will be found in Dana F. White, "Education in the Turn-of-the-Century City: The Search for Control," *Urban Education* 4, no. 2 (1969): 169–82.

9. "Current Literature: The City Wilderness," Review of *The City Wilderness*, ed. Robert A. Woods, *Gunton's Magazine* 16 (February 1899): 137.

10. Samuel T. Dutton, "Educational Resources of the Community," *Journal of Social Science* 38 (December 1900): 118,121, 122–23.

11. "Life and Education," *Citizen* 3 (August 1897): 127.

12. In "Country Boy versus Town Boy," *The Social Economist* 3 (July–September 1892): 11–22, 98–107, 179–84, J. M. Welding contended that the city boy's major drawback came from the "discouragement of having always dinned into him the utter hopelessness of his efforts in competing with his country cousin" (p. 12).

13. W. M. Beckner, "City Schools as Compared with Country Schools," *Journal of Social Science* 21 (September 1886): 226.

14. Taylor, "American Childhood," p. 50.

15. Sadie American, "The Movement for Vacation Schools," *American Journal of Sociology* 4 (November 1898): 309, 310–25.

16. Sadie American, "The Movement for Small Playgrounds," *American Journal of Sociology* 4 (September 1898): 170.

17. Stoyan Vasil Tsanoff, "Children's Playgrounds," *Municipal Affairs* 2 (June 1898): 293, 294.

18. Charles Zueblin, "Municipal Playgrounds in Chicago," *American Journal of Sociology* 4 (September 1898): 145.

19. William Paul Gerhard, C. E., "A Plea for Rain Baths in the Public Schools," *Journal of Social Science* 38, (December 1900): 40, 35–36.

20. Charles B. Todd, "The City History Club of New York," *Gunton's Magazine* 18 (May 1900): 444, 444–50.

21. "Military Drill for Boys' Clubs," *Charities Review* 4 (March 1895): 235–39. The plan for boys' brigades, which was formulated first in Glasgow in 1883, was introduced in the United States in 1890; by 1895, there were a thousand companies with 25,000 in various American cities (Aaron I. Abell, *The Urban Impact on American Protestantism, 1865–1900* [Cambridge, Mass.: Harvard University Press; London, Eng.: Oxford University Press, 1943], pp. 208–09.

22. Lila Verplanck North, "The St. Paul's Guild House and the Boys' Brigade of Baltimore," *Open Church* 2 (October 1898): 362.

23. See John P. Diggins, "Flirtation with Fascism: American Pragmatic Liberals and Mussolini's Italy," *American Historical Review* 71 (January 1966): 487–506, for an analysis of the authoritarian leanings of some twentieth-century Progressive reformers.

24. Charles Barnard, "What Is He Going to Do About It?" *The Social Economist* 5 (September 1893): 146–48.

25. Florence Kelley, "The Working Boy," *American Journal of Sociology* 2 (November 1896): 358, 365.

26. John Beverly Robinson, "The School Buildings of New York," *Architectural Record* 7 (January–March 1898): 359.

27. Henry W. Thurston, "Family Social Status and Secondary Education," *The Commons* 5, no. 49 (August 15, 1900): 1–4.

28. Ernest Crosby, "Ninety-nine in the Shade," *American Federationist* 7 (August 1900): 233.

29. Henry Powers, "How the Other Half Lives," *The Social Economist* 1 (April 1891): 104. Jacob A. Riis wrote a new series of essays for the *Atlantic Monthly* on the general subject of the tenement house problem in 1899: "The Battle with the Slum," 83 (May): 626–34; "The Tenement House Blight," (June): 760–71; "The Tenement: Curing Its Blight," 84 (July): 18–28; "The Tenant," (August): 153–63; "The Genesis of the Gang," (September): 302–11; "Letting in the Light," (October): 495–505; "Reform by Humane Touch," (December): 745–53.Since these essays are basically repetitive of his earlier writings and since others have analyzed his contributions to the movement in great detail (e.g., Roy Lubove in "Jacob A. Riis: Portrait of a Reformer," *The Progressives and the Slums: Tenement House Reform in New York City, 1890–1917* [Pittsburgh: University of Pittsburgh Press, 1962], pp. 49–80), no attempt has been made here to examine these essentially reportorial essays.

30. "Civics and Education: What to do for the Slums," *Gunton's Magazine* 14 (May 1898): 320.

31. Mary E. Herrick, "The Tenement-House: Its Influence Upon the Child," *Journal of Social Science* 29 (August 1892): 25–26.

32. Julius M. Mayers, "Sweating System in New York City," *Gunton's Magazine* 11 (August 1896): 104; (October 1896): 277–85.

33. Kelley, "The Working Boy," p. 360.

34. Anna S. Daniel, "Conditions of the Labor of Women and Children. Observed by a Dispensary Physician of New York, in 1892," *Journal of Social Science* 30 (October 1892): 73, 85.

35. Charles J. Wingate, "Workingmen and Sanitation," *American Federationist* 4 (March 1897): 6.

36. Joseph Lee, "The Sweating System," *Charities Review* 2 (December 1892): 100–104.

37. Walter L. Creese, *The Search for Environment. The Garden City: Before and After* (New Haven, Conn.: Yale University Press, 1966), p. 288. As Charles Abrams has suggested, "It may have to be conceded that in the formative years of industrialization, the slum will be the inevitable by-product of urban development, like the abdominal distortion that precedes birth and growth. The trouble has been that reformers have always called the swelling a cancer to be excised wherever it appears" (*Man's Struggle for Shelter in an Urbanizing World* [Cambridge: MIT Press, 1964], p. 125).

38. W. D. McCracken, "Giving Work," *The Public* 3 (October 6, 1900): 410.

39. George E. Bissel, "Enrichment of Cities," *Public Improvements* 2 (January 1, 1900): 101.

40. Arnold Eilvart, "An Attempt to Give Justice," *Charities Review*, 3 (May 1894): 345–46.

41. Kemper Bocock, "Tenement Houses and Their Tenants," *The Social Economist* 6 (February 1894): 112, 114–15. Bocock's harsh indictment against grasping landlords was an indication of his attitude toward slum dwellers, most of whom, he asserted, moved willingly and happily from one substandard hovel to another.

42. Harold Kelsey Estabrook, "Some Slums in Boston," *Charities Review* 8 (July 1898): 243, 242.

43. Frances Buckley Embree, "The Housing of the Poor in Chicago," *Journal of Political Economy* 8 (June 1900): 354, 355. While she regretted that Chicagoans had not created a model city upon the ashes left by the Chicago Fire of 1871, Embree was quick to point out that the civic conscience of Chicago was incomparably better developed than was that of its municipal rival, New York.

44. "San Francisco's Opportunity," *California Municipalities* 2 (July 1900): 174.

45. "Editorial Crucible," *The Social Economist* 4 (February 1893): 120.

46. Henry White, "Effects of New York Sweatshop Law," *Gunton's Magazine* 18 (April 1900): 345.

47. Lawrence Veiller, "The Tenement House Problem," *Public Improvements* 2 (March 1, 1900), 198–99. See Lubove, *The Progressives and the Slums*, pp. 151–84, for a perceptive analysis of "The Age of Veiller" and his direction of the movement for mode tenements.

48. Lawrence Veiller, "The Tenement-House Exhibition of 1899," *Charities Review* 10 (March 1900): 19, 23–24, 25.

49. Veiller, "Tenement Problem," pp. 198–200. Roy Lubove has observed that the housers were no radicals "toying with imaginative reconstructions of the social and economic order. Their aim was more modest—to provide safe, comfortable, and even pleasant housing for low-income groups within the framework of the capitalist-profit system. . . . The model tenement represented no challenge whatever to economic orthodoxy. It was a painless and ostensibly effective solution to the housing problem" (*The Progressives and the Slums*, p. 37).

50. E. R. L. Gould, "The Housing Problem," *Municipal Affairs* 3 (March 1899): 108, 109, 111.

51. E. R. L. Gould, "The Housing Problem in Great Cities," *Quarterly Journal of Economics*, 14 (May 1900): 378, 379. For the exhibition, see Lubove, *The Progressives and the Slums*, pp. 115–16.

52. Gould, "Housing Problem," pp. 115–16.

53. Ibid., pp. 114–15, 124. A description of this system is provided in Lubove, *The Progressives and the Slums*, pp. 105–06.

54. Margaret Andrews Allen, "Jennie Collins and Her Boffin's Bower," *Charities Review* 2 (December 1892): 105–115. Jennie Collins, an ex-"Lowell girl," had chosen the name for her home from Dickens' *Our Mutual Friend*: "Old Betty Higden, in her horror of the poorhouse, and Lizzie Hexam, in her heroic self-sacrifice to save Eugene Wrayburn from lowering his social position by a marriage with her, are just such characters as Jennie Collins loved, and we can see how strongly the book must have moved her" (p. 107). We can see, further, that such modest views were remarkably conservative and must have appealed to reformers who advocated class segregation.

55. Annie Marion MacLean, "Homes for Working Women in Large Cities," *Charities Review* 9 (July 1899): 228. Such homes already existed, MacLean pointed out, in Atlanta, Baltimore, Boston, Buffalo, Chicago, Louisville, New York, Philadelphia, St. Louis, and San Francisco.

56. "Editorials," *The Public* 2, no. 57 (May 6, 1899): 5, 5–6.

57. Davis Allyn Gorton, M.D., "The Perils that Menace Popular Government," *American Magazine of Civics* 9 (January 1897): 488. This particular article, it should be noted, which espoused the single tax and a redistribution of wealth through socialism, represented a minority viewpoint.

58. John H. Pryor, "The Tenement and Tuberculosis: Apropos of the Movement for Better Housing Conditions in New York," *Charities Review* 10 (December 1900): 441–42.

59. C. T. C., "The Ethical Side of Tenement House Reform," *Open Church* 2 (October 1898): 366–67.

60. Scott Greer, *Urban Renewal and American Cities: The Dilemma of Democratic Intervention* (Indianapolis: The Bobbs-Merrill Company, Inc., 1965), p. 156.

61. Benjamin Doblin, "The Problem of the Great Unwashed," *The Public* 1, no. 49 (March 11, 1899): 13, 14.

62. William Nelson Black, "Various Causes for Bad Architecture," *Architectural Record* 2 (October–December 1892): 153, 149–52.

63. "Rapid Transit Subways in Metropolitan Cities," *Municipal Affairs* 4 (September 1900): 480.

64. "Civics and Education: . . . the Slums," *Gunton's Magazine* 14 (May 1898): 323–24.

65. Lawrence M. Friedman, *Government and Slum Housing: A Century of Frustration* (Chicago: Rand McNally Company, 1968), p. 4.

66. These terms are defined in, respectively, Gideon Sjoberg, "Cities in Developing and in Industrial Societies: A Cross-Cultural Analysis," *The Study of Urbanization*, ed. Philip M. Hauser and Leo F. Schnore (New York: John Wiley & Sons, Inc., 1965), p. 232, and Lyle W. and Magdaline Shannon, "The Assimilation of Migrants to Cities: Anthropological and Sociological Contributions," in *Urban Research and Policy Planning*, ed. Leo F. Schnore and Henry W. Fagin (Beverly Hills, Calif.: Sage Publications, Inc., 1967), p. 72.

67. "Work, Not Charity," *American Federationist* 1 (March 1894): 11. Not charity, but public works should be sponsored by the community: "The cities or towns may build school houses, parks, roads, canals, waterways, docks or any other tangible improvements. They may expend millions of dollars in these works, but after the idle have been put to work and the improvements have been completed the cities and towns are not

poorer. It is true that the money has been expended, but it is in the hands of its citizens, and the intrinsic value of its own property has become so enhanced and its facilities to obtain more wealth has [sic] become so much greater as to far overbalance the money expended'' (pp. 11–12).

68. Bolton Hall, "The Disease of Charity," *American Journal of Politics* 4 (March 1894): 225, 226, 228, 229.

69. Edward Cummings, "Charity and Progress" [Address before the National Conference of Unitarian and Other Christian Churches, Saratoga, N.Y., September 1897], *Quarterly Journal of Economics* 12, (October 1897): 27.

70. Homer Folks, "Municipal Charities," *Municipal Affairs* 3 (September 1899): 517–18, 527. In "The Unemployed in American Cities," *Quarterly Journal of Economics* 8 (January, July 1894): 168–217, 257–60, 453–77, 499–502, Carlos E. Closson, Jr., summarized the findings of his exhaustive study—based on over 1,200 questionnaires distributed nationally—of contemporary public and private relief measures. Closson categorized and analyzed welfare programs under four headings: "permanent charity organizations," "established municipal or county agencies of relief," "citizen committees or other agencies," and "municipal governments" or public works (the category that he favored). His concluding judgment of "the various relief measures" was that "while some of them have been developed only by great effort and devotion on the part of those in charge, none of them have been individually of extraordinary magnitude. Taken in the aggregate, however, they represent a vigorous effort on the part of the community to afford relief to those of its members suffering most severely from the industrial depression" (p. 477).

71. "Benevolent Investment," *The Social Economist* 1 (March 1891): 11.

72. "Free and Paid Medical Service," *The Social Economist* 7 (December 1894): 353.

73. Marvin Gettleman, "Charity and Social Classes in the United States, 1874–1900," *American Journal of Economics and Sociology* 22 (April 1963): 316.

74. Edward Everett Hale, "The Prevention of Pauperism," *Charities Review* 1 (November 1891): 40, 41.

75. Charles J. Bonaparte, "What a Charity Organization Society Can Do and What it Cannot," *Charities Review* 1 (March 1892): 204, 208.

76. Alfred Bishop Mason, "Things to Do," *Charities Review* 1 (March 1892): 212.

77. Washington Gladden, "The Plain Path of Reform," *Charities Review* 1 (April 1892): 254–55, 253, 256.

78. Frederic Almy, "The Problem of Charity, From Another Point of View," *Charities Review* 4 (February 1895): 179–80.

79. Charles F. Weller, "Friendly Visiting—A Social Force," *Charities Review* 7 (November 1897): 750.

80. Positive statements of purpose, moreover, gave way increasingly to analytical surveys of charitable work in the nation's cities. Among the more valuable of these later analyses were "City Problems," *Charities Review* 9 (November 1899): 358–66; Edward T. Devine, "American Philanthropy in the Nineteenth Century: Relief and Care of the Poor in Their Homes," *Charities Review* 10 (May–October 1900): 118–28, 183–90, 221–30, 261–72, 306–12, 334–45; Joseph Lee, "Preventative Work. (American Philanthropy of the Nineteenth Century)," *Charities Review* 10 (November, December 1900): 376–88, 469–85 [continued into 1901]. The studies by Devine and Lee, both prominent COS

leaders, are especially important for the detail they provided on antebellum and late-century charitable work.

81. Woods Hutchinson, "Darwinsim and Philanthropy," *Charities Review* 7 (January 1898): 897.

82. "Editorial Chit-Chat," *Charities Review* 6 (April 1897): 181, 182. An editorial sponsoring "A Co-operative Coal Club," *Charities Review* 8 (July 1898): 214, gave further evidence of that journal's often gelid attitude to the plight of the poor. The success of coal cooperatives, it was argued, ought to encourage the establishment of cooperative shoe clubs: "To induce weekly savings for shoes among those families whose children give as an excuse for not attending the public schools that they have no shoes."

83. J. S. Menken, "Organized Charity," *Charities Review* 7 (November 1897): 751, 752.

84. Frederick Howard Wines, "Salutatory," *Charities Review* 6 (March 1897): 2.

85. Jeffrey R. Brackett, "The Charity Organization Movement," *Charities Review* 4 (June 1895): 399.

86. Military terminology was employed frequently in this journal. An editorial entitled, "Charity Organization in Times Extraordinary," *Charities Review* 3 (April 1894): 275–81, was typical in its selection of the martial metaphor: "It is the wise man, said Horace, who in time of peace prepares the things necessary for war. And it is the wise city by encouraging thrift among its people, but by provision against the imposition of unthrift, not only by laying up stores and ammunition, but by teaching the economical and wise use of these. Some communities when the hard times came this winter, and the army of the unemployed swept through the streets, were panic-stricken, the inhabitants fortified themselves behind soup-houses, and threw loaves of bread out upon the besiegers; naturally the siege continued" (p. 275).

87. Helen Bosanquet, "Methods of Training," *Charities Review* 10 (November 1900): 391, 393–94.

88. This disparaging sobriquet is quoted by Samuel Rezneck in "Patterns of Thought and Action in the American Depression, 1882–1886," *American Historical Review* 61 (January 1956): 297.

89. "Miscellany. The Slum Baby. By Frank Parsons" [reprinted from *The Kingdom*], *The Public* 1, no. 30 (October 29, 1898): 11.

90. "Editorials," *The Public* 3 (December 15, 1900): 561.

91. "Miscellany," *The Public* 3 (June 30, 1900): 191.

92. "Editorials," *The Public* 3 (December 1, 1900): 529.

93. Katherine Lente Stevenson, "Teach Us, Today," *Chicago Commons* 1, no. 9 (December 1896): 1.

94. Emma Playter Seabury, "Behold I Stand at the Door and Knock," *The Commons* 2, no. 14 (June 1897): 1.

95. George Howard Gibson, "Christian Commonwealth," *The Commons* 3, no. 30 (October 1898): 4.

96. John R. Commons, "The Church and the Problem of Poverty in Cities," *Charities Review* 2 (May 1893): 347, 348–56.

97. Thomas R. Slicer, "Relation of the Church to Municipal Politics," *Municipal Affairs* 4 (June 1900): 386.

98. Walter Laidlaw, "A Plea and Plan for a Cooperative Church Parish System in Cities," *American Journal of Sociology* 3 (May 1898): 796.

99. "For a National Church," *The Commons* 2, no. 23 (March 1898): 13. Hunting-

ton's analysis was described in the following terms: "Three types of natural temperament and conviction divide the churches by local autonomy, the principles of representation and unity of administration. They might all be conserved, the author thinks, by a 'county church,' having a 'master missionary' or county pastor ('bishop') [,] a county council ('presbytery'), representing autonymous local churches ('congregations'). Differing groups of worshippers could even use the same sanctuary and its better equipment. A triennial state convention of county pastors and local clergy and laity, and a decennial national congress, with two houses, each having lay and clerical members, completes the 'National Church.' "

100. J. D. Davis, "Foreign Missions at Home" [reprinted from the Chicago *Advance*], *Chicago Commons* 1, no. 4 (July 1896): 3, 4.

101. "Tabernacle Church. Its Notable History and Its Great Opportunity," *Chicago Commons* 1, no. 8 (November 1896): 1.

102. Walter Rauschenbusch, "The Stake of the Church in the Social Movement," *American Journal of Sociology* 3 (July 1897): 29–30.

103. Edward T. Devine, "The Shiftless and Floating City Population," *Annals of the American Academy of Political and Social Science* 10 (September 1897): 160–64.

104. "Architectural Aberrations. The Salvation Army Building," *Architectural Record* 6 (July–September 1896): 77.

105. W. J. Ashley, "General Booth's Panacea," *Political Science Quarterly* 6 (September 1891): 538. For Charles Booth's contributions, see above, "A Social Survey."

106. Laidlaw, "A Plea and Plan," p. 799.

107. Gilbert, "The Down-Town Church Again," p. 288.

108. Thomas J. Ducey, "Religion and the Labor Question," *Metropolitan Magazine* 12 (August 1900): 259, 256–58. This is not to say that Ducey was representative of the Catholic clergy in his liberalism. Most probably, Thomas M. Mulry's "Catholic Co-operation in Charity," *Charities Review* 8 (October 1898): 383–86, which was delivered first as a paper at a COS meeting and then reprinted in *Catholic Reading Circle Review*, was more typical of the clerical viewpoint. Far less sophisticated than Ducey's essay, this paper is interesting for its self-conscious defense of Catholic charitable work and for its hesitant probes toward accommodation with Protestant agencies. Thus Mulry complained that Catholic charities were unable to compete with their Protestant counterparts: "They had the wealth; we had the poor" (p. 384); however, "our catholic institutions compare favorably with any other, whether they are public or private" (p. 386); and yet, denominational competition "created a sort of piracy among the charities" (pp. 383–84), and cooperation was badly needed. Here was the voice of the uncertain minority—boastful, defensive, wary, but seeking acceptance.

109. Abell, *Urban Impact*, p. 163.

110. Everett D. Burr, "Methods of an Open and Institutional Church," *Open Church* 1 (April, May, June 1897): 97, 98.

111. Ibid., pp. 99, 97–99.

112. Rev. Joseph Jansen Spencer, "Open and Institutional Work in the Village Church. A New England Experiment," *Open Church* 3 (January, February, March 1899): 8. Institutionalism was possible in the rural church, the author concluded, but it had to depend there almost entirely upon voluntary support. See also, "The Institutional Village Church" [anon. letter to the editor], *Citizen* 1 (November 1895): 212–13.

113. "Editorial Table: Some Misconceptions," by C.L.T., *Open Church* 1 (October 1897): 200.

114. Burr, "Methods of an Open and Institutional Church," p. 98.

115. Charles A. Dickinson, "Editorial Table: The Church and the Average Man," *Open Church* 1 (July, August, September 1897): 154.

116. The Rev. Gerald H. Beard, "Church Work for Men," *Open Church* 2 (July 1898): 324–26; see also the Rev. Charles Stelzle, "Boys' Club Work," *Open Church* 3 (January, February, March 1899): 18–21, for another example of this mixed military and business imagery.

117. John Clark Hill, "Men's Clubs," *Open Church* 2 (January 1898): 216.

118. H. Richard Niebuhr, *The Kingdom of God in America* (New York: Harper & Brothers, 1937, 1959), esp. Chapter 5. Niebuhr concluded that the evolution from the early transcendental to the later secularized kingdom resulted in "A God without wrath [who] brought men without sin into a kingdom without judgment through the ministrations of a Christ without a cross" (p. 193). See also Dana F. White, "A Summons for the Kingdom of God on Earth: The Early Social-Gospel Novel," *South Atlantic Quarterly* 67 (Summer 1968): 469–85.

119. Elias B. Sanford, "The Relation of the Church to the Kingdom of God" [a paper read at the Convention of the Open and Institutional Church League, 1898], *Open Church* 3 (January, February, March 1899): 29, 30–31.

120. Rauschenbusch, "The Stake of the Church," p. 26.

121. The movement's eventual decline is analyzed in Robert D. Cross, ed., *The Church and the City* (Indianapolis: Bobbs-Merrill Co., 1967), pp. xxxvi–xxxix.

122. Edward Cummings, "University Settlements," *Quarterly Journal of Economics* 6 (April 1892): 257. A definition of settlements in an editorial in *Citizen* was typical of this uncritical approach; settlements were, it read, "now operative in our largest cities, [and were] a noble attempt to strengthen the brotherhood of men, rich and poor, cultured and ignorant, to know what the poor think and feel, to extend their mental view and light the drudgery of labor with a sense of its purpose and sacredness" ("Life and Education," 3 [August 1897]: 128–29). For the popularity of the "in darkest Africa" metaphor, see Chapter 4.

123. Cummings, "University Settlements," pp. 259, 258, 261, 277. In his history of the movement, Allen F. Davis estimated that there were six settlements in the United States in 1891, seventy-four in 1897, over one hundred by 1900, more than two hundred in 1905, and over four hundred by 1910 (*Spearheads for Reform: The Social Settlements and the Progressive Movement 1890–1914* [New York: Oxford University Press, 1967], p. 12).

124. Cummings, "University Settlements," pp. 263, 271, 263, 273–74, 277, 273–74.

125. Robert A. Woods, "University Settlements: Their Point and Drift," *Quarterly Journal of Economics* 14 (November 1899): 67. Perceptive portraits of Woods may be found in Arthur Mann, *Yankee Reformers in the Urban Age: Social Reform in Boston, 1880–1900* (Cambridge: Harvard University Press, 1954), pp. 114–23, and in Barbara Miller Solomon, *Ancestors and Immigrants: A Changing New England Tradition* (Cambridge: Harvard University Press, 1956), pp. 140–43.

126. Woods, "University Settlements," pp. 69–70, 72, 73–76, 79, 78.

127. Robert A. Woods, "Settlement Houses and City Politics," *Municipal Affairs* 4 (June 1900): 395–96.

128. Woods, "University Settlements," p. 86.

129. Christopher Lasch, ed., *The Social Thought of Jane Addams* (Indianapolis: The Bobbs-Merrill Co., 1965), p. xxvi. Horace Spencer Fiske's poem "The Genius of Hull

House," which was prominently displayed on the front page of *The Commons*, all but fused together the famous founder and her settlement (5, no. 47 [June 30, 1900]: 1).

130. Jane Addams, "The Function of the Social Settlement," *Annals of the American Academy of Political and Social Science* 12 (May 1899): 325, 326.

131. Herman F. Hegner, "Scientific Value of the Social Settlements," *American Journal of Sociology* 3 (September 1897): 178–80.

132. For a comprehensive statement of the organization, aims, and methods of church-affiliated settlements, see Anson P. Atterbury, "The Church Settlement," *Open Church* 1 (October 1897): 161–73. For a detailed analysis of one such institution, see Mary Brownson Hartt, "Westminster House. The Social Settlement of Westminster Church, Buffalo," *Open Church* 2 (July 1898): 309–16. Church-directed settlements served primarily as missions for the parent congregations in lower-class districts of the city; thus, while Buffalo's Westminster Presbyterian Church was located on the West Side's fashionable Delaware Avenue, its settlement, Westminster House, was situated on the impoverished East Side's Monroe Street. One last type of settlement was described by John P. Gavit in "Rural Social Settlements," *The Commons* 4, no. 34 (May 1899): 5–6.

133. Frank Luther Mott, *A History of American Magazines* vol. 4: *1885–1905* (Cambridge: Harvard University Press, 1957), p. 743.

134. John P. Gavit, "Story of Chicago Commons," *Chicago Commons* 3, no. 31 (November 1898): 4. A valuable biography of Taylor is Louise Wade's *Graham Taylor: Pioneer for Social Justice, 1851–1938* (Chicago: University of Chicago Press, 1964).

135. Graham Taylor, "The Settlement Name," *Chicago Commons* 1, no. 1 (April 1896): 6–7.

136. "Our Purpose and Scope," *Chicago Commons* 1, no. 1 (April 1896): 1.

137. "A Settlement Warning," *Chicago Commons* 1, no. 5 (August 1896): 4.

138. "A Word of Caution," *Chicago Commons* 1, no. 11 (February 1897): 8. Proletarian romanticism, the editors of *The Commons* cautioned, no matter how well-intentioned it might be, was a poor substitute for insight into the brutalization of the masses. The sins of the plutocracy were many, but "the greed, the grasping disregard of elementary rights of fellowmen, the clutch after the tawdry brass buttons which make up the outward show of 'wealth' (so miscalled) is as finely and unquestionably displayed among poor people as among the rich. . . . Allow all you will for the social conditions of environment which have put a premium upon tiger-qualities and compelled men to be greedy beasts in order to stay on earth at all, there remains the equally evident fact that there did lie more or less dormant in character the tiger-qualities and the beastly greed which came to the surface at the first opportunity" ("The Kingdom Within," *The Commons* 4, no. 38 [September 1899]: 8–9). With the tiger, urban America thus added still another species to its zoological metaphors.

139. "The New Envoys" [reprinted from *The New Age*], *The Commons* 2, no. 18 (October 1897): 1.

140. "The Children's Concert," *Chicago Commons* 1, no. 3 (June 1896): 5.

141. "Socializing Education," *The Commons* 5, no. 53 (December 1900): 14.

142. "Our Neighborhood Church," *Chicago Commons* 1, no. 1 (April 1896): 2.

143. Edwin Burritt Smith, "The Morals of the Crowd," *The Commons* 5, no. 48 (July 15, 1900): 1. To support this claim, Charles M. Sheldon in "Work With Humanity at First Hand. Impressions of Chicago Commons," *The Commons* 5, no. 53 (December 1900): 6, wrote: "I may also truthfully say that my first thought of the character of the 'Bishop' in 'In His Steps' [his best-selling novel] was suggested to me there. If any souls

have felt the encouragement and inspiration of such a character, and of such a work, it is due to the life and work of him who has put his life and means into the Commons.'' For an examination of this novel, see White, ''A Summons,'' *South Atlantic Quarterly*, Summer 1968.

144. John P. Gavit, ''Chicago Commons Free Floor Labor Discussions,'' *The Commons* 5, no. 51 (October 1900): 9.

145. ''The Standard of Living,'' *The Commons* 4, no. 44 (March 31, 1900): 6.

146. ''Students At The Settlement. Growing Use of the Opportunities on the Field— Demand for Public Presentations,'' *The Commons* 2, no. 19 (November 1897): 11.

147. Robert A. Woods, ''The Settlement State of Mind'' [remarks at Chicago Commons, May 18, 1899], *The Commons* 4, no. 35 (June 1899): 2–3.

148. *The Commons* 4, no. 40 (November 30, 1899): 3–4.

149. Hegner, ''Scientific Value,'' p. 175.

150. Lewis Mumford, *The City in History: Its Origins, Its Transformations, and Its Prospects* (New York: Harcourt, Brace & World, Inc., 1961), p. 500; Arthur Mann, ''British Social Thought and American Reformers of the Progressive Era,'' *Mississippi Valley Historical Review* 42 (March 1956): 684–85; Davis, *Spearheads for Reform*, pp. 40–59, 75–76, 86–89.

151. Luther H. Gulick, *The Metropolitan Problem and American Ideas* (New York: Alfred A. Knopf, 1962), pp. 110–12.

152. Ray Ginger, *Altgeld's America: The Lincoln Ideal Versus Changing Realities* (New York: Funk & Wagnalls Company, 1958), p. 113.

AGENDA FOR A NEW CENTURY

During the final thirty-five years of the nineteenth century, Americans were trying to learn how to live in cities, a mode of existence that, as one turn-of-the-century urbanist noted, had not been "a very easy art to master."[1] City dwellers of the post–Civil War years were to witness, during the 1870s and 1880s, the transformation, by century's end, of their essentially preindustrial order into a modern urban culture. Responding to these changes in the civic order, the magazines of the period printed millions of words concerning the shaping, managing, and organizing of the American municipality—an enormous body of literature which is, in itself, of great importance to historians of the period and, more especially, to urban historians and latter-day urbanists.

The tellers of the tale of the booming cities had an important story to tell and they told it with a force, brashness, and sense of excitement that were hallmarks of their cities. They wrote with gusto and took themselves and their message so seriously, indeed, that the present-day reader must tend, at times, to respond with irritation, if not outright hostility, to so self-satisfied a generation. Victorian hypocrisy, puritanical zeal, a surplus of respectability, and an ingenuous faith in progress were characteristics of a period that seems almost beyond comprehension today. These were years of extremes that cannot readily be balanced one against the other. The failures were glaring, but the triumphs were monumental. Not the least of the attainments of the age was its characteristically vigorous acceptance of the promise of the future metropolis.

In transcending the bounds of a single city, the late-century urbanist broke sharply with immediate postwar observers to advance from observation to investigation, from reporting to analysis, from the limits of the specific locale to the aggregate of urban America. His focus was mainly on the central city, but he looked out hopefully as well beyond its walls to the suburban reaches spreading out around it. His search for environment encompassed the total urban area, with core and rings together comprising a metropolitan universe. He recognized change as inherent in the urbanization process and developed an open-ended approach to planning for the future. The future became his area of specialization.

What seems to have united these writers was less a sense of class identity than a common language and frame of reference: in short, a shared subculture. Indeed, a significant majority of them shared similar attitudes and approaches, which cut across political, economic, and social lines. They evidenced a self-confidence in their own ideas and an optimism concerning the future of their society. Theirs was an activist generation, one that had great faith in the power of educated elites and experts to improve and control their environments by means of a general science of behavior, one which was often antimajoritarian and, in the extreme, aggressively authoritarian in its philosophy, methods, and

plans. There is, in short, much to fault and much to praise in their commitment
to the reordering of society. But still it must be recognized that they chose to
live in cities and that their cities were for them sources of pride and commitment.
Their investments in cities of money, energy, and love—exceeded those of
previous and even later generations.

Modern cities, Chauncey D. Harris and Edward L. Ullman have noted in a
classic essay on the subject, are "the focal points in the occupation and utilization
of the earth by man," but they are also "paradoxes": "Their rapid growth and
large size testify to their superiority as a technique for the exploitation of the
earth, yet by their very success and consequent large size they often provide a
poor local environment for man."[2] Late-century urbanists attempted to unravel
and solve this paradox: that they did not succeed in doing so can come as no
surprise to later generations which have witnessed subsequent "urban crises"
and proposed similar semisuccessful solutions of their own. Whether the achievements of the late twentieth century will eclipse those of the century before remains
to be seen, but the spirit of the earlier age, its dedication and faith, ought not
to be overlooked today: it might serve both as inspiration and as warning. The
first lessons were summed up best by a contemporary at the turn of the century:

American cities have been exceedingly slow to realize the importance and seriousness of
municipal problems, but there is no disputing the vigor with which specific propositions
are carried out when once public sentiment reaches the point of really undertaking them.
There have been many hopeful signs in the last few years of an awakening civic spirit.
At first it is taking the form of handling the great rough problems of the physical necessities
of municipalities; we seem destined to wait a good while before the less obvious but
equally vital problems of educational, social and political conditions are taken up in a
similarly wholesome, thorough-going way. But it is great deal to have made a beginning.[3]

It was no mean beginning, but it also marked the beginning of an end.

"Some decades ago—and I am deliberately vague about the date," historian
Oscar Handlin suggested in a seminal methodological essay, "a significant
change appeared": "To put it bluntly, the urbanization of the whole society
may be in process of destroying the distinctive role of the modern city."[4] This
latest transformation, arguably as profound as the earlier one from preindustrial
to urban-industrial, has been dated variously during the opening decades of the
present century; nevertheless, as I have written elsewhere, "1915 may serve
here as a logical starting point. After 1915, 'the urbanization of the whole society'
progressed to such a degree that the term *city* was no longer comprehensive
enough to circumscribe the totality of urban life and form; after 1915, the process
of urbanization created what has been described variously as the modern *city
state*, the *metropolis*, the *federal city*, and *megalopolis*."[5] Significantly, for
present purposes, by 1915 urbanists had developed a body of theory of such
size, scope, and sophistication that it endured—challenged, but dominant—into
the mid–1950s when it was confronted by a new urban revival. Its gospel, as

promulgated by the editors of *Fortune*, was set forth spiritedly in *The Exploding Metropolis*.[6]

PLAN, PROMO, AND PROSPECTUS

A cluster of three texts emanating from Chicago—that "vast sociological laboratory," according to a contemporary; a "Dreiserian city," according to a recent critic—encapsulates neatly the ideas and visions of late-century urbanists and carries them forward to the transformation that meant the urbanization of the whole society.[7] They are Daniel H. Burnham's 1909 plan for Chicago, Walter D. Moody's 1911 tract for promoting it, and Robert E. Park's 1915 prospectus for a social scientific research design of Burnhamesque proportions.

If the 1902 McMillan Plan for Washington was indeed "born," as Frederick Gutheim has suggested, "before its time," its 1909 descendant for Chicago issued forth at a most propitious moment.[8] If Burnham's role in the former was that of the Baptist, in the latter he played Messiah. As the Washington volume describing the plan was splendid, its Chicago counterpart was spectacular, surpassing its progenitor in every measure: the 9 1/4- by 6-inch size was enlarged to 12 by 9 inches; the black-and-white illustrations were replaced with sepia tones and three- or four-color separations; the format of the handsome report was transformed, in sum, into that of a souvenir volume or coffee-table book.[9] In planning terms, the Chicago effort stood as a transitional document. In concept and vision, it drew directly on the McMillan Plan. In scope, it far exceeded its antecedent by encompassing all of metropolitan Chicago within a sixty-mile radius of the Loop within its purview. Historically, "not only was it the first metropolitan plan, and hence the first to be predicated on an understanding of the unity of the city and its metropolitan context," historian Carl W. Condit has explained, "but it also marked the transition between the strictly geometric planning of the Renaissance and Baroque periods and the three-dimensional, organic, and functional planning of the present day." Paradoxically, Conduit continues, it also "marked the last phase of the geometric, Neo-Platonic planning of the Renaissance, with balance, axiality, and monumental vistas deployed in a hierarchical arrangement—the surviving symbols of the mathematical harmonies underlying the divine order, a cosmos in which mankind by the nineteenth century had ceased to believe."[10] Paradoxically too, this Janus-like creation, facing back toward the ideal of the ordered city and forward to the reality of sprawling conurbations, would exert a dominating influence for a half-century to come—as model and target both for those who sought to shape metropolitan America.

The Chicago Plan dwarfed its Washington antecedent not only in presentation and scope, but also in promotion. Within days of its release, a Chicago Plan Commission of over 300 members, covering a broad spectrum of political and business interests, was appointed by the city council to guide the plan's future. The largely ceremonial commission, which convened annually, was actually managed by an executive committee of twenty-six, under the chairmanship of

Charles Wacker. By January 1911 this businessman-booster turned over the day-to-day management of the promotional campaign to Managing Director Walter D. Moody. Lauded by a contemporary as the "Chief of all Pushers," Moody, according to historian Michael P. McCarthy, "was a professional organizer, one of the new breed of executives who made careers out of managing civic organizations. . . . He was aggressive, zealous, and persistent."[11] He was an urbanist skilled at translating planning ideals into political realities through business methods. Communication was his forte.

Burnham's beautiful book was a logical enough beginning point, but as its senior author confessed, it "proved very costly indeed, no other of like scope and illustration having ever been attempted before"; consequently, fewer than 2,000 copies were ever distributed.[12] From it, Moody produced in June 1911 an inexpensive booklet entitled *Chicago's Greatest Issue*, which he had distributed to all city property holders and any tenants paying rents of over $25 a month: 165,000 copies reached 40 percent of the city's voters.[13] From them, the Chief of all Pushers turned to their progeny and generations yet to come, owners and renters alike, by having a unit on the Chicago Plan introduced into the public school curriculum, a course based on a Moody-managed text: *Wacker's Manual of The Plan of Chicago* appeared in December of the year of the managing director's appointment, a productive year indeed.[14]

"Chicago is destined to become the center of the modern world," the opening sentence of *Wacker's Manual* promised, "*if* the opportunities in her reach are intelligently realized, and *if* the city can receive a sufficient supply of trained and enlightened citizens." The conditional conjunction *if* was carefully targeted, as the next sentence confirmed: "the author has mapped out the part Chicago school children are to play in creating the greater Chicago of the future." That part began with information, as students developed "a sharp, clear, vivid interest in . . . cities, in their history, in their growth, in their present and in their future"; advanced to recognition of a common heritage, "this new and growing feeling of civic patriotism," "a revival, under modern conditions, of a patriotism as old as civilization itself"; and ended with faith, "in the hearts of the city's future citizens."[15] *Wacker's Manual* imparted knowledge through broad topical coverage; encouraged civic patriotism through illustration (Figures 9 and 10), with an average of almost one picture per page; and inculcated belief through catechization—with questions posed *and* correct answers provided for the student-reader at the close of each section. For Chicago's parochial school students especially, *Wacker's Manual* must have seemed familiar, with its "Prefatory Note" and chapter ends resembling a stock *Baltimore Catechism*. For Chicago school children generally, the lesson must have seemed self-evident: Catholic kids knew that if you couldn't answer the religious questions word-for-word, you went straight to Hell; other Chicago kids probably suspected, too, that if they didn't learn the answers, the same direction threatened their city, which otherwise was "destined to become the center of the modern world." Their Civic Catechism, as it were, so well embodied the ideas and ideals and vision

Figure 9

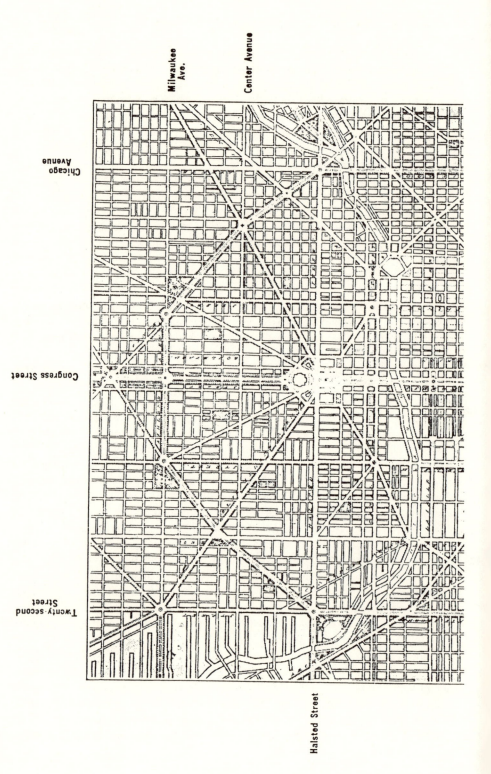

258

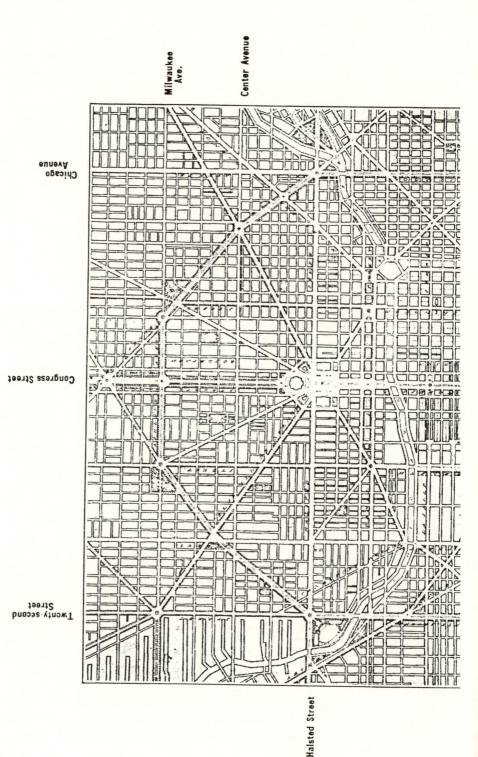

Figure 9

Milwaukee Ave.

Center Avenue

Chicago Avenue

Congress Street

Twenty-second Street

Halsted Street

258

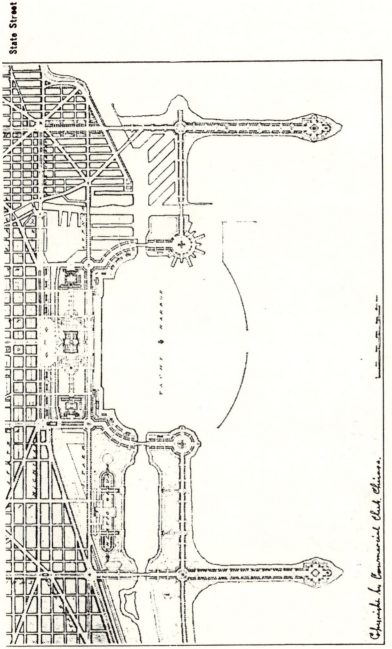

State Street

Michigan Avenue

CHICAGO. Plan of the complete system of street circulation; railway stations; parks, boulevard circuits and radial arteries; public recreation piers; yacht harbor and pleasure boat piers; treatment of Grant Park; the main axis and the Civic Center, presenting the city as a complete organism in which all its functions are related one to another in such a manner that it will become a unit.

[Copyrighted by the Commercial Club.]

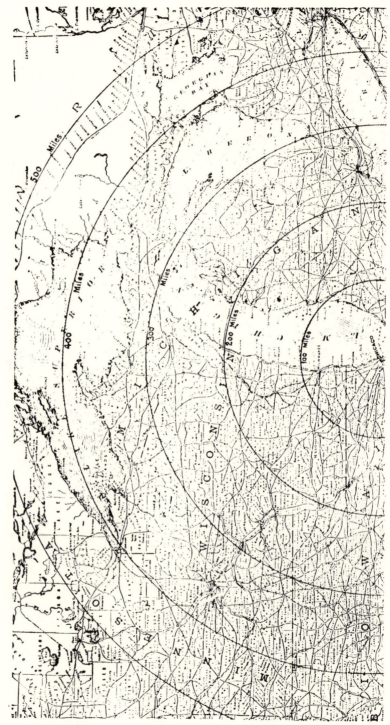

Figure 10

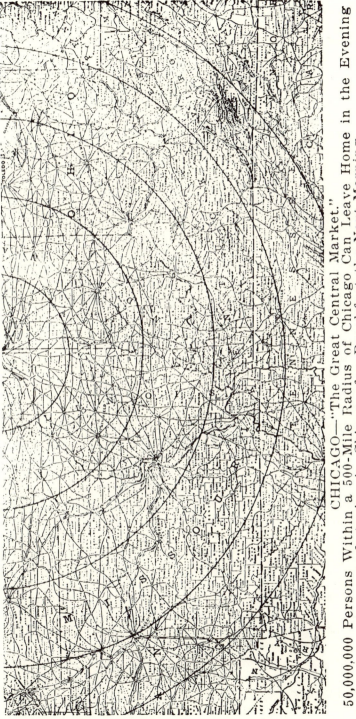

CHICAGO—"The Great Central Market."

50,000,000 Persons Within a 500-Mile Radius of Chicago Can Leave Home in the Evening and Arrive in Chicago for Breakfast the Next Morning.
[Especially prepared for the Chicago Association of Commerce.]

261

of late-century urbanists that it served, almost without exaggeration, as a sacred text.

From "Dreiserian" Chicago, there was promulgated, four years later, a sociological manifesto of surpassing significance. Its author, Robert E. Park, was born in 1864, four years earlier than W.E.B. Du Bois; began studies at Harvard in 1898, three years after Du Bois had been awarded the Ph. D. there; and left for Germany to study sociology in 1899, five years after Du Bois's return. From then on, the correspondences between their professional lives became opposites. To begin with, their career directions were almost reversed: Du Bois, a scholar-teacher through his mid-forties, became at that point a fulltime activist; Park, a journalist-organizer into his late-forties, turned then to the more contemplative order of the academy. Then, too, although both wrote about race, each came to the subject from a different starting point. As an African-American, Du Bois was born into the "Negro Problem." As a muckraking journalist, Park discovered it during 1903–1904 in the Belgian Congo, where he was investigating racial abuse, and followed it in 1905 to Tuskegee, Alabama, where he served for the next half-dozen years as press agent for Du Bois's nemesis Booker T. Washington. In 1912, on the basis of a reputation earned at Tuskegee, Park was invited to lecture on the "Negro in America" at the University of Chicago, where he would soon establish himself as *the* force in the wider field of urban sociology. This "impressario of research," this "captain of inquiry" shared with W.E.B. Du Bois the ambition to create a long-term, problem-oriented, city-based research effort.[16] In 1915, he outlined its component parts in "The City: Suggestions for the Investigation of Human Behavior in the City Environment."[17]

"The City," for Park, was "not a mere congeries of persons and social arrangements, but an institution." It was, moreover, "a mechanism—a psychophysical mechanism" and a "growth"—"the undesigned product of the labors of successive generations of men."[18] To examine it, Park drew upon the best minds of his age—philosophers, economists, sociologists, urbanists: William Graham Sumner, Robert A. Woods, Georg Simmel, Walter Bagehot, W. I. Thomas, Charles Horton Cooley, James Bryce, and Sigmund Freud. To comprehend it, he offered a four-part outline of topics for inquiry. "I. The City Plan and Local Organization" (pp. 578–84) opened, Chicago-style, with an introduction to *"The city plan"* (really physical geography, natural advantages, and layout—as opposed to formal planning), then proceeded to *"The Neighborhood"* and *"Colonies and segregated areas."* Each subheading opened with a textbook-like explanation and concluded with questions intended to inspire research. "II. Industrial Organization and the Moral Order" (pp. 584–93) turned to the "modern city" as a liberating force, as expressed in that "old German adage . . . that 'city air makes men free' (*Stadt Luft macht frei*)" or, in Park's terms: "The city offers a market for the special talents of individual men."[19] The subheadings to II were: *"Vocational classes and vocational types," "News and the mobility of the social group,"* and *"The stock exchange and the mob."* "III. Secondary Relations and Social Control" (pp. 593–607) focused upon "the fact that the growth of cities has been accompanied by the substitution of indirect, 'secondary,' for direct, face-to-face, 'primary' relations in the associations of individuals in the community."[20] Its subcategories were: "*The church, the school, and the family*," "*Crisis and the courts*," "*Commercialized vice and the liquor traffic*," "*Party politics and publicity*," and "*Advertising and social control.*" "IV. Temperament and the urban environment" (pp. 607–10) describes "great cities" as "melting-pots of races and of cultures. Out of the vivid and subtle interactions of which they have been the centers," Park proposed, "there have come the newer breeds and the newer social types."[21] They are the subject of his final subheadings: "*Mobilization of the individual man*," "*The moral region*," and "*Temperament and social contagion.*" Such, then, are Robert E. Park's "Suggestions for the Investigation of Human Behavior in the City Environment." As a totality, they are unquestionably comprehensive, if not totally comprehensible; breath-taking, if not mind-blowing, in scope and range.

Park's prospectus for the study of the city, as with Burnham's plan for it, achieved continuity through institutionalization. As the Chicago Plan Commission guided the 1909 conceptualization into actualization, the University of Chicago's Department of Sociology developed a distinctive "Chicago style" to address the questions raised in Park's 1915 essay.[22] What came to be called the Chicago School of Sociology provided, Maurice Stein has noted, "a tremendously exciting atmosphere for social scientists," "an atmosphere of true continuity and accumulation, with the key to both largely in Park's hands."[23] So charged was this atmosphere that in 1945, at the high point of the Chicago School, novelist Richard Wright could claim confidently in his introduction to *Black Metropolis*, one of the finest monographs to come out of the department, that "Chicago is the *known* city; perhaps more is known about it . . . than any other city in the world."[24] That knowledge was a long time building, but its agenda had been set in 1915.

1915 . . . 1957

In its April 1915 issue *The American City* included an advertisement for "A Municipal Exhibition" (Figures 11 and 12). The prototype for this show was Newark, New Jersey, but its approach was so flexible, so universalistic that it was said to be applicable to any American city. The exhibition package claimed to cover the full range of civic concerns—government, education, city planning, civicism. It offered, in sum, mail-order reform.

"A Municipal Exhibition" was almost a cartoon-like view of the ideas and expressions of turn-of-the-century urbanists. As Burnham's plan, Moody's promotion, and Park's prospectus had, among them, encapsulated and institutionalized the major concepts of the closing years of the century into the framework of a single municipality, *The American City's* fill-in-the-blanks exhibition nationalized them for any urban place within the United States. The challenge of self-recognition that had faced urban America following the Civil War had been

264

Figure 12

Interior of Newark City Hall, as decorated for the Exhibition.

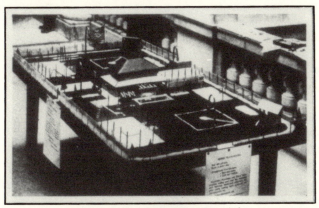

Exhibit of the Newark Playground Commission.

Eight of the 154 panels in the American City Bureau's Exhibit.

265

addressed so successfully by late-century urbanists and those who followed them, that by 1915 it seemed possible to locate, describe, and prescribe for Anycity, U.S.A.

The year *1915* represents, then, a logical transition point: it was a year when, on the one hand, a coherent enough body of theory, method, and achievement was in place so as to suggest authority; and, on the other hand, a year that marked a new urban transformation, the urbanization of the whole society. The urban America conceptualized by this first generation of urbanists, consequently, was a pre–1915 entity; nevertheless, their conceptualization of it would dominate the planning and running of cities for the next half-century. That this would lead to reaction was inevitable.

The year *1957* marks a transition. When *The Exploding Metropolis*, the bell-wether of our most recent urban renascence, appeared in paperback, a cover blurb described it as "A Study of the Assault on Urbanism and How Our Cities Can Resist It." Interestingly, the assailants were exponents of the conventional wisdom of the first generation of urbanists: planners projecting Burnham, promoters practicing Moody, social scientists parroting Park. During the following decade, this counterattack continued, with the targets the same. That the times had changed, that urban America had undergone a new transformation was seldom acknowledged. That the old answers no longer sufficed seemed obvious, but that the questions they addressed were valid was ignored.

This new generation of urbanists, those of the 1950s and 1960s, rejected their intellectual forebears; still, they resembled them more often than not, and more closely—both in approach and effect—than they ever comprehended. Indeed, the correspondences between the two generations of urbanists, despite changes over time, recalls the penetrating observation of Chicago's sage Mr. Dooley: "I see gr-reat changes takin' place ivry day, but no change at all ivry fifty years."[25]

NOTES

1. David Starr Jordan, "A Continuing City," *California Municipalities* 1 (February 1900): 230–31.

2. Chauncey D. Harris and Edward L. Ullman, "The Nature of Cities," *Annals of the American Academy of Political and Social Science* 242 (November 1945): 7.

3. "Civic and Educational Notes: Signs of Civic Spirit," *Gunton's Magazine* 18 (March 1900): 255.

4. Oscar Handlin, "The Modern City as a Field of Historical Study," in *The Historian and the City*, ed. Oscar Handlin and John Burchard (Cambridge, Mass.: MIT Press and Harvard University Press, 1963), p. 24.

5. Dana F. White, "The Urbanization of Society," *Urban Education* 2 (1966): 115–16.

6. Editors of *Fortune, The Exploding Metropolis* (Garden City, N.Y.: Doubleday & Company, Inc., 1957 and 1958).

7. Albion W. Small, "Scholarship and Social Agitation," *American Journal of So-

ciology 1 (March 1896): 581; Philip Fisher, *Hard Facts: Setting and Form in the American Novel* (New York: Oxford University Press, 1985), p. 131.

8. Frederick Gutheim, "Daniel Burnham, Then and Now," in *Historical Perspectives on Urban Design: Washington, D.C., 1890–1910*, ed. Antionette J. Lee, Occasional Paper No. 1, Center for Washington Area Studies (Washington, D.C.: George Washington University, 1984), p. 25.

9. Daniel H. Burnham and Edward H. Bennett, edited by Charles Moore, *Plan of Chicago* (Chicago: The Commercial Club, 1909; New York: Da Capo Press, 1970). My reference is to the more accessible facsimile edition in the Da Capo Series in "Architecture and Decorative Art," Vol. 29.

10. Carl W. Condit, *Chicago, 1910–29: Building, Planning, and Urban Technology* (Chicago: University of Chicago Press, 1973), pp. 64–65.

11. Michael P. McCarthy, "Chicago Businessmen and the Burnham Plan," *Journal of the Illinois State Historical Society* 63 (Autumn 1970): 247–48, 253–54. In "Burnham's *Plan* and Moody's *Manual*: City Planning as Progressive Reform," Thomas J. Schlereth has provided "a textual analysis of Moody's widely promulgated book as an early classic in city planning promotional literature," pp. 75–99, in Donald A. Krueckeberg, ed., *The American Planner: Biographies and Recollections* (New York and London: Methuen, 1983), p. 76.

12. McCarthy, "Chicago Businessmen," pp. 246, 254. In "Burnham, Guerin and the City as Image," Robert Bruegmann has examined the Plan's "presentation . . . as essentially a picture book," pp. 16–28 in John Zukowsky, ed., *The Plan of Chicago: 1909–1979* (Chicago: The Art Institute of Chicago, 1979), p. 16.

13. McCarthy, "Chicago Businessmen," pp. 254–55.

14. Walter D. Moody, *Wacker's Manual of The Plan of Chicago; Municipal Economy*, Especially Prepared for Study in the Schools of Chicago; Auspices of the Chicago Plan Commission (Chicago: The Henneberry Company, 1911 & 1915). On the copyright page of this 1915 edition is the information: *"The Retail Price of this book is 75 cents."*

15. Ibid., "Introduction"; italics added.

16. Robert E. L. Faris, *Chicago Sociology, 1920–1932* (Chicago: University of Chicago Press, 1967 & 1970) pp. 87, 107.

17. Robert E. Park, "The City: Suggestions for Investigation of Human Behavior in the City Environment," *American Journal of Sociology* 20 (March 1915): 577–612.

18. Ibid., pp. 577, 578.

19. Ibid., pp. 584, 585.

20. Ibid., p. 593.

21. Ibid., p. 607.

22. My reading of Park has been influenced strongly by Fred H. Matthews's brilliant *Quest for an American Sociology: Robert E. Park and the Chicago School* (Montreal & London: McGill-Queen's University Press, 1977).

23. Maurice Stein, *The Eclipse of Community: An Interpretation of American Studies* (New York: Harper Torchbooks, 1960 & 1964), pp. 13, 14.

24. "Introduction" to St. Clair Drake and Horace R. Cayton, *Black Metropolis: A Study of Negro Life in a Northern City* (New York: Harcourt, Brace and Company, 1945), p. xviii. The book's dedication is to "The Late Professor Robert E. Park of Tuskegee, the University of Chicago, and Fisk; American Scholar and Friend of the Negro People."

25. Finley Peter Dunne, *The World of Mr. Dooley*, edited and with an Introduction by Louis Filler (New York: Collier Books, 1962), p. 20.

Appendix:

A Note on Method

"The Self-Conscious City: A Survey and Bibliographical Summary of Periodical Literature on American Urban Themes, 1865–1900" is the basis for the present study. That work, completed in 1969, began with a team effort at George Washington University to survey the literature of social awareness for the period 1865–1917.[1] Initially, my part in the project entailed surveying all periodical literature from 1865 to 1900 that touched on urban themes, recording and organizing this material, and outlining patterns of urban awareness and development of seminal ideas for these thirty-five years, on a year-by-year or decade-by-decade basis. It soon became apparent that this could not be accomplished. To begin with, the period resisted neat compartmentalization. In terms of urban development, 1865 could be justified readily enough as a beginning point, but any direct line aimed at 1900 soon wavered. What is more, the magazines themselves compounded the problem. The more than 10,000 periodicals that appeared between 1865 and 1900 varied widely in publishing and editorial practices, in quality and quantity of material printed, and in the locales and interests that they represented.[2] In order to select a representative sample from this mass of material, it would have been necessary either to survey the entire field or to rely on available scholarly and bibliographical sources as guides. Neither alternative seemed feasible: the former was beyond the capacity and endurance of any one scholar; the latter seemed unsound methodologically.

Periodical literature presents special problems. The vast number of magazines published; the time-devouring task of covering adequately even a single journal over any extended period of publication; the bother of hefting large numbers of heavy, often corroding, and sometimes disintegrating bound volumes; poor or sketchy indexes (if any); incomplete runs of holdings even in the best libraries; changes in titles and numbering: all have combined to lead scholars into neglecting these sources entirely, scanning them hurriedly, or selecting from their number indiscriminately.

Scholarly guides have their limits. The most comprehensive history of American magazines, Frank Luther Mott's five-volume work, for all its virtues, is essentially a literary survey which, while it provides excellent accounts of individual journals and useful sections on special categories of periodical literature, is of limited value for a multifaceted subject such as the modern city. Indeed, many of the most important urban journals covered in these pages received only a few lines or else were buried in Mott's notes. Bibliographical guides, too, have their problems. That old standard *Poole's Index to Periodical Literature* offered the convenience of its topical headings, an obvious appeal in the high quality of its listings, and a sense that it was somehow representative. In fact, Poole's is nothing more than a selection of selections. Its urban listings are few and, given their reformist bias, totally unrepresentative.

My starting point for the study of urban periodical literature was the authoritative *Bibliography of Municipal Problems and City Conditions* by Robert Clarkson Brooks.[3] A massive compendium of sources, primarily periodical, Brooks's work offered a number of advantages over any challengers: it was a reference bibliography compiled between 1897 and 1901 in the nation's first specifically urban journal, *Municipal Affairs*; it was intended for the use of municipal officials, experts, designers, and active citizens; it was published in 1901 under separate cover and achieved wide circulation; it exerted considerable influence upon contemporary urban thought; and, most important for my purposes, it listed in its opening pages the major periodicals publishing articles on urban affairs. The Brooks bibliography provided me with a purposive sample of periodicals and an alternative periodization.

Brooks confirmed that 1885 was the inevitable transition point between 1865 and 1900. Based on his listings, I selected thirty-seven periodicals: twenty-six of them appeared first after 1885, and provided the basic information for ''The Self-Conscious City''; the other eleven magazines were started before 1885 (see Table 1). Although the post–1885 periodicals predominate here, both in number and in the space allotted them, my broader objective was to view the development of urban awareness over the entire thirty-five years and to analyze the formation, late in the century, of what I have described as an urban frame of mind. In the shaping of this set of attitudes, the specialized post–1885 journals were in the vanguard, but this approach to urban thought had its roots in the post–Civil War decades.

To represent the entire thirty-five-year period, I chose two prestigious, general-interest magazines: *Atlantic Monthly* and *North American Review*. Boston's *Atlantic* merited special attention as a model for high-quality monthly magazines, while *North American*, founded in the same city, reflected changes in contemporary publishing trends as it shifted first from a quarterly to monthly format and, next, moved from the old capital of letters in New England to the new in the Empire City. Two specialized journals were chosen to supplement these general magazines. *Banker's Magazine* and *Journal of Social Science* were forerunners, in a sense, of late-century professional periodicals, in that they were limited in their appeal and circulation to a smaller and more homogeneous readership than were *Atlantic* and ''Old *North*.'' Proponents all of serious and informative literature, these four periodicals served as sounding boards for the discussion of urban matters throughout the thirty-five-year period. But they are not enough. Major weeklies, such as *Nation* and *Harper's Weekly*, despite their appeal, had to be excluded, since a thorough examination of even one of them would have been prohibitive in terms of time and effort. In addition, it was impossible to identify representative examples of the immense religious press of the period. In order to address these deficiencies, additional short-run magazines were selected.

For 1865–1885, a complement of seven periodicals were selected to fill in some of these gaps. *Every Saturday, Galaxy, Hours at Home,* and *Scott's Monthly Magazine* were chosen to supplement the material already available for the decade of least attention to urban affairs, 1865–1875. Regional representation was another consideration: *Scott's*, in addition to its relevant periodicity, was also one of the few quality magazines published in the South during the post–Civil War years; similarly, *The Western*, to a degree, represented mid-America for the succeeding decade; whereas *The Continent*, which was removed to New York City after its initial publication in Philadelphia, typified, as did *North American*, the sometimes reluctant, but nonetheless compelling shifts from lesser cities to the magazine Mecca of the age. *Galaxy* was a quality New York monthly that successfully challenged the intellectual leadership of Boston's *Atlantic Monthly* for over a decade. *Every Saturday*, for its part, was a manageable weekly. And finally, *The Manhattan* drew attention as a prototype of the journal of urban manners, in that it was a forerunner of the blasé, somewhat snobbish, yet cosmopolitan magazine handbook—to which the present-day *New Yorker* is heir—for the metropolitan sophisticate.

For 1885–1900, a cluster of twenty specialized journals was selected to represent the ideas of those whom I came to identify as urbanists.[4] The weight of this selection is, nonetheless, heavy on magazines that adopted a social science approach to urban affairs, and light upon those with a technical or design emphasis; thus, I included virtually all the social science journals listed in Brooks, but only *Architectural Record* and *Public Improvements* among those with a technological bent. My justification for this seeming imbalance is threefold: first, the social science journals, by the very nature of their approaches, were more analytical, more likely to fit a specific subject into a broader municipal framework and, hence, more valuable as indicators of urban awareness; second, the technical journals were so specialized and so narrowly focused that there was a great deal of repetition in their subject matter and in their handling of that material; and third, technical subjects were often covered extensively by nontechnical journals such as *California Municipalities, Municipal Affairs,* and *Municipality* (all a part of this study).

For 1885–1900, what is more, six other magazines were included to match those of 1865–1885. *The Public*, a Chicago weekly devoted to the single tax, and *World's Work*, a weekly news magazine in the *Time* and *Newsweek* format, were both featured conspicuously in Brooks. *Bookman* and *Everybody's Magazine* were high-circulation monthlies, typical of the dozens of such publications spawned during the magazine revolution of the 1880s and 1890s. *Metropolitan Magazine*, a mildly salacious monthly, was a logical followup to the earlier *Manhattan*. *Yellow Kid* was typical of the comic press that developed in the cities. And, lastly, *Open Church* served to represent the emerging interdenominational religious mood of the period as applied to urban affairs.

After the magazines had been selected, a volume-by-volume, issue-by-issue, page-by-page survey was initiated. Each entry was classified under three general headings: "Urban Theory and Form," "Government and Politics," and "Socioeconomic Patterns." Each of these general headings was broken down further into from four to six separate subheadings.

A bibliographical summary, which included general historical information and the facts of publication, was prepared for each magazine. To each summary was appended a numerical account of the entries previously surveyed and classified under the appropriate general headings and subheadings. From all of this material, a "Descriptive Compendium of Magazines" was assembled to provide a numerical summary of the total entries by period and topic.[5]

What this rather primitive foray into cliometrics demonstrates is that magazines and journals devoted a good bit of their prime commodity, space, to urban matters. What is more, it shows just what categories filled that space. Finally, all this suggests that the

Table 1

TITLE	PLACE OF PUBLICATION	DATES
American Federationist[1]	New York, Indianapolis & Washington	1894-1919
American Journal of Sociology[1]	Chicago	1895-current
American Magazine of Civics & American Journal of Politics[1]	New York	1892-1897
Annals of the American Academy of Political and Social Science[1]	Philadelphia	1890-current
Architectural Record[1]	New York	1891-current
Atlantic Monthly[3]	Boston	1857-current
Banker's Magazine[1]	New York	1846-1943
Bookman[3]	New York	1895-1933
California Municipalities[2]	San Francisco	1899-1932
Charities Review[2]	New York	1891-1901
Citizen[1]	Philadelphia	1895-1898
The Commons and Chicago Commons[2]	Chicago	1896-1905
Continent and Our Continent[3]	Philadelphia & New York	1882-1884
Direct Legislation Record[1]	New York & Newark	1894-1906
Every Saturday[3]	Boston	1866-1874
Everybody's Magazine[3]	New York	1899-1929
Galaxy[3]	New York	1866-1878
Good Government[1]	Washington & New York	1892-current
Gunton's Magazine and The Social Economist[1]	New York	1891-1904
Hours at Home[3]	New York	1865-1870

Table 1 (Continued)

TITLE	PLACE OF PUBLICATION	DATES
Journal of Political Economy[1]	Chicago	1892-current
Journal of Social Science[1]	New York	1869-1909
The Manhattan[3]	New York	1883-1884
Metropolitan Magazine[3]	New York	1895-1911
Municipal Affairs[2]	New York	1897-1902/03
Municipality[2]	Madison, Wisconsin	1900-current
North American Review[3]	Boston & New York	1815-1939/40
Open Church[2]	New York	1897-1899
Political Science Quarterly[1]	New York	1886-current
The Public[3]	Chicago	1898-1919
Public Improvements[2]	New York	1899-1903
Publications of the American Statistical Association[1]	Boston	1888-current
Quarterly Journal of Economics[1]	Cambridge, Massachusetts	1886-current
Scott's Monthly Magazine[3]	Atlanta	1865-1869
The Western[3]	St. Louis	1875-1881
World's Work[3]	New York	1900-1932
Yellow Kid and Yellow Book	New York	1897-1898

Categories:

1 professional/trade

2 urban

3 general public

Publication sites are included only for the years 1865-1900; dates of publication, on the other hand, include the entire cycle of each magazine.

surface has just been scratched, that urbanists today must dig deep, indeed, to uncover their roots, and that the periodical press is a promising site for literary archaeology.

NOTES

1. The project, inspired by the work of Lisle A. Rose and named in his honor, has been housed at George Washington University for the past two decades. Portions of it have been published by Greenwood Press.

2. Frank Luther Mott has estimated that there were between 8,000 and 9,000 periodicals published in the United States between 1865 and 1885, that some 7,500 new ones were founded between 1885 and 1905, and that nearly 11,000 different periodicals were published in the latter twenty-year period; see his *History of American Magazines* vol. 3: *1865–1885*, p. 5, and vol. 4: *1885–1905*, pp. 11–12 (Cambridge: Harvard University Press, 1938 & 1957).

3. Robert Clarkson Brooks, *A Bibliography of Municipal Problems and City Conditions* (New York: Reform Club, Committee on City Affairs, 1901); also to be found under the same title in *Municipal Affairs* 5 (March 1901): 1–346. Brooks attempted to assemble works by not only American, Canadian, and English writers, but also gathered materials published in Germany, France, Italy, Austria, Spain, Russia, Holland, Switzerland, and elsewhere. There are some 12,000 entries in the alphabetical subject index; about 8,000 titles referred to in the author index and 4,500 authors represented in all.

4. See above, "The Urbanist, 1885–1900" following Chapter 1.

5. White, "The Self-Conscious City," pp. 542–620.

Bibliographical Essay

When I was writing "The Self-Conscious City" during the late 1960s, little that could be described as urban history was in print; as I work at *The Urbanists* now, this special field has seemingly completed a full cycle of discovery, self-definition, expansion, maturation, and stagnation. In "The Self-Conscious City," I used editorial footnotes as cachés for rare and stray bibliographical references. For *The Urbanists*, I have gone light on such notes. To begin with, they often distract attention from the text; then, too, given the expanse of the field of study, extended bibliographical notes would burden this text with an unacceptable bulkiness; and, finally, with the present availability of review articles on urban history, such citations would be redundant. Shortly after completing "The Self-Conscious City," for instance, I began writing "The Underdeveloped Discipline: Interdisciplinary Directions in the Study of American Urban History," *American Studies: An International Newsletter* 9, no. 3 (Spring 1971): 3–16, which was reprinted and expanded upon in Robert H. Walker, editor, *American Studies: Topics and Sources* (Westport, Conn.: Greenwood Press, 1976), pp. 152–70; a supplement to the first two "editions" subsequently appeared in "The Underdeveloped Discipline: A Summary Perspective," in Jefferson B. Kellogg and Robert H. Walker, editors, *Sources for American Studies* (Westport, Conn.: Greenwood Press, 1983), pp. 454–69, which, in turn, reappeared (updated) in "The Underdeveloped Discipline: Directions/Misdirections in American Urban History," *American Studies International*, 22, no. 2 (October 1984): 122–40. While I lack the temerity to claim that mine is the best introduction to the field, I can at least boast that it is probably the longest running.

"The Self-Conscious City" contained thirty pages of citations that ranged from the general to the specific: from such global perspectives on American life and culture as those of Merle Curti, Ralph Henry Gabriel, and David M. Potter, on the one hand; to, on the other, the ABC's of urban living—from art, baseball, city councils, . . . on down to zoos. Rather than excerpting from that sizable compilation, never mind replicating it, I shall concentrate here upon works that are either central to or that might direct the reader beyond *The Urbanists*.

Theoretical "how-to-do-it" guides are a necessary starting point. Concerning categories and levels of interpretation, see social psychologist Anselm L. Strauss's *Images of the American City* (New York: The Free Press of Glencoe, 1961) for an analysis of image and metaphor in common usage, including magazine prose; planner Kevin Lynch's *The Image of the City* (Cambridge, Mass.: MIT Press, 1960), together with urban design critic Grady Clay's *Close-Up: How to Read the American City* (New York: Praeger, 1973) for patterns in the perception of the built environment; cultural analyst and critic Raymond Williams's *Keywords: A Vocabulary of Culture and Society* (New York: Oxford University Press, 1976) for shifts in word meanings as measures of cultural change; literary critic Steven Marcus's *Engels, Manchester, and the Working Class* (New York: Random House, 1974) for how to adapt techniques of textual analysis to nonliterary works; and intellectual historian William G. McLoughlin's *The Meaning of Henry Ward Beecher: An Essay on the Shifting Values of Mid-Victorian America, 1840–1870* (New York: Alfred A. Knopf, 1970) for the inner meanings of the genre biography. For methodological essays on English cities, which are often suggestive about their American counterparts, see H. J. Dyos and Michael Wolff, editors, *The Victorian City: Images and Realities*, 2 vols. (London & Boston: Routledge & Kegan Paul, 1973), especially: G. H. Martin and David Francis, "The Camera's Eye," 1: 227–46, and Steven Marcus, "Reading the Illegible," 1: 257–76; Nicholas Taylor, "The Awful Sublimity of the Victorian City: Its Aesthetic and Architectural Origins," 2: 431–47, E.D.H. Johnson, "Victorian Artists and the Urban Milieu," 2: 449–74, and Michael Wolff and Celina Fox, "Pictures from the Magazines," 2: 559–82.

For author identification, topic coverage, and ready reference, the volumes of Frank Luther Mott and Blake McKelvey stand out: one for the medium, the other the message. Mott's *A History of American Magazines*, 5 vols. (Cambridge, Mass.: The Belknap Press of Harvard University Press)—especially volumes 3: *1865–1885* (1938); 4: *1885–1905* (1957); and 5: *Sketches of 21 Magazines, 1905–1930* (1968), which contains a 243–page cumulative index for all five volumes—remains the irreplaceable encyclopedia for the genre. McKelvey's *The Urbanization of America, 1860–1995* and *The Emergence of Metropolitan America, 1915–1966* (New Brunswick, N.J.: Rutgers University Press, 1963 & 1968) approach the encyclopedic both in coverage and treatment, with a paragraph often encompassing what a chapter might be expected to contain. As dictionaries of their respective fields then, Mott and McKelvey complement each other neatly.

Concerning magazines and magazinists, John Tomsich's *A Genteel Endeavor: American Culture and Politics in the Gilded Age* (Stanford, Calif.: Stanford University Press, 1971), Theodore P. Greene's *American Heroes: The Changing Models of Success in American Magazines* (New York: Oxford University Press, 1970), and David Mark Chalmers's *The Social and Political Ideas of the Muckrakers* (New York: The Citadel Press, 1964) illustrate, each in its own manner, the transformation of periodical publication during the late nineteenth and early twentieth centuries. Howard R. Weiner's dissertation on "The Response to the American City (1885–1915) as Reflected in Writings Dealing with the City in Scholarly and Professional Serial Publications" (New York University, 1972) resembles "The Self-Conscious City" fairly closely in periodization, journal selection, and subject identification; unfortunately, Weiner did not make reference to my work and thereby missed the opportunity for potentially enlightening comparison. Finally, John Gross's *The Rise and Fall of the Man of Letters: A Study of the Idiosyncratic and the Humane in Modern Literature* (New York: The Macmillan Company, 1969), while its subject is exclusively literary England, has much to say about the genre within a wider Anglo-American framework.

By characterizing the organizing force of urban America as *The Search for Order, 1877–1920* (New York: Hill and Wang, 1967), Robert H. Wiebe provided a clear focus for the professionalization and associationalism that produced urbanists. In his historical account *Modernization: The Transformation of American Life, 1600–1865* (New York: Hill and Wang, 1976), Richard D. Brown traced the roots of these forces. In his sociological analysis of *The Professions: Roles and Rules* (New York: Russell Sage Foundation, 1970), Wilbert E. Moore, in collaboration with Gerald W. Rosenblum, detailed their structural characteristics (and provided an extensive bibliography, as well); and in her *The Rise of Professionalism: A Sociological Analysis* (Berkeley: University of California Press, 1977), Margali Sarfatti Larson offered a transatlantic perspective by comparing developmental patterns in England and the United States. For the nascent social sciences, see Thomas L. Haskell, *The Emergence of Professional Social Science: The American Social Science Association and the Nineteenth-Century Crisis of Authority* (Urbana: University of Illinois Press, 1977), and Mary O. Furner, *Advocacy and Objectivity: A Crisis in the Professionalization of American Social Science, 1865–1905* (Lexington: University of Kentucky Press, 1975). For the emerging design professions, unfortunately, there are no comparable studies; however, the critical perspectives provided by M. Christine Boyer in *Dreaming the Rational City: The Myth of American City Planning* (Cambridge, Mass.: MIT Press, 1983) and Galen Cranz in *The Politics of Park Design: A History of Urban Parks in America* (Cambridge, Mass.: MIT Press, 1982) raise many questions that could set the agenda for such studies. For a singular approach to the professional in motion, rather than as a type, see Donald A. Schön, *The Reflective Practitioner: How Professionals Think in Action* (New York: Basic Books, 1983), which examines the workings of such present-day professions as city planning, engineering, architecture, management, and engineering; and which, in the process, suggests ways of reexamining their historical precursors. The compilation of a profession-by-profession catalog of sources here would be laborious and, given the wealth of bibliographic guides, redundant. For additional sources on any particular profession, consult appropriate chapter endnotes in the text, which include references to such areas of specialization as public administration, social work, sanitary science, and others.

Urban America's mind, mood, style, and character—the optimum term would include all of the above—were best expressed by contemporaries in words, pictures, and plans. For insights into the intricacies of these expressions, a miscellany of recent scholarly works may be suggested: Gunther Barth's *City People: The Rise of Modern City Culture in Nineteenth-Century America* (New York: Oxford University Press, 1980) for the attempt to identify what was uniquely urban in urban America; Jane Allen Shikoh's "The 'Higher Life' in the American City of the 1890s: A Study of Its Leaders and Their Activities in New York, Chicago, Philadelphia, St. Louis, Boston, and Buffalo" (New York University dissertation, 1972) for localized applications of many of the general propositions presented in magazines and journals; Paul Boyer's *Urban Masses and Moral Order in America, 1820–1920* (Cambridge, Mass.: Harvard University Press, 1978) for a summary perspective on the uplift of the masses by the classes; Stow Persons's *The Decline of American Gentility* (New York: Columbia University Press, 1973), John G. Sproat's *"The Best Men": Liberal Reformers in the Gilded Age* (New York: Oxford University Press, 1968), and John Tomsich's previously cited *A Genteel Endeavor* for group portraits of urban Americans reacting to modernization; Jean B. Quandt's *From the Small Town to the Great Community: The Social Thought of Progressive Intellectuals* (New Brunswick, N.J.: Rutgers University Press, 1970) for a systematic analysis of nine early urbanists; and Samuel Haber's *Efficiency and Uplift: Scientific Management in the Progressive Era, 1890–1920* (Chicago: University of Chicago Press, 1964) for insights not only into the thought of the period, but also into the very process of thinking. A study that I wish had been available to me when I began research on urban self-consciousness would have been an American equivalent to Walter E. Houghton's brilliant explication of English thinking in *The Victorian Frame of Mind, 1830–1870* (New Haven: Published for Wellesley College by Yale University Press, 1957); at this late date, I'd still welcome it.

The individuals who expressed the ideas, the plans they prepared, and the places they planned for—all have informed my reading of this generation of urbanists. A number of them have been introduced in the Interludes here; more of them will be featured in a companion volume to the present one—one that will carry their story down to the recent past.

Index

Abbott, Lyman, 167–68
Abell, Aaron I., 232, 245 n.21
Abrams, Charles S., 246 n.37
Adams, Charles Francis, Jr., 11
Adams, Henry, 144
Addams, Jane, 195, 204, 236–37, 251–52 n.129
Advertising, 161–63; agencies, 161–62, 188 n.51; promotions, 188 n.50
African-Americans, 179–81; advertising, figure in, 188 n.50; Atlanta Conference on Negro City Life, 180–81; *The Philadelphia Negro* (W. E. B. Du Bois), 195–205; segregation of, 179, 193 n.136; South, condition in, 190 n.85, 193 n.137; suffrage, 181
Agar, John G., 130
Agriculture, 15, 45, 63–64, 170–71; agricultural discontent, 154, 170; agricultural workers commuting from cities, 85 n.128
Almy, Frederick, 226
American, Sadie, 210–11
American City, 263–66
American Civil War, as transition period, 1–3, 12, 13, 107, 175, 226
American Federationist, 40, 170, 173, 189 n.73, 223

American Journal of Politics. See American Magazine of Civics
American Magazine of Civics (also *American Journal of Politics*), 187 n.30
An American Positivist, 24–25
Anarchy, threats of, 164, 168
Andrews, Charles M., 116
Annals of the American Academy of Political and Social Science, 180
Apartment house, 54–55
Aptheker, Herbert, 197
Architectural League of New York: building height limitations proposed, 80–81 n.57; "The Planning of Cities" series, 72–73
Architectural Record, 51, 54, 55–56, 157, 230; series on "Architectural Aberrations" and "Provincial Architecture," 82 n.76
Architecture, 152; building height limitations, 51, 80–81 n.57; *École des Beaux Arts*, as model for American architecture, 56, 75; Fifth Avenue mansions, 165; styles of, 55, 82 n.76
Articles of Confederation, U.S., 116
Ashley, W. J., 230
Associationalism, 10, 13, 35–36, 44, 70, 102–3, 113–15, 119–20, 223, 226, 227

Astor, John Jacob, 189 n.71
Astor, William Waldorf, 168, 189 n.71
Atlanta, 12, 30 n.64
Atlanta Conference on Negro City Life, 180–81
Atlanta University, 196
Atlanta University Publications, 204–5
Atlantic Monthly, 11, 35, 113; Jacob A. Riis series on slums and tenements, 245 n.29
Automobile, 38, 77 n.5

Bacon, Francis, 14, 31 n.74, 32 n.95
Bagehot, Walter, 262
Baker, M. N., 125
Baltzell, E. Digby, 188 n.56, 197
Balzac, Honoré de, *Scenes from Political Life*, 101
Banker's Magazine, 8, 19–20, 23, 26, 66–67, 114, 115, 119, 157; municipal development, future of, 154–56
Banks, as guarantors of social stability, 186 n.19
Barth, Gunther, ix, 2, 36; department stores, 187 n.37
Bartlett, J. F., 176
Baseball, 76–77 n.2, 137 n.78; as inspiration for loyalty, as with political clubs, 114
Beckner, W. M., 210
Behan, Brendan, 20–21
Bemis, Edward W., 64
Benson, Eugene, 3
Berg, Louis De Coppet, 51
Bernheim, A. C., 114
Biltmore House, Asheville, North Carolina, 189 n.62
Birkenhead Park, England, 94, 97 n.17
Bissel, George E., 45, 216
Black, William Nelson, 57, 221–22
Black Metropolis, 263
Blackmar, Frank W., 65, 208
Blacks. *See* African-Americans
Blaine, James G., 19
Blashfield, Edwin Howland, 58, 58–59, 152
Bocock, Kemper, 217
Bonaparte, Charles J., 225–26

Booth, Charles, 195–97, 204, 231
Booth, General William, 205 n.4, 231
Bosanquet, Helen, 227
Boss, 24; "boss idea," 124. *See also* Tammany Hall
Boston, 7, 10–11, 97 n.16; growth, 42, 45–46, 48–49; model housing, 220; parks, 95, 96, 96 n.4; tenements, 217
Boys' Brigade of Baltimore, 212–13; Glasgow origins, 245 n.21
Brace, Charles Loring, 26, 27
Bradford, Amory H., 43
Bradford, Gamaliel, 126
Briggs, Asa, 52, 84 n.104, 173
Broderick, Francis L., 202
Brooks, Robert Clarkson, 110
Brosius, Marriott, 64
Brown, A. Theodore, 2, 68
Bryan, William Jennings, 110
Bryce, James, viscount, 99, 262
Buffalo, New York, 91–95, 96, 97 n.16; Westminster House Settlement, 252 n.132
Burnham, Daniel Hudson, 71, 142–44, 195; Chicago Plan, 256–57; Washington Plan, 142, 144–45
Burr, Everett T., 232, 233
Burton, Charles E., 186 n.30
Bush-Brown, H. K., 72
Business, 107, 108; business state, 154; management techniques for municipal administration, 125–26; political involvement, 122

Caesar's Column (Ignatius Donnelly), 170
California: urbanization, 38–39, 87 n.154; slum clearance, 217–18
California Municipalities, 38, 40–41, 120, 125, 217–18
Carnegie, Andrew, 106
Carter, Kate, 179
Cassedy, James H., 195
Cemeteries, 17; mausoleums in, 165
Centennial Exposition of 1876, 3, 5
Central city, 44–45, 151–52, 221
Central Park, New York City, 16, 17–18, 60, 89

Chamberlin, C. D., 153–54

Chapman, John Jay, 122–23

Charities Review, 104, 183, 212; as organ of the Charity Organization Society, 225–27

Charity, 26–27, 242–43; Charity Organization Society, 223–27; friendly visitors, 226, 227; public works, in lieu of, 247–48 n.67; surveys of, 248 n.70, 248–49 n.80

Charity Organization Society (C. O. S.), 225–27; critics of, 249 n.88

Chicago, 8, 11–12, 103, 246 n.43; civil service reform in, 127; "Dreiserian city," 256, 262; labor violence in, 172; parks, 60–61; politics, 109, 109–10, 120–21; Tabernacle Church, 230; tenements, 217

Chicago Commons. See The Commons

Chicago Commons Settlement, 185–86 n.13, 237–41; political stance of, 121

Chicago Plan (1909), 149 n.12; artistic presentation in, 267 n.12; Plan Commission, 256–57

Chicago School of Sociology, 262–63

Children's Aid Society, New York City, 27

Chinese immigrants, 192 n.128; in San Francisco, 217

Church, John A., 14

Churchill, John Spencer, ninth duke of Marlborough, 164–65

Citizen, 210

City and Suburban Homes Company, New York City, 219

City Beautiful, 57, 70, 132, 142. *See also* Planning

City Club of New York, 121

City councils, 126

City Efficient, 132–33

City History Club of New York, 211–12

City-state relations, 117–19

Civic Federation of Chicago, 120–21, 139 n.112

Civic pride, 52, 74, 104, 121, 212, 217, 257–58; in England, 124

Civic religion, 104

Civil service, 127–28

Class: "American metropolitan upper class," 164; and caste, 239; conflict, 25–28, 169; consciousness, 54; "hothouse aristocracy," 164; new rich, 24–25, 163–69; stratification, 169

Clemens, Samuel L. (Mark Twain), 33 n.113

Cleveland, Grover, 172

Cliff dwellers, 54–55, 221

Coan, Titus Munson, 4–5, 25, 26, 34 n.140

Coleman, William, 77 n.10

Coler, Bird S., 37–38

Coleridge, Samuel T. ("The Ancient Mariner"), 61–62

Collins, J. A., 67

Commons, John R., 39, 99–100, 122, 131, 229

The Commons (also *Chicago Commons*), 66, 107–8, 121, 168, 175–76, 195, 229–30; as organ of the Chicago Commons Settlement, 237–40

Commercial spirit, 188 n.51

Communications revolution, 145

Conant, Charles A., 155

Concentration, 153–54. *See also* Trusts, 153–54, 155, 226

Condit, Carl W., 256

Continent (also *Our Continent*), 10, 16

Cooley, Charles Horton, 262

Cowboy, as unskilled labor, 213

Cranz, Galen, 17, 59

Creese, Walter L., 44, 57, 68, 91, 216, 222, 254

Crevècoeur, Hector St. Jean de, 4

Croker, Richard, 174; criticized, 111–12; "Tammany Hall and the Democracy," 112–13, 115–16

Croly, Herbert, 185 n.5

Crosby, Ernest, 159, 239

Crowell, John Franklin, 208–9

Crystal Palace, England, 80 n.44

Cullen, Michael J., 195

Cummings, Edward, 224, 234–35

Curtin, Louis, 52

Cutting, R. Fulton, 128

Dana, M. Mc'G., 119

"Dangerous classes," 25–26, 100, 182

Daniel, Anna S., 215
Davis, Allen F., 241
Davis, J. D., 229–30
Deming, Clarence, 116
Democracy, 3, 100; in municipal politics, 22–23
Department stores, 159–61; Big Store advertisement, 163; John Wanamaker and associates, 187 n.39
Desmond, Henry W., 55
Devine, Edward T., 65, 182–83, 230
Dewey, John, 236
Dewey Arch, New York City, 56–57, 82 n.81; advertisement in vicinity of, 162–63
Dickens, Charles: *David Copperfield*, 84 n.111; *Our Mutual Friend*, 220
Dickinson, Charles A., 233
Dietrick, Ellen Battelle, 181
Disenfranchisement of non-property holders, 23
Donnelly, Ignatius (*Caesar's Column*), 170
Douglass, Frederick, 204
Downtown, 151–52, 217
Du Bois, W. E. B., 180, 195–96, 262; *The Philadelphia Negro*, 195–205
Ducey, Thomas J., 231
Dude, 166, 188 n.50, 189 n.73
Dugdale, R. L. (*The Jukes*), 15, 65
Dunne, Finley Peter (Mr. Dooley), 173, 266
Durand, E. Dana, 123, 126
Dutton, Samuel T., 45, 209–10

Eaton, Dorman B., 22, 113
Eberhartt, Gilbert L., 67
Education, 27, 242; as socialization, 209–14; urban-rural comparisons, 210
Eidlitz, Leopold, 56
Eilvart, Arnold, 216–17
Elevators, hydraulic, 51, 152
Elseffer, L., 101
Ely, Richard T., 138 n.101
Embree, Frances Buckley, 217
Emerick, C. E., 65, 157
Emerson, Ralph Waldo, 1, 10, 62, 89, 119, 231

Estabrook, Harold Kelsey, 217
Ethnicity, theories of, 176–79; "ethnic type," 176. *See also individual ethnic names*
Eugenics, 27
Europe, 130, 153; advertising in, 162; impact upon American cities, 5, 164, 176–79; municipal management, 126; municipal socialism, 128–29; municipal statistics, 123–24; promenades in cities, 90; socialism, 157
Every Saturday, 7–8, 11, 14, 15, 18, 21–22, 30 n.48
Everybody's Magazine, 50
The Exploding Metropolis (editors of *Fortune*), 256, 266

Fairlie, John Archibald, 123
Field, Kate, 11
Flagg, Ernest, 56
"Floating population," 182–83
Folks, Homer, 224
Ford, Paul Leicester (*The Honourable Peter Sterling*), 102
"Foreign" influence in municipal politics, 101, 103, 137 n.80. *See also* Immigration
Foulke, William Dudley, 105
The Four Hundred, New York City, 165–66, 189 n.73
Frederickson, George M., 13
"French flat," 54
Freud, Sigmund, 262
Friedman, Lawrence M., 222
Frontier, 63–67; closing of, 66, 100; conditioning factor, 178; as safety valve, 64, 170–71
Fuller, Henry B., 139 n.112

Gabriel, Ralph Henry, 183
Galaxy, 3, 7, 11, 15–16, 24, 26, 35
Gangs, streetcorner, 211; as training ground for politics, 114
Garden city, 88, 89, 91, 96, 142
Garden of Eden, 64
Gardens, urban, 61, 83–84 n.99
Gaston, Paul M., 12
Gavit, John P., 237–38

Genteel politics, 21–24, 101
George, Henry, 111, 157; New York City election of 1886, 136 n.65
George, Henry, Jr., 100, 191–92 n.113
German free cities, 117
Gettleman, Marvin, 225
Gibson, George Howard, 229
Giddings, Franklin H., 42, 169
Gilbert, Levi, 42, 169, 231
Ginger, Ray, 109, 243
Glaab, Charles N., 2, 68
Gladden, Washington, 104, 185 n.13, 226
Glass, Ruth, 195
Godkin, Edwin L., 24, 64, 102, 130, 135 n.32
Good Government, 102, 105, 119, 121
Good roads movement, 66
Goodnow, Frank J., 126
Goodwin, Grace, 44
Gould, E. R. L., 59, 219–20
Grady, Henry Woodfin, 12
Graffenreid, Clare de, 176
Gratacap, L. P., 134 n.13, 137 n.80
Gray, John H., 108, 119, 130
Greater New York, 50, 124–25
Greer, Scott, 221
Gulick, Luther H., 241
Gunton, George, 153, 185 n.5
Gunton's Magazine (also *The Social Economist*), 48, 50, 59–60, 65, 69, 101, 103, 105–6, 110, 111, 114–15, 125, 126, 129, 152, 153–54, 157, 160, 173, 185 n.5, 209, 214, 218, 222, 224–25
Gutheim, Frederick, 74, 145, 256

Hale, Edward Everett, 225
Hall, Bolton, 224
Hall, Lucy M., 65–66
Halstead, Leonora H., 78 n.29, 102
Hamilton, Gail (Mary Abigail Dodge), 5
Hamilton, James H., 74
Hamlin, A. D. F., 56
Handlin, Oscar, 255
"Hard times parties," 166–67
Harder, Julius F., 70–72, 72, 73
Harris, Chauncey D., 255

Harris, Elisha, 14
Harrison, Benjamin, 144
Hart, Albert Bushnell, 67
Hauser, Philip M., 119
Hawthorne, Julian, 6
Haymarket Riot, Chicago, 172
Haynes, George H., 118
Hays, Samuel P., 133
Health. *see* Sanitation
Hegner, Herman F., 237
Heinz Company advertisement, 163
Henderson, Charles R., 208
Herrick, Mary E., 215
Herron, George D., 231
Hewitt, Abram S., 80 n.49, 121
Hill, George, 157
Hill, John Clark, 233
Hines, Thomas, 143–44
Historical exemplars, references to: Jesus Christ, 167–68, 190–91 n.94, 212, 228–29, 244 n.4; Thomas Jefferson, 64; Napoleon, 108, 167; George Washington, 167
Historical periods, references to: American Revolution, 121, 216; Ancient/Biblical, 41, 45, 53, 101, 108, 168, 177, 190–91, 210, 214, 229, 230, 233, 235; Classical, 39, 47, 51, 55–56, 100, 102, 106, 117, 122, 126, 130, 152, 155, 165, 168, 174, 177, 181, 182, 192, 218, 221, 249; Eighteenth Century, 39, 130, 168; English, 64, 166–67, 173, 225; French Revolution, 112–13, 116, 130, 164, 190; Medieval, 39, 51, 58, 117, 130, 152, 158, 159, 164–65, 232, 233, 236; preindustrial, 41, 58, 104, 214, 233, 235, 239; Puritan New England, 116–17; Renaissance, 55, 58–59, 181, 256
History, lessons of, 173, 177
Hoffman, Frederick L., 41
Holmes, George K., 67–68, 169
"Homeless," 221
Homes, 18–19; ownership of, 66–69, 221; scale of, 53–54
Homestead, Pennsylvania, 172
Hours at Home, 9, 15
Housing, 242–43; by class, 219–20; crit-

ics of, 221–22; economics of, 216, 222–23
Howard, Ebenezer, 91
Hubbard, C. M., 208
Hudson River, 16–17; homes along, 189 n.62
Hull House, Chicago, 195, 213, 237, 251–52 n.129
Hunt, Richard Morris, 54; Biltmore Estate, 189 n.62
Huntington, W. R., 229
Hutchinson, Woods, 226
Hyman, Harold M., 13

Immigration, 176; competition among groups, 192 n.127; manual labor, 213; restriction proposed, 27, 77 n.10, 181–82
Imperialism, 155–56, 158, 159
Independent citizen leagues, 139 n.114
Institutional church, 231–34, 243; rural, 250 n.112
International influence, urban America, 155–56, 162, 186 n.17
Irish, 32–33 n.112, 177; in politics, 20–21, 23, 111–16

James, Edmund J., 124, 126
James, Lewis G., 137 n.80
James, William, 236
Jews, 172–73, 177–78
Jones, Samuel M., 115, 124
Jordan, David Starr, 126, 254
Journal of Political Economy, 171
Journal of Social Science, 8, 26, 27, 88–91
The Jukes (R. L. Dugdale), 15, 65
"Juvenile criminality," 61

Kansas City "Patch" (Armourdale), 175–76
Kantor, Harvey A., 87 n.153
Keasbey, Lindley M., 156
Kelley, Florence, 213, 215
Kelly, Edmond, 100, 104
Kelly, John, 111, 113
Kennedy, William, 151
Kimball, Richard B., 25

Kingsbury, Frederick L., 47–48, 134 n.8
Kip, Leonard, 9, 19, 29 n.31
Kipling, Rudyard, 159, 191 n.104

Labor, 215–16; civil service, attitudes toward, 127–28; politics of, 122; urban-based, 170–71
Laidlaw, Walter, 229, 231
Lakewood, New Jersey, 174–75
Lamb, Charles Rollinson, 56–57, 57–58
Lamb, Frederick S., 58, 73, 156
Lasch, Christopher, 236
League of California Municipalities, 120
League of Wisconsin Municipalities, 120
Lee, Guy Carleton, 179
Lee, Joseph, 172–73, 216
Leland, Charles G., 8
Leo XIII (pope), 231
Lewis, Alfred Henry, 112
Lewis, William Draper, 117, 118
Library facilities, in parks, 61
Lindholm, S. V., 172
Lindsay, Samuel M., 43–44
Lloyd, Henry Demarest, 231
"Local municipal state," 117
Loeb, Joseph, 40, 129
Loeb, Morris, 61
Low, Seth, 106–7, 126, 127
Lowell, Francis C., 113
Lowell, Massachusetts, 171, 190 n.92, 247 n.54
Lubove, Roy, 187 n.42, 245 n.29, 246 nn.47, 49

McAllister, Ward, 165
McCarthy, Justin, 4, 11–12
McCarthy, Michael P., 257
McCook, John J., 183
McCracken, W. D., 216
M'Creary, E. D., 171
Machine politics, 111–16, 231
McKelway, St. Clair, 123
McKim, Charles F., 142, 145
MacLean, Annie Marion, 160–61, 220–21
McLean, Francis H., 37
MacMaster, John Bach, 134 n.22

McMillan Plan, Washington, D. C., 142–
  43, 144–49, 256
MacVeagh, Franklin, 107
Macy, Jesse, 101
Magazines, x, 184; selection of, 269–74;
  transformation, 2, 27–28, 35–36, 62–
  63, 84 n.106, 163–64, 207, 254–55
Maltbie, Milo Ray, 128–29
The Manhattan, 8, 18
Mann, Arthur, 241, 251 n.125, 253
  n.150
Martin, William R., 29 n.39
Mason, Alfred Bishop, 226
Maurice, Arthur Bartlett, 101, 173–74
Maxon, William D., 104
Mayers, Julius M., 215
Mayo-Smith, Richard, 178
Mencken, H. L., 63, 88
Menken, J. S., 227
Merchants' Association, San Francisco,
  122
Merwin, Henry Childs, 113–14
Metropolitan Magazine, 51, 63, 161,
  164–65
Military drill, 212–13
Military in cities, 100; barrack plan hous-
  ing as model, 182
Miller, Herbert, 130
Mitchell, Donald Grant, 16, 17, 18
Monroe, Charles E., 108
Moody, Walter D., 257–58
Moore, Charles, 145
Morgan, Horace H., 6
Mosby, Speed, 168
Moses, Adolph, 130, 134 nn. 8, 12
Moses, Robert, 127, 142
Mott, Frank Luther, x, 2, 35, 237
Mowry, Duane, 106
Moynihan, Daniel Patrick, 21
Mugwump, 105–6, 112, 116, 140 n.137;
  press, 115
Mulry, Thomas M., 250 n.108
Mumford, Lewis, 75, 78 n.18, 97 n.15,
  253; Olmsted, Frederick Law, about,
  88, 91, 95
Municipal administrative academies, 119,
  138 n.101
Municipal Affairs, 49, 50, 61, 72, 222

Municipal annexation, 124–25, 125. *See
  also* Greater New York
Municipal art, 57–59, 152
Municipal beautification, 57–59
Municipal corruption, 20–22, 99–103,
  107–16. *See also* Boss; Tammany Hall
"A Municipal Exhibition," Newark,
  New Jersey, 263–66
Municipal experimentation, 119
Municipal improvement associations, 70,
  139 n.114
Municipal indebtedness, 19
Municipal lodging houses, 182–83
Municipal management, 125–27
Municipal opera, 74
Municipal parties, 122–23
Municipal rivalry, 6–13, 124–25, 140 n.
  132, 144, 155–56
Municipal scientists, 119
Municipal socialism, 40, 128–30
Municipal theater, 74
Municipality, 40, 120
Mutualism, 170, 181
Myrdal, Gunnar, 204

Nast, Thomas N., 32–33 n.112
National Association for the Advance-
  ment of Colored People (NAACP), 196
National character, 2–6, 24, 28 n.6
National Conference of Municipal Re-
  formers, 120, 138 n.108
National Conference of City Planning and
  the Problems of Congestion (1909),
  70
National Consumers League, 160–61
National Municipal League, 120, 126,
  138 n.108
Nationalism, 144, 212–13, 236; in reli-
  gion, 229–30, 249–50 n.99
Nativism, 27–28, 177–78, 187 n.31
Nature, 15, 60, 88, 210–11
Nebraska, 64
New England town government,
  116–17
New towns. *See* Garden city
New York City: architecture, 51–54,
  152–57, 165; beautification, 57–58,
  69–70; class differentiations, 164–67,

173–75; Dongan Charter, 125; finances, 20, 32 n.10; growth, 6–7, 8,
9–10, 37–38; housing, 43–44, 53–56,
80–81 n.57, 214–20; international role,
152–53, 155; investigative committees
on, 110, 215–16; parks, 16, 17–18,
60, 89–90; planning, 70–73, 80 n.45;
politics, 20–23, 101–2, 110–16; as
publishing center, 2; sanitary conditions, 13, 215–16; slums, 182–83,
214–20; statehood, 138 n.96; transportation, 49–50
New York City Federation of Churches,
229
Newspapers, 170; municipal ownership,
129
Niebuhr, H. Richard, 233–34
Nietzsche, Friedrich, 57, 75, 191 n.110
Noise abatement, 46, 79 n.36
Nordau, Max, 191 n.110
North, Edward P., 72
North American Review, 9, 21, 23,
112

Oberholtzer, Ellis Paxson, 117, 118
Ocean Grove, New Jersey, 131
Octavia Hill method of rent collecting,
220, 247 n.53
Office building, 156–57
Olmsted, Frederick Law, 18, 60, 61,
142, 144, 189 n.62; "Justifying Value
of a Public Park" (author), 17–18;
"Public Parks and the Enlargement of
Towns" (author), 88–96
Olmsted, Frederick Law, Jr., 142
Olmsted Brothers, 97 n.15, 142
Open and Institutional Church League,
231–34; parish model, 231; Ruggles
Street Church, Boston, as model, 232–
33
Open Church, 65, 167, 221; organ of the
Open and Institutional Church League,
231–34
Oppenheim, Nathan, 225
Osborn, Frederic J., 88, 97 n.15
Osborn, Henry Leslie, 61–62
"Other half," 169–83, 235
Our Continent. See Continent

Paine, Robert Treat, 27, 182
Palisades, Hudson River, 73, 87 n.152
Park, Robert E., 262–63, 267 n.22
Parkman, Francis, 22
Parks, 17–18, 59–62, 210–11; compre-
hensive planning, role in, 88–96; plea-
sure grounds, 18, 59; reform parks, 59;
signage, 124; small parks, ranking of,
83 n.12
Parkside, Buffalo, 94, 96
Parkway, 90–91
Parsons, Frank, 228
Parthenon, 57; Ictinus, designer of, 55–
56
Patten, Simon N., 66, 116, 117, 118
Paxton, Sir Joseph, 80 n.44, 94
Peck, Harry Thurston, 63
Peckham, Grace, 46, 69
Peets, Elbert, 88
Peters, Absalom, 17
Peters, Alfred H., 117
Peterson, Jon A., 145
Peterson, Lorin, 106
Phelan, James D., 106
Phelps, Edward J., 127
Philadelphia College Settlement, 196,
202
Philadelphia Gas Works, 109
Philadelphia Municipal League, 120
The Philadelphia Negro, 195–205
Pickard, C. E., 100
Pingree, Hazen, 83–84 n.99
Pittsburg Survey, 195
Planning, 70–75; Daniel Hudson, Burn-
ham, 142–49, 256–67; Frederick Law,
Olmsted, 88–96; "The Planning of
Cities" series, 72–73. *See also* City
Beautiful
Platt, Walter B., 46–47
Playgrounds, 182, 210–11
Poetry of the city, 62–63
Pond, George E. ("Philip Quilibet"), 5,
24, 25
Poor, "worthy," 184, 219–20
Porter, Robert P., 8, 20
Post, George B., 72, 73, 81 n.57
Post, Louis, 106, 158
Potter, David M., 161

Potts, William, 127

Professional classes, 158, 159, 170, 244

Professors, as civic leaders, 244 n.5

Progress, 156, 157, 171; voice of, 173

Progressive ideals: authority, 245 n.23; efficiency, 133; order, 212–13

Proportional representation, 141 n.160

Prospect Park, Brooklyn, 17

Prostitution, 161, 176

"Protective state," 121–22, 139 n.117

Protestant: charity, 224; ideal of the Kingdom, 104, 105, 128, 233–34, 239; laymen, 105; ministers, 34 n.140, 105; proselytizing, 192 n.128; reform activities, 27

Pryor, John H., 115, 124–25

The Public, 37, 74–75, 77 n.3, 106, 107, 110, 111–12, 114, 158–59, 160, 167, 167–68, 168–69, 170–71, 172, 176, 180, 189 n.71, 221, 228–29, 244 nn.93, 94

Public Improvements, 37, 48, 51, 61, 66, 179, 186 n.17; "The Planning of Cities" series, 72–73

The public interest, 132–33

Puddefoot, W. G., 103, 182

Quincy, Josiah, 83–84 n.99

Race, theories of, 177–78. *See also* Ethnicity

Rauschenbusch, Walter, 230, 234

Recreation, 61, 90

Recreation piers, 87–88 n.151

Reeves, Robert N., 163–64

Reform, 106, 107–8, 114, 122–23, 128; age of, 123; mail-order, 263; political bosses, 115

Reissman, Leonard, 2

Retail revolution, 161–63

Richard, Frank P., 119

Richardson, Benjamin Ward ("Hygeia, or the City of Health"), 14

Richardson, H. H., 94

Riis, Jacob, 214; slums and tenements, *Atlantic Monthly* series, 245 n.29

"Ring," 20–24, 99–103, 111

Ripley, William Z., 45

Riverside, Illinois, 91, 94

Robinson, Charles Mulford, 145

Robinson, James Argyle, 49–50

Robinson, John Beverly, 213

Rockerfeller, John D., 168

Roman Catholic Church, 101, 103, 231, 250 n.108

Roosevelt, Theodore, 105, 185 n.5

Root, Frederick Stanley, 119

Root, John Wellborn, 143

Rosenberg, Charles E., 13

Rothschild family, 173

Rousseau, Jean-Jacques, 170

Rovit, Earl H., 68

Rowe, Leo S., 39, 76, 119

Rowland, Irene, 179

Ruggles Street Church, Boston, 232–33

Rural, 15, 47–48, 61–66, 103, 139 n.114, 153, 156, 165–66, 209, 244 n.12; improvement societies, 16

Ruskin, John, 58, 63

St. Gaudens, Augustus, 142

Salvation Army, 205 n.4, 230–31

Sanborn, Edwin W., 42

Sanford, Charles L., 9

Sanford, Elias B., 234

Sanitation, 47–48, 89, 208–9, 224; American Social Science Association, role in, 47–48, 89; rain baths promoted, 211; rural conditions, 65–66; "Sanitary elite," 13–14; statistics on, 79–80 n.42; U.S. Sanitary Commission, 13–14

Schorske, Carl, 54

Schurz, Carl, 128

Schuyler, Montgomery, 51–52, 53–54

Scott's Monthly Magazine, 3–4, 7, 9, 10, 12, 24

Scruggs, William L., 23

Seabury, Emma Playter, 228

Sears, A. F., 154

Sedgwick, William T., 48

See, Milton, 73

Self-help, 181

Seligman family, 173
Senner, Joseph H., 181
Settlements, 234–41, 243; church-affili-
ated, 252 n.132; elan of, 235, 238; po-
litical role of, 121; rural, 252 n.132;
statistics on, 251 n.123
Shaw, Albert, 124, 182
Sheldon, Charles M., 252–53 n.143
Shepard, Edward M., 137 n.80
Sherman, Sidney A., 161–62
Simmel, Georg, 262
Single tax, 100, 157–58, 247 n.57
Skyscrapers, 51–52; proposed ban on, 81
n.57
Slicer, Thomas R., 105, 229
Slum, 174, 214–16
Slum clearance, 217–18
Small, Albion W., 45–46, 120, 169,
256
Smalley, Eugene Virgil, 27
Snow, R. W., 108
Social Darwinism, 129, 190 n.85, 204,
224, 226–27; "law of urban elimina-
tion," 178
*The Social Economist. See Gunton's
Magazine*
Social gospel, 231–34
Society for Checking the Abuses of Pub-
lic Advertising, England, 163
Spanish-American War, 168, 188 n.50
Speculation, evils of, 185–86 n.13
Spencer, Herbert, 39
Starett, Paul, 143
Steffens, Lincoln, x
Stein, Maurice, 263
Stevenson, Mrs. Cornelius, 39–40
Stevenson, Katherine Lente, 228
Strauss, Anselm, 53
Strong mayor, 23, 33 n.117, 100, 126
Submerged tenth, 235, 236
Suburbs: annexation of, 124–25; lifestyles
in, 16–17, 42–43; suburban towns, 41,
91–96, 97 n.16; suburbanization, 37–
44, 68, 75–76, 86 n.149
Sullivan, Louis, 142–43
Summer vacations, 16, 31 n.81
Sweat shops, 171, 215–16

"Sweater," 172–73, 215–16
Swisshelm, Jane Grey, 6

Taft, William Howard, 107
Tammany Hall, 20–22, 102, 105, 111–
16, 136 n.65, 140 n.148, 209, 234;
Hogan & Slattery, architectural firm
employed by, 56
Taxation, 130–31; as basis for suffrage,
33 n.113; of nonprofit organizations,
32 n.98; taxpayers as governing body,
33 n.117
Taylor, Graham, 238; biography of, 252
n.134
Taylor, Henry Ling, 207–8, 210
Telephone, 48, 152
Tenants associations, 217
Tenements, 27, 190 n.85, 219–21; New
York Charity Organization Society
Tenement Committee, 217–19, 246
n.51
Theocritus, 65
Thomas, W. I., 262
Thoreau, Henry David, 16
Thurston, Henry W., 213–14
Tocqueville, Alexis de, 5
Tolstoi, Leo, 167
Totem, 114, 157
Tourgée, Albion W., 10
Tower of Babel, 53, 69, 81 n.62
Townsend, Edward W., 173–74
Toynbee Hall, London, 234, 235, 237
Trachtenberg, Alan, 25–26
Tramps, 171, 182–83, 194 n.155
Transportation: automobile, 38, 77 n.5;
bicycle, 78–79 n.29; coaching, 80
n.46; elevated rail, 49, 80 n.48; public
transit, advertising on, 163; public
transit, franchises, 21, 109; public
transit, racial segregation of, 179, 193
n.136; rail, 78–79 n.29; revolution, 49;
streetcars, 18, 31, 32, 49; subway, 49;
suspension bridges, 50
Trenholm, William L., 12
Trusts, 153–54, 155; as model for charity
management, 226
Tryon, Thomas, 57
Tsanoff, Stoyan Vasil, 211

Tweed, William Marcy, 24, 99, 101–2,
111–12, 113, 134 n.7; exposure of
Ring (1871), 21–22
"Two nations," in England, 152, 166,
227
Typewriter, 152

Ullman, Edward L., 255
United States Constitution, 116, 117,
130
United States Sanitary Commission, 13–
14
University of Berlin, Sociology faculty,
202
Unwin, Raymond, 88
Uptown, 217
Urban imagery, 29 n.23, 39–40, 48–49,
49, 52–53, 57, 58, 71, 81 nn.63, 66
109, 112–12, 119, 122, 125, 156, 173,
190–91 n.94, 208, 209, 210, 217,
222–23, 225, 226, 227, 230, 233, 234,
235–36, 240–41, 249, 251, 252,
262
Urban theory, 6–13, 35–36, 70, 115–16,
131–32, 185, 209, 219, 242, 262–63;
anti-city, 47–48; ideal city, 69, 70, 75;
modern city, ix, 2, 14, 47, 76, 120,
208, 235; urbanism, 3, 18–19, 45–48,
48–49, 106–7, 262–63; urbanization,
7–8, 35, 37–42, 79 n.30, 154, 220–22;
urban-rural continuum, 61–62, 66, 88–
96, 154
Urban university, 244 n.5

Vacation schools, 210–11
Vanderbilt, Consuelo, 164–65
Vanderbilt, Cornelius, 165
Vanderbilt, George Washington, 189
n.62
van Rensselaer, Mariana Griswold, 88
Vaughan, Robert, 35
Vaux, Calvert, 17, 89
Veiller, Lawrence, 218–19; biography of,
246 n.47
Violence, 216; Haymarket, 172; Home-
stead, 172
Voluntaryism. See Associationalism

Wacker, Charles, 257
Wacker's Manual of the Plan of Chicago,
257–58; textual analysis of, 267 n.11
Walker, Robert H., 62–63, 103, 107,
110
Wall Street, 155–56
Ward, Lester Frank, 138 n.101
Waring, Colonel George E., Jr., 14, 38,
115, 126–27
Warner, John DeWitt, 50, 152,
162–63
Washington, Booker T., 204, 262
Washington, D. C., 52; building height
limitations, 51; government, commis-
sion form of, 131, 144; L'Enfant-Elli-
cott Plan, 86 n.142, 144; McMillan
Plan, 142, 144–45, 256
Weber, Adna F., 41, 124; The Growth of
Cities in the Nineteenth Century (re-
view), 44–45
Weideman, U. M., 173
Welch, J. Herbert, 50
Weller, Charles F., 226
Welsh, Herbert, 102, 108, 122, 127
Wendell, Barrett, 197
The Western, 27
Westminster House Settlement, Buffalo,
252 n.132
White, Arnold, 178
White, Henry, 209, 218
White, Lucia, 86 n.138
White, Morton, 86 n.138
White, Richard Grant, 18
Whitman, Walt, 2–3, 17, 173, 191
n.104
Whyte, William H., 86 n.137; Exploding
Metropolis (editor), 256, 266
Wiebe, Robert H., 35, 207
Wilcox, Delos F., 129
Will, Thomas E., 39, 47, 100–101, 101,
176
Williams, Raymond, 77 n.10
Winchell, James Manning, 16–17
Wingate, Charles F., 14, 215–16; articles
on Tweed Ring, 32 n.111
Winship, A. E., 48
Women in cities, 89–90; African-Ameri-
can gender imbalances, 202; churches,

active in, 233; clerical work, 213; military drill, leadership in, 212–13; saleswomen, department stores, 160–61; settlements, influence of, 241; underpaid, 159; as urbanists, 207
Woodruff, Clinton Rogers, 109, 123–24, 125
Woods, Robert A., 99, 121, 195, 235–36, 237, 241, 251 n.125, 262
Wordsworth, William, 18
Work, Monroe N., 180
World's Columbian Exposition, Chicago (1893), 70, 143, 144

World's Work. 75
Wright, Richard, 263

Yellow Book. See Yellow Kid
Yellow Kid (also *Yellow Book*), 42–43, 63, 108, 156, 165–66, 177
Yerkes, Charles T., 109–10
Young, Edward, *Night Thoughts*, 17
Young, James T., 131

Zoning, 46
Zueblin, Charles, 60, 211

About the Author

DANA F. WHITE is Associate Professor of Urban Studies at Emory University. He is the co-editor, with V. Kramer, of *Olmsted South: Old South Critic/New South Planner* (Greenwood, 1979). His articles have appeared in *American Studies International*, *The Journal of Urban History*, *The Atlanta Historical Journal*, and *Technology and Culture*.

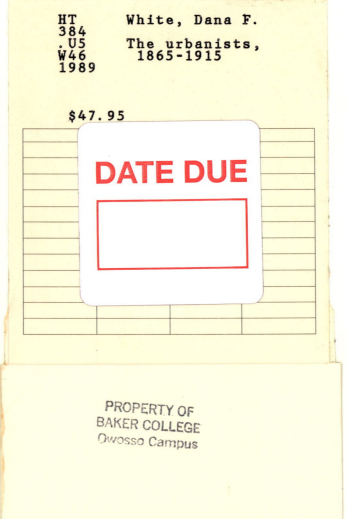